AF778248

The Supply Chain Differentiation Guide

Erik Hofmann · Patrick Beck
Erik Füger

The Supply Chain Differentiation Guide

A Roadmap to Operational Excellence

Springer

Erik Hofmann
Kerkhoff Competence Center
of Supply Chain Management
Chair of Logistics Management
University of St. Gallen
St. Gallen
Switzerland

Erik Füger
Inova Management AG
Wollerau
Switzerland

Patrick Beck
Chair of Logistics Management
University of St. Gallen
St. Gallen
Switzerland

ISBN 978-3-642-31935-8 ISBN 978-3-642-31936-5 (eBook)
DOI 10.1007/978-3-642-31936-5
Springer Heidelberg New York Dordrecht London

Library of Congress Control Number: 2012943972

© Springer-Verlag Berlin Heidelberg 2012
This work is subject to copyright. All rights are reserved by the Publisher, whether the whole or part of the material is concerned, specifically the rights of translation, reprinting, reuse of illustrations, recitation, broadcasting, reproduction on microfilms or in any other physical way, and transmission or information storage and retrieval, electronic adaptation, computer software, or by similar or dissimilar methodology now known or hereafter developed. Exempted from this legal reservation are brief excerpts in connection with reviews or scholarly analysis or material supplied specifically for the purpose of being entered and executed on a computer system, for exclusive use by the purchaser of the work. Duplication of this publication or parts thereof is permitted only under the provisions of the Copyright Law of the Publisher's location, in its current version, and permission for use must always be obtained from Springer. Permissions for use may be obtained through RightsLink at the Copyright Clearance Center. Violations are liable to prosecution under the respective Copyright Law.
The use of general descriptive names, registered names, trademarks, service marks, etc. in this publication does not imply, even in the absence of a specific statement, that such names are exempt from the relevant protective laws and regulations and therefore free for general use.
While the advice and information in this book are believed to be true and accurate at the date of publication, neither the authors nor the editors nor the publisher can accept any legal responsibility for any errors or omissions that may be made. The publisher makes no warranty, express or implied, with respect to the material contained herein.

Printed on acid-free paper

Springer is part of Springer Science+Business Media (www.springer.com)

Foreword and Acknowledgements

The *Supply Chain Differentiation Guide* (*SCD Guide*) at hand is the outcome of a long-term research project conducted by the Chair of Logistics Management at the University of St. Gallen and several practicing partners from Switzerland and Germany. The project started at the end of 2009 and lasted until the end of 2011. It was funded by the Commission for Technology and Innovation (CTI) located at the Federal Department of Economic Affairs (FDEA), Switzerland (http://www.evd.admin.ch). The CTI promotes projects in the areas of R&D, knowledge transfer, and business formation and establishment. Our project was located within the CTI Enabling Sciences, which contribute to knowledge transfer from research institutions to companies.

Schweizerische Eidgenossenschaft
Confédération suisse
Confederazione Svizzera
Confederaziun svizra

Eidgenössisches Volkswirtschaftsdepartement EVD
Kommission für Technologie und Innovation KTI
Förderagentur für Innovation

Conceptual and integration partners:

- Inova Management AG, a consultancy specialized in supply chain management, was the implementing partner and supported the research project with their almost 20 years of experience in supply chain management projects.
- GS1 Switzerland, the leading association dedicated to the design and implementation of global standards and solutions to improve efficiency and visibility of supply chains and demand management. GS1 Switzerland was the project's disseminating partner.

• Mercuri Urval GmbH (Germany) ensured that special requirements in supply chain management with respect to human resources were taken into consideration in the project.

The consumer goods industry was represented by Emmi AG. The companies Bühler AG, Reichle & De-Massari AG, Soplar sa and Wild & Küpfer AG represented the machinery and plant engineering industry.

In addition, the logistic service providers Damco Germany GmbH and the Sieber Group participated in the project. Mega Verbund AG also supported the project with its knowledge in commerce.

Besides the project just introduced, a further reason for publishing the present *SCD Guide* is our strong conviction that the "one-size-fits-all" approach does not satisfy the modern requirements of supply chain management. Several internationally active firms in industry and consulting report their efforts or the efforts of their clients to differentiate their supply chains. Support from academia, however, has been lacking. The *SCD Guide* is a first step to bridge this gap. It offers a comprehensive approach, starting with customers, aligning all value adding steps and suppliers to serve customers according to their specific needs.

We would like to thank all our partners for their constructive collaboration and support. Furthermore, special thanks go to the students and interns who supported the development of this book.

St. Gallen, Switzerland, September 2012 — Erik Hofmann, Patrick Beck

Zurich, Switzerland, September 2012 — Erik Füger

Preface

The supervision of value adding networks involving several companies has been drawing a lot of attention in research and practice for over a decade, under the concept of supply chain management. There appears to be a broad consensus with respect to the central guiding principle of supply chain management, which encompasses the integration of materials, goods, and information flows across multiple value chains, and the alignment of all value adding activities with the requirements of consumers. However, in companies of different sectors and sizes, there is still considerable potential for reducing costs, increasing performance, improving quality, increasing flexibility, and improving risk management by means of supply chain management. A major reason for the discrepancy between the perceived and actual relevance of supply chain management can be seen in the challenge of identifying and selecting which initiatives as well as actions should be executed in the supply chain management context. This is especially the case for small- and medium-sized companies. However, a trend that affects multinational companies as well as small- and medium-sized enterprises is the rapidly changing and diversifying character of customer needs. Some companies in the consumer industry, nowadays, offer customization approaches even for goods perceived as commodities by most customers. Furthermore, enterprises in the plant and machinery building industry are forced to invent new business models, since their customers demand the opportunity to purchase the production capacity, know-how, and innovation instead of buying an investment good. Modern supply chain management offers a solution for such a market requirement: supply chain differentiation.

Supply chain differentiation means the simultaneous operation of several supply chains for effectively and efficiently dealing with customer needs. It is an undeniable trend, especially in supply chain management practice. While some market leaders already have implemented a differentiated supply chain, many other companies struggle in even identifying suitable approaches for analyzing whether or not a differentiated supply chain is an appropriate solution for their company. The work presented here, *The Supply Chain Differentiation Guide*, offers approaches for investigating such issues in a holistic and integrated manner. The book covers a wide range of subjects and provides an overview of topics relevant to supply chain management as well as supply chain differentiation. The Inova

Management AG has already successfully applied the *Supply Chain Differentiation Guide* in its consulting practice. I am confident that the *Guide*'s readers will find suggestions and inspirations for improving supply chain management in their own companies.

St. Gallen, Switzerland, September 2012

Wolfgang Stölzle
Chair of Logistics Management
University of St. Gallen

Contents

Part I Conception of the Supply Chain Differentiation Guideline

1 Introduction . . . 3
- 1.1 Why do We Need a Supply Chain Differentiation Guideline? . . . 3
- 1.2 Supply Chain Assessments: What is Currently Available? . . . 9
  - 1.2.1 The Supply Chain Scan Approach . . . 9
  - 1.2.2 The Supply Chain Diagnostic Tool . . . 10
  - 1.2.3 Supply Chain and Operations Audits . . . 12
  - 1.2.4 What is Missing? . . . 13
- 1.3 Principles and Advantages of the Supply Chain Differentiation Approach . . . 14
- 1.4 The Structure of the SCD Guide . . . 16
- 1.5 Scalability of the Approach . . . 22
- 1.6 The Morphological Box for Supply Chain Differentiation . . . 23
- 1.7 Exemplary Cases . . . 26
- 1.8 Challenges of an Application of the Supply Chain Assessment and Differentiation Guideline . . . 29
- References . . . 31

Part II Phase 1: Description of a TO-BE Supply Chain

2 SCD Guide Preparation . . . 35
- 2.1 Internal Analysis: Company Strategy . . . 35
  - 2.1.1 Elaboration of Vision, Mission and General Principle . . . 35
  - 2.1.2 Portfolio Analysis of Products and Product Groups in the Supply Chain . . . 35

2.1.3 Product Life Cycle Position 36
2.1.4 Description of Generic Strategy in the Supply Chain 37
2.2 External Analysis: Company and Environment. 38
2.2.1 Evaluation of the Environmental Factors 38
2.2.2 Industry Structure Analysis 38
2.2.3 Analysis of Strategic Groups in the Market 40
2.2.4 Examination of the Strongest Competitors 41
2.2.5 Core Competency Assessment 41
2.3 Summary of Strategic Internal and External Analysis 42
2.4 Application Example and Possible Output of Company Strategy Analysis 43
References 45

3 CM1: Customer Segmentation and Supply Chain Strategy 47
3.1 Goals of Content Module 1 47
3.2 Customer Requirements and Segmentation. 47
3.2.1 Customer Requirements Categorization Based on a Hierarchical Structure 47
3.2.2 Customer Segmentation. 50
3.2.3 Customer Segmentation Through Qualitative Analysis. 54
3.2.4 Customer Segmentation Through Quantitative Analysis. 56
3.2.5 Geography as a Descriptive Dimension 61
3.3 Assignment of Supply Chain Strategies to Customer Segments 64
3.3.1 Customer Segment Characteristics and Supply Chain Strategies. 64
3.3.2 Customer Segment Requirements and Supply Chain Strategies. 67
3.3.3 Adjustment of Business Unit Strategy and Supply Chain Strategies. 68
3.3.4 Choosing the Right Supply Chain Strategy for a Customer Segment 69
3.3.5 Customer Order Decoupling Point 71
3.4 Application Example of SCD Guide CM1 and Possible Output 74
3.4.1 Customer Segmentation. 74
3.4.2 Strategic Supply Chain Orientation 76
References 78

4 CM2: Manufacturing Strategy and Supply Chain Management . . . 81
4.1 Goals of Content Module 2 . . . 81
4.2 Product Modularization . . . 82
4.2.1 Principle of Product Modularization . . . 82
4.2.2 The Process of Product Modularization . . . 85
4.3 Modularization and Deciding the Value of the Real Net Output Ratio . . . 86
4.3.1 Process for the Outsourcing Decision . . . 88
4.3.2 Outsourcing Procedure . . . 88
4.3.3 The Execution of Outsourcing . . . 91
4.4 Alternative to Modularization: The Formation of Material Groups . . . 92
4.5 Manufacturing Strategies . . . 93
4.5.1 Make-to-Stock . . . 94
4.5.2 Assemble-, Make- and Build-to-Order . . . 95
4.5.3 Engineer-to-Order . . . 96
4.6 Manufacturing Strategies and Supply Chain Strategies . . . 96
4.7 Supply Chain Strategies and Customer Order Decoupling Point . . . 98
4.8 Application Example of SCD Guide CM2 and Possible Output . . . 101
References . . . 103

5 CM3: Supplier Segmentation and Supply Strategy . . . 107
5.1 Goals of Content Module 3 . . . 107
5.2 Buyer–Supplier Relationships . . . 107
5.2.1 General Classification of Suppliers . . . 108
5.2.2 Distribution of Power in Buyer–Supplier Relationships . . . 109
5.2.3 Combination of Buyer–Supplier Relationship Types with the Distribution of Power . . . 110
5.3 Implications of Buyer–Supplier Relationships on the Sourcing Procedure . . . 111
5.3.1 The Merging of Item Categorization and Buyer–Supplier Relationship Types . . . 113
5.3.2 Purchasing Portfolio Matrix . . . 114
5.3.3 Integrated Supplier Relationship Management Procedure . . . 115
5.4 Supplier Management and Supply Chain Strategies . . . 117
5.5 Alternative Approach to Managing Suppliers: The ABC Analysis . . . 119
5.6 Application Example of SCD Guide CM3 and Possible Output . . . 121
References . . . 122

6 **CM4: Activity Allocation and Supply Chain Process Definition** . . . 125
6.1 Goals of Content Module 4 . . . 125
6.2 Producing Internationally . . . 126
6.2.1 Different Ways of Operating in an International Context . . . 127
6.2.2 Internationalization and Supply Chain Strategies . . . 128
6.2.3 Structuring the Network Design Decision . . . 129
6.2.4 Allocation of Supply Chain Processes to Respective Geographical Regions . . . 131
6.3 Implications of Manufacturing Strategies for Supply Chain Processes . . . 132
6.3.1 The SCOR Framework . . . 132
6.3.2 Aligning Supply Chain Processes With Manufacturing Strategies . . . 133
6.4 Supply Chain Processes in a Differentiated Supply Chain Context—The case of Dell . . . 135
6.5 Application Example of SCD Guide CM4 and Possible Output . . . 137
References . . . 140

7 **CM5: Supply Chain Governance** . . . 141
7.1 Goals of Content Module 5 . . . 141
7.2 Supply Chain Governance Structure . . . 141
7.2.1 Supply Chain Governance Typology . . . 142
7.2.2 Relationship Management Framework . . . 143
7.2.3 Customer Relationship Management . . . 145
7.2.4 Supplier Relationship Management . . . 146
7.3 Information Sharing in Supply Chains . . . 147
7.3.1 Characteristics of Information Sharing in the Supply Chain . . . 148
7.3.2 Different Levels of Information Sharing . . . 149
7.3.3 Supplier and Customer Relationship and Information Sharing . . . 149
7.3.4 Positive Effects of Information Sharing . . . 150
7.3.5 Negative Effects of Information Sharing . . . 151
7.3.6 Enabling Information Sharing via IT Systems . . . 152
7.3.7 Information Sharing in Practice . . . 152
7.4 Application Example of SCD Guide CM5 and Possible Output . . . 154
References . . . 156

8 CM6: Supporting Activities—Project Management and Human Resources 159
8.1 Goals of Content Module 6 159
8.2 Supply Chain Project Management 159
8.2.1 The Project Management Maturity Model 160
8.2.2 Challenges of Supply Chain Management Projects 163
8.2.3 Inter-Organizational Boards 163
8.3 Human Resources in Supply Chain Management 165
8.3.1 The Role of Human Resource Management in Supply Chain Management 165
8.3.2 Human Resource Risks in Supply Chain Management 166
8.3.3 Prevention of Human Resource Risk in Supply Chain Management 167
8.3.4 Human Resource Planning in Supply Chain Management 169
8.3.5 Human Resource Development and Training 170
8.3.6 Supply Chain Manager Development and Training 171
8.3.7 Employee Competencies in Supply Chain Management 172
8.4 Application Example of SCD Guide CM6 and Possible Output 175
References 176

Part III Phases 2 to 5: From the AS-IS Analysis to the Selection and Implementation Preparation of Specific Corrective Actions

9 Phase 2: Identification of AS-IS Supply Chain and Analysis 179
9.1 Goals of SCD-Phase 2 179
9.2 Content Module 1a: Analyzing the Customers 180
9.2.1 Customer Segmentation 180
9.2.2 Customer Characteristics and Customer Requirements 183
9.2.3 Distribution Channels 185
9.3 Content Module 1b: Analyzing the Supply Chain Strategy 187
9.3.1 Fundamental Aspects of Strategic Supply Chain Orientation 187
9.3.2 Determining the Supply Chain Strategy 188

9.4 Content Module 2: Analyzing the Manufacturing Strategy . . . 191
9.4.1 Fundamental Aspects of Manufacturing Strategy . . . 191
9.4.2 Product Modularization . . . 193
9.4.3 Outsourcing . . . 194
9.4.4 Determining the Manufacturing Strategy and Decoupling Point . . . 195
9.5 Content Module 3: Analyzing the Suppliers . . . 198
9.5.1 Fundamental Aspects of Supplier Management . . . 198
9.5.2 Categorization of Modules and the Classification of Suppliers . . . 200
9.6 Content Module 4: Analyzing Supply Chain Processes . . . 202
9.6.1 Geographic Process Allocation . . . 202
9.6.2 Configuration of Source, Make and Deliver Processes . . . 204
9.7 Content Module 5: Analyzing the Supply Chain Governance . . . 208
9.7.1 Relationship Management and Level of Information Sharing: Customers . . . 208
9.7.2 Relationship Management and Level of Information Sharing: Supplier Side . . . 211
9.8 Content Module 6: Analyzing the Supporting Activities in the Supply Chain . . . 211
9.8.1 Project Management Within the Supply Chain Context . . . 212
9.8.2 Human Resource Perspective . . . 214
9.9 Approach for Key Performance Indicators Selection . . . 215
9.10 Application Example of SCD-Guide SCD-Phase 2 and Possible Output . . . 225
References . . . 228

10 Phase 3: Supply Chain Gap Analysis in the SCD-Guide . . . 231
10.1 Goals of SCD-Phase 3 . . . 231
10.2 CM1: Customer Segmentation and Supply Chain Strategy . . . 232
10.2.1 Customer Segmentation and Customer Requirements 232
10.2.2 Derivation of the Supply Chain Strategy . . . 233
10.3 CM2: Modularization and Vertical Range of Manufacture . . . 233
10.3.1 Service Offerings Per Customer Segment . . . 233
10.3.2 Specification of the Different Modules Within a Product . . . 236
10.3.3 Make-Or-Buy Decision Per Module and the Vertical Range of Manufacture . . . 236
10.4 CM3: Supplier Segmentation and Supply Strategy . . . 236
10.5 CM4: Allocation of Supply Chain Activities . . . 238

10.6 Functional Supply Chain Processes 238
10.6.1 Plan Process 238
10.6.2 Deliver Process 239
10.6.3 Make Process 239
10.6.4 Source Process 239
10.6.5 Return Process 240
10.7 CM5: Supply Chain Governance 240
10.7.1 Customer Relationship Management and Information Sharing 240
10.7.2 Supplier Relationship Management and Information Sharing 242
10.8 CM6: Supply Chain Project Management and Human Resources Perspective 243
10.8.1 Supply Chain Project Management 243
10.8.2 Supply Chain Process Management: Human Resources Perspective 244
10.9 Collection of Corrective Actions 245
10.9.1 Corrective Actions: Plan Process 245
10.9.2 Corrective Actions: Source and Make Processes 245
10.9.3 Corrective Actions: Deliver Processes 252
10.10 Supply Chain Resources 255
10.11 Application Example of SCD-Guide SCD-Phase 3 and Possible Output 257
References 260

11 Phase 4: Supply Chain Prioritization and Selection of Corrective Actions 261
11.1 Goals for SCD-Phase 4 261
11.2 Prioritization Procedure for Corrective Actions 261
11.3 Step 1: Goal Prioritization 262
11.4 Step 2: Identification of Corrective Actions 264
11.5 Step 3: Pre-Selection of Corrective Actions 266
11.6 Step 4: Evaluation and Prioritization of Corrective Actions 268
11.6.1 Existence of Prior Experience 268
11.6.2 Extent of Intra- and Inter-Organizational Implementation 268
11.6.3 Interdependencies and Logical Hierarchies 269
11.6.4 Weighted Score Method 269
11.6.5 Analytic Hierarchy Process 272

11.7 Application Example of SCD-Guide SCD-Phase 4 and Possible Output 276
11.7.1 Identification of Corrective Actions 276
11.7.2 Pre-Selection of Corrective Actions 277
Reference 281

12 Phase 5: Preparation of Implementation of Supply Chain Differentiation 283
12.1 Goals for SCD-Phase 5 283
12.2 Step 1: Project Conception. 284
12.2.1 Description and Content of the Phase 284
12.2.2 Methods. 285
12.3 Step 2: Project Specification 288
12.3.1 Description and Content of the Phase 288
12.3.2 Detailed Descriptions and Methods 288
12.4 Step 3: Project Planning 292
12.4.1 Description and Content of the Phase 292
12.4.2 Methods. 293
12.5 Application Example of SCD-Guide SCD-Phase 5 and Possible Output 301
References 303

Appendix 305

Index 337

Part I
Conception of the Supply Chain Differentiation Guideline

1 Introduction

1.1 Why do We Need a Supply Chain Differentiation Guideline?

The awareness of the importance of supply chain management has increased significantly in recent years. In most industries and sectors, supply chain management has climbed up organizational agendas. One reason for this development results from the increased complexity of supply chains due to the outsourcing trend in recent decades. In the late 1980s for example, outsourcing in U.S. industries contributed to nearly 60 % of total production costs. However, the development of supply chain management is, in addition to such internal motives, also driven by various external factors including the constant growth of globalization, decreasing international trade barriers, improvements in information availability, and government regulations such as the establishment of a single European market (Gunasekaran et al. 2004).

The overriding objective of supply chain management is the generation of revenue and, if possible, the increase of market share during the integration of procurement, production, distribution and logistics functions across company borders. More precisely, to generate revenue the organization and its affiliated supply chain partners must provide a product or a service to the customer (Childerhouse and Towill 2000). In other words, in current-day business the success or failure of supply chains is defined in the marketplace by the end customer. The development of a strategy which meets the requirements of the supply chain and the end customer is only possible if the needs and constraints of the markets are understood. Thus, customer satisfaction and marketplace understanding are crucial when elaborating a new supply chain strategy (Christopher and Towill 2001).

However, in recent years, the focus of supply chain management lay significantly on cost optimization, which is legitimate as logistic costs have increased in recent years and are expected to continue to do so. Thus, it is crucial to prevent supply chain expenditures and the tying up of working capital including inventories. However, in order to ensure the sustainability or improvement of a

E. Hofmann et al., *The Supply Chain Differentiation Guide*,
DOI: 10.1007/978-3-642-31936-5_1, © Springer-Verlag Berlin Heidelberg 2012

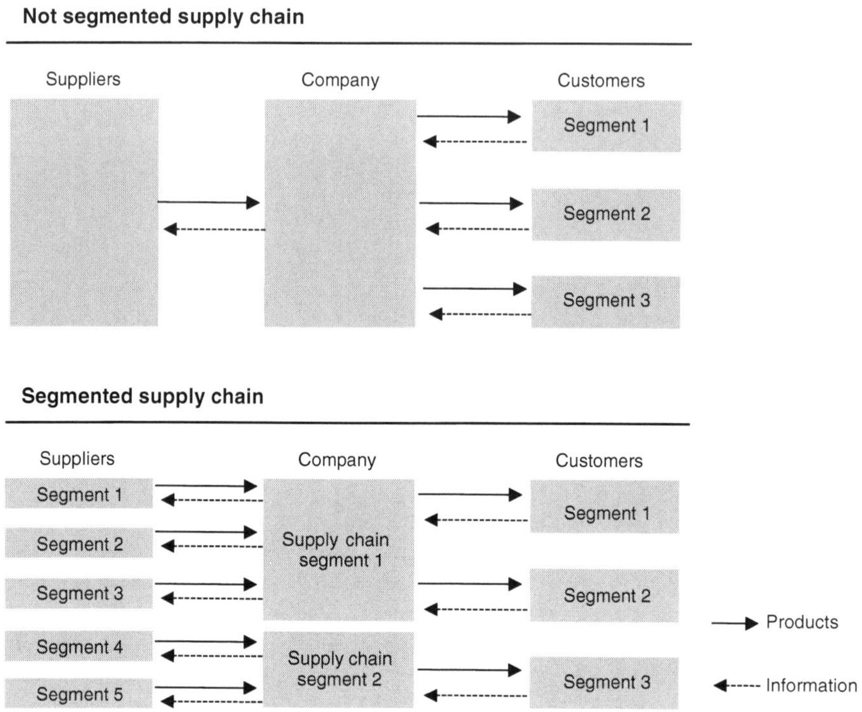

Fig. 1.1 Segmented and non-segmented supply chains

company's competitive position, the enhanced customer requirements in terms of supply availability, delivery reliability, and delivery lead time must be taken into account. This trade-off between reducing costs and satisfying customer requirements has to be resolved, something that has gained importance as the shape of the economy has become less stable (Mayer et al. 2009).

With regard to the importance of an increased focus on customer requirements, it is crucial to differentiate between different customer segments. Satisfying customer requirements in many cases cannot be achieved by one single supply chain as customer requirements differ and vary across various marketplaces.

If a "one-size-fits-all" approach is applied, then not only are all customers of an organization treated in a similar manner, but all suppliers are also managed in a similar way. These factors lead to ineffectiveness in supply chain management. Hence, a clear focus of supply chain management should be the satisfaction of the various customer requirements accomplished by a segmented supply chain; here compare Childerhouse and Towill (2000) as depicted in Fig. 1.1.

The relevance of supply chain differentiation, which encompasses supply chain segmentation, has also been confirmed by a 2009 study. Companies segmenting their supply chain instead of applying a "one-size-fits-all" supply chain are clearly more successful. More than two-thirds of the companies in the sample already

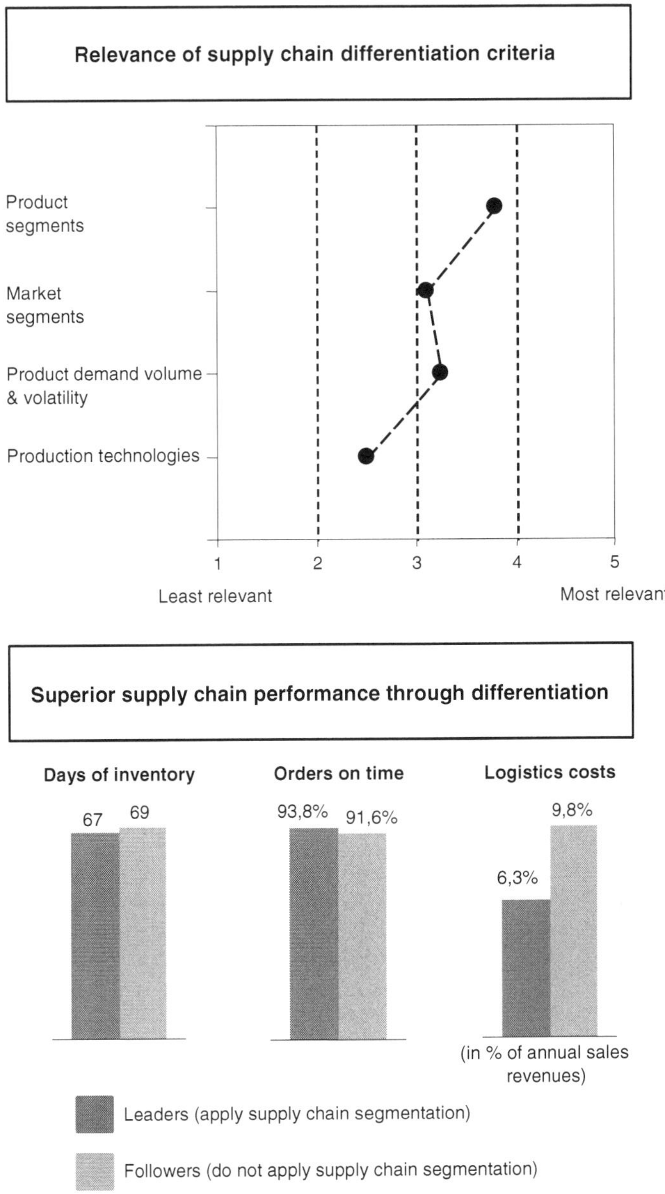

Fig. 1.2 Superior supply chain, performance supply chain performance through differentiation (Mayer et al. 2009)

make successful use of a differentiated supply chain. On the one hand, the study analyzed whether companies employing a segmented supply chain achieve a better supply chain performance. The results revealed a better supply chain performance

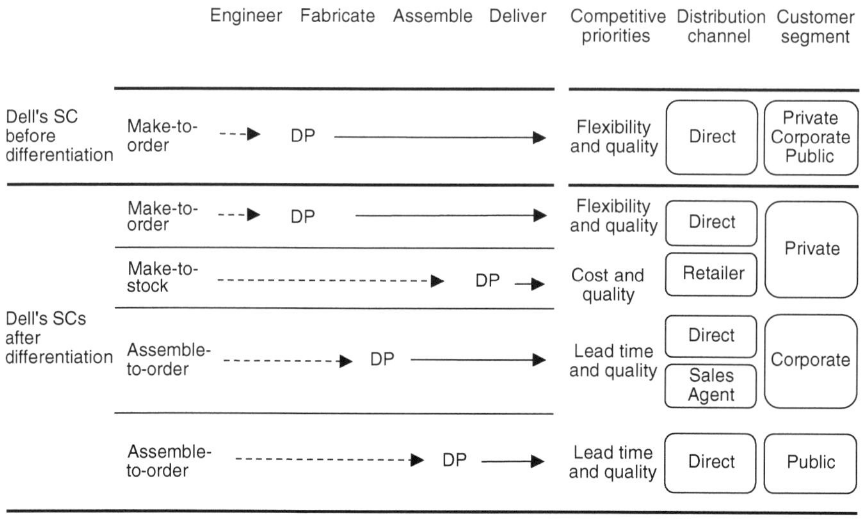

Fig. 1.3 Supply chain differentiation of Dell before and after the consideration of customer requirements. *DP* decoupling point, *SC* supply chain

for companies applying clear segmentation logic with subsequently customized processes and structures. Due to segmentation according to criteria regarded as important for product and market segments, companies can offer a better delivery service at lower logistics costs by keeping inventory low. Hence, the superior supply chain performance in terms of the categories "days of inventory", "orders on time" and "logistics costs" of companies applying segmentation compared to companies taking a "one-size-fits-all" approach is depicted on the right hand side of Fig. 1.2. Segmentation by "product segments" and "product demand volume and volatility" plays an important role. Segmentation by "production technologies" is considered less relevant as illustrated on the left hand side of Fig. 1.2.

A prominent example of a differentiated supply chain approach is the case of the popular computer manufacturer Dell. The company was faced by decreasing margins over a number of years. By analyzing the problem, Dell observed that not all of its customers require and value Dell's complex make-to-order strategy which allowed its customers to purchase a product customized to their specifications. After analyzing its customer requirements in detail, the company realized that public and corporate customers appreciate predictability and reliable delivery in contrast to private customers who value multiple sales channels and low price options more. In addition, public customers demand less variety of product variants than corporate customers. The private customers, however, demand a rather high diversity of product variants (Davis 2010). Based on this insight, Dell developed a differentiated supply chain strategy based on the three identified customer segments. Every supply chain is designed to meet the requirements of a specified customer segment as depicted in Fig. 1.3 (for simplicity's sake, only four

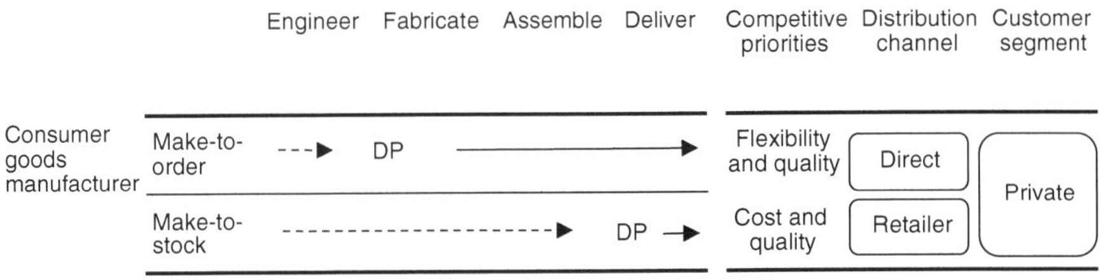

Fig. 1.4 Supply chain differentiation of a consumer goods manufacturer

of the six different supply chains established by Dell are illustrated). Thus, the supply chain strategy differentiates according to the specific requirements of a customer segment. If, for example, flexibility and quality are the main requirements, a make-to-order approach is suitable which implies the positioning of the decoupling point (DP) fairly far upstream in the value chain. The decoupling point is traditionally defined as the point in the value chain where a product is linked to a specific customer order (for a more detailed description of the decoupling point, please see Chaps. 3 and 4).

By differentiating the supply chain configuration in alignment with identified customer requirements, Dell was able to provide its products to its customers as demanded. Moreover, the company was able to reduce complexity as the configuration of its products was reduced in the supply chain. Furthermore, Dell was able to lower its operational costs by approximately $1.5 billion from 2008 to 2010 (Davis 2010).

The case of Dell is a good example for illustrating on a simplified level the impact and benefits of a differentiated supply chain. Regarding present-day business, getting the right product at the right time and price to the right costumer has become the key to competitive advantages as whole supply chains compete against each other instead of just individual companies (Christopher and Towill 2001). Thus, a "one-size-fits-all" approach is no longer sufficient for differentiating a company from its competitors.

In consumer goods manufacturing, there are various companies such as Adidas, Nike and Oakley which are already successfully performing supply chain differentiation. As can be seen in Fig. 1.4, the supply chain of consumer goods has changed over time. Due to the low price of consumer goods, companies have made greater use of make-to-stock approaches. The successful implementation of supply chain differentiation by prominent consumer goods manufacturers has shown that it can be applied to that area as well. It affirms that supply chain differentiation is relevant for all price ranges of products within manufacturing companies.

Table 1.1 Overview of supply chain assessment approaches

Author(s), year	Methodology of definition put forth
Brun et al. (2006)	An information system for advanced planning/scheduling and supply chain management with a focus on supply chain value assessment.
de Vries (2007)	Systemized and integrated approach toward analyzing inventory management systems and a conceptual framework which aims at assessing and redesigning inventory management systems.
Foggin et al. (2004)	A supply chain diagnostic tool to determine problems, inefficiencies, or needed improvements in a client's, or a potential client's supply chain that the third party logistics provider can effectively address.
Gunasekaran and Kobu (2007)	The key performance measures and metrics to manage logistics and supply chain operations.
Kannan and Tan (2002)	Effective supplier selection and assessment for companies and the identification of relationships between criteria and a buying firm's business performance.
Naim et al. (2002)	A guide for conducting Quick Scan, a supply chain oriented business diagnostics.
New (1996)	A conceptual framework for analyzing supply chain improvement.
Payne and Peters (2004)	The product supply characterization model assesses the alignment of the type of product clusters with the type of distribution channels delivering the products.
Rajala and Savolainen (1997)	Two different ways of coping with process variations through simulation modeling or value analysis (VA). Radical improvements can be achieved when applying VA to business process re-engineering.
Fahmy Salama et al. (2009)	Supply chain and operations audits represent a fundamental step for systematically capturing market changes and for adequately supporting improvement projects in this way.
Naim (2000)	Supply chain assessment methodology based on the supply chain proficiency model that can be used to set realistic supply chain objectives.
Verma and Pullman (1998)	The study examines the difference between managers' rating of the perceived importance of different supplier attributes and their actual choice of suppliers using the Likert scale set of questions and a discrete choice analysis.
Wei et al. (2007)	A framework with three main phases for selecting an adequate supply chain management project that incorporates the strategies and operating routines of a supply chain, including a strategic objective analysis phase, a systems analysis phase, and group decision making phase.

1.2 Supply Chain Assessments: What is Currently Available?

Supply chain assessment is a crucial part of the supply chain differentiation process. In the following an introductory overview will be given, which includes the most important approaches to supply chain assessments. Three methods will be discussed in further detail in order to provide a picture of the scope of operations following the implementation of these methods. The Table 1.1 as well as the following description of selected approaches does not intend to be exhaustive, but only to give an overview regarding currently available supply chain assessment approaches.

1.2.1 The Supply Chain Scan Approach

The approach taken by Naim et al. (2002) is a guide for performing a supply chain oriented business diagnostics called Quick Scan. Quick Scan is the first step in identifying change management opportunities in the supply chain.

Before implementing information and communication technologies, the author underscores that it is important to thoroughly analyze the supply chain via the quick scan process. This supply chain diagnostic approach collects and synthesizes qualitative and quantitative data from the supply chain. The objective of the quick scan implementation is to advise companies of the direction and magnitude of change required in their supply chains at the start of a change program.

Different factors can be taken into account in the quick scan analysis, such as material flows, information flows and information and communication technology (ICT), measures of performance, organizational structures, and relationships and attitudes. The data collection and analytical techniques are used to evaluate how well the supply chain processes of the company meet end customer requirements. In the following a comprehensive overview of the different steps involved in the quick scan process is presented. Figure 1.5 shows the different tasks which have to be performed during the process, starting with identification of the supply chain business process and getting a buy in of the business champion, followed by the conducting of the actual quick scan via data collection techniques and analysis of the findings.

It's stated that a complete quick scan process can be finished within a two-week period. Once this is done, a feedback presentation is conducted during which opportunities and improvements are discussed. The quick scan is therefore of importance, since it helps in fully comprehending the current state of the supply chain and in determining those actions that will yield maximum benefit which can be implemented before or with the automation process. The approach however, is not sufficiently strategic, can only be seen under operative circumstances and does not explicitly mention supply chain differentiation.

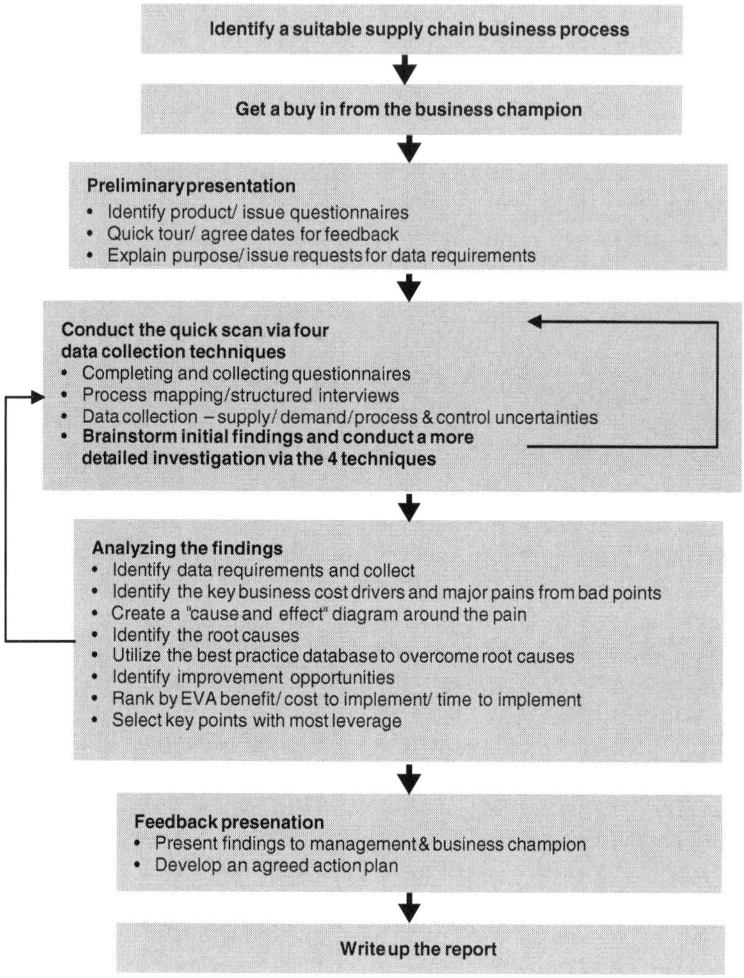

Fig. 1.5 Supply chain scan analysis, according to Naim et al. (2002)

1.2.2 The Supply Chain Diagnostic Tool

The supply chain diagnostic tool put forth by Foggin et al. (2004) determines the problems, inefficiencies, or needed improvements in a client's, or a potential client's supply chain that the third party logistics provider (3PL) can effectively address. Most tools describing the problems of supply chains are too large, time-consuming or quantitative. The approach employed by Foggin et al. (2004) is a much quicker qualitative method for analyzing areas of inefficiencies.

3PL–client relationships are fraught with risk and have a high failure tendency. The most common reason for this inefficiency is nonperformance. There are

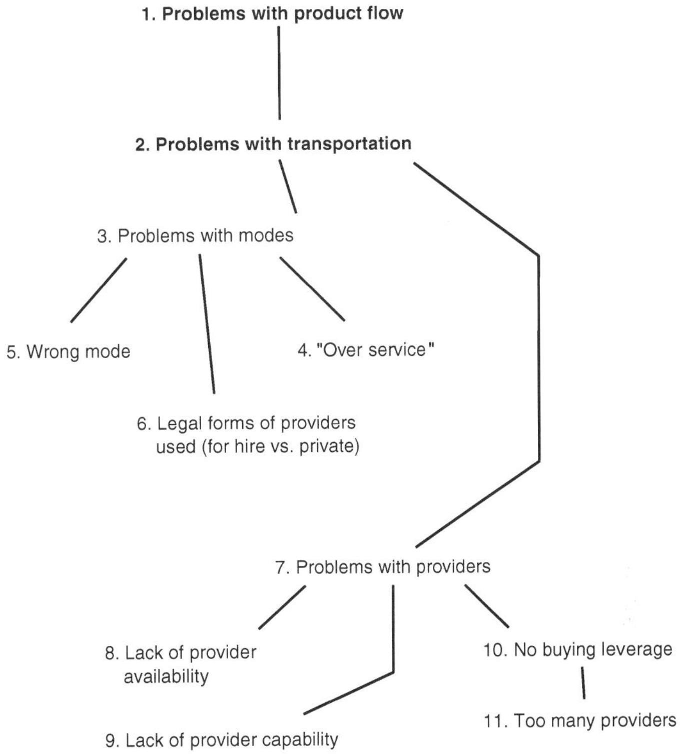

Fig. 1.6 Identifying key inventory issues with the supply diagnostic tool, according to Foggin et al. (2004)

continuous reports of various failures and breakdowns in 3PL–client relationships. Two-thirds of 3PL–client relationships fail within the first 5 years of the relationship. As a result of these failures, companies either find new contracting partners or decide to bring the competencies back in-house.

This shows the need for a diagnostic tool which can help to examine the customer supply chain in an early stage of the relationship. The distinct separation of customers who do not need help, who cannot be helped or customers who will potentially turn into a viable relationship needs to be undertaken before more cost-intensive and time-consuming measures are taken.

The diagnostic tool developed by Foggin et al. (2004) is easy to handle and is structured to be completed within an hour. It solely involves data that can be easily obtained. The method is thereby qualitative in nature. The supply chain diagnostic tool is a questionnaire that helps to quickly identify problems and diagnose the current problems existing in a potential customer's supply chain. The following overview (Fig. 1.6) shows an approach to the areas of interest to identify key issues within inventory management. It is thereby only an abstract of the full questionnaire and shows an example of the chain of cause and effect given within the supply chain diagnostic tool.

The questionnaire includes different areas of interest starting with general questions about the nature of the supply chain, inventory issues, customer service issues, organizational issues, system/information issues and product flow issues.

It is a relatively quick, effective and comprehensive tool for diagnosing the potential client's supply chain problems and for detecting the overall ability of the 3PL–client relationship to solve those problems. The ability to diagnose potential 3PL–client relationship problems beforehand will lead to a more efficient process at a later point in time and will help eliminate inefficiencies at an early stage of the relationship. This approach is, however, only operative and does not take the strategic approach into account. Furthermore the approach does not sufficiently consider supply chain differentiation.

1.2.3 Supply Chain and Operations Audits

Fahmy Salama et al. (2009) introduce a tool to improve supply chain and operations by conducting supply chain and operations audits. Organizations today face highly dynamic markets which are characterized by agility, adaptability and alignment. The authors suggest that a rising need for supply chain and operations audits becomes apparent. Supply chain and operations audits support improvement projects and can be carried out in two different approaches. One focuses on the problems found as its starting point and the other starts with prospective solutions or enablers.

The diagnostic stage is the central element of the auditing approach. Here assessment is aimed at the interaction between an organization and its "others" (whether people, processes and technology) as it affects market-driven performances. The identification of causal relationships is a fundamental step for project success. The diagnostic stage considers the following steps: defining the scope of analysis; identifying market drivers and competitive positions; creating causal relationship maps; investigating critical processes; and tune, weigh and validate causal relationship maps. It uses predefined master causal relationship maps based on current best practices to identify the as-is situation. The final result shows a qualitative mapping of the as-is situation and the gap between it and best practices. Thus, the most important output of this framework is the development of an explanatory causal relationship map.

Figure 1.7 shows a simplified version of the master best practice relationship map to give an example of the methodology's diagnostic process. The results of the diagnosis stage then help to identify "enablers" or "solutions" (technology- or management-related solutions) which tend to change continuously over time. The lack of identification of causal relationships forms a major threat to the project's success, regardless whether an approach is taken aimed at finding the pains or one aimed at identifying the solution and its enablers. The weak aspects of this

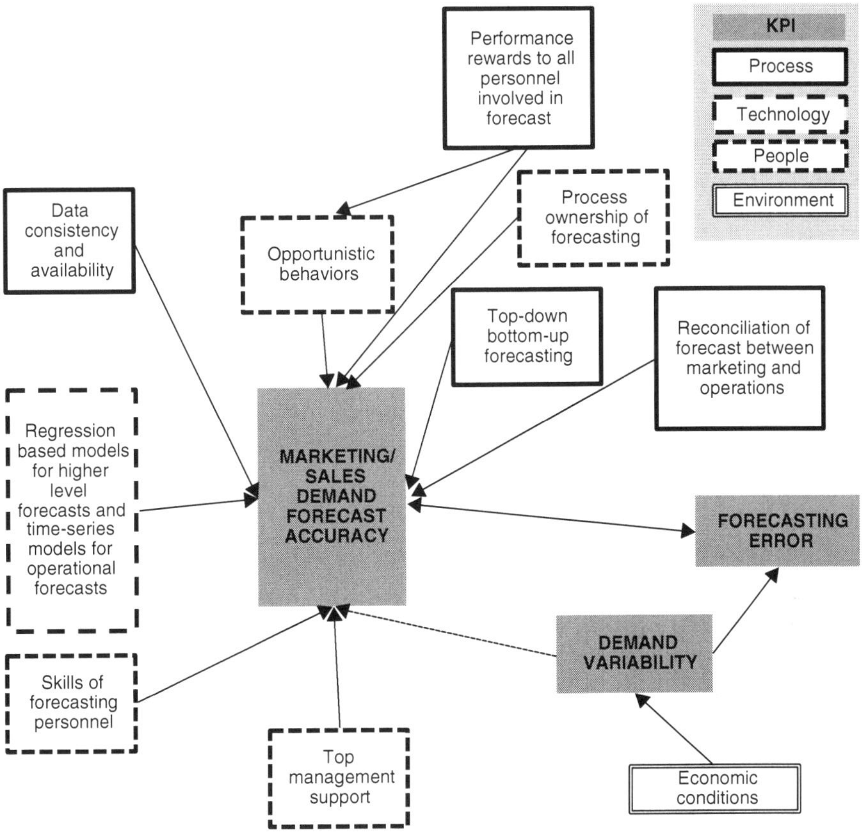

Fig. 1.7 Supply chain and operations audit, according to Fahmy Salama et al. (2009). *KPI* key performance indicators

approach are its missing operative approach, its less strategic approach and the fact that differentiation as such has not been explicitly recognized.

1.2.4 What is Missing?

As the heading of this subsection already indicates, the approaches presented by Naim et al. (2002), Foggin et al. (2004) and Fahmy Salama et al. (2009) are purely of operational nature. Furthermore, the approaches neglect supply chain segmentation/differentiation as a means of dealing with varying customer needs and requirements while operating each supply chain in an efficient manner. The supply chain assessment and differentiation guideline introduced in this book addresses this deficiency, this gap, and, by doing so, presents a holistic and customer-oriented approach to supply chain management.

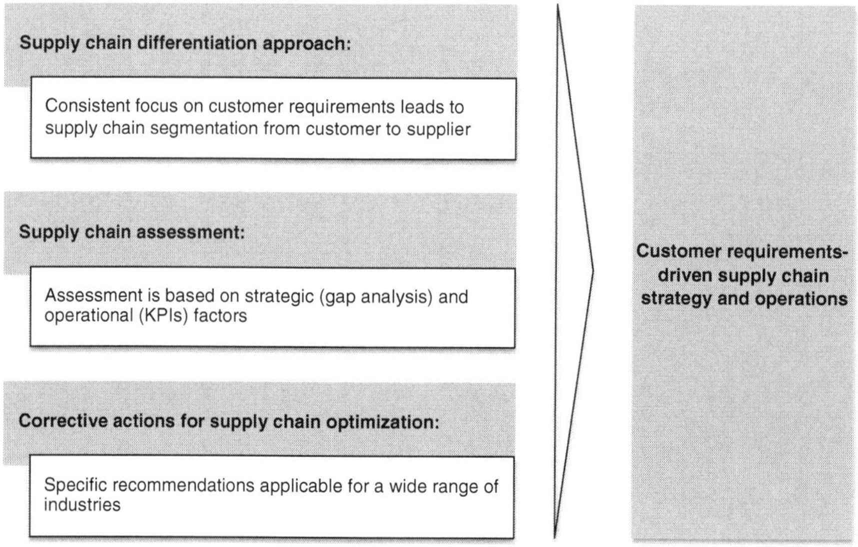

Fig. 1.8 Principles of the SCD Guide

1.3 Principles and Advantages of the Supply Chain Differentiation Approach

The overarching goal of our guideline is to execute supply chain management based on customer requirements by applying a **supply chain differentiation approach**. Thus, as depicted in Fig. 1.8, the consistent focus on customer requirements throughout the approach leads to a supply chain segmentation from the customer to the supplier. This is realized by elaborating first a TO-BE supply chain configuration based on defined customer segments and their corresponding requirements such as product quality, product availability, price, service, or service response time, to mention just a few. Furthermore, the AS-IS situation is identified in order to gather structured information about the current configuration of the supply chain, a process which is equally based on identifying an organization's customer segments and their requirements. The impacts of these requirements on the supply chain strategy for each customer segment, its product modules, process allocation and definition, as well as on the suppliers are ascertained in order to come up with a consistent supply chain differentiation strategy and mode of operation.

Moreover, to reveal the possible improvement potentials of the prevailing supply chain, a **supply chain assessment** based on a gap analysis and a self-benchmarking based on adequate key performance indicators (KPIs) is conducted. The gap analysis as a strategic factor results from the deduced TO-BE configuration compared to the AS-IS situation of the supply chain. Just like the gap

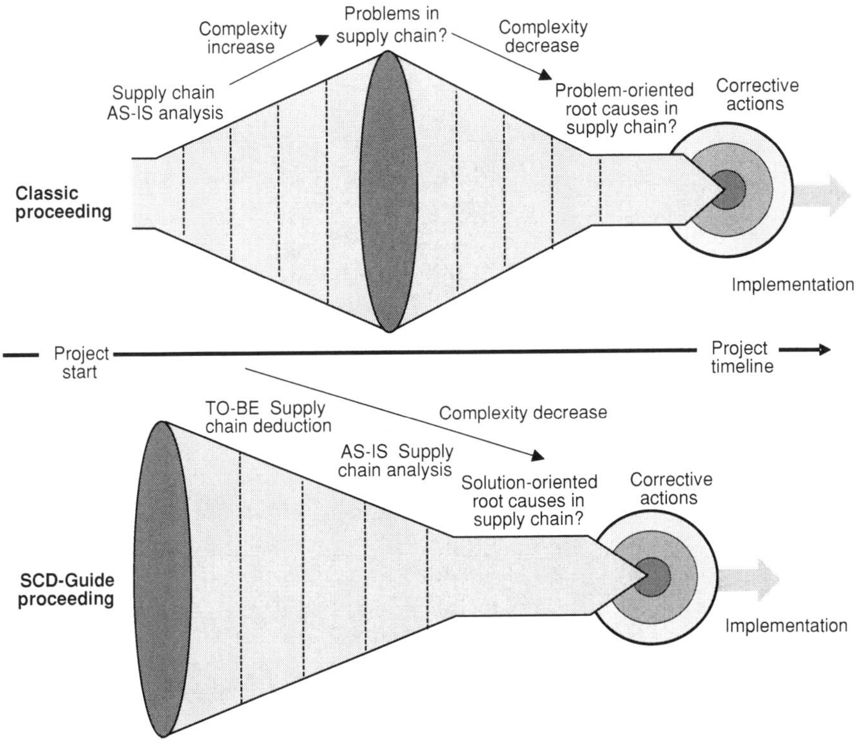

Fig. 1.9 The SCD Guide versus the classic approach

analysis, self-benchmarking as the operational factor, which is based on the organization's strategic supply chain orientation and its desired competitive priorities such as quality, cost, lead time, and flexibility, reveals differences between the desired and the actual state. The **corrective actions for supply chain optimization** that result from the gap analysis and self-benchmarking allow for specific recommendations which are applicable to a wide range of industries, since these corrective actions are generic in character.

The main advantage of the SCD Guide compared to classic procedures is its solution-oriented approach. Right from the beginning the guideline focuses on the formulation of a TO-BE supply chain. The derivation of such a desired supply chain, accomplished in the first phase of the methodology, leads to a clear **solution-oriented** focus. This allows one to bypass time-consuming problem and AS-IS analysis and not lose sight of available resources and solution potentials. While classic approaches increase complexity in the initial analysis until the problems are identified, the SCD Guide starts off with a higher level of complexity, since the user has to learn and transfer the structure of the SCD Guide to his or her case example. In this way the SCD Guide approach yields corrective actions faster than classic approaches, as depicted in Figs. 1.9 and 1.10.

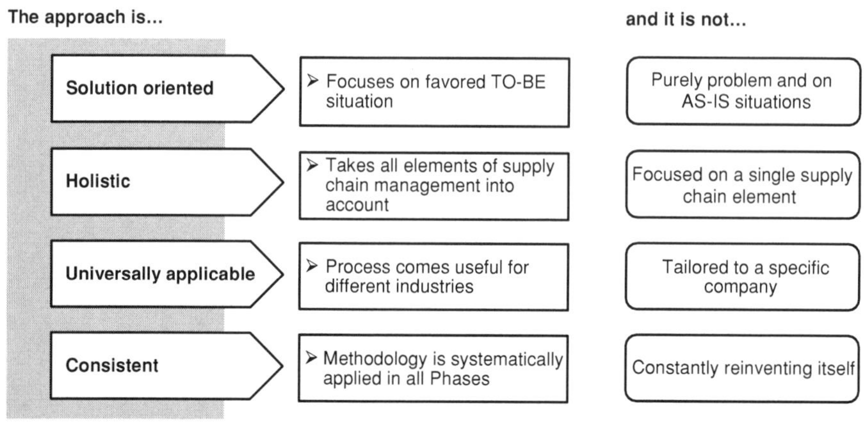

Fig. 1.10 Advantages of the SCD Guide

Besides its solution orientation, the SCD Guide is characterized as follows:

- The approach has a **holistic** claim as all relevant aspects of supply chain management are considered from both a strategic and an operative viewpoint. This includes customer and supplier segmentation, product modularization, supply chain process configuration including deliver-, make-, source-, plan- and return-processes, the allocation of the different processes, vertical range of manufacturing, distribution processes, as well as supply chain governance. In addition, supporting activities such as project management and human resources are considered. Those aspects of supply chain management can be found in the content modules (CM) of the guideline, depicted in Fig. 1.11.
- Another advantage of the generic guideline is its **universally applicable** approach to companies. Thus, the approach is of use for a variety of industries and company sizes because it is not tailored to a specific company. However, the main focus of the approach lies on industrial enterprises, since topics like manufacturing are covered in the approach. Once this focus put aside, the guideline is equally applicable to other companies. However, this would require a greater degree of adaptation.
- A final advantage of the guideline is its **consistent** application of the same methodology to all six phases it describes. Thus, as illustrated in Fig. 1.11, every phase of the approach consists of the same six CMs. This allows one to avoid unnecessary complexity and confusion, and the methodology needs not constantly reinvent itself.

1.4 The Structure of the SCD Guide

The structure of the guideline consists of five main phases, where every phase contains the same six content modules (CM), as depicted in Fig. 1.11. These CMs do not claim to be complete. Companies may see the need to analyze further areas

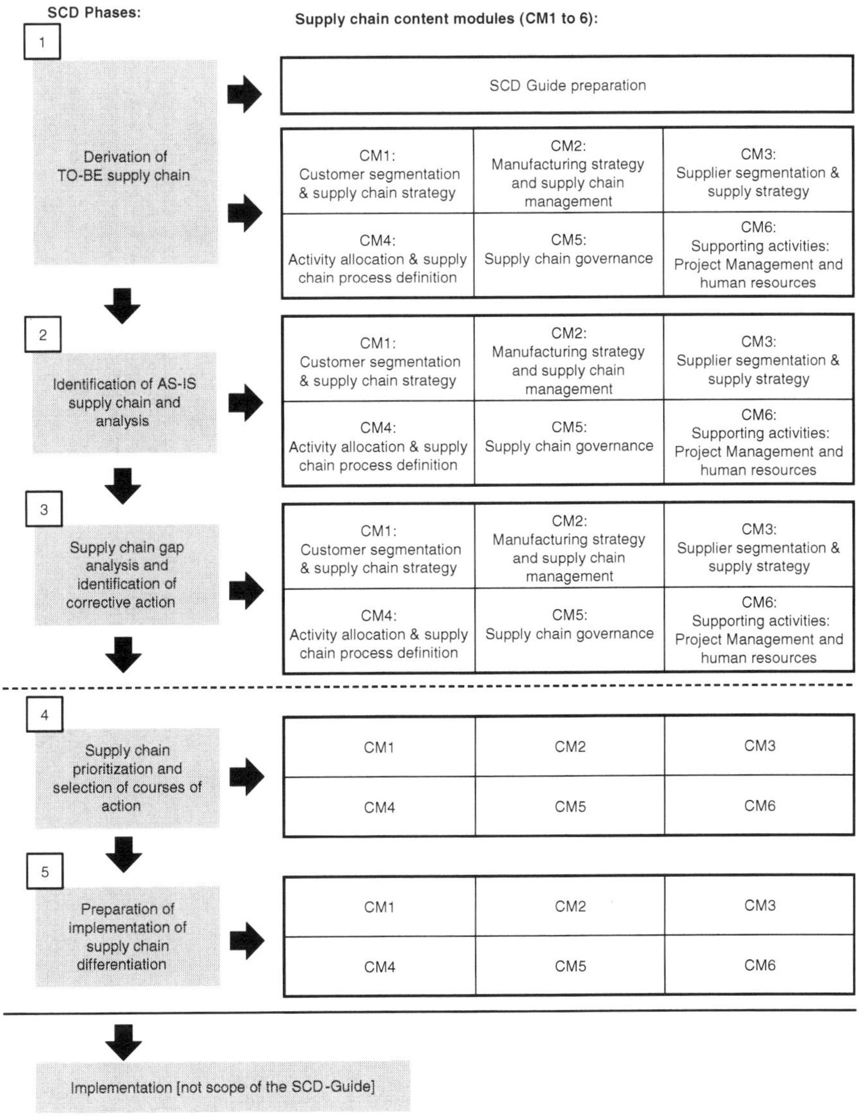

Fig. 1.11 General structure of the SCD Guide

for the consideration of supply chain differentiation. For example, one could examine value streams through the supply chain. The SCD Guide is easily expandable with respect to further CMs.

The structure of the content of SCD Phase 1 differs slightly from the structure of SCD Phases 2–5. In the first phase, where a possible TO-BE supply chain is systematically deduced, based on a customer requirement analysis, its content is

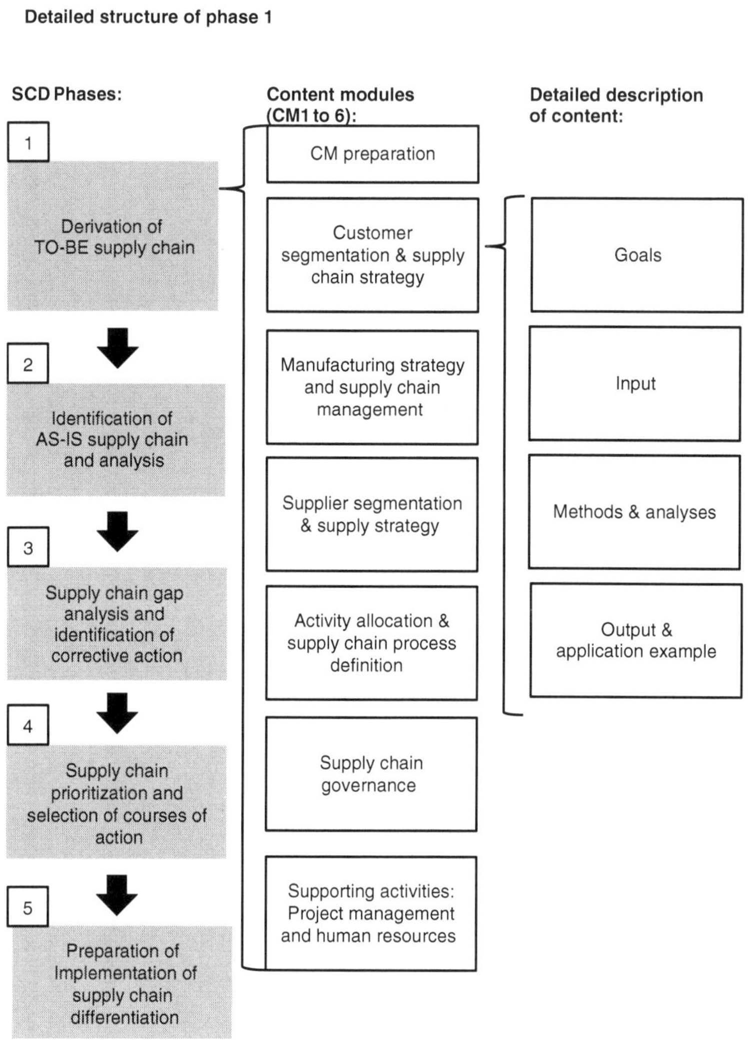

Fig. 1.12 Differences in the detailed structure of SCD Phase 1 (shown here) and that of SCD Phases 2–5 (shown in Fig. 1.13) of the SCD Guide

structured in six content modules which are described in detail by their goals, inputs, methods and analyses, output, and examples, as shown in Fig. 1.12.

This contrasts to the description of the subsequent SCD Phases 2–5, which focus on the identification and analysis of the present supply chain and the comparison between the derived TO-BE and the identified AS-IS supply chain, as well as on the prioritization of corrective actions and a preparation for implementation. These phases, namely, are described directly by the corresponding

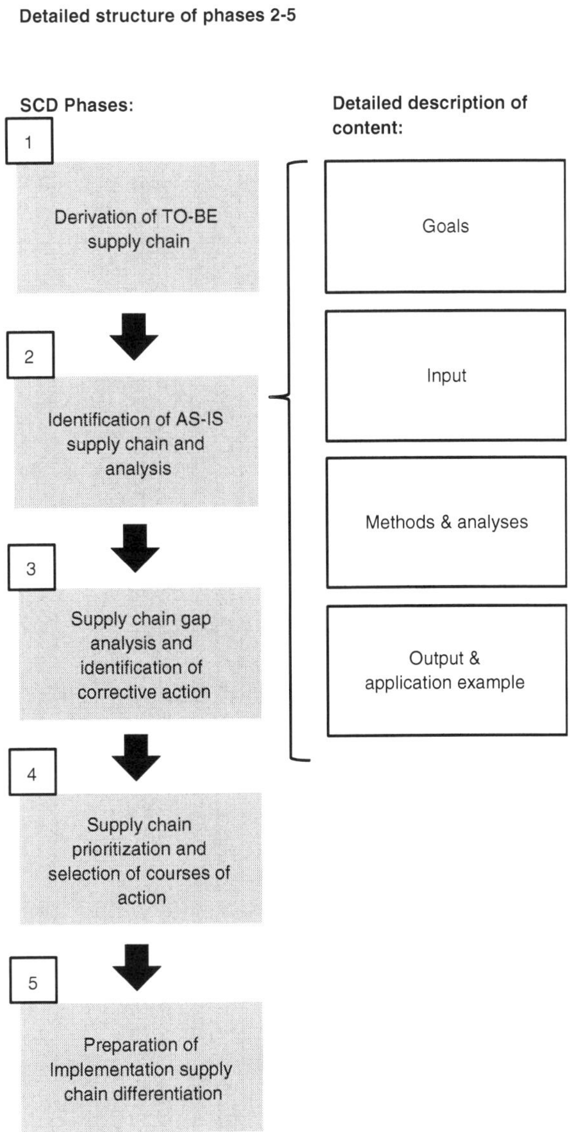

Fig. 1.13 Differences in the detailed structure of SCD Phase 1 (see Fig. 1.12) and that of SCD Phases 2–5 (shown here) of the SCD Guide

goals, inputs, methods and analysis, and by means of examples and output (see Fig. 1.13). This differentiation in the structure is implied, as the first phase is regarded as the most extensive, representing, as it does, the key phase, and thus, requiring a more detailed description. However, within SCD Phases 4 and 5, not all content modules necessarily have to be made use of. The gap analysis indicates in which areas there is a need for action. SCD Phase 4 prioritizes these needs and therefore reveals which content modules should be considered in SCD Phase 5.

The following paragraph gives a short overview with respect to the subject matter of the different phases and CMs. The subsequent sections focus on a more detailed description of the six content modules in SCD Phase 1 and the derivation of a TO-BE supply chain, as well as on the content covered in the following SCD Phases 2–5.

- In the **CM preparation** the company analyzes the current status of the supply chain using different methods and analyses. Furthermore, in doing so, the competitor's situation is taken into account in order to compare different supply chains with one another.
- The **CM1** in SCD Phase 1 covers the topics of customer segmentation and supply chain strategy which includes the classification of customers according to their sales volume and the value of the sold product. In order to be able to derive an adequate supply chain orientation based on an analytical hierarchy process (AHP) for each customer segment determined, customer needs are analyzed such as product quality and availability, service quality, delivery reliability, and price. Moreover, product characteristics and the business unit strategy for each segment are determined. This process allows one to specify a ranking of the alternatives of quality, costs, flexibility, or lead time which, in turn, permits one to allocate more of a lean or agile strategic supply chain orientation to each customer segment (Christopher and Towill 2001; Ketchen et al. 2008; Vitasek et al. 2003).
- **CM2** covers the manufacturing area and the breaking down of the different products into modules and their corresponding components if applicable. If not, different material groups are considered. Moreover, the vertical range of manufacturing is considered for the different products.
- **CM3** covering supplier segmentation and supply strategy focuses on the classification of the identified modules in order to rate and segment the corresponding supplier according to the importance of the purchase and the complexity of the respective supply market, for example according to Kraljic (1983).
- **CM4,** which covers the allocation of processes within the supply chain to respective geographic regions, seeks to evaluate where, for example, the distribution processes for an identified customer segment are located. Moreover, it involves a detailed discussion of which kind of deliver, make, and source processes have to be implemented. Hence, it is determined, for instance, whether the delivery process describes the delivery of stocked products, make-to-order products, or engineer-to-order products.
- **CM5,** covering the topic of supply chain governance, includes the management of customer relationships and supplier relationships. In doing so, it focuses on determining the level of information sharing between the company considered and its different customer and supplier segments.
- The final CM, **CM6,** focuses on project management and human resources. Here, on the one hand, a company's supply chain project management style is classified in order to determine which company level the project normally

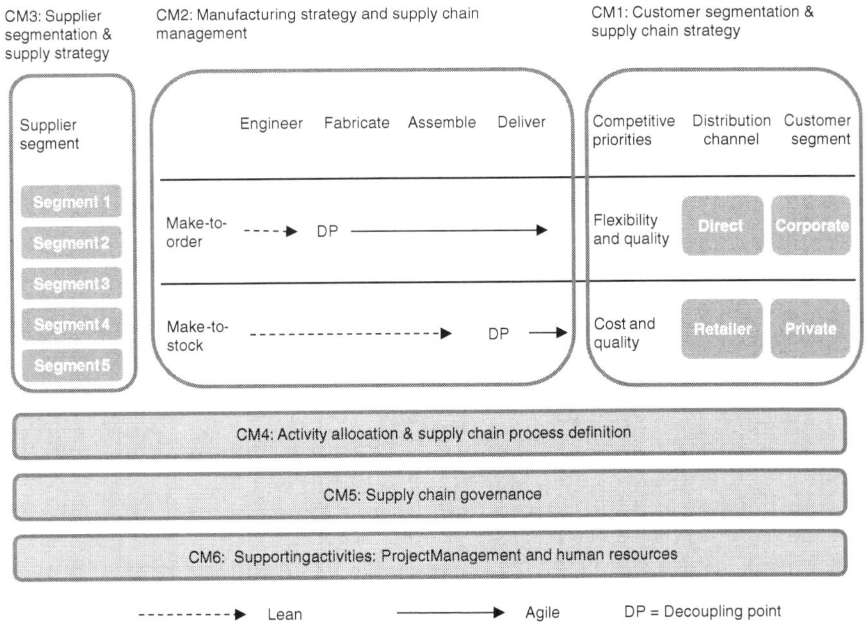

Fig. 1.14 Position of content modules in the value adding process

should affect and whether the projects are supposed to be strategic or non-strategic. On the other hand, the project management is described, for instance, in terms of organizational awareness and management support in order to determine a company's maturity level. Regarding human resources, topics such as strategic HR planning, HR training and development, and the retention of personnel in key positions and at all other organization levels are considered.

The described content is equally applied in all five phases by means of the same CMs. Thus, in SCD Phase 2 for example, the topics of the CMs are applied with respect to the AS-IS situation of supply chain management in the company analyzed. Figure 1.14 describes which stages of the value adding process the CMs are applied to. CM1–CM3 are applied to specific areas of the value adding process. CM4 and CM5 span across all steps in the value adding process. CM6 is a supporting activity which is not directly related to the value adding process.

Within each CM in SCD Phase 1 a morphological box is completed which records the TO-BE situation. The same is performed in SCD Phase 2, where the AS-IS situation is recorded in the morphological box. An example of the morphological box can be found in Sect. 1.6. In SCD Phase 3, the filled morphological boxes from SCD Phases 1 and 2 are compared within the gap analysis.

- **SCD Phase 2** focuses on the analysis of the AS-IS situation by gathering structured information about the current configuration of the supply chain.

Moreover, a main focus of this phase is on compiling and selecting relevant KPIs based on the strategically desired TO-BE states. Here the aim is to enable managers to use these KPIs to conduct a self-benchmarking of their organization's performance.

- **SCD Phase 3** includes the aforementioned gap analysis which results from the comparison of the TO-BE and the AS-IS states of the supply chain recorded in the previous two phases in order to identify areas requiring optimization. This comparison is achieved by filling the results from SCD Phase 1 as well as from SCD Phase 2 into a morphological box. This allows for a clear illustration of the deficit arising from the comparison of the TO-BE and AS-IS situation. Based on the analysis of the strategic and operative gap and a KPI benchmarking, suitable corrective actions to all supply chain processes, if necessary, are selected.
- **SCD Phase 4** aims to prioritize the identified corrective actions in SCD Phase 3 by a more detailed analysis. Its goal is to clarify the measures' strengths and weaknesses and to define their rank order by a qualitative and quantitative prioritization. In this way, two decision making methods are suggested which differ in scope and level of complexity. Moreover, this phase assesses the availability of different resources required by the identified corrective actions.
- The last phase, **SCD Phase 5,** focuses on the preparation of implementation, considering aspects such as time scheduling, responsibility check, and resource allocation.

1.5 Scalability of the Approach

Regarding the applicability of the guideline with its five phases and six CMs, the modular structure of the guideline, as depicted in Fig. 1.15 enables it to scale its contents as applied to a specific company. One opportunity to **reduce the number of analyzed customer segments** arises by applying all phases depicted in Fig. 1.11, but conducting the analysis for just one customer segment, one product, or one business unit.

A second option allows one to diminish the scope by **reducing the number of content modules considered**. Thus, all phases would be applied, but only to a limited number of CMs such as customer segmentation and supply chain strategy, or supply chain governance.

Lastly, by applying all phases to all identified customer segments and products but with a **reduced depth of steps performed** on each, a reduction of complexity can be achieved.

However, the approach may not only be reduced with respect to the regarded content modules, it is also possible to expand the number of content modules. In this way, further areas for analysis may be introduced to the approach.

1 Reduce number of analyzed customer segments

Apply all of the framework's steps but reduce the number of customer segments considered

- ➢ Conduct analysis for just one customer segment / one product / one business unit

2 Reduce number of content modules considered

Apply all of the framework's steps but only to a limited number of content modules

- ➢ Be aware of possible module interdependency

3 Reduce depth of steps performed

Apply all steps to all customer segments and products, but each with reduced depth

- ➢ Cut back complexity

Fig. 1.15 Scalability of the supply chain differentiation approach

1.6 The Morphological Box for Supply Chain Differentiation

In this section an exemplary morphological box is presented. The morphological box illustrated in Figs. 1.16 and 1.17 is a recommendation for possible analysis to be applied to a supply chain differentiation approach. Thus, the structure of the morphological box depends on the chosen analysis as well as on the applied CMs within the guideline. As mentioned in Sect. 1.5, the approach is scalable due to its modular structure and hence, not all CMs must be applied.

Every analysis within a CM leads to one dimension (row) in the morphological box and determines the possible values or conditions for each dimension (the columns). If, for example, the dimension "Relationship management" highlighted in Fig. 1.16 is considered, the analysis is characterized by four possible results. However, the possibility would also exist to illustrate eight possible results. For this reason the characteristics of an analysis may vary.

However, the structure of the morphological box also depends on the detail depth of the applied content of the guideline. This can be illustrated by taking the dimension "Product modules" depicted in Fig. 1.16 as an example. In this morphological box, the products for a customer segment are subdivided into their modules. In addition, for each of the identified modules it would equally be possible to determine their components. This would imply additional dimensions in the morphological box for each product. Thus, if a company is producing three

Customer segment 1

Descriptive part	Geographic distribution	Europe	Asia	North America	South America	Africa	Australia
Descriptive part	Demanded products	Product 1	Product 2	Product 3			
Descriptive part	Requirements ranking	Product quality	Product availability	Service quality	Delivery reliability	Price	
Descriptive part	Distribution channels	Direct	1-tier: Retailer	2-tier: Wholesaler	3-tier: Sales Agent	…	
Customer area	Competitive priorities	Quality	Cost	Flexibility	Lead time		
Customer area	Strategic supply chain orientation	Agile	Lean				
Customer area	Relationship management	Transaction based	Standardized process	Strategic customer relationship	Strategic alliance		
Customer area	Information sharing	Low	Low-medium	Medium-high	High		
Customer area	Delivery proc. (Process type)	Deliver stocked products (D1)	Deliver make-to-order product (D2)	Engineer-to-order(D3)			
Customer area	Delivery proc. (Process allocation)	Europe	Asia	North America	South America	Africa	Australia
Manufacturing area	Product 1 modules (MoB)	Module 1	Module 2	Module 3	Module 4	Module 5	Module n
Manufacturing area	Product 1 (Module categorization)	Noncritical	Leverage	Bottleneck	Strategic diversify	Strategic balance	Strategic exploit
Manufacturing area	Product 2 modules (MoB)	Module 1	Module 2	Module 3	Module 4	Module 5	Module n
Manufacturing area	Product 2 (Module categorization)	Noncritical	Leverage	Bottleneck	Strategic diversify	Strategic balance	Strategic exploit
Manufacturing area	Product n modules (MoB)	Module 1	Module 2	Module 3	Module 4	Module 5	Module n
Manufacturing area	Product n (Module categorization)	Noncritical	Leverage	Bottleneck	Strategic diversify	Strategic balance	Strategic exploit
Manufacturing area	Make process (Process type)	Make-to-stock (M1)	Make-to-order (M2)	Engineer-to-order (M3)			
Manufacturing area	Make proc. (Process allocation)	Europe	Asia	North America	South America	Africa	Australia
Manufacturing area	Decoupling point	Engineer-to-order	Source-to-order	Make-to-order	Assemble-to-order	Make-to-stock	

Fig. 1.16 Example of the morphological box (MoB) for supply chain differentiation, first part

different products, each consisting of six modules off our components each, this would imply a total of 18 further dimensions and 72 additional characteristics within these dimensions.

Customer segment 1

Area	Category	Dimension						
Suppliers area		Source process (Process allocation)	Europe	Asia	North America	South America	Africa	Australia
Suppliers area	Noncritical	Relationship management	Transaction-based	Standardized process	Strategic supplier relationship	Strategic alliance		
Suppliers area	Noncritical	Information sharing	Low	Low–medium	Medium–high	High		
Suppliers area	Noncritical	Source process (Process type)	Source stocked product (S1)	Source make-to-order product (S2)	Source engineer-to-order product (S3)			
Suppliers area	Leverage	Relationship management	Transaction-based	Standardized process	Strategic supplier relationship	Strategic alliance		
Suppliers area	Leverage	Information sharing	Low	Low–medium	Medium–high	High		
Suppliers area	Leverage	Source process (Process type)	Source stocked product (S1)	Source make-to-order product (S2)	Source engineer-to-order product (S3)			
Suppliers area	Bottleneck	Relationship management	Transaction based	Standardized process	Strategic supplier relationship	Strategic alliance		
Suppliers area	Bottleneck	Information sharing	Low	Low–medium	Medium–high	High		
Suppliers area	Bottleneck	Source process (Process type)	Source stocked product (S1)	Source make-to-order product (S2)	Source engineer-to-order product (S3)			
Suppliers area	Strategic	Relationship management	Transaction based	Standardized process	Strategic supplier relationship	Strategic alliance		
Suppliers area	Strategic	Information sharing	Low	Low–medium	Medium–high	High		
Suppliers area	Strategic	Source process (Process type)	Source stocked product (S1)	Source make-to-order product (S2)	Source engineer-to-order product (S3)			
		Supply chain project management (PM)	No discernible PM	Common language	Common process	Singular method-ology	Bench-marking	Continuous improve-ment
		Supply chain human resource risks	Shortage risk	Risk of quitting	Adaptation risk	Motivation risk		
		Supply chain manager competencies	Social competencies	Conflict competencies	Motivation competencies	Leadership competencies		
		Supply chain competencies	Cooperation competencies	Business process competencies	Customer competencies			

Fig. 1.17 Example of the morphological box for supply chain differentiation, second part

Another example highlights how the structure of the morphological box for supply chain differentiation may vary depending on the depth of the applied analysis. Taking the dimension "Decoupling point" into account as depicted in Fig. 1.16, the structure may differ depending on the following three approaches on how to evaluate the decoupling point:

- Determining the decoupling point for the whole value network.
- Determining the decoupling point for each product.
- Determining the decoupling point for each module level.

Hence, if the decoupling point is determined for the whole value network, the morphological box for supply chain differentiation will appear as depicted in Fig. 1.16. However, if the decoupling point is defined for each product, this would imply an additional dimension for each product. The third approach, determining the decoupling point for each module level, would add 18 additional dimensions to three products and six content modules.

After having explained the variability of the morphological box, the layout will be briefly explained. The morphological box consists of one **descriptive part** and three decision areas such as the **customer area**, **manufacturing area**, and **supplier area** as depicted on the left hand side in Figs. 1.16 and 1.17.

- The **descriptive part** covers issues determining, for example, the product demanded for a defined customer segment. Moreover, it includes customer requirements such as product quality or price and defines which distribution channel fits best for the considered customer segment. However, this part takes into account the major points in the morphological box and thus, may vary depending on the preferences of a company.
- The **customer area** contains dimensions such as the strategic supply chain orientation of a company in order to decide whether the supply chain is agile or "leagile". Furthermore, it is determined which competitive priorities are essential and if the product shall be delivered as a stocked product, make-to-order product, or engineer-to-order product.
- The second decision area, the **manufacturing area**, implies dimensions containing topics concerned with the products. Thus, the number of modules for each product is recorded as well as whether the modules are categorized as noncritical or strategic exploit. Moreover, the process type is recorded (make-to-stock, make-to-order, or engineer-to-order) and it is decided where the decoupling point shall be positioned within the value chain.
- The last decision area, the **supplier area**, is depicted in Fig. 1.17. This area determines, first of all, which geographical region the source process is allocated to. Then, supplier areas (segments) are classified according to the importance of the purchase and the complexity of the respective market. This classification is based on Kraljic (1983). Thus, it is decided whether a supplier area is, for example, noncritical or a leverage area. Within this dimension, it is then recoded how the relationship management is characterized and how intense the information sharing between the company and its supplier area is. Further, the source process is specified (Kraljic 1983).

1.7 Exemplary Cases

In the following, there are five different examples of companies which are interested in implementing the supply chain differentiation process. This allows us to see which parts of the SCD Guide the companies need to identify and implement according to their individual needs.

Case 1: Professional introduction of the supply chain management approach
A small- or medium-sized enterprise (SME) is interested in establishing and professionalizing its supply chain management. The key components, such as the purchasing department and the marketing and sales department, are already in place, but up until now there has not been an integrative approach to supply chain management within its business operations. Therefore the SME wants to establish an approach which is in alignment with the other areas of the supply chain. The company is advised to follow all the different steps of the supply chain differentiation process with a special focus on customer orientation. A supply chain which is not customer oriented fails to provide the most important objective of a supply chain. Customer orientation is the key element in differentiating a supply chain.

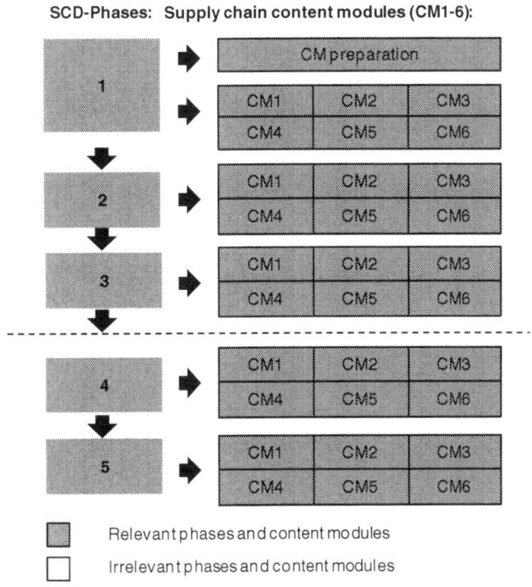

Case 2: Determine a supply chain strategy for one or more segments
A major international corporation is interested in aligning its supply chain strategy with one or more customer segments. It is important to note whether customer segmentation has taken place or not. If customer segmentation has not yet taken place, it is important to do so before the modification of other segments takes place. If the mere objective of the company is to determine the supply chain strategy, the application of SCD Phase 1 (CM1–CM3) will be sufficient. On the other hand, if the objective of the company is to identify and implement this strategy within its operations, SCD Phase 1 to SCD Phase 5 and CM1 to CM3, respectively, have to be considered.

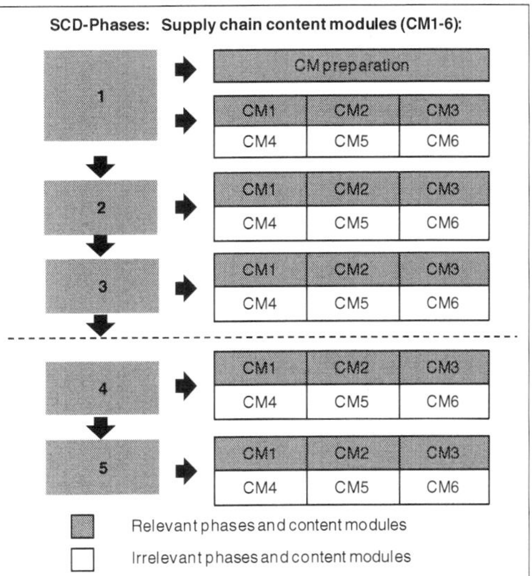

Case 3: Modification of the supplier–customer interface
An SME is interested in professionalizing procurement and supply management within its operations. Procurement is one of the key aspects of supply chain management today. Acquiring goods and services at a minimal cost at the right time, quantity, quality and location is a major success factor of supply chain management within a company. The increasing challenges the company faces in the procurement process are significant. In the implementation process of new procurement measures, the SME is advised to look at CM3 within each of the SCD Phases 1 to 5.

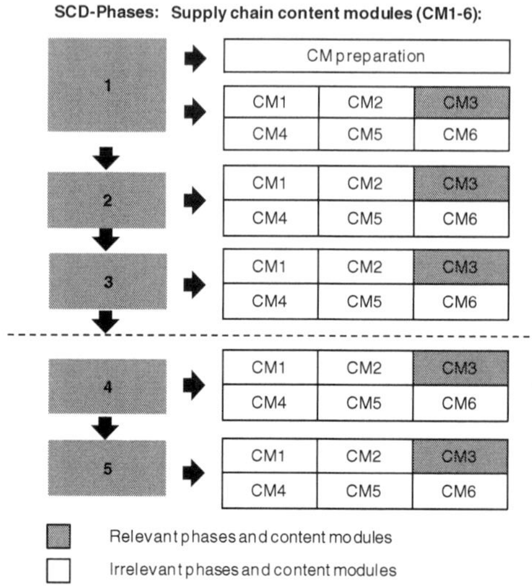

Case 4: Establishing a supply chain performance measurement system
An SME is trying to implement a supply chain performance measurement system to assess the performance of its supply chain. The company wants to measure the efficiency of its operations and the attainment of its objectives with the given resources. In case a strategic supply chain orientation is not yet in place, the company can implement SCD Phase 1 CM1 before starting to implement the other components. Otherwise the implementation performance measurement system in SCD Phase 2 cannot be realized. In that phase, the company accumulates business ratios in order to evaluate the efficiency of their processes.

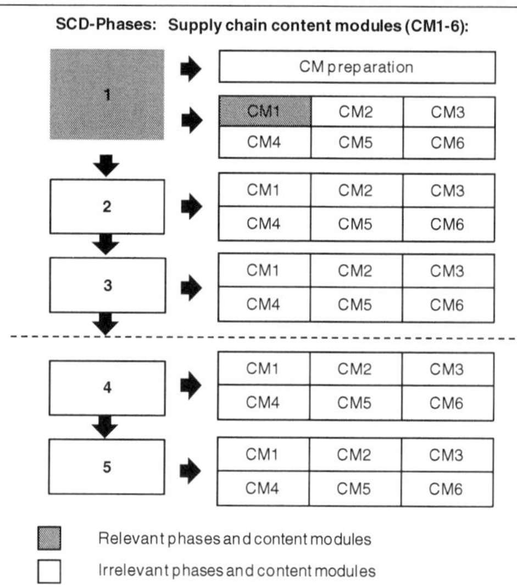

Case 5: Development and implementation of supply chain differentiation
A multinational corporation wants to implement supply chain differentiation within its operations. All the areas of the supply chain differentiation process are relevant for the corporation. Furthermore it is necessary to place a focal point on customer orientation. The assessment of customer segmentation is of crucial importance since a false segmentation can lead to an ineffective outcome. Since the whole approach lies within customer orientation, the process needs to begin with the customer segmentation process, if not already completed. Thereafter the whole process, from derivation of the TO-BE supply chain up until the preparation for the implementation phase of supply chain differentiation, can be conducted.

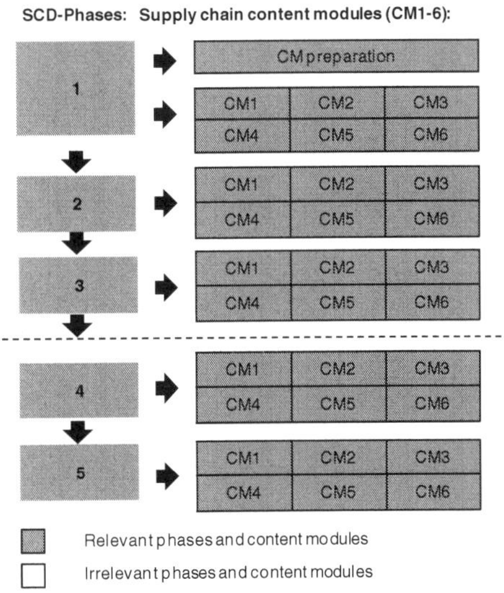

1.8 Challenges of an Application of the Supply Chain Assessment and Differentiation Guideline

Every project faces different challenges up until its completion and thus, certain requirements should be satisfied in order to facilitate a successful realization of an application of the guideline at hand. This can be reached by taking pre-requisites of project management and methodology-specific pre-requisites into account, as depicted in Fig. 1.18.

Regarding **project management pre-requisites** it must be stated that the complexity of the projects has significantly increased in the last few years. The reasons for this recent development are manifold. Time and resources are scarcer and product life cycles are growing shorter. Furthermore, project contents are more and more diverse, interdisciplinary and interconnected. Different stakeholders bring their interests to bear with more self-confidence, and regional as well as cultural differences are self-evident. In daily business, a vast number of projects fail to reach their aims fully or even fail completely. The main reasons are the absence of the required support and insufficient understanding of project management. Moreover, the complexity of the project is often underestimated (Kuster et al. 2008).

- It is absolutely critical that **top management support** is ensured as certain fundamental strategic decisions have to be considered regarding the development of a customer requirement driven supply chain strategy and operation. Moreover, such support allows priority to be given to projects and helps to provide the necessary resources, which often cannot be allocated by the project leader himself due to a lack of power.

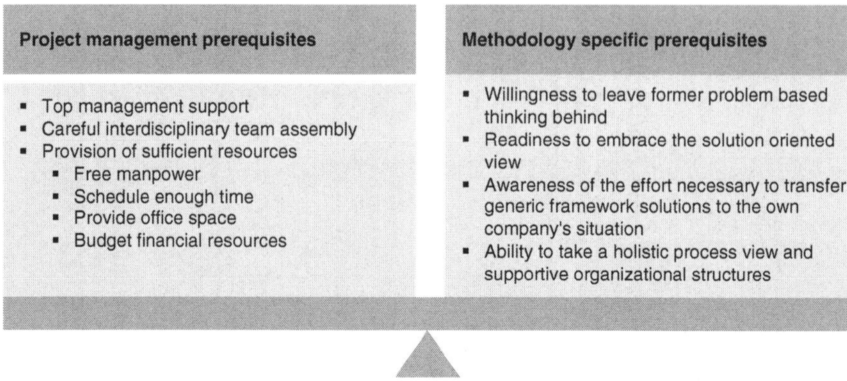

Fig. 1.18 Project management and methodology-specific pre-requisites for the supply chain differentiation guideline

- In addition, emphasis should be given to **careful team assembly** in order to ensure that the project leader disposes over supply chain and project management knowledge and the project team contains experts from the affected supply chain function. This is crucial as, on the one hand, the involved personnel need to have a vision on how a TO-BE supply chain should look and, on the other hand, they must have knowledge about how the current AS-IS supply chain looks in order to be able to identify possible gaps. Furthermore, a vague distribution of tasks and insufficient understanding on the part of the involved employees regarding their allocated roles should be avoided. This will ensure an interdisciplinary process.
- The **provision of sufficient resources** includes having free manpower available and scheduling enough time for the whole project scope. Moreover, office space must be provided and financial resources budgeted in order to avoid a shortage of these resources, which could jeopardize the project.

Focusing on the **methodology-specific pre-requisites** four main points arise which need to be taken into account for an effective and efficient implementation:

- The willingness to **leave former purely problem-based thinking behind** and the **readiness to embrace a solution-oriented view** are essential requirements as the guideline starts with a definition of a TO-BE supply chain and, thus, are entitled to be solution oriented.
- Moreover, both the employees involved and management must be **aware of the effort necessary** to transfer the generic solutions to a specific company. Thus, before applying the provided analysis and methods of the guideline, companies need to familiarize themselves with its contents to ensure a successful result.
- Additionally, the provided morphological box is based on a generic solution. Hence, if the contents of the guideline are to be tailored to a specific company, this certainly implies necessary adjustments concerning the box. A last point which is essential regarding methodology-specific requirements is the **ability to take a holistic process view** and the existence of a supportive organizational structure.

References

Brun, A., Caridi, M., Fahmy Salama, K., & Ravelli, I. (2006). Value and risk assessment of supply chain management improvement projects. *International Journal of Production Economics, 99*(1–2), 186–201.

Childerhouse, P., & Towill, D. (2000). Engineering supply chains to match customer requirements. *Logistics Information Management, 13*(6), 337–345.

Christopher, M., & Towill, D. (2001). An integrated model for the design of agile supply chains. *International Journal of Physical Distribution and Logistics Management, 31*(4), 235–246.

Davis, M. (2010). *Case study for supply chain leaders: Dell's transformative journey through supply chain segmentation*. Gartner Research ID Number: G00208603.

de Vries, J. (2007). Diagnosing inventory management systems: an empirical evaluation of a conceptual approach. *International Journal of Production Economics, 108*(1–2), 63–73.

Fahmy Salama, K., Luzzatto, D., Sianesi, A., & Towill, D. R. (2009). The value of auditing supply chains. *International Journal of Production Economics, 119*(1), 34–45.

Foggin, J. H., Mentzer, J. T., & Monroe, C. L. (2004). A supply chain diagnostic tool. *International Journal of Physical Distribution and Logistics Management, 34*(10), 827–855.

Gunasekaran, A., & Kobu, B. (2007). Performance measures and metrics in logistics and supply chain management: a review of recent literature (1995–2004) for research and applications. *International Journal of Production Research, 45*(12), 2819–2840.

Gunasekaran, A., Patel, C., & McGaughey, R. E. (2004). A framework for supply chain performance measurement. *International Journal of Production Economics, 87*(3), 333–347.

Kannan, V. R., & Tan, K. C. (2002). Supplier selection and assessment: their impact on business performance. *Journal of Supply Chain Management, 38*(4), 11–21.

Ketchen, D. J., Rebarick, W., Hult, G. T. M., & Meyer, D. (2008). Best value supply chains: a key competitive weapon for the 21st century. *Business Horizons, 51*(3), 235–243.

Kraljic, P. (1983). Purchasing must become supply management. *Harvard Business Review, 61*(5), 109–117.

Kuster, J., Huber, E., Lippmann, R., Schmid, A., Schneider, E., Witschi, U. (2008). *Handbuch Projektmanagement*. Berlin: Springer.

Mayer, S., Thiry, E., Frank, C.-B. (2009). *6th European A.T. Kearney/ELA Logistics Study 2008/2009: Supply chain excellence amidst the global economic crisis.*

Naim, M. M. (2000). Supply chain assessment methodology. *Hospital Material Management Quarterly, 22*(1), 15.

Naim, M. M., Childerhouse, P., Disney, S. M., & Towill, D. R. (2002). A supply chain diagnostic methodology: determining the vector of change. *Computers and Industrial Engineering, 43*(1–2), 135.

New, S. J. (1996). A framework for analysing supply chain improvement. *International Journal of Operations & Production Management, 16*(4), 19–34.

Payne, T., & Peters, M. J. (2004). What is the right supply chain for your products? *International Journal of Logistics Management, 15*(2), 77–92.

Rajala, M., & Savolainen, T. (1997). Exploration methods in business process re-engineering. *Computers in Industry, 33*(2–3), 367.

Verma, R., & Pullman, M. E. (1998). An analysis of the supplier selection process. *Omega, 26*(6), 739.

Vitasek, K. L., Manrodt, K. B., & Kelly, M. (2003). Solving the supply-demand mismatch. *Supply Chain Management Review, 7*(5), 58.

Wei, C.-C., Liang, G.-S., & Wang, M.-J. J. (2007). A comprehensive supply chain management project selection framework under fuzzy environment. *International Journal of Project Management, 25*(6), 627–636.

Part II
Phase 1: Description of a TO-BE Supply Chain

2 SCD Guide Preparation

The following chapter serves as an orientation for analyzing a company's current internal and external situation. This chapter and its implementation are not compulsory for the assessment of the supply chain or the subsequent differentiation process, but it is meant as a practical support for understanding both the company and its environment (Fig. 2.1).

2.1 Internal Analysis: Company Strategy

2.1.1 Elaboration of Vision, Mission and General Principle

Defining the **vision, mission and general principle** of a company is helpful before starting to assess the company's situation. Questions which need to be asked involve the key principles and core values of the company. The identity of a company derives from its mission statement and its core principles. Furthermore it is important to define the fields of activity as well as the strategic objectives of your company. Besides defining its identity, this will help to assess the future direction of the company within supply chain management.

2.1.2 Portfolio Analysis of Products and Product Groups in the Supply Chain

The portfolio analysis is a well-known strategic management concept developed by the Boston Consulting Group. Herewith the company can assess which product segments exist and how to balance the product portfolio and subsequently the distribution of financial resources.

The product portfolio analysis has two different indicators: market share and market growth. Products are placed within this matrix according to these indicators. The optimal strategies can be depicted from the matrix, in which case the

E. Hofmann et al., *The Supply Chain Differentiation Guide*,
DOI: 10.1007/978-3-642-31936-5_2, © Springer-Verlag Berlin Heidelberg 2012

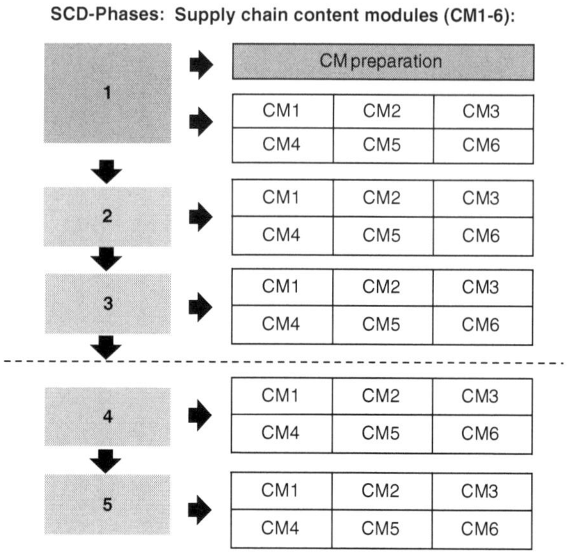

Fig. 2.1 Position of Chap. 2 in the SCD guide

company invests in the "star" customers and disinvests from the "poor dog" customers. "Cash cows" stay in the same position and, depending on the resources left, the company can decide whether to invest them in the "question mark" customers (cf. also Fig. 3.4). The portfolio analysis helps to improve the balance in cash flow within the supply chain.

2.1.3 Product Life Cycle Position

Products have a life cycle which includes different phases: the **introduction, growth, maturity and decline phase** (Fig. 2.2).

The cycle starts with the product idea, the product test and finally the **introduction** into the market. In the beginning major costs accumulate due to the development of the product. When customers see the benefits of the product, the purchasing begins and the **growth** phase starts. Revenue starts to increase and profit increases to a positive level. The market reaches saturation in the **maturity** phase, which leads in the following to an intensified competition between products. The curve reaches the point of inflection and an overall decrease in profit and revenue starts to set in. In the **decline** phase profit decreases further and loss sets in; here it becomes necessary to either take the product from the market or start relaunching the product through different performance features. Another possibility is the introduction of a new product onto the market.

In the analysis each individual product of the product portfolio in the supply chain can be placed within a given stage of the product life cycle. The company

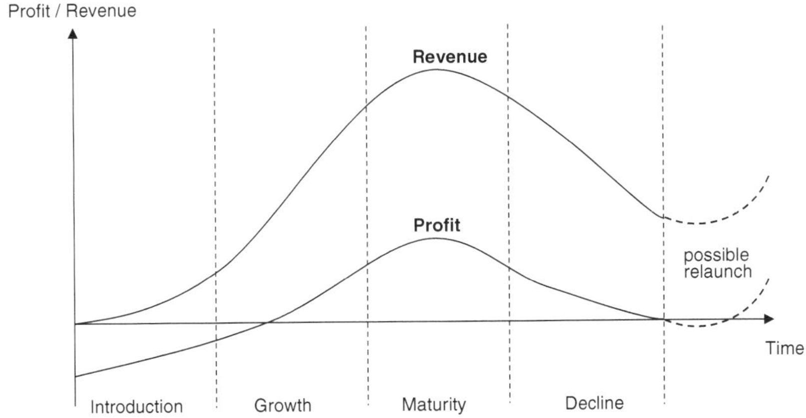

Fig. 2.2 The product life cycle and implications on profits, according Müller-Stewens and Lechner (2005)

can therefore develop individual strategies for individual products. Assessing the product life cycle can help to prevent future risks and find ideas and solutions to upcoming problems at an early stage. This will help secure the future positions of a company and help to identify the position of the company within its competing products and align the performance to the needs of the customers.

2.1.4 Description of Generic Strategy in the Supply Chain

The following generic strategy model by Porter shows that a company either focuses on product differentiation or product cost leadership as a core element. Focus strategies address a niche market and have to distinguish the company from other competitors in the market segment; the strategy either makes it a cost leader or differentiates it substantially from competitors in the niche market.

Differentiation is especially advised when a special need has not been satisfied by the market and can be realized by the company. These kinds of products are usually cost inelastic. It is furthermore possible that a company has a cost advantage within the given segment compared to the industry competitors. In the following figure, Fig. 2.3, the generic strategy matrix is outlined. With this model the company can determine its product strategy within supply chain management and whether it is more of a cost-related strategy or a differentiation strategy. The company can determine the strategy for each individual product in its product line with the help of the generic strategy model and the product's location within the matrix.

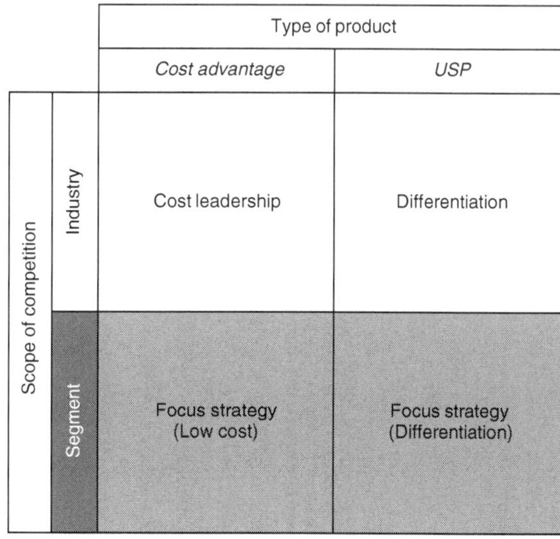

Fig. 2.3 Generic strategy matrix to identify supply chain strategy in accordance with Porter (1980)

2.2 External Analysis: Company and Environment

2.2.1 Evaluation of the Environmental Factors

The business environment can be divided into different segments varying along **political and legal, economic, sociocultural** and **technological (PEST)** lines. Through this environmental analysis, the factors influencing the business itself can be determined and possible challenges detected. The earlier the main influencing factors can be determined, the earlier the company can react to their implications.

A company can analyze its business environment by applying the PEST analysis and determine the influencing factors as seen in Fig. 2.4. This method is helpful in order to get a better understanding of the company's environment within supply chain management.

2.2.2 Industry Structure Analysis

Following Porter's five forces model, Fig. 2.5 shows the five main forces which are influencing a company's ability to react. Here we have **industry rivalry**, **potential entrants, substitute products, buyers** and **suppliers**. The model clearly shows that the company is constantly exposed to different forces. The company strategy needs to be aligned according to these forces.

- **Growing bargaining power of suppliers**.
  In this section, the relationship with the suppliers is considered and a general examination of the supply chain up until now is undertaken. A possible

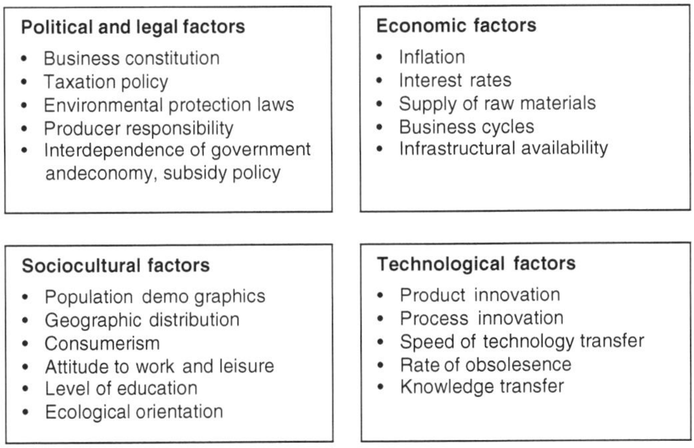

Fig. 2.4 PEST analysis to evaluate the company environment (Müller-Stewens and Lechner 2005)

Fig. 2.5 Porter's five forces model to identify the company's environment within the supply chain

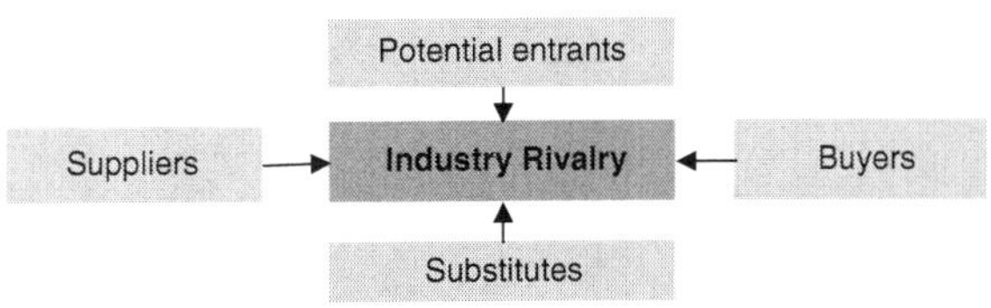

consolidation of suppliers in the industry as well as the tendency to forward integration needs to be examined. Furthermore there may be declines in the flow of information from suppliers and the number of possible substitutes as well as a possible lack of coordination with producers.

- **Growing bargaining power of buyers**
  In this section, the relationship with the buyers is considered and a general examination of the supply chain up until now is undertaken. A possible consolidation of customers in the industry as well as a tendency toward backward integration needs to be examined. Furthermore the information flow from suppliers and possible new distribution channels are taken into consideration.
- **Threat of substitute products**
  In this section the threat of substitute products is assessed. The question that arises concerns the prediction of new products entering the market. The price and performance proportion of the substitutes and the user-friendliness of substitutes may improve. The entrance barriers for substitutes need to be taken into consideration.
- **Threat of new entrants**
  In this section the threat of new competitors entering the market is assessed. Questions which can be asked concern the decline of economies of scale or customer homogeneity, the sunk costs (irreversible fixed costs for the entrance into the industry) and conversion costs (costs for the conversion to new technologies, which are necessary to compete in the relevant industry).

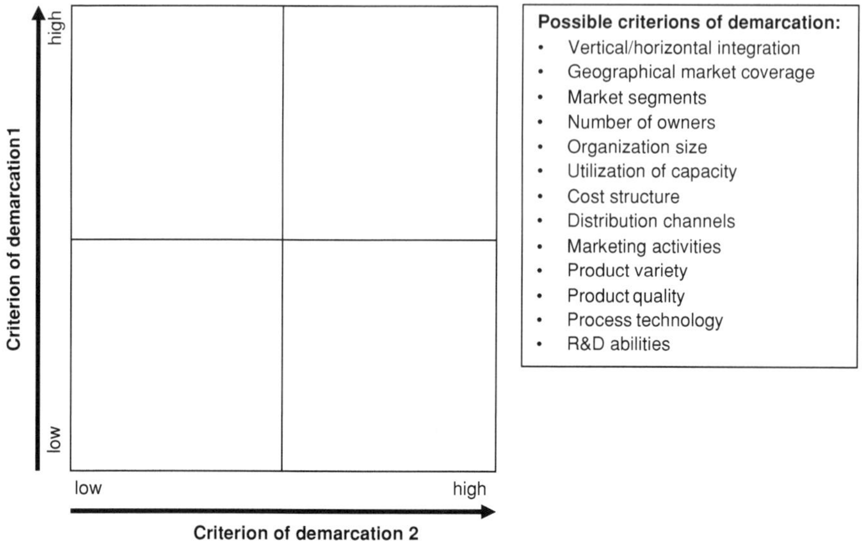

Fig. 2.6 Demarcation matrix to identify relevant criteria and levels of demarcation

- **Competitive rivalry within an industry**
  In this section the rivalry within an industry is closely examined. Questions which concern the company are market growth, relative proportion to fixed costs and the appearance of any dominant designs or products. Furthermore the consolidation in the industry as well as fragmentation in the market is part of this assessment.

2.2.3 Analysis of Strategic Groups in the Market

In the analysis of strategic groups in the market, the position of the company compared to its competitors is classified. The adequate criteria of demarcation for the establishment of strategic groups in the relevant market are determined via the matrix shown in Fig. 2.6. The most adequate criteria can be chosen and placed within the matrix. The same can be done for the competitors. The matrix shows the relationship of two criteria in order to place them within the product groups. It is therefore possible to evaluate one's own strategy compared to the strategy of competitors.

Figure 2.7 shows an exemplary analysis of strategic groups within the automotive industry. Here the two different demarcation variables which best distinguish the business strategy and competitive position of the company, product range and geographical scope, are used for the analysis.

By using this analysis, it is usually possible to identify two or more groups of companies that have adopted similar strategies. Three different strategic groups have

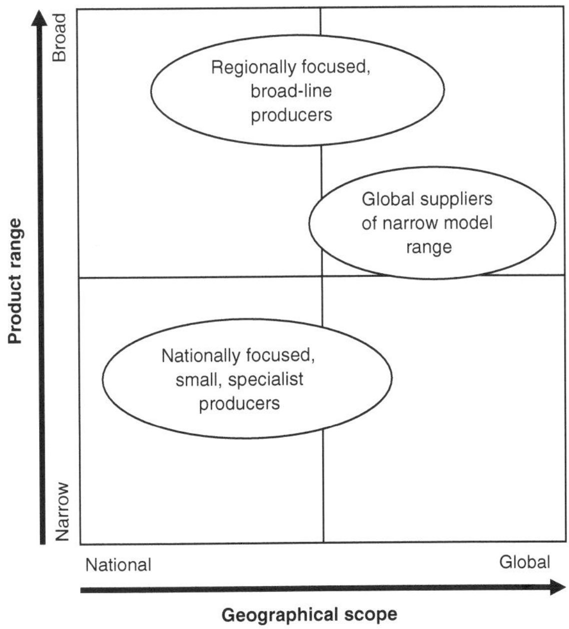

Fig. 2.7 Exemplary segmentation of strategic groups in the automotive industry

been identified by the analysis. First the regionally focused, broad-line producers, the global suppliers of a narrow model range and the nationally focused small, specialist producers. The strategic group analysis helps to identify the similarities between different companies and competitors. This contributes to the understanding of industry structure, firm strategy and industry evolution (Grant 2002).

2.2.4 Examination of the Strongest Competitors

An examination of the strongest competitor can help to directly compare one's own strategy with the strategy of the competitor. In order to make a thorough analysis of the competitors, the competitor has to be analyzed according to its **objectives, assumptions, strategy, abilities and prognoses**. The analysis of the competitor should include future strategies and objectives, estimating the reactions of the competitor to one's actions and how the behavior of the competitor can be influenced through strategy.

2.2.5 Core Competency Assessment

In the supply chain assessment the company can evaluate how strong its competencies are compared to the strongest and second strongest competitor in different areas of the supply chain. Examples can be given which indicate the core

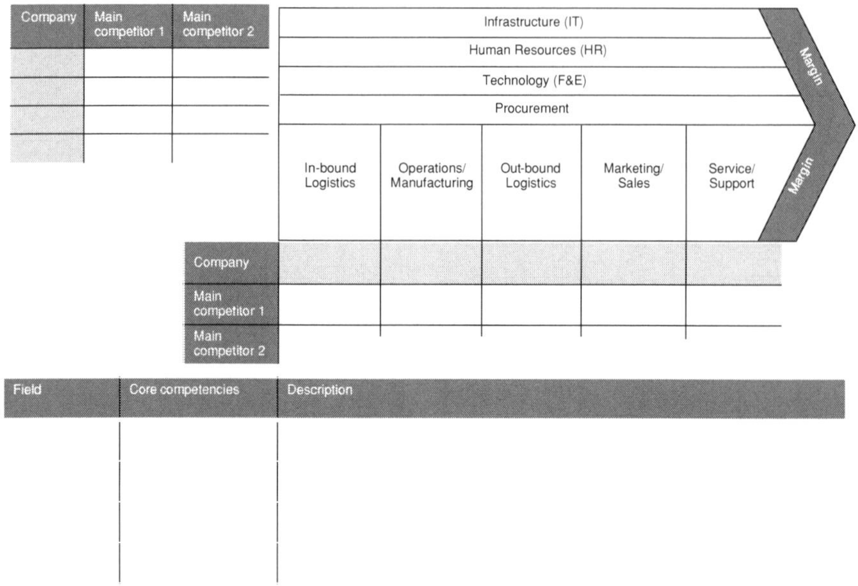

Fig. 2.8 Assessing the company's competencies by means of Porter's value chain analysis

competencies of the company in different areas. By the comparing of supply chains, this assessment will help to analyze where the competitive advantage of the company lies compared to its competitors.

In this assessment the companies can analyze their competencies in the supply chain according to their competitors. They can determine the company's competencies according to the indicators weak, rather weak, average, rather strong and strong and compare them with the competencies of their competitors. Hereby one possible way of determining one's own main competitors is to compare them relative to the industry average. Figure 2.8 shows examples of core competencies. In the following a brief description of the competencies can be given. Carrying out this method will help to position the company within the industry.

2.3 Summary of Strategic Internal and External Analysis

The SWOT analysis shows the output of previous analyses which were done in order to assess the company's internal and external situation within its industry. The process of analyzing the company and its environment can help to further assess the implementation factors of the supply chain differentiation process. This will give an overview of the company's strengths and weaknesses as well as its environment.

In the following the company can place the outcome of the analyses within one chart (Fig. 2.9). This shows a compact overview of the main **strengths** and

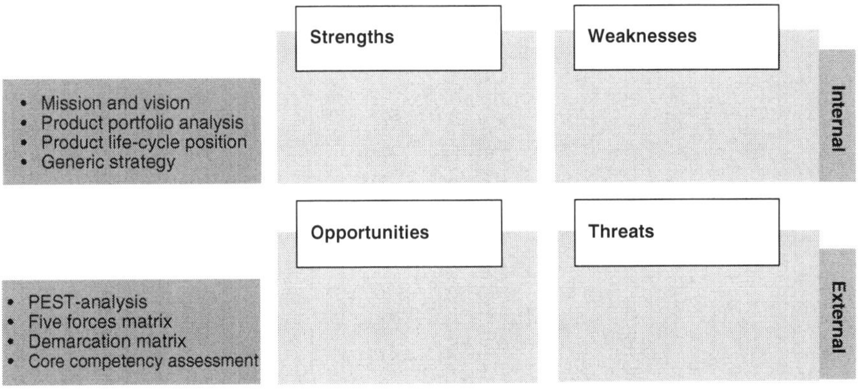

Fig. 2.9 Analyzing internal and external factors according to the outcome of analyses

weaknesses on the internal side of the company as well as the **opportunities and threats** on the external side when looking at the company's environment.

The concepts and methods outlined within CM preparation are **intra-organizational**, meaning that they were solely applied to the company's situation and its environment. A further **inter-organizational** assessment can be conducted by applying the concepts to supply chain components within different companies. The given methods can be applied analogically. By doing so, the core competencies within the supply chain of the company and the competencies of the competitor's supply chain can be assessed.

2.4 Application Example and Possible Output of Company Strategy Analysis

The following case study shows how a fictive example of a firm named "PC Manufacturing Inc." can implement the supply chain differentiation process.

PC Manufacturing Company is a multinational corporation in the IT systems industry that intends to apply the supply chain differentiation process. Due to changes in customer channel preferences, emerging markets, declines in component costs, a capable supply base and globalization, the company has to analyze its supply chain process in order to stay competitive on the market. Customer demands have become increasingly complex, which shows in the market demands predictability, customization, services and precision delivery. Processes are much more complex and different customer requirements create a need for multiple supply chains. The supply chain strategy and the core competencies of the company consist of configure-to-order (CTO) manufacturing, just-in-time inventory and a high cash-to-cash conversion cycle. Due to higher demand and competition, the company wants to apply an integrative differentiated supply chain process.

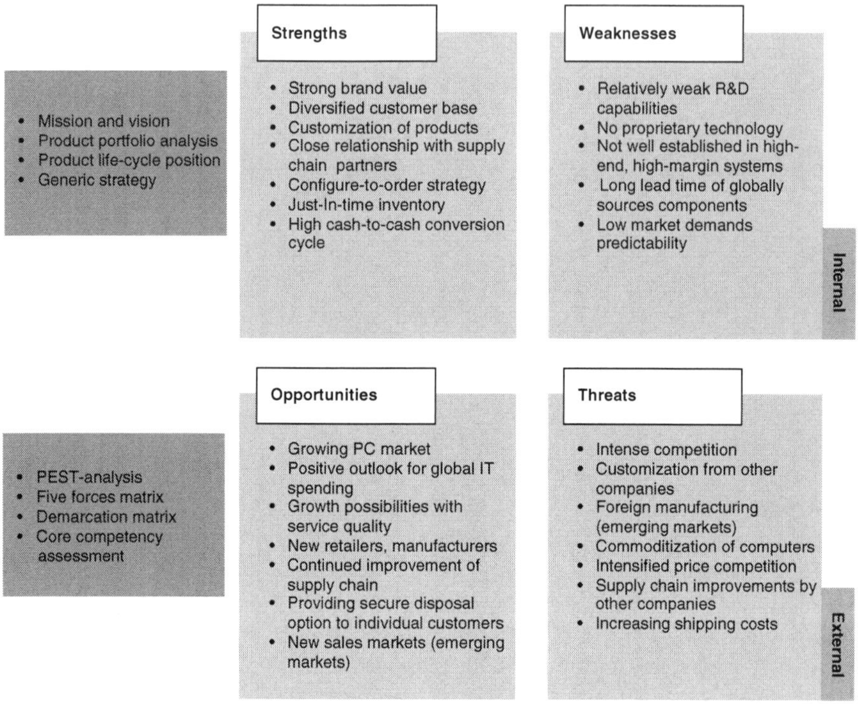

Fig. 2.10 Example—Internal and external factors influencing the success of PC Manufacturing Inc

The differentiation process provides multiple offerings focused on cost efficiency, choice of features and personalization and/or services. Since the customers are looking for multiple channel options, there is a strong need to transform the former supply chain strategy within the corporation.

- In CM preparation it is necessary to scrutinize the company and its environment. In order to provide an example of the analysis in CM preparation, one can apply Porter's **generic strategy** in order to distinguish the different product segments and strategies. This case study will mainly focus on the computer segment as the main product group of the large variety of products within the product portfolio of the company, disregarding the other product groups and mentioning them solely where necessary. In the generic strategy developed by Porter, one can distinguish the strategies of all products and product groups. Porter's generic model analyzes the company's strategy and shows that companies are either focused on product differentiation or on cost leadership. The characteristics of a differentiation strategy are a large variety of products or niche products, low price sensitivity and a strong brand management. The company can either compete in mass markets or target a few markets while focusing on innovation. Due to the large variety of products in information technology, business related services, infrastructure technology, consulting and applications and business process services and a strong brand image, the company is clearly focusing its strategy on differentiation rather than cost leadership.

- The **SWOT analysis** of the supply chain of PC Manufacturing Inc. in Fig. 2.10 shows the strengths and weaknesses as internal factors of the company and the opportunities and threats as external factors influencing the company and involving its environment. The output of the analysis of the different measures outlined in CM preparation can be seen within the SWOT analysis. The computer manufacturer has recognized the need for a differentiated supply chain model because of its diversified customer base and its customization of products.

Especially in an industry with continuous product innovation, PC Manufacturing Company has to consider its long-term strategies and continually refine its product portfolio. Therefore the outlook for the next three years is crucial. The customer needs and supporting global customer groups are classified. Due to high complexities of products and processes, there is a need for complexity reduction while maintaining a responsive mindset. In regard to changing business strategies, product commoditization, intense competition, foreign manufacturing, supply chain improvements by other companies and multichannel sales, the company needs to design its supply chain around the new environmental circumstances by applying the supply chain differentiation process.

References

Grant, R. M. (2002). *Contemporary strategy analysis* (4th ed.). Malden: Blackwell.

Müller-Stewens, G., & Lechner, C. (2005). *Strategisches Management: Wie strategische Initiativen zum Wandel führen; der St. Galler General Management Navigator* (3rd ed.). Stuttgart: Schäffer-Poeschel.

Porter, M. E. (1980). *Competitive strategy: Techniques for analyzing industries and competitors*. New York: Free Press.

3 CM1: Customer Segmentation and Supply Chain Strategy

3.1 Goals of Content Module 1

The target of the CM1 is a homogeneous segmentation of the current customers of a company into separate segments. Furthermore, the customer segments are merged with supply chain strategies to present options for the design of various pipelines within a supply chain (Fig. 3.1).

Thus, in a first section a method is presented on how to identify customer requirements in order to be able to satisfy those segments. Moreover, different analyses on how to effectively segment customers are demonstrated. This second section covers both quantitative and qualitative methods. Due to the fact that these two themes are better covered by the field of marketing, they do not belong to the core of this guideline, but shall nonetheless be mentioned as they represent a crucial element in developing a differentiated supply chain strategy. In a third and final section, for each derived customer segment a corresponding supply chain strategy is identified by using different methods, such as the analytical hierarchy process.

3.2 Customer Requirements and Segmentation

3.2.1 Customer Requirements Categorization Based on a Hierarchical Structure

Marketplaces have manifold requirements for alternative products as well as services. Such requirements are customer specific and crucial to understand in order to be able to satisfy various customers of a single company. Thus, a focus is required to adjust supply chains to match customer requirements (Childerhouse et al. 2002). However, identifying customer needs and requirements is a complex but crucial task in a business environment. Studies among customers normally reveal 200–400 different customer needs. Hence, in order to structure the vast number of

E. Hofmann et al., *The Supply Chain Differentiation Guide*,
DOI: 10.1007/978-3-642-31936-5_3, © Springer-Verlag Berlin Heidelberg 2012

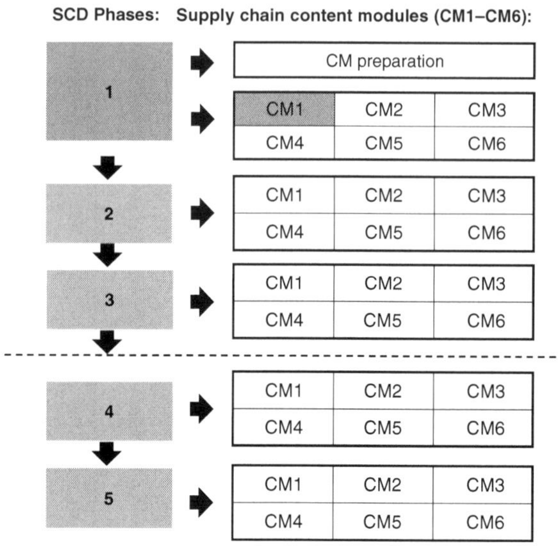

Fig. 3.1 Position of Chap. 3 in SCD guide

options, a **categorization based on a hierarchical structure** is suggested (Griffin and Hauser 1993).

There are but a few primary needs (5–10) and they are on a high level of abstraction. These needs have a high strategic significance, as they are relevant to the strategic direction of a company. Each of the primary needs can be elaborated into secondary, tactical needs, which offer complementary information about the successful satisfaction of the primary needs. Additionally, tertiary needs provide information on an operational level. These needs are specifications of the tactical needs and give detailed inputs to specific functions (e.g. R&D). In the context of this guideline, the primary needs are most important, as all elaborations take place on a strategic level, and will thus be subject to these elaborations.

A survey on evaluating important aspects of customer service, which is shown in Table 3.1, names 35 different needs that are regarded as relevant aspects in customer service.

The most often desired service element is **delivery time**, followed by **quality, after-sales service, delivery information** and **price**. Assuming that after-sales service and delivery information can be combined to **flexibility**, it is discovered that all of the successively listed elements (e.g. **order accuracy, availability** or **delivery reliability**) could be allocated to one of the first elements, which therefore are considered as primary or strategic needs, namely: **delivery time, quality, flexibility** and **price**.

The identified strategic needs in customer service also hold true for those in a supply chain environment. From the vendor's perspective, it is claimed that focusing on the end user brings forth a lot of issues that have to be taken into

Table 3.1 Important aspects of customer service (Gilmour et al. 1994)

Customer service element	Number of times customer service element mentioned
Delivery time	21
Quality	20
After-sales service	16
Providing the customer with information about delivery	14
Price	12
Competence and availability of technical representatives	11
Order accuracy	9
Correct specifications	9
Availability	6
Supplier assistance during initial use of product	6
Assistance with design changes	5
Satisfactory warranty provisions	4
Packaging	4
Delivery reliability	4
Credit and provision to return goods	4
Friendly attitude	3
Accurate documentation	3
Providing the customer alternative sources if out of stock	2
Providing published material	2
Prompt claims procedure	2
Priority given to urgent orders	2
Correct installation	2
Availability of spare parts	2
Opportunity to test the product prior to purchase	2
Delivery reliability	1
Honesty	1
Help with forecasting product changes	1
Wide product range	1
Ability to fill the complete order	1
Prompt quotation	1
Priority given to advance orders	1
Realistic dates provided for back orders	1

(continued)

Table 3.1 (continued)

Customer service element	Number of times customer service element mentioned
Help with training operators	1
Reasonable delivery estimates	1
Assistance with safety considerations	1

account. However, all these requirements can be subsumed under the four already highlighted strategic needs (Naylor et al. 1999):

- Lead time, which is considered as a term that integrates the different aspects of the dimension better than delivery time, mainly describes the speed of a company. That includes, for example, the time for delivery, replenishment or adaptation of new technologies. Moreover, availability is an absolutely fundamental aspect of service to the customers, as well as a flexibility to create customized solutions.
- Quality largely means the product or service quality that a customer requires and is willing to pay for. However, today's consumers may not only be interested in a high-quality end product, but also in the processes and side products, for instance, in terms of energy and resource sustainability.
- Flexibility describes all the tasks that accompany the supplier–buyer interaction. Here examples include customer and product support.
- The price plays a crucial role in the customers' considerations. In addition to the price of the product (or service), the costs, for example, of utilization, maintenance and recycling are also of importance.

These four dimensions will therefore be used as the strategic needs of the customers.

In the following section, after giving an overview of the most common customer needs and requirements, some variables are presented to describe customer segments in more detail and with a clear supply chain focus. Thereafter different customer segmentation models, both qualitative and quantitative, are presented followed by a short analysis of geographic segmentation aspects. Finally, while considering the various aspects of customer segmentation, suitable supply chain strategies are discussed and suggestions for assigning them to different segments are provided.

3.2.2 Customer Segmentation

Up to today, market segmentation remains a very commonly applied tool in marketing science. Its purpose is to group the various types of customers and their needs and requirements into clusters according to specific characteristics

(Albert 2003). As a result of effective segmentation, a company is endowed with comprehensive information about its customers and their requirements and needs, as well as about the company's competitive position and opportunities (Cooil et al. 2008). Closely related to the concept of market segmentation is the concept of customer segmentation. Here, an additional emphasis is put on the customers and their behavior (Marcus 1998).

Two types of segmentation in marketing sciences can be distinguished; one type is concerned with a structural analysis of the existing customer segments, in order to maintain and improve the service. The second type is more oriented towards the market, i.e., it is investigated whether there are attractive markets for current or newly developed products (Ansoff 1957; Cooil et al. 2008). Moreover, the importance of analyzing a company's current customers is highlighted, as the allocation of resources and the competitive positioning are an integral part of a firm's strategy development process (Campbell and Cunningham 1983).

Two distinct methodological approaches can be found with regards to segmentation: **a priori** and **post hoc** segmentation. In a priori segmentation, the characteristics of the segments, i.e., their number, size and description (Green and Krieger 1991), are identified **before** data are collected (Cooil et al. 2008). By contrast, in post hoc segmentation the segments are defined **after** the data collection (Green and Krieger 1991), and the segmentation is achieved through the analysis of existing data (Cooil et al. 2008). Especially the latter approach has received increased attention among academics and practitioners (Marcus 1998), as the collected data enable analysts to focus either on the segments and their characteristics themselves, or on the development of predictive models as an auxiliary tool for improving customer service performance (Cooil et al. 2008).

The actual segmentation of a firm's customers (and markets), be it before or after the data collection, can be performed on the basis of various different factors. It is claimed that the most traditional categorization is based on demographic data (Marcus 1998). Furthermore, geographic, psychographic and behavioral factors can be used (Cooil et al. 2008). Customer preferences are also a means for segmentation, as well as the motivation of purchase and situational aspects, such as purchase patterns and usage (Cooil et al. 2008; Marcus 1998). Due to the fact that the supply chain differentiation framework is not aiming at greenfield projects, but at firms in which processes are already running (i.e., at existing data), with already existing customer structures, post hoc customer segmentation is assumed as being the most conducive.

3.2.2.1 DWV^3 Classification Variables

Dependent on the attributes chosen for segmentation and on general circumstances, not all of the attributes presented in this section are equally important or even exist for all businesses. Nevertheless, some dimensions are assumed to be prevalent in the majority of supply chains. These dimensions will briefly be addressed in this section and are illustrated in Table 3.2.

Table 3.2 Customer classification variables according to the DWV^3 approach (Childerhouse et al. 2002)

Classification variables	Some key reasons for their use in classifying demand chain types
Duration of product life cycle	Short life cycles require rapid time to market.
	Short life cycles require short end-to-end pipelines to enable demand to be continuously replenished during the life cycle.
	Short life cycles require a demand chain to be able to 'fast track' product development, manufacturing and logistics to exploit ever decreasing windows of opportunity.
	Replenishment lead times need to be matched to stage of the product life cycle, so as to reduce lost sales and risks of obsolescence.
Window for delivery	Rapid response is required to replenish fashionable goods that are selling well at a particular point in time.
	Competitive pressures are continually reducing acceptable response times, with many demand chains competing on the basis of very short windows for delivery of customized products.
Volume	Products aimed at high volume mass markets allow for lean-type production and make-to-forecast strategies to take advantage of economies of scale.
	Lower volume markets benefit from flexibility both in production and in the entire demand chain.
Variety	Greater variety results in a larger number of stock keeping units because the volume is split between alternatives.
	Continuous appraisal of the proportional breakdown between variants must be conducted during the product life cycle because those variants popular at the introductory stage may be less popular in the decline stage.
Variability	Variability relates to spikiness of demand and unpredictability.
	Spikiness drastically effects capacity utilization and resultant production techniques.
	Unpredictability increases the risk of obsolescence and lost sales and can be addressed via information enrichment (Mason-Jones and Towill 1997), consultative forecasting (Fisher 1997) and lead time reduction (Watson 1994).

Central to the supplier–buyer transaction is the type of **product**. However, besides the product, several other dimensions of customer segments can be found, which are all more or less strongly tied to the type of product. For the purpose of capturing the most relevant of these dimensions, a concept called **DWV^3** (Duration of life cycle, window for delivery, volume, variety and variability), which consists of five variables, will be successively presented. The DWV^3 classification variables are used to categorize products of a company into clusters with related

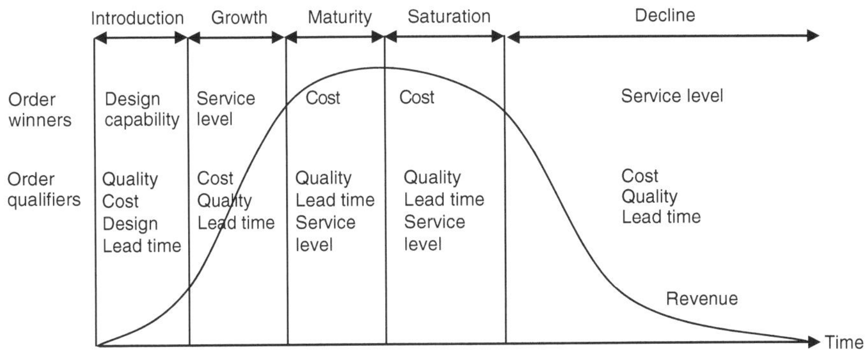

Fig. 3.2 Market criteria and the product life cycle, following Childerhouse et al. (2002)

characteristics. Thus, the classification leads to a clear definition of requirements regarding demand channels (Childerhouse et al., 2002).

- The first variable is the **duration of the product life cycle**. The length of the cycle and the stage the product is actually in provide a firm with exploitable knowledge about the customer. Dependent on the life cycle stage, a firm can estimate what the future contribution of a customer (segment) will be to the profit of the firm, i.e., if the profit margin will continue to rise or if it has already passed its high point. Moreover, the different stages of the life cycle represent different order winning and order qualifying criteria. The following connection between the product life cycle and the distinguishing criteria is found as Fig. 3.2 shows. The graph clearly points out that the criteria most highly demanded by customers vary throughout the life cycle. Therefore, according to the current position of the product, necessary insight into the connection of a customer segment with the product life cycle can be gained, and practicable managerial implications can be derived. Moreover, if, for example, segmentation was undertaken with regard to the point of entry of the customers (Rogers 1995), the product life cycle reveals viable information. Innovators and early adopters accompany a product from the very introductory phase onwards and therefore have different preferences than the majority has.
- The second characterizing variable is the **window for delivery**. This variable describes how quickly the supply chain has to and is able to react to demand. Different customer segments, and different products, require varying speed of delivery. In connection with the speed of delivery, a company sets its depth of unfinished products and the position of the decoupling point (Naylor et al. 1999).
- A further specifying aspect of customer segments is the **volume** of products demanded by a segment. Naturally, the volume of purchased items is strongly related to the **size** of the specific segment. Besides, there are products that are demanded more regularly than others, which increases the volume sold. Clearly, segments that purchase high-volume products have to be treated

differently from those customer segments asking for smaller quantities. Effects such as economies of scale and learning curve effect have an impact on the production process as well as on the supply chain strategy choice determinants.

- As a fourth variable, the **variety** of a firm's product range is to be considered. The higher the number of independent products or product derivatives a specific customer segment is willing to purchase, the more prepared the supplying firm has to be to satisfy the shifting market.
- Finally, the **variability** of demand plays an important role in describing the customer segments. More precisely, variability stands for the variations in demand and the unpredictability it is accompanied by. Uncertain demand forecast strongly influences the layout of the entire production process.

Unpredictable demand is a consequence of diverging product characteristics. Moreover, external factors (e.g., seasonal variation) complicate the estimation of customer behavior (Fisher 1997).

3.2.3 Customer Segmentation Through Qualitative Analysis

Qualitative customer analysis is an easily accomplishable type of customer segmentation. The allocation of customers to segments is not based on figures, but rather on soft factors such as demographic, geographic, psychographic and behavioral factors (Cooil et al. 2008). Despite its simplicity, this type of segmentation provides practical and rapid information about customer composition.

3.2.3.1 Descriptive Methods

As an initial approach, one-dimensional descriptive segmentation is presented. Here, segmentation is achieved by applying only one distinguishing dimension (Kotler and Bliemel 2001). Consequently, the number of segments depends on the level of detail of the chosen criterion. Frequently, producing companies utilize their product range as one option for segmenting their customers. Although very basic, this option provides a lot of exploitable knowledge, as the different attributes of the products reveal the inherent preferences and intentions of their customers.

As a further example of this type of segmentation, the technology adoption life cycle is presented. This concept is defined as "the degree to which an individual or other unit of adoption is relatively earlier in adopting new ideas than the other members of a system" (Rogers 1995). Accordingly, five categories of adopters are common:

1. Innovators
2. Early adopters
3. Early majority
4. Late majority
5. Laggards

These categories can also be utilized for the purpose of segmentation. In this way, in a simple and quick manner, different groups of customers can be

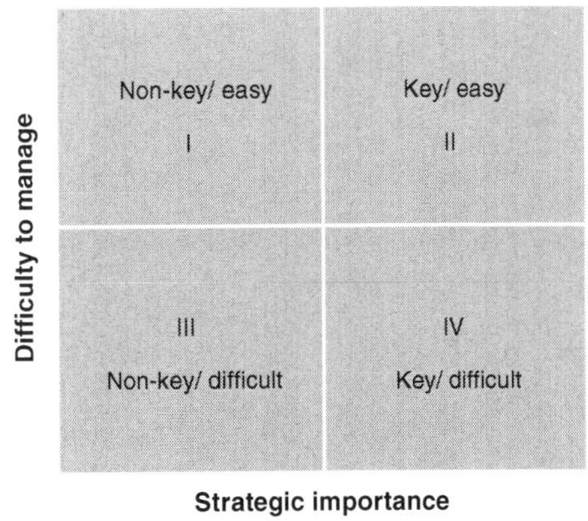

Fig. 3.3 Customer portfolio, following Yorke and Droussiotis (1994)

generated. Nevertheless, although rather elementary, it can support managerial decision making with helpful insights about customer structure and characteristics.

3.2.3.2 Customer Portfolio Analysis

Portfolio models are a very common tool in customer segmentation. The applied parameters for this type of segmentation can be purely qualitative, but also mixed combinations or purely quantitative dimensions are possible (see customer value matrix in Marcus 1998).

The so-called **customer portfolio models or matrices (CPM)** are targeted at allocating resources to identified groups of customers (Zolkiewski and Turnbull 2002). Normally, market share, market growth, market attractiveness and competitive position serve as key dimensions for the segmentation (Yorke and Droussiotis 1994).

As an example of this type of segmentation, an exemplary CPM is depicted in Fig. 3.3. Here, **strategic importance** and **difficulty to manage** are used as key dimensions.

In a subsequent step, a more detailed analysis of the identified segments is carried out; again, two variables are employed, the customer's business attractiveness (high, medium, low) and the relative stage of the present buyer/seller relationship (strong, medium, weak). Particularly the latter dimension, also known as power balance, which is used as a means for assessing the relative power of customers and sellers, is a commonly used measurement in qualitative customer segmentation (see Fig. 3.4).

Summarizing, it can be said that using portfolio models for qualitative customer segmentation offers an effective and rather simple way of evaluating the allocation of resources to specific customers (Terho and Halinen 2007). Moreover, it is also an appropriate option to combine qualitative and quantitative dimensions, for instance, by considering customer lifetime value (CLV) (Campbell and Cunningham 1983).

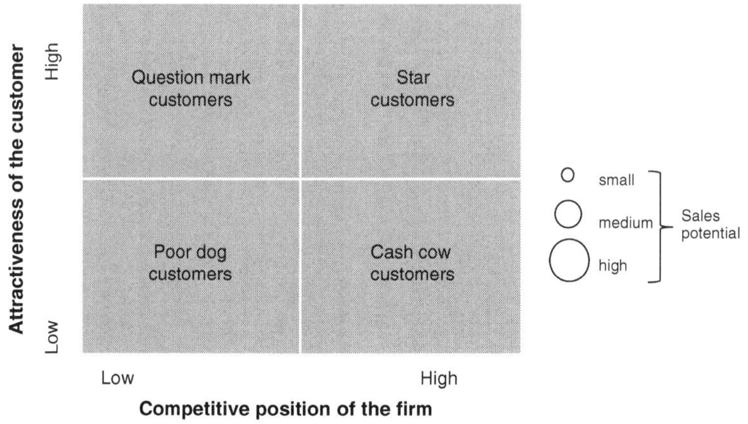

Fig. 3.4 Adaptation of the BCG matrix, following Homburg and Krohmer (2006)

However, the simplicity of the concepts also bears potential for critique. It is claimed that portfolio models serve only for visualization, but not for an analytical and prescriptive treatment of the data (Yorke and Droussiotis 1994). Moreover, practically speaking, this type of business analysis is relatively rarely performed for grouping customers into segments. Furthermore, the simplification of complex systems excludes crucial influencing factors, such as network effects (i.e., the linking up of business participants) (Yorke and Droussiotis 1994; Terho and Halinen 2007).

3.2.4 Customer Segmentation Through Quantitative Analysis

In contrast to the former type of analysis, quantitative analyses rely on figures and measures that are extracted from running businesses. Again, comparable to the qualitative segmentation concepts, different levels of sophistication can be pursued, depending on the purpose of segmentation and the available data.

3.2.4.1 ABC Analysis

The ABC analysis is a very classic and basic tool of segmentation and can be applied to a wide variety of purposes, be it, for example, in production or marketing. Due to the fact that it is based on simple, non-arithmetic principles, it can easily be performed. Nonetheless, it offers understandable results and easy-to-implement managerial decision-making aids.

As the ABC analysis is a commonly utilized method, a great number of textbooks can be found which describe it. From among a range of fairly equal options, the decision was made to take the excellent book by Homburg and Krohmer (2006) as the point of reference for the following explanation of ABC customer segmentation.

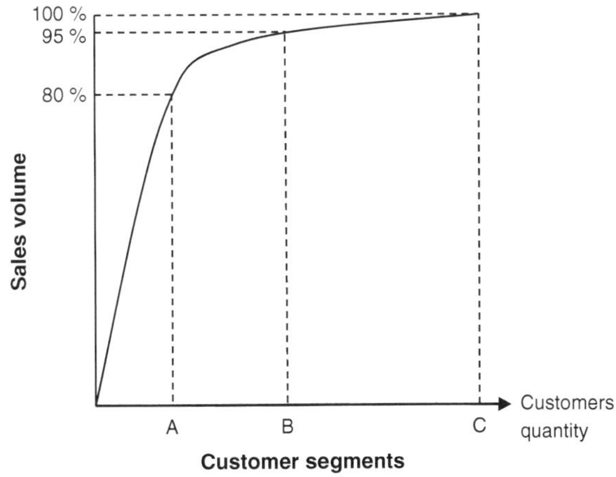

Fig. 3.5 ABC analysis (1 of 2)—comparing customers to the sales volume

For the purpose of this guide, customer segmentation through ABC analysis is two-fold: in a first step, the traditional ABC segmentation is presented, achieved by successively ranking the customers according to their purchasing volume and the value of sold products. In the following step, the two analyses are combined. This results in a 3 × 3 matrix, from which new and more reliable customer segments can be drawn. Starting with the first ABC analysis, the specific sales volume of each customer is set in proportion to the accumulated volume of purchased products. Figure 3.5 depicts the typical distribution.

The distribution of purchasing volume as compared to customer structure is traditionally characterized through the **Pareto principle**. This law describes the 80:20 rule, meaning that 80 % of the dependent variable (here: purchasing volume) can be assigned to 20 % of the independent variable (here: customers) (Koch 1997). Besides the already identified segment, two more segments are proposed (Homburg and Krohmer 2006). Hence, the assignment of customer segments to a company's purchasing volume can be specified as follows:

- Customer segment A stands for 80 % of the sales volume,
- Customer segment B stands for 15 % of the sales volume, and
- Customer segment C stands for the remaining 5 % of the sales volume.

However, as the Pareto law already indicates, the size of the segments A, B and C is inversely correlated to the volume of purchase; therefore, although purchasing only 5 % of the entire volume, segment C consists of the largest number of customers.

To make the segmentation sounder, the same procedure is repeated, but now the customers are not ranked according to their respective purchasing volume, but to the **value of products sold**. Again, it is likely that the diagram shows the distribution depicted in Fig. 3.6.

In this comparison it is also expected that a rather small group of customers is accountable for the great majority of the value sold. By contrast, the majority of the customers account for relatively little value of the products sold.

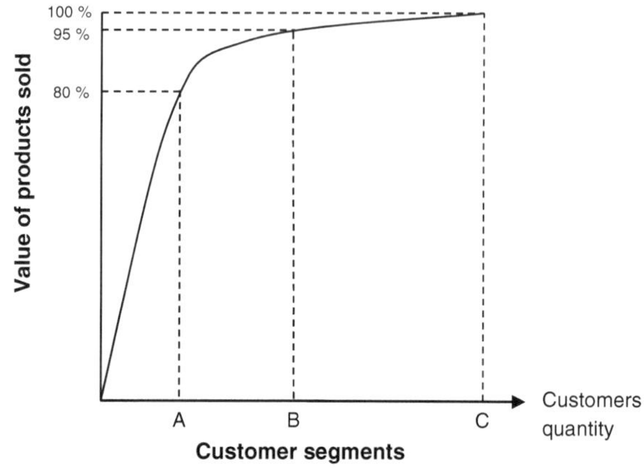

Fig. 3.6 ABC analysis (2 of 2)—comparing customers to the value of products sold value of sold products

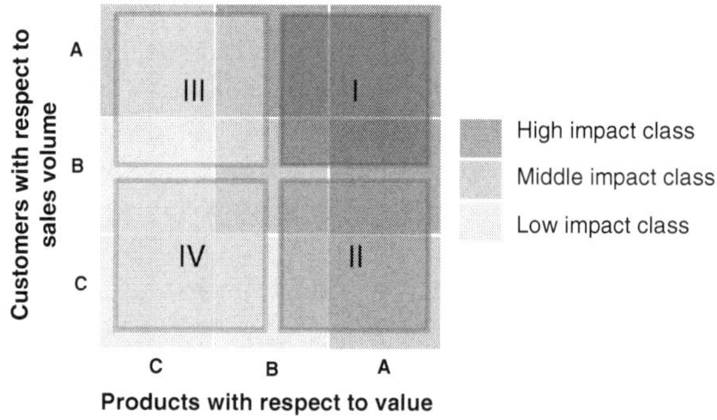

Fig. 3.7 Customer segments derived by means of a combined ABC analysis

Following the previous analyses, in total six segments have been identified. However, it is assumed that there is a significant degree of overlapping between the two analyses, that is, that customers grouped in segment A in the first analysis will probably appear in segment A (or B) in the second analysis.

Nonetheless, to sharpen the distinction among the segments, in a subsequent step the two ABC analyses are combined. Due to the fact that both analyses are based on the same independent variable, the two dependent variables can be contrasted. This results in a 3 × 3 matrix (Fig. 3.7). The previously derived six segments are transferred here into a new segmentation scheme:

- High impact class (combination of segments A–A, A–B, and B–A)
- Middle impact class (combination of segments B–B, A–C, and C–A)
- Low impact class (combination of segments C–C, B–C, and C–B)

In this way, customer segmentation comprises not just one, but two factors. Thus, because it captures more data, the evidence and consistency of the segmentation is increased.

In Fig. 3.7 there are four different quarters representing the products with respect to their value while considering the customers with respect to sales. Quarter I shows the top products that have the highest profits, highest revenue and

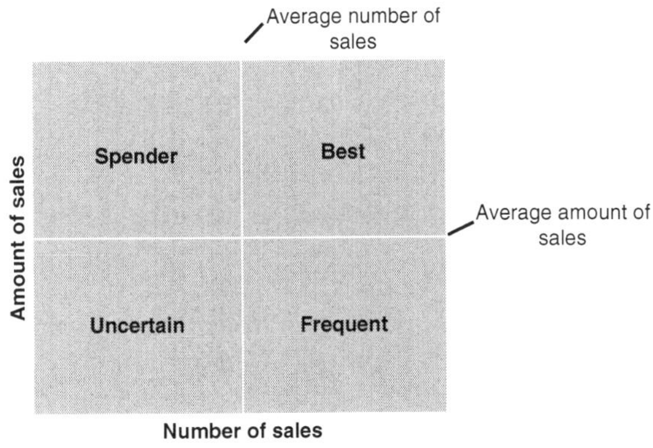

Fig. 3.8 The customer value matrix, following Marcus (1998)

are generally the most expensive products. Quarter II shows standardized products which generally generate solid profits. Quarter III represents the enabled products generally used for A and B customers. Quarter IV shows products which generally generate losses. They can either be "eliminated" or optionally sustained due to connections with other products or product groups.

Summing up, the ABC analysis enables a clarification and visualization of the different customer segments and their respective size and importance with relatively little effort. Moreover, it provides descriptive and compact information about the economic relevance of various customers. It can thus be seen as a beneficial tool to quickly reduce complexity, and can easily be extended for more detailed results (as the combination of two analyses and the emerging segmentation shows). On the other hand, ABC analyses only include a very small number of correlations (one or two) as a means for customer segmentation. Various other influencing factors are not considered, which impairs the evidence and consistency, nor are qualitative factors included, which also weakens the soundness of the analysis.

3.2.4.2 Customer Value Matrix

A method that is rather similar to the ABC analysis in terms of applicability and simplicity is the customer value matrix. The concept of the customer portfolio matrix, as described in an earlier section, also underlies this tool; however, here quantitative dimensions have been chosen.

For obtaining the quadrants, the average values of the two factors, frequency (**number of purchases**) and monetary value (**amount of purchase**), are calculated and accordingly each factor is split up into two parts (Marcus 1998). In this way, four equally sized segments are formed (see Fig. 3.8). It becomes obvious that the importance of the segments decreases from the top right to the bottom left quadrant. Logically, each particular segment requires a distinct strategy, be it in marketing or supply chain management. For achieving this, the four different segments can be analyzed regarding different characterizing aspects, for instance, geographic distribution or predictability of demand (in a supply chain management context).

In general, the principle of the customer value matrix can be utilized for various analyses. As an extension, additional factors such as geographical, demographic or purchase-related factors (e.g., recency, length of customer relationship) are suggested (Marcus 1998).

3.2.4.3 Customer Lifetime Value (CLV)

In this segmentation method, the focus is put on the contribution that each specific customer makes to the profit of the company, with segments being formed on this basis (Kim et al. 2006). CLV is an arithmetic method for which, depending on the purpose it is used for, several sophisticated and specialized approaches exist. However, for the purpose of this guide, only the basic model is presented in this context.

CLV can be defined as "the net profit or loss to the firm from a customer over the entire life of transactions of that customer with the firm" (Jain and Singh 2002). More precisely, the value of a customer is composed of the total revenue per customer, reduced by the costs of sales (processing the customer order) and promotion costs (retention costs), and under consideration of a discount rate. In addition, for achieving a long-term perspective, the yearly values are summed up. Written as an equation, CLV is defined as follows (Jain and Singh 2002).

$$CLV = \sum_{i=1}^{n} \frac{(R_i - C_i)}{(1+d)^{i-0.5}}$$

where

- i the period of cash flow from customer transaction
- n the total number of periods of projected life of the customer under consideration
- R_i revenue from the customer in period i
- C_i total cost of generating the revenue R_i in period i
- d Is the yearly discount rate (appropriate for marketing investments)

Obviously, this basic model is not designed to capture all the different aspects that have an impact on customer life time value. For example, acquisition costs are not included; furthermore, it is assumed that all cash flow transactions take place at the same point of time (Jain and Singh 2002). Nevertheless, even just the basic model offers a suitable opportunity for segmenting customers according to their economic importance to the company. Furthermore, by creating a list, customers can be segmented according to their customer life time value (Fig. 3.9).

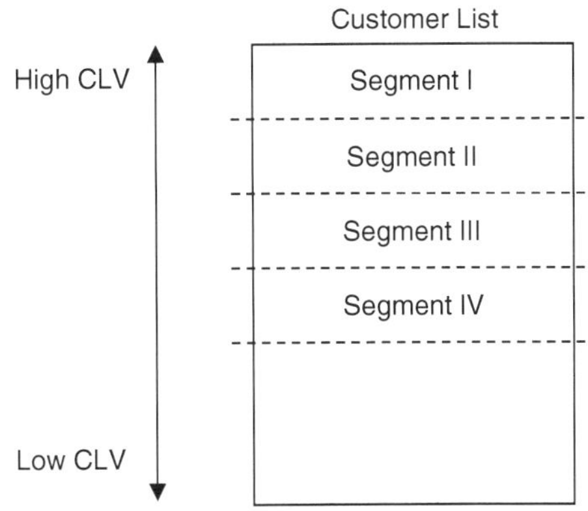

Fig. 3.9 Customer segmentation using customer life time value (*CLV*) after Kim et al. (2006)

After having generated a list, segments can easily be detected, by defining how to divide the entire group into smaller entities (Kim et al. 2006). In this way, customers can be analyzed and treated more appropriately with regard to their impact on a firm's success, and future strategies can be deduced (Jain and Singh 2002).

3.2.5 Geography as a Descriptive Dimension

A dimension that has not yet sufficiently been regarded is the regional distribution of segments. Nowadays, most supply chains act on an international level, and the customer structure is often highly international as well. The question arises whether segmentation stops at national borders or if segments can be identified that span across several countries. Due to the current relevance of this issue, it was decided to add this dimension to the description of customer segments, as it provides crucial data for making supply chain strategy choices in an international context. Due to the fact that each national market has its own cultural and behavioral peculiarities, customer needs and thus customer segments differ from those in other countries. However, several exceptions exist where segments are found to exist across national borders, i.e., where groups of customers from several countries share similar needs and requirements (Mentzer et al. 2004).

The still very common practice to define segments within national borders neglects both the homogeneity that can be found between customer groups in different countries as well as the heterogeneity of demand within a market. Therefore, **cross-national segmentation** is recommended, which ignores national borders and just regards the characteristics of the customers. Nevertheless, it has to be borne in mind that some nations are closer to one another (geographically, historically, and so on) than others. Thus, a distinction has to be made, dependent on the spatial association of the specific countries (Ter Hofstede et al. 2002).

Hence, customer segmentation in an international context can be performed both horizontally (across national borders) and vertically (within a market), with each having its advantages: on the one hand, cross-national segmentation displays a preference for analysis by segment rather than by country, which allows for a more diversified view of a market and increased customer satisfaction. Moreover, costs can be reduced as redundant logistics service offerings are avoided through their customization to specific segments (Mentzer et al. 2004). On the other hand, as some countries have more in common than others, segmentation across borders only makes sense to a certain degree of similarity (Ter Hofstede et al. 2002).

3.2.5.1 Distribution Channels

After having identified different customer segments, it is crucial to determine, in order to align a suitable supply chain strategy with a given customer segment, which distribution channels are suitable for which customer segment. Although this task is regarded as marketing related (Homburg and Krohmer 2006) and thus, will not be covered further in this section, it plays an important role for the definition of a supply chain strategy. Hence, considering the example of Dell explained and depicted in Part A, for the private customer segment, a product may be distributed directly to the end customer or indirectly via a retailer. This implies two different supply chains for the same customer segment and therefore needs to be considered when developing a differentiated supply chain strategy. This fact is also crucial for the completion of the morphological box. Hence, the number of boxes which need to be filled into conduct the gap analysis is based, on the one hand, on the number of identified customer segments and, on the other, on the different distribution channels (Chopra and Meindl 2007). If the example of Dell is considered, three different customer segments exist, which implies the completion of three morphological boxes. However, the private customer segment is served by two different distribution channels as explained above. Hence, for this specific customer segment, two morphological boxes are required as two different supply chains exist in order to fulfill its requirements.

Summary sheet

CM1a: Customer requirements and segmentation

Goals of SCD Guide CM1a

The goal of this section of the SCD Guide CM1 is the identification of customer requirements and a homogeneous segmentation of the present customers into separate customer segments. In the following you can find analysis and methods to identify customer requirements and customer segmentation.

Methods and analysis for SCD Guide CM1a

Customer requirements:

- Geographic distribution
- Categorization based on a hierarchical structure

Customer segmentation:

- DWV^3
- Customer portfolio analysis
- ABC analysis
- Customer value matrix
- Customer life time value (CLV)

Input per method for SCD Guide CM1a

	Input from other CMs			
Description of customer requirements	(None)	**Geographic distribution** • Geographic distribution in percentages according to continents	**Categorization based on a hierarchical structure** • Information generated by customer survey	
Methods for customer segmentation	(None)	**DWV^3** • Duration of product life cycle • Window for delivery • Volume, variety and variability of demand	**Descriptive methods** • Customer behavior with respect to categorization of criterion (e.g., demand regarding product range)	**Customer portfolio analysis** • Attractiveness of customer business • Competitive position of the firm
	(None)	**ABC analysis** • Buying volume per customer/ customer segment • Value of sold products	**Customer value matrix** • Average purchased amount • Number of purchases	**Customer lifetime value** • Total revenue per customer • Cost of sales (cost of processing customer orders) • Promotion costs (retention costs)

Output from SCD Guide CM1a

- Customer requirements ranking per customer segments
  Dimension in the morphological box: Requirements ranking
- Homogeneous customers segmentation
  For each customer segment a morphological box is filled in

3.3 Assignment of Supply Chain Strategies to Customer Segments

In this section, the previous elaborations are merged and the core idea of this chapter is addressed, i.e., the combination of supply chain strategies and different customer segments, in order to present the various options of pipeline development within a supply chain. For this purpose, the concepts introduced in the literature review in the introduction are consulted, which contain exploitable information about the different aspects and forces in supply chain management.

3.3.1 Customer Segment Characteristics and Supply Chain Strategies

This part of the section deals with the follow-up discussion of the DWV^3 variables introduced above for describing customer segments and their connection to supply chain strategy theory. Particularly the conditions required for choosing a hybrid strategy might become challenging in some cases. Nonetheless, it is believed that the assignment offers an opportunity to adjust supply chains more effectively.

3.3.1.1 DWV^3 and Supply Chain Strategies

The assignment of **product** categories to supply chain strategies is rather simple, as previous research has already frequently dealt with this topic. Thus, technologically advanced and newly launched products with high demand unpredictability are assigned to agile supply chains. On the other hand, everyday products that satisfy the basic customer needs, traditionally have a highly foreseeable demand and are therefore manageable through a lean supply chain. A leagile strategy is needed if the product is composed of various components and the product flow up- and downstream from a decoupling point has to be managed separately (Christopher et al. 2006). A model for assigning products to suitable supply chains, is the so called DWV^3-model (duration of product life cycle, window for delivery, volume and variability of demand as well as variety of products):

- Regarding the **duration of the product life cycle**, innovative products tend to have a short life cycle, whereas that of functional products is rather long (Christopher et al. 2006). Consequently, the strategies are identified analogously to the type of product. Thus, when investigating the different stages of the product life cycle and corresponding supply chain strategies, it became apparent that the type of product has a significant impact. For example, regarding functional and hybrid products, the supply chain strategy does not change over the duration of the life cycle. In contrast, for innovative products the strategy has to be adapted to the changing life cycle stages. During the stages of introduction and growth, which normally (particularly with innovative products) are characterized by uncertainty in terms of demand and the optimal production process, agility is crucial to react quickly to emergent changes, thus, an agile supply chain strategy is suitable. Later in the product life (maturity, saturation and decline), when all the determinants are known, potentials for optimization can be exploited and thus the strategy can be switched to a more cost-efficient layout, i.e., a less agile, leagile or even lean orientation (Childerhouse et al. 2002). Here, the type of product (and the strongly connected demand) again dictates the strategy. Normally, the initially innovative product soon becomes less innovative, as it is copied by competitors and therefore cost becomes increasingly important. Furthermore, as the market matures, demand can be more precisely estimated. Nevertheless, the degree of demand predictability still determines how cost-efficiently the supply chain can be organized. If volatility of demand continues to be prevalent, a leagile strategy suits best, whereas if good forecasting is possible, even a lean supply chain can be implemented. For the decline stage, a transformation of the supply chain back into an agile design, to slowly let production phase out while satisfying the last customers' demand is recommended (Aitken et al. 2003). However, the decline stage can have different characteristics; it can thus also be possible that demand remains stable on a lower level and only a few competitors stay in the market (Anderson and Zeithaml 1984). Here, keeping a lean supply chain can be the most appropriate solution.

- The impact of the **window for delivery** on the supply chain strategy choice has constantly been rising over the past few years. Time has gained increased significance as a competitive variable, particularly due to the rise of global sourcing and the extended delivery lead times accompanying it. However, as long as demand is predictable, the time for delivery does not necessarily influence the supply chain strategy. If forecasts can be based on sound data, the delivery times of supply just have to be integrated into the calculations; a lean supply chain is easily accomplishable. On the contrary, if demand is hard to predict, long delivery times can greatly hamper a lean strategy. Therefore, an agile strategy is most feasible. Finally, if lead times are short and demand volatile, a leagile supply chain design can be applied (Bruce and Daly 2004; Childerhouse et al. 2002).
- Products that are produced in high **volumes** are likely to be managed in a lean way. Due to scale effects and the elimination of unnecessary parts, a high level of cost efficiency can be obtained. On the other hand, if only low quantities are demanded, it is less probable that a smooth production flow can be achieved; hence, the lean methods for cost-saving cannot be sufficiently implemented. In addition, high flexibility is the required key concept in this case, which leads to an agile supply chain strategy. Traditionally, the volume that is produced via a leagile supply chain lies in between the two poles. Nonetheless, higher quantities can also be produced with this type of supply chain strategy; in this case, further factors need to be considered, such as the following one, for example (Childerhouse et al. 2002).

- Increasing **variety** is a condition that many of today's companies are facing (Childerhouse et al. 2002). Complexity is increased not only by the rise of mutually independent products, but even more so by the differentiation and customization of products. To cope with this challenge, a leagile supply chain strategy is an effective approach; here, the concept of postponement is applied, which means that up to a certain point in the supply chain only standardized product components are produced, which serve as the basis for the various product derivatives. Generally, it can be presumed that a higher product range requires a higher level of flexibility in the supply chain. Therefore, a lean strategy is only expedient if a company offers a limited range of products. On the other end of the continuum, a multitude of different and separate products has to be handled in an agile manner.
- For reasons of simplification, the two attributes, type of product and demand **variability**, are interconnected; however, it is believed that demand uncertainty is not only an effect of the type of product and has therefore also be treated separately (Christopher et al. 2006). Of course, as the discussion above has shown, the product category has a significant impact on demand variability. Nevertheless, beyond that, additional factors have to be considered. It is assumed that commodity items also exist that are subject to demand volatility. However, logically, the implications regarding demand predictability are equally valid in this context: predictable demand allows lean supply chain management, whereas unpredictable demand requires a more flexible organization, i.e., an agile supply chain. Partially predictable demand is best managed through a leagile supply chain.

The influences of **geographic aspects** have, up until today, barely been subject to supply chain management research. However, in the strongly related logistic service sector, "diverse regulations across borders, longer lead times, and increased transportation costs all add to the difficulty of managing logistics services internationally"Mentzer et al. 2004). It is believed that this estimation can be directly transferred to the supply chain management context. Keeping in mind that cross-national segments, though similar in most of their characteristics and requirements, still are likely to have cultural peculiarities, high complexity is expected. Thus, high flexibility is needed, which indicates an agile or leagile supply chain strategy. Especially the latter strategy is assumed to master specific (national) features within an international segment through the concept of postponement, which eases differentiation. Due to the fact that lean supply chain organization is normally not designed to handle major complexity of demand, cross-national segments are not regarded as a suitable combination with this type of strategy, but rather different pipelines for different countries.

However, it has to be pointed out that all these assignments in Figure 3.10 are not fixed, but judged as tendencies. Generally, the transition from one supply chain strategy to another is continuous. Moreover, it is expected that exceptions exist (Agarwal et al. 2006).

Descriptive characteristics	Supply chain strategies		
	Lean	Leagile	Agile
Product	Functional	Hybrid	Innovative
Duration of product life cycle	Long	Short	Short
Prevalent strategies in the particular product life cycle stages	Introduction Growth Maturity Saturation Decline	Introduction Growth Maturity Saturation Decline	Introduction Growth Decline (dependent on market characteristics)
Window for delivery (lead times)	Dispensable	Small	Large
Product volume	High	Medium to High	Low
Product variety	Low	Medium to High	High
Demand variability (unpredictability)	Low	Medium	High
Geographic distribution of segments	National	National and Cross-national	National and Cross-national

Fig. 3.10 Customer segments' characteristics and corresponding supply chain strategies (1/2)

3.3.2 Customer Segment Requirements and Supply Chain Strategies

Naturally, **customer requirements and needs** could also have been added to the attributes of customer segments presented above. However, it was decided to discuss them separately, highlighting the customer orientation that is advocated by today's supply chain management researchers.

Regarding the four strategic needs price, lead time, flexibility and quality have been identified. These four strategic needs perfectly accord with the **four value-generating criteria** of a business (Johansson et al. 1993), which Hill (1993) has employed in their order winner/order qualifier framework. Therefore, the insights of this research can be referred to when working out the connection of strategic needs to the various supply chain strategies.

If customers define price as their core requirement, it is normally accompanied by a market environment that allows cost orientation, which means, for instance, predictable demand of high-volume commodity goods. Thus, a lean strategy can be implemented. As it was explained in the literature review, in this case the market winner is cost (which of course is very closely related to price), whereas quality, lead time and flexibility are market qualifiers (Christopher and Towill 2000). In contrast, short lead time and high availability expectations can best be satisfied with a flexible, agile organization (Agarwal et al. 2006). To satisfy the customer drivers, flexibility is regarded as the order winning criterion, relying on cost, lead time and quality as order qualifiers (Christopher and Towill 2000). If a high level of flexibility is demanded, a leagile strategy is suggested; here, both the two previous market winning criteria cost and lead time are considered as providing a competitive edge, while lead time and quality are

Descriptive characteristics	Supply chain strategies		
Customer drivers	Price	Flexibility	Lead time (high availability)
Market winning criteria	Cost	Cost Flexibility	Flexibility
Market qualifying criteria	Lead time Flexibility Quality	Lead time Quality	Cost Lead time Quality
	Lean	Leagile	Agile

Fig. 3.11 Customer segments' characteristics and corresponding supply chain strategies (2/2)

prerequisite for competing. It becomes apparent that the fourth strategic need, quality, does not appear as a customer driver in any of the supply chain strategies. That is because it is rated as a prerequisite (market qualifier) for all of the supply chain strategies, but does not excel as a customer driver, as customers generally assume a high level of quality (Christopher 2000; Agarwal et al. 2006); see Fig. 3.11.

3.3.3 Adjustment of Business Unit Strategy and Supply Chain Strategies

Finally, the different supply chain strategies are discussed with regard to the strategy of the focal company. Here, "[s]upply chain management must be aligned with firm strategies to contribute to a sustainable competitive advantage" (Hofmann 2010). Particularly, the business units' strategies are significant for achieving a competitive advantage (Hofmann 2010), which will thus be subject to explanation. In general, a supply chain strategy cannot directly be assigned to a business unit's strategy. Nonetheless, some of the strategies seem a better match than others.

Thus, a model consisting of three generic strategies that companies can apply in order to outperform competitors is presented (Porter 1980).

- The first strategy, **overall cost leadership**, is characterized by an aggressive cost efficiency concept, which results in lower costs than those of their rivals. Consequently, the corresponding supply chain strategy is lean; requirements like cost reductions through scale or experience effects are most likely with this type of supply chain. Nevertheless, also if circumstances (e.g., demand) dictate a leagile or agile organization, and cost reduction cannot extensively be implemented, cost leadership is a possible strategy, as long as the competitors face similar obstacles.
- The second generic strategy is **differentiation**. This concept employs a striving for uniqueness of products within the industry. Through this strategy, above-average returns can be accomplished. It becomes obvious that this business unit strategy does not share objectives with lean management. Therefore, agile or

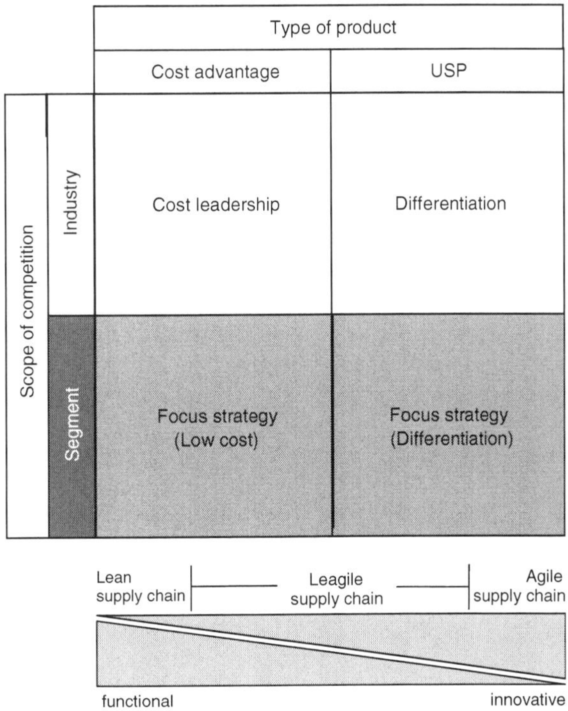

Fig. 3.12 Linking the supply chain strategy with the generic strategy matrix

leagile strategies seem to be more suitable, particularly bearing in mind the ability of the latter to offer a broad variety of products at competitive costs.

- The third generic strategy is named **focus**. Here, the focal business unit focuses "on a particular buyer group, segment of the product line, or geographic market" (Porter 1980). Within its target segment, the firm can pursue cost leadership or differentiation or both. Therefore, all of the three generic supply chain strategies might be most suitable, depending on the strategy within the focus segment. If the aim is both cost leadership and differentiation, a leagile supply chain strategy might work best. In conclusion, the different strategies are illustrated in Fig. 3.12.

3.3.4 Choosing the Right Supply Chain Strategy for a Customer Segment

In the previous sections, various interrelations between supply chain strategies and the business environment have been discussed, both from the customers' and the focal company's perspective. For the purpose of achieving an integrated, holistic solution, a decision-making tool is briefly presented that includes all the different aspects discussed.

3.3.4.1 The Analytical Hierarchy Process

Another method for solving multi-criteria decision-making problems is the analytic hierarchy process (AHP). Just like the weighted score method, the AHP organizes problems into a hierarchy, with an overall goal at the top (in our situation, the goal to identify a ranking of different corrective actions), alternative methods of reaching the goal (the different corrective actions), and several criteria against which the alternatives have to be measured (utility, feasibility, etc.). In most cases all these steps have to be taken, but in particular situations the company has to decide which of these steps are most relevant.

The most creative decision-making process involves prioritizing the hierarchy. There are different steps in elaborating a hierarchy according to Saaty (1996).

(1) Identify the overall goal. What are you trying to accomplish? What is the main question?
(2) Identify the subgoals of the overall goal. If relevant, identify time horizons that affect the decision.
(3) Identify criteria that must be satisfied to fulfill the subgoals of the overall goal.
(4) Identify sub criteria under each criterion. Note that criteria or sub criteria may be specified in terms of ranges of values of parameters or in terms of verbal intensities such as high, medium, low.
(5) Identify the actors involved.
(6) Identify the actors' goals.

Table 3.3 shows a comparison of the relationships between two elements that share a common parent. The set of judgments can be shown in a square matrix in which the set of elements is compared with itself. There are two questions which are considered: Which of the two elements is more important with respect to a higher-level criterion, and how much more important, using the 1–9 scale in Table 3.3 for the element at the top matrix? (Saaty 1996).

Regarding the analytical hierarchy process, pairwise comparisons of the various relevant factors on different hierarchic levels with regard to an overall goal are performed. In each step of the process, the different attributes identified at a particular hierarchic level are compared with respect to the level above, in a descending order from the top level on. The prioritizations of each level are then combined and a final ranking of priorities is obtained (Saaty 1994).

For the present context, the hierarchical structure for the AHP is shown in Fig. 3.13. On the top level, the business unit strategy, product characteristics and customer needs are rated against each other with respect to the overall goal. Thereafter, on the next lower level, the different factors are compared with regard to the corresponding factor of the next higher level. For example, the diverse customer needs are ranked. Finally, a pairwise comparison of the four **value**

Table 3.3 The fundamental scale is a scale of absolute numbers used to assign numerical values to judgments made by comparing two elements, with the smallest element used as the unit and the larger one assigned a value from this scale as a multiple of that unit (Saaty 1996)

Intensity of importance	Definition	Explanation
1	Equal importance	Two activities contribute equally to the objective
3	Moderate importance	Experience and judgment slightly favor one activity over another
5	Strong importance	Experience and judgment strongly favor one activity over another
7	Very strong or demonstrated importance	An activity is favored very strongly over another, its dominance demonstrated in practice
9	Extreme importance	The evidence favoring one activity over another is of the highest possible order of affirmation
2, 4, 6, 8	For compromise between the above values	Sometimes one needs to interpolate a compromise judgment numerically because there is no good word to describe it
Reciprocals of above	If activity *i* has one of the above nonzero numbers assigned to it when compared with activity *j*, then *j* has the reciprocal value when compared with *i*	A comparison mandated by choosing the smaller element as the unit to estimate the larger one as a multiple of that unit
Ratios	Ratios arising from the scale	If consistency were to be forced by obtaining *n* numerical values to span the matrix

generating criteria at the bottom is undertaken, in each case according to the factor on the upper level.

3.3.5 Customer Order Decoupling Point

The positioning of the customer order decoupling point (CODP) is increasingly becoming an issue of strategic interest (Olhager 2003). Traditionally, the CODP is defined as "[…] the point in the value chain for a product, where the product is linked to a specific customer order". Thereby, the CODP, sometimes called the order penetration point, divides the flow of the material which is forecast driven (upstream of the CODP) from the material flow driven by customer orders (downstream from the CODP). Moreover, it represents the last point at which strategic inventory is held without order reverence (Olhager 2010). Thus,

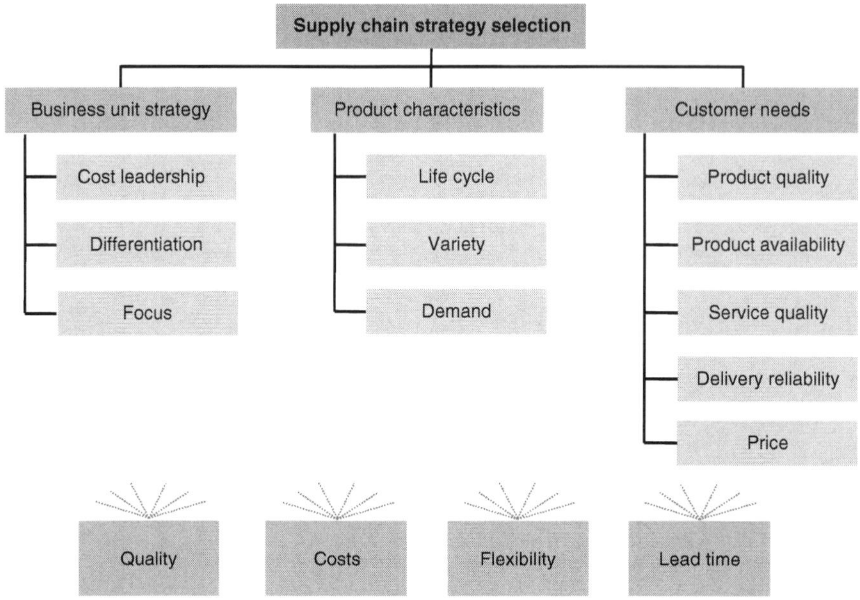

Fig. 3.13 Schematic hierarchy of the supply chain strategy, selected *sources* Christopher and Towill (2001), Fisher (1997), Ketchen et al. (2008) and Vitasek et al. (2003)

inventory is held, for example, in a modular form and only assembled when the precise customer requirement is known (Christopher and Towill 2001).

The positioning of the CODP in the value chain is affected by different factors which can be divided into three categories: **market-related factors**, **product-related factors**, and **production-related factors**.

- Regarding **market-related factors**, product demand volatility specifies to what extent the products is made to order or to stock. Thus, if volatility is high, forecasting is relatively difficult and products are typically made to order. Conversely, low volatility means the items can be forecast driven.
- For the **product-related factors**, customization plays a role in positioning the CODP. Hence, if the customization offered enters the product at an early stage of the production, the CODP needs to be positioned upstream in the value chain.
- An example of a **production-related factor** is represented by the production lead time. This factor needs to be considered regarding the delivery lead time requirements determined by the market, as this relationship places a constraint on the positioning of the CODP. If the lead time is reduced, the constraint can be relieved and a wider range of CODP positioning is possible (Olhager 2003).

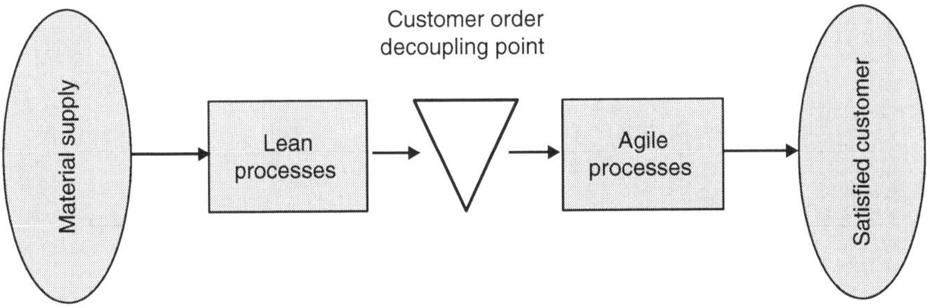

Fig. 3.14 Decoupling point in a supply chain (Mason-Jones et al. 2000)

The CODP allows for a differentiation of supply chain strategy before and after the defined point. Companies may utilize a lean strategy up to the CODP and an agile strategy beyond it as depicted in Fig. 3.14 (Christopher and Towill 2001).

The lean method is applied upstream of the CODP as the demand is straight and standardized products flow through a number of value streams. Downstream, the agile method is suitable, as customer demands vary significantly and the product variety per value stream has increased. A good example is offered by the case of Hewlett Packard, where a U.S. factory produced printers for the global market. After their production, the generic printers were customized to meet various national specifications and shipped to regional distribution centers. Especially in Europe, with its small national markets, this approach was problematic. Due to the fact that the stockholding point of the market-specific products is located at the distribution centers, the situation often arose that one country found itself out of stock, while another was overstocked. Thus, the target of the company was to redesign its supply chain in order to overcome the issue of variability in customer demand by increasing the agility of the supply chain beyond the CODP. This was achieved by positioning the decoupling point as far downstream as possible and performing product differentiation at that specific point. Concretely this meant that the generic product was distributed to the individual distribution centers as buffer stock and then differentiated for each national market. In this way, the supply chain of Hewlett Packard went from a completely lean orientation to a supply chain which incorporated agility beyond the CODP (Naylor et al. 1999).

For further information about the CODP, please see Chap. 4 on manufacturing and supply chain processes.

Summary sheet

CM1b: Supply chain strategy

Goals of SCD Guide CM1b

The target of this section of the SCD Guide CM1 is a differentiated supply chain strategy derived in accordance with the identified customer segment. Here methods and analysis are presented which determine supply chain strategies according to the different customer segments as well as the positioning of the customer order decoupling point.

Methods and analysis for SCD Guide CM1b

- DWV^3 and supply chain strategies
- Analytical hierarchy process (AHP)
- Customer order decoupling point (CODP)

Input per method for SCD-Guide CM1b

	Input from other CMs	DWV^3 and supply chain strategies	Analytical hierarchy process (AHP)
Method for selecting supply chain strategies	CM1	• Customer requirements with respect to DMV^3 variables	• Product characteristics • Customer requirements • Business unit strategy

The customer order decoupling point is presented in CM4.

Output from SCD Guide CM1b

- Differentiated supply chain strategy for each identified customer segment
  Dimensions in morphological box: Competitive priorities and strategic SC orientation

3.4 Application Example of SCD Guide CM1 and Possible Output

PC Manufacturing Inc. has identified customer requirements which are ranked from product quality, price, product availability, and delivery reliability to service quality. Products can be ordered by means of different distribution channels via direct orders by mail or telephone, on its online platform, or through retailers.

3.4.1 Customer Segmentation

In a **DWV^3- analysis**, the company defines its product requirements according to the five variables shown in Figs. 3.15 and 3.16 need for focus. The existing product portfolio can be realized and thereby reach maximum competitiveness for each

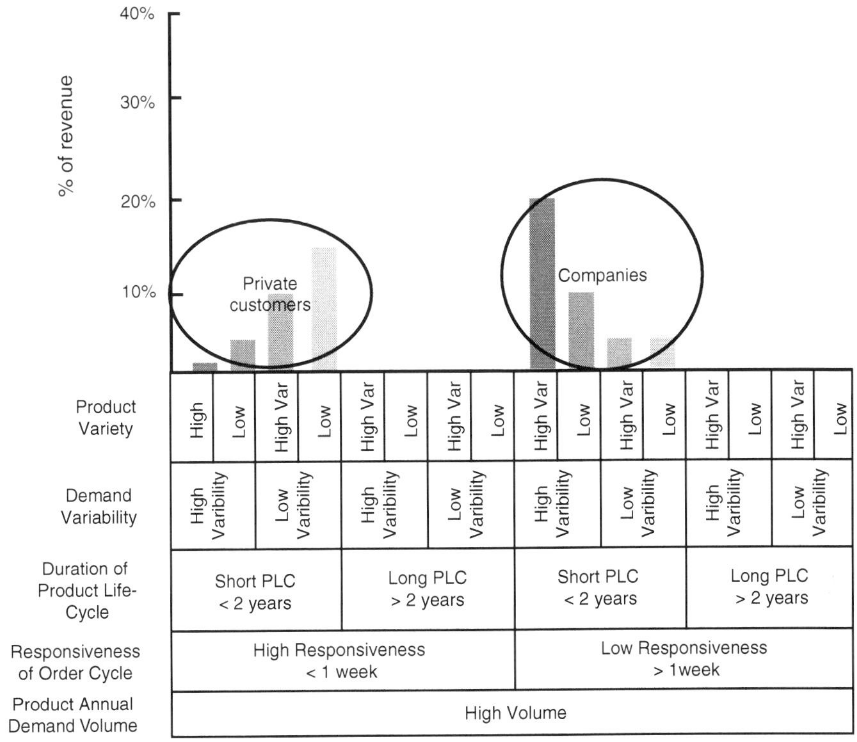

Fig. 3.15 DWV^3 analysis to define customer segments for the case company PC Manufacturing Inc. (1/2)

individual product. The five variables are product variety, demand variability, duration of product life cycle, responsiveness of order cycles, and volume of annual product demand.

Figures 3.15 and 3.16 show three different clusters in relation to the five different variables. The aim here is to reach a near perfect combination between theory and practice.

In practice the computer company has identified three different customer segments, namely, private customers, companies and the public sector. The SCD Guide requires entries in the morphological box for each of these customer segments. The clusters derive from the revenue that the products achieve and their requirements in regard to the five different variables. Data collection and analysis have identified that businesses have a lower demand for variety than private customers and therefore do not need a large diversity of products. The company has a strategy which leaves it with very short lead times. For example if the product volume of companies is exceptionally high, the product life cycle is short and the variety of the products is low. Private customers demand a high level of

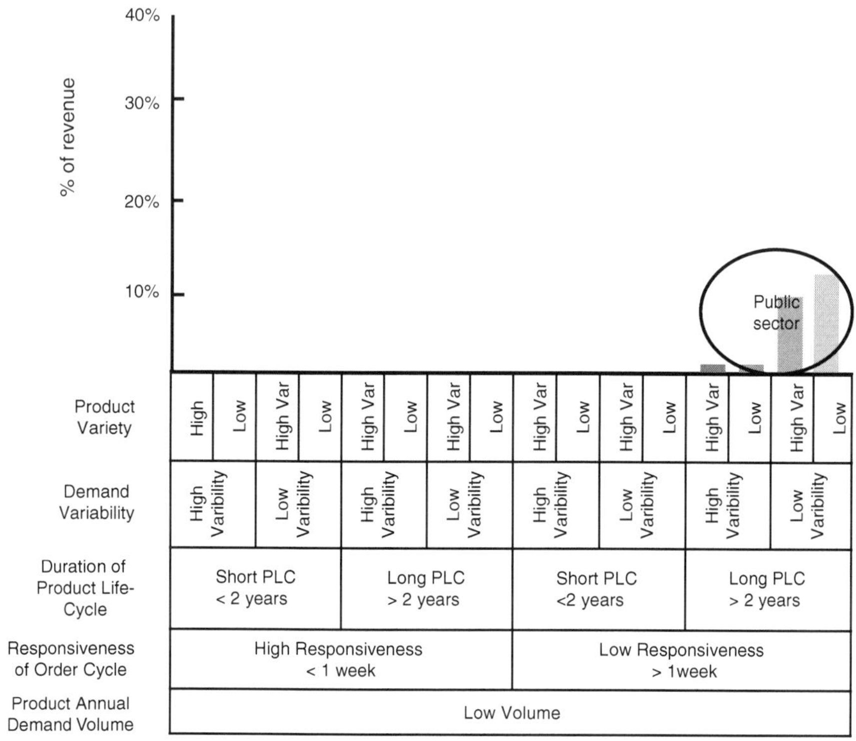

Fig. 3.16 DWV^3 analysis to define customer segments for the case company PC Manufacturing Inc. (2/2)

customized products, which results in a large variety of different products since they allocate their products via the online sales platform.

3.4.2 Strategic Supply Chain Orientation

In what follows the PC Manufacturing Inc. will make use of the SCD Guide for the customer segment "private".

The **AHP analysis** defines which of the three different supply chain strategies is advisable for the manufacturing of Tec 1. The same process needs to be carried out separately for each of the product groups. The value-generating criteria—quality, costs, flexibility and lead time—are evaluated in terms of business unit strategy, product characteristics and customer needs. The relevant supply chain strategy is derived from this assessment. In the following table, one can see the outcome of different value-generating criteria, expressed in percentages Table 3.4.

Table 3.4 Ranking of value-generating supply chain criteria (Example)

Value-generating supply chain criteria	%	Ranking (1–4)
Quality	75	Flexibility
Costs	70	Quality
Flexibility	100	Costs
Lead time	60	Lead time

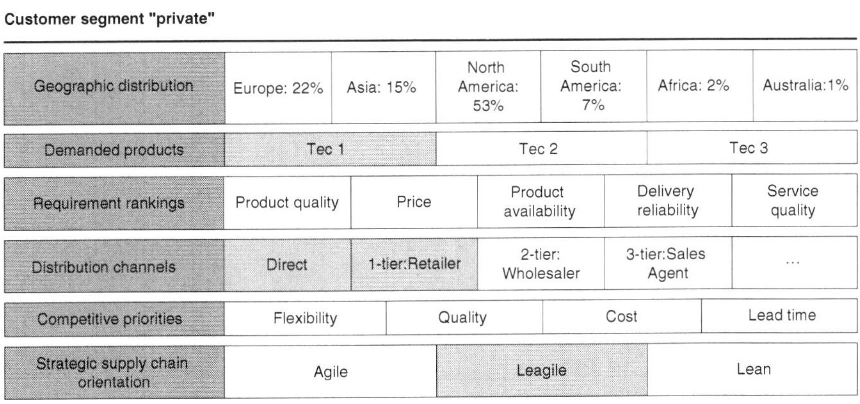

Fig. 3.17 Exemplary morphological box for identifying customer requirements and segments of Tec 1

The ranking is generated from the percentages derived in the AHP analysis. It shows the relative importance of the value-generating criteria and prioritizes the different values from 1 to 4. With flexibility as the highest priority PC Manufacturing Inc. is advised to apply a leagile strategic supply chain orientation, with a stronger focus on agility as opposed to a strictly lean or agile orientation.

Since the leagile strategy has been defined for product 1 of the computer manufacturer, it is now important to take a closer look at the position of the **customer order decoupling point (CODP)**, which will take place in CM2, but can be considered when looking at the determination of the supply chain strategy.

The assessment and morphological box of PC Manufacturing Company within CM1b has shown that geographic distribution lies mainly in North America as well as Europe. In addition, a significant proportion of the products are distributed in Asia. There are three different customer segments, as the business, private and public sector. Three different product groups have therefore been determined. Furthermore, appointing flexibility as the most important value-generating criteria makes the leagile strategic supply chain orientation the most appropriate one for the customer segment "private". The SCD Guide demands that a morphological box be filled in for each of these customer segments (since this would be too extensive, we will only fill in one morphological box in the application examples Fig. 3.17).

References

Agarwal, A., Shankar, R., & Tiwari, M. K. (2006). Modeling the metrics of lean, agile and leagile supply chain: an ANP-based approach. *European Journal of Operational Research, 173*(1), 211–225.

Aitken, J., Childerhouse, P., & Towill, D. (2003). The impact of product life cycle on supply chain strategy. *International Journal of Production Economics, 85*(2), 127–140.

Albert, T. C. (2003). Need-based segmentation and customized communication strategies in a complex-commodity industry: a supply chain study. *Industrial Marketing Management, 32*(4), 281–290.

Anderson, C. R., & Zeithaml, C. P. (1984). Stage of the product life cycle, business strategy, and business performance. *Academy of Management Journal, 27*(1), 5–24.

Ansoff, I. (1957). Strategies for diversification. *Harvard Business Review, 35*(5), 113–124.

Bruce, M., & Daly, L. (2004). Lean or agile a solution for supply chain management in the textiles and clothing industry? *International Journal of Operations & Production Management, 24*(2), 151–170.

Campbell, N. C. G., & Cunningham, M. T. (1983). Customer analysis for strategy development in industrial markets. *Strategic Management Journal, 4*(4), 369–380.

Childerhouse, P., Aitken, J., & Towill, D. R. (2002). Analysis and design of focused demand chains. *Journal of Operations Management, 20*(6), 675–689.

Chopra, S., & Meindl, P. (2007). *Supply chain management: strategy, planning, and operation* (3rd ed.). Upper Saddle River: Pearson Prentice Hall.

Christopher, M. (2000). The agile supply chain. *Industrial Marketing Management, 29*(1), 37–44.

Christopher, M., & Towill, D. R. (2000). Marrying lean and agile paradigms. Ghent, Belgium, Proceedings of EUROMA: 114–121.

Christopher, M., & Towill, D. R. (2001). An integrated model for the design of agile supply chains. *International Journal of Physical Distribution & Logistics Management., 31*(4), 235–246.

Christopher, M., Peck, H., & Towill, D. R. (2006). A taxonomy for selecting global supply chain strategies. *International Journal of Logistics Management, 17*(2), 277–287.

Cooil, B., Aksoy, L., & Keiningham, T. L. (2008). Approaches to customer segmentation. *Journal of Relationship Marketing, 6*(3/4), 9–39.

Fisher, M. L. (1997). What is the right supply chain for your product? *Harvard Business Review, 75*(2), 105–116.

Gilmour, P., Borg, G., Duffy, P. A., Johnston, N. D., Limbek, B. E., & Shaw, M. R. (1994). Customer service: differentiating by market segment. *Journal of Physical Distribution and Logistics Management, 24*(4), 18–23.

Green, P. E., & Krieger, A. M. (1991). Segmenting markets with conjoint analysis. *Journal of Marketing, 55*(4), 20–31.

Griffin, A., & Hauser, J. R. (1993). The voice of the customer. *Marketing Science, 12*(1), 1–27.

Hill, T. (1993 [1st ed. 1985]). Manufacturing strategy: text and cases. 2nd ed. Blue Ridge Ill: Irwin Professional Publishing.

Hofmann, E. (2010). Linking corporate strategy and supply chain management. *International Journal of Physical Distribution & Logistics Management., 40*(4), 256–276.

Homburg, C., & Krohmer, H. (2006). *Marketingmanagement: Strategie—Instrumente—Umsetzung—Unternehmensführung* (2nd ed.). Wiesbaden: Gabler.

Jain, D., & Singh, S. S. (2002). Customer lifetime value research in marketing: a review and future directions. *Journal of Interactive Marketing, 16*(2), 34–46.

Johansson, H. J., McHugh, P., Pendlebury, A. J., & Wheeler, W. A. (1993). *Business process reengineering: breakpoint strategies for market dominance*. Chichester: Wiley.

Ketchen, D. J., Rebarick, W., Hult, G. T. M., & Meyer, D. (2008). Best value supply chains: a key competitive weapon for the 21st century. *Business Horizons, 51*(3), 235–243.

Kim, S.-Y., Jung, T.-S., Suh, E.-H., & Hwang, H.-S. (2006). Customer segmentation and strategy development based on customer lifetime value: a case study. *Expert System with Applications, 31*(1), 101–107.

Koch, R. (1997). *The 80/20 principle: the secret of achieving more with less*. London: Nicholas Brealey Publishing.

Kotler, P., & Bliemel, F. (2001). *Marketing-Management* (10th ed.). Stuttgart: Schäffer-Poeschel Verlag.

Marcus, C. (1998). A practical yet meaningful approach to customer segmentation. *Journal of Consumer Marketing, 15*(5), 494.

Mason-Jones, R., & Towill, D. R. (1997). Information enrichment: designing the supply chain for competitive advantage. *Supply Chain Management, 2*(4), 137–148.

Mason-Jones, R., Naylor, B., & Towill, D. R. (2000). Lean, agile or leagile? matching your supply chain to the marketplace. *International Journal of Production Research, 38*(17), 4061–4070.

Mentzer, J. T., Myers, M. B., & Cheung, M.-S. (2004). Global market segmentation for logistics services. *Industrial Marketing Management, 33*(1), 16–20.

Naylor, J. B., Naim, M. M., & Berry, D. (1999). Leagility: integrating the lean and agile manufacturing paradigms in the total supply chain. *International Journal of Production Economics, 62*(1–2), 107–118.

Olhager, J. (2003). Strategic positioning of the order penetration point. *International Journal of Production Economics, 85*(3), 319–329.

Porter, M. E. (1980). *Competitive strategy: techniques for analyzing industries and competitors*. New York: Free Press.

Rogers, E. M. (1995). *Diffusion of innovations* (4th ed.). New York: The Free Press.

Saaty, T. L. (1994). How to make a decision: the analytic hierarchy process. *Interfaces, 24*(6), 19–43.

Saaty, T. L. (1996). *Multicriteria decision making: planning, priority setting, resource allocation* (2nd ed.). Pittsburgh: University of Pittsburgh.

Ter Hofstede, F., Wedel, M., & Steenkamp, J. B. E. M. (2002). Identifying spatial segments in international markets. *Marketing Science, 21*(2), 160–177.

Terho, H., & Halinen, A. (2007). Customer portfolio analysis practices in different exchange contexts. *Journal of Business Research, 60*(7), 720–730.

Vitasek, K. L., Manrodt, K. B., & Kelly, M. (2003). Solving the supply-demand mismatch. *Supply Chain Management Review, 7*(5), 58.

Watson, G. H. (1994). *Business systems engineering: managing breakthrough changes for productivity and profit*. New York, Chichester, Brisbane, Toronto, Singapore: Wiley.

Yorke, D., & Droussiotis, G. (1994). The use of customer portfolio theory—an empirical survey. *Journal of Business and Industrial Marketing, 9*(3), 6–18.

Zolkiewski, J., & Turnbull, P. (2002). Do relationship portfolios and networks provide the key to successful relationship management? *Journal of Business and Industrial Marketing, 17*(7), 575–597.

4 CM2: Manufacturing Strategy and Supply Chain Management

4.1 Goals of Content Module 2

The target of CM2 is the explanation of the concept product modularization in the context of supply chain management. Outsourcing is derived as a consequence of the concept of product modularization. Therefore, this chapter includes a thorough discussion of the implications of an outsourcing decision. Furthermore the concept of product modularization as well as the outsourcing decision are embedded into the supply chain strategies (Fig. 4.1).

The first section identifies the concept of product modularization as a vital part of the manufacturing process. Product modularization is explained in further detail, whereby the benefits of modularization are clearly demonstrated.

The second section explains outsourcing as a self-explanatory consequence of modularization. The different implications of the buy-or-make decision are outlined in this section.

The third section deals with the outsourcing decision process made by the relevant company, whereas the core competencies of the company play a significant role in the choice of the final outsourcing strategy. First, the four different stages of the outsourcing process are defined and in the following analyzed. The goal is to offer an outline of the significance involved in the outsourcing decision and a brief description of the outsourcing process itself which can be adapted to any given company.

The fourth part depicts an alternative to modularization, namely, the formation of material groups, since some of the structural conditions circumvent the use of product modularization.

E. Hofmann et al., *The Supply Chain Differentiation Guide*,
DOI: 10.1007/978-3-642-31936-5_4, © Springer-Verlag Berlin Heidelberg 2012

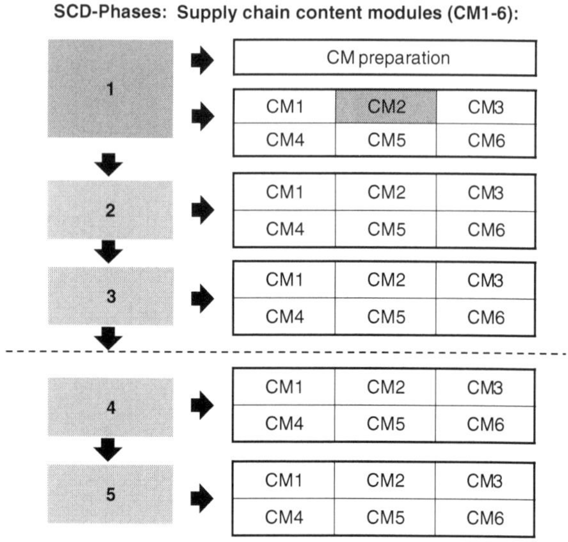

Fig. 4.1 Position of Chap. 4 in SCD Guide

4.2 Product Modularization

4.2.1 Principle of Product Modularization

Modularity describes the division of products into subsystems, so-called **modules**, in order to increase the flexibility of both the firm and the users (Baldwin and Clark 1997). A given product consists of various sub-parts, which can therefore be depicted by a **product architecture**. The concept can be defined as follows: "Product architecture is the arrangement of the functional elements of a product into several physical building blocks, including the mapping from functional elements to physical components, and the specification of the interfaces among interacting physical components" (Mikkola 2003). Thus, complex tasks are decomposed into homogeneous elements in order either to manage them independently or to continue operating them as a whole. The more independent the different parts are from one another, the more likely is the option to utilize them separately, thus increasing the degree of modularity (Mikkola 2003).

Modularization in supply chain management is needed in order to implement supply chain strategies as well as manufacturing strategies. The assemble-to-order strategy can only be implemented if there is a modular design of products. The end product can then be assembled out of a small number of products. According to the modules, a decision can be made whether to make or to outsource certain modules to other suppliers and focus more on core competencies. In the next section this is discussed in further detail.

The benefits of modularization are multifaceted. Modularity can help a firm increase the number of products offered while simultaneously lowering costs.

Through a modular organization not only economies of scale, but also economies of scope such as customization or product variation can be achieved (Mikkola 2006). Furthermore, a firm disposes over increased capability to provide a broader range of products when modularization is applied (Halman et al. 2003). In addition, time to market of new products can significantly be reduced through composing a product of modules, and new product development can also be accomplished with more flexibility (Baldwin and Clark 1997). Finally, the frequent combination of standardized and approved components induces a high level of product performance (Halman et al. 2003).

Within a given firm the concept of modularization is naturally most important to the research and development (R&D) department (Ulrich 1995). Since it has, however, a significant impact on various central strategic issues such as the variety of products or the degree of standardization, diverse other functional areas are affected by modularization. For instance, Christopher (2000) mention that reduction of complexity through modularization should be of significant importance for the adjustment of the marketing and logistics departments.

In general, the scope of product architecture can be defined rather arbitrarily (Ulrich 1995). Two main requirements are identified that need to be fulfilled if a successful modular structure of the product range is to be implemented (Halman et al. 2003). On the one hand, the product structure has to permit the division of elements; on the other hand, parts of the product architecture have to support standardization. A framework for categorizing the prevalent aspects of product architecture has the following aspects: On the top level, the **functional elements** are arranged; this describes what the products characteristics are. These elements are linked to **physical components**, which are connected by **interfaces** that specify the interaction of the physical components. The connection of physical components can be further split up into two types: **modular** and **integral**.

- "A **modular** architecture includes a one-to-one mapping from functional elements in the function structure to the physical components" (Ulrich 1995), which means that each component is highly independent of each other and the connecting interfaces, and thus easily substitutable (Halman et al. 2003). Regarding the term **decoupling**, meaning that the change of one component does not affect its connected components (Ulrich 1995), product architectures serve as flexible platforms, which lead to cost efficiencies and a constant preservation of state-of-the-art products through rapid and easy substitutability (Mikkola 2003).
- By contrast, an **integral** architecture is characterized by a more complex interrelationship between functional elements, components and interfaces; decoupling is not given to the same extent as when a modular structure is pursued (Ulrich 1995). Because of the higher interdependencies of components and the resulting lower degree of modularization, costs for customization are traditionally higher than those of modular architecture. On the other hand, this type of structure supports the exchange of knowledge among the involved parties, as product design is carried out jointly (Mikkola 2003). Moreover, the interconnectedness of the aspects creates an idiosyncratic character to product

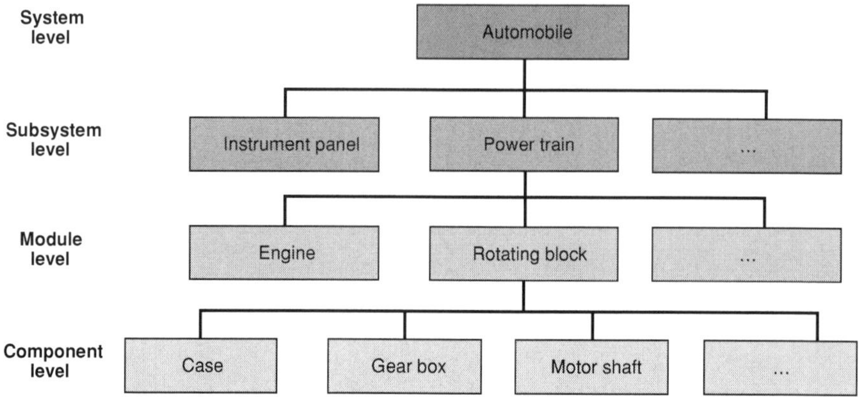

Fig. 4.2 Schematic product architecture of an automobile, after Mikkola (2006)

architecture, which makes it complicated for competitors to copy and thus establishes a competitive advantage (Mikkola 2006).

In conclusion, a graphic is presented that provides a concrete visualization of the concept of modularization. For this purpose Fig. 4.2 depicts an exemplary product architecture. The system chosen for this example is the automobile. The automobile qua system can be split up into various subsystems, such as the instrument panel or the power train. Next, the subsystems consist of diverse modules; for instance, the power train is made up, among other things, of the engine and the rotating block. Lastly, a module is composed of different components. For example, the rotating block is composed of components such as the case, the gear box and the motor shaft.

At the component level, it distinguishes between **standard** (STD) and **new to the firm** (NTF) components. This distinction determines the perspective of product architectures. The utilization of standardized items generates significant cost efficiencies through economies of scale; beyond this, the investments in the product structure are generally reduced. By contrast, components that are new to the firm can improve the characteristics and performance of a product, while cutting production costs. Moreover, newly developed components might, at least in the short term, endow the firm with a competitive advantage. However, it must be acknowledged that an accumulation of NTF components can hamper fast product time to market, as both the component development and the integration into the product structure can involve complexity (Mikkola 2006). In general, the increased variety of products and product configurations that is a result of modularization does not necessarily add benefit to a company; on the one hand, an augmented effort of coordination takes place, and, on the other, the confusion of the customers increases as to which product to choose.

4.2.2 The Process of Product Modularization

To attain a product architecture as described above, a modularization framework is proposed that details the different steps necessary for breaking down the product into its components (Shamsuzzoha 2011).

4.2.2.1 Modularization Framework

The modularization framework is a guideline for breaking the production process down into its individual components. Here different steps have to be carried out, starting with the functional level, analysis and evaluation, and sensitivity analysis.

- Starting on the **functional (system or subsystem)** level, the product is analyzed regarding its functional requirements and design objectives, and accordingly decomposed into its components. Through this step, the interrelationships between the product functions and the corresponding physical parts are clarified. Subsequently, the identified components are bundled into modules, addressing the diverse design objectives. However, "in general, the primary objective of modular design architecture is to cluster the components into modules in which the dependencies among components are localized based on functional interactions" (Shamsuzzoha 2011). For this purpose, various grouping attributes can be applied, such as technological characteristics or cost aspects.
- Consequently, the following step in the modularization process deals with the **analysis and evaluation** of the devised modules. Principally, the analysis considers the costs of the particular modules, specifically, the costs of manufacturing and reusability. Whereas, the first are specified by the costs that can be rooted in the manufacturing process, which also includes the convenience of assembly through standardized interfaces, the costs of the latter are determined by the appropriateness of modules for multiple usages, with regard to various objectives.
- In a third step, a **sensitivity analysis** is carried out. Here, the defined key modules are assessed with regard to their costs and manufacturability. Furthermore, other important factors as, for example, resource availability, technological requirements and the potential for outsourcing parts of the manufacturing process are included in the analysis. Moreover, the modules' suitability for assembly is the subject of the sensitivity analysis. If the results of the analysis indicate any insufficiency, the module development process has to be repeated.

Once the modules have passed the sensitivity analysis, they are, in a final step, analyzed regarding the dependency of their respective components. The dependency of components is then ranked according to the level or strength of their dependency.

Finally, the coordination of resource requirements and customer preferences has to be borne in mind during the entire modularization process (Shamsuzzoha 2011, Fig. 4.3).

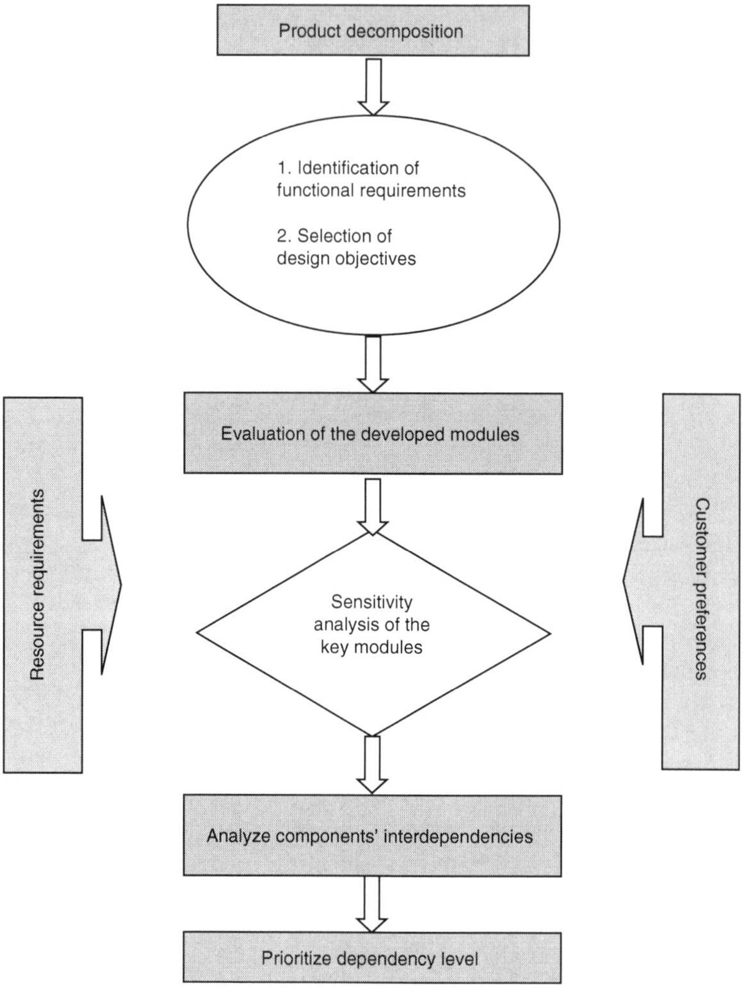

Fig. 4.3 The process of product modularization in supply chain management, after Shamsuzzoha (2011)

4.3 Modularization and Deciding the Value of the Real Net Output Ratio

Following upon the investigation of the concept of modularization including its various facets and characteristics, this section is concerned with the decision of setting the value of the real net output ratio (which is, roughly speaking, the level of non-outsourced production) as a self-evident consequence of modularization. Outsourcing can be described as purchasing a certain part from another company instead of making it by yourself (Womack et al. 1990). In this sense, a shift of responsibility is made, as the suppliers gain an increased strategic importance for the focal producing firm (Zsidisin 2003). Consequently, the buyer–supplier relationship becomes tighter (Mikkola 2003).

Outsourcing is significantly facilitated and advanced through modularization (Mikkola 2003). Due to augmented specification of components and interfaces, which already takes place in the design phase, interchangeability of parts rises. As a consequence, an increased modularity goes hand-in-hand with simplified outsourcing of parts (Ernst and Kamrad 2000). The outsourcing decision can affect various functions of a firm; in their survey, Kakabadse and Kakabadse (2002) found out that European and U.S. companies primarily outsource their basic services (e.g., the canteen service), followed by information technology (IT), human resources (HR) and telecommunication services. However, put into a manufacturing context, Sako (2003) states that original equipment manufacturers (OEMs) should outsource their functions in a bunched way: either design and development, or production and assembly, or both.

Several reasons for outsourcing can be presented. For instance, von Hippel (1994) recognizes that, if a product is composed of parts that require varying technological capabilities, it might be beneficial to divide the production into modules and distribute those parts to specialists that require competencies lacking in the firm. This view is supported by the insight of Henderson and Clarkt (1990), who claim that firms struggle and regularly fail, if they try to change their production structure to cope with the challenges of demand or competition, instead of focusing on their conventional strengths. Moreover, concentrating on specific modules allows a more intensive handling of them (Baldwin and Clark 1997).

Besides focusing on what is often called the ‘core competencies’ (Prahalad and Hamel 1990) of a firm, a great majority of the outsourcing companies regard cost effects, such as economies of scale, as a key driver (Kakabadse and Kakabadse 2002). A study by Ro et al. (2007) in the U.S. car sector provides evidence of this conclusion: it is not the satisfaction of the customer, but the reduction in costs that is the primary goal of outsourcing. For example, the forwarding of demand uncertainty effects—which traditionally increase production costs—to the supplier(s) are a reason for outsourcing (Mikkola 2003). However, not only the production costs are reduced through outsourcing, but also costs and efforts related to the coordination and management of diverse in-house activities (Mikkola 2003).

As a further advantage, outsourcing can reduce the time to market of a product, due to synchronized innovation efforts of buyer and supplier(Kakabadse and Kakabadse 2002). Depending on the management of component outsourcing, the degree of buyer–supplier interdependency varies, which in turn has an impact on the composition of the product and consequently on the pace of innovation and time to market (Mikkola 2003; treated in greater detail in a later part of this section).

However, the question arises why it is decided to outsource some modules or components, while others are left in-house. The main benefits of outsourcing have already been stated above. Nonetheless, these aspects are embedded parts of an

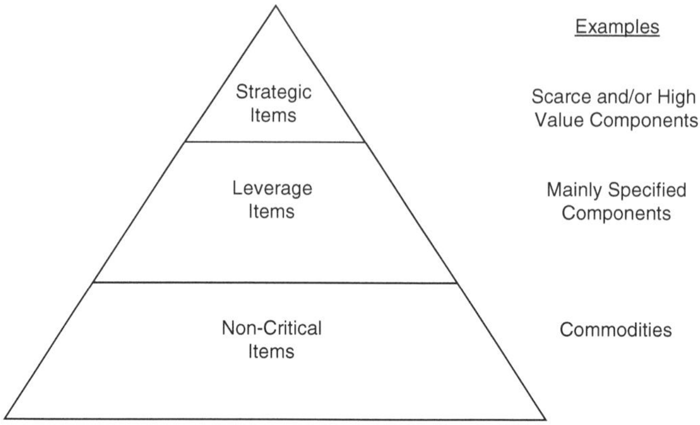

Fig. 4.4 Hierarchy of strategic importance, adapted from McIvor and Humphreys (1997)

overarching outsourcing or make-or-buy decision-making concept. This concept will now briefly be introduced.

4.3.1 Process for the Outsourcing Decision

For this purpose an outsourcing process framework, consisting of four successive stages, is taken and adapted to the present discussion (McIvor 2000).

4.3.2 Outsourcing Procedure

4.3.2.1 Stage 1: Defining the "Core" Items

Of high relevance is the clarification of the strategic importance of the item of interest (component or module), in other words, determining what position it has in the firm's product architecture.

Here, the identification of **core competencies** plays an important role. If a firm possesses a unique position compared to its competitors, it is very likely that the firm possesses a core competence in producing particular products or technologies. These competencies are not of a physical nature, but capabilities, knowledge or processes that are inherent in the structure of a firm and thus difficult for competitors to uncover and copy (McIvor 2000; Prahalad and Hamel 1990). Based on these facts, different items of a firm can be classified into three different groups (McIvor and Humphreys 1997), as shown in Fig. 4.4.

One identified item is of high strategic importance for the success of the firm. The two remaining items are considered less important and thus of lower strategic significance. Consequently, depending on which role an item plays in the firm's product architecture, a decision is made. If the technologies and competencies involved belong to the core competencies, the item is considered part of the

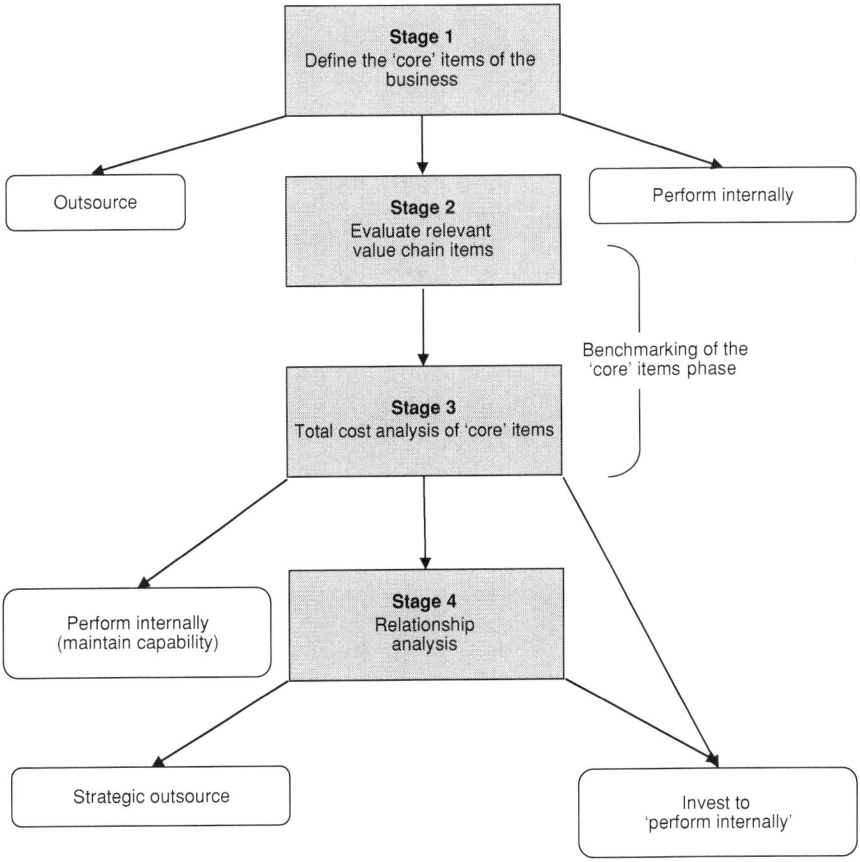

Fig. 4.5 A practical framework for evaluating the outsourcing decision, after McIvor (2000)

proprietary core of the firm and thus stays in-house. If not, the recommendation is made to purchase the item (McIvor 2000).

However, it is not self-evident that such an extreme position reflects a firm's particular situation, as a part inextricably connected to its environment; therefore, aspects such as relations or long-term contracts within the industry might constrain the outsourcing decision (McIvor 2000) (Fig. 4.5).

4.3.2.2 Stage 2: Evaluate Relevant Value Chain Items

Next, decision making proceeds with the evaluation of the identified core items. The purpose of this and the subsequent step is to compare the firm's items not only to direct competitors, but also to competitors within the same value chain (i.e. suppliers, McIvor 2000).

Even if the product or technology belongs to the core competencies of the focal firm, it still has to honestly appraise if producing the product or technology in-house really provides the firm with a sustainable competitive advantage over horizontal and/or vertical competitors (McIvor 2000). Barney (1991) has made this notion popular, stating that it comes into existence if a firm has a "value creating strategy not simultaneously being implemented by any current or potential competitors and when these other firms are unable to duplicate the benefits of this strategy". To be considered as a sustainable competitive advantage, Barney (1991) proposes four attributes that a resource has to fulfill:

- Valuable (provide a firm with increased effectiveness and efficiency)
- Rare (not possessed by a large number of competitors)
- Imperfectly imitable (not acquirable for competitors)
- Non-substitutable (no resource with similar effect existing).

In the case of the outsourcing decision, the situation might be that, although the item is regarded as a core competence, direct competitors have a competitive edge in providing the same product (McIvor 2000). Therefore, the in-house activities have to be thoroughly assessed by benchmarking them against competitors' capabilities, including not only the product, but also the processes and skills behind it (McIvor 2000).

Nevertheless, this second step does not directly result in a make-or-buy recommendation, but has a strong impact on the following considerations.

4.3.2.3 Stage 3: Total Cost Analysis of "Core" Items

Directly related to the analysis of the firm's benefit from producing a certain product, the costs of providing a product, naturally, have a central role in the make-or-buy decision-making process. The cost estimation takes into account not only purchasing and production costs, but all the costs generated throughout the entire supply chain (from suppliers to end customers) and all functions that are affected by the production process (McIvor 2000). Additionally, in order to benchmark the focal firm's competitive position, its competitors' efforts and costs also have to be estimated. Logically, this step requires significant time and effort; however, the comprehensive analysis benefits the firm in the long-term, as high awareness of internal processes increases productivity and reduces inefficiencies, and knowledge of the competitors' processes, including their strengths and weaknesses, helps in the strategic positioning of the firm (McIvor 2000).

As a result of the last two stages, which have highlighted the competitive position of a focal firm from two different angles, two different scenarios arise (cf. McIvor 2000).

If the analyses have revealed that the company is more capable than the other players in the market, the obvious strategy is to keep the item in-house. Nevertheless, to strategically outsource is also regarded as an option. This means that, if a company does not believe that its competitive advantage is sustainable in the long run, outsourcing parts of the item or the processes behind it can be an early step in proactively responding to expected competition. Lastly, if a firm, for some reason, still wants to outsource a core item, Stage 4 will be the logical step.

The second scenario involves a situation in which the focal firm's core activities are inferior to those of its direct competitor(s). As a solution, a company may improve its internal capabilities, achieved by investing in its core competencies (McIvor 2000). This might be an option if the gap is fairly small and the potential for bridging it is assumed to exist. However, the more prevalent alternative is outsourcing—Stage 4.

4.3.2.4 Stage 4: Relationship Analysis

Finally, the case is developed that the focal firm has decided, for reasons discussed above or other, individual reasons, to outsource its core item. It is expected that the intention is to keep parts of the capability, such as design or technological skills, in-house, while other parts, such as, for instance, manufacturing, are purchased (McIvor 2000). In general, several variants of buyer–supplier relationships exist, with different degrees of interdependence between the parties. This issue will be addressed in more detail in the following section.

A restrictive option that has to be borne in mind is that outsourcing cannot occur due to a shortage of capable suppliers. Then, although a firm is willing to purchase parts of its items, it has to keep production internal, and possibly invest in the activity, unless it is willing to take the risk of jeopardizing the existence of the product (McIvor 2000).

4.3.3 The Execution of Outsourcing

As indicated in Stage 4 of the last section, different methods of outsourcing exist. Following the core competence/competitive advantage discussion (see previous section), the outsourcing organization depends to a large extent on the sensitivity of the outsourced activity, as well as on the capability of the supplier (Mikkola 2003).

In order to explain the diverse options of outsourcing parts and the impacts on the buyer–supplier relationship, an operationalized concept is depicted in Fig. 4.6 (cf. Mikkola 2003).

- Starting with the highest degree of interchangeability, **commodity parts** are put forward. These are normally characterized by the lowest buyer–supplier interdependence, i.e., the coupling between buyer and supplier is loose.
- For **detail-controlled parts**, which are placed next on the buyer–supplier interdependency continuum, the design and development work of the component is completely performed by the buyer. The supplier has to carry out the production of the part solely based on instructions (blueprints, etc.) given by the buyer. This type of relationship is expedient if the buyer does not want to reveal closer details of the product and its characteristics. Moreover, high design quality can be guaranteed. By contrast, dependency exists with respect to the supplier's precision in manufacturing.

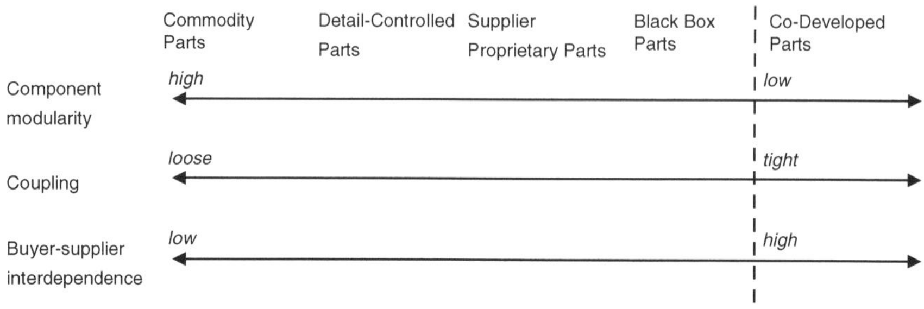

Fig. 4.6 Characteristics of component outsourcing, adapted from Mikkola (2003)

- One step further along in terms of interdependency is the transaction of **supplier proprietary parts**. The supplier develops these parts completely on its own. Due to the fact that the buyer does not contribute to the development of the item, the supplier traditionally possesses a superior position, which brings the buyer into dependency and a weak bargaining position.
- **Black box parts** specify the tightest buyer–supplier connection. In this case, the buyer defines the functions of the items, and, accordingly, the supplier is concerned with their detailed engineering and manufacturing. The advantage for the buyer is that it keeps control over the overall process while benefiting from the supplier's expertise. As both parties are involved in the development process, added value can be generated through the combination of competencies.

In addition to the proposed buyer–supplier relationships that are relevant in case one company purchases items from another, a further relationship is possible that goes beyond the hierarchical concepts hitherto presented: the co-development of parts. Here, buyer and supplier act as partners in a strategic alliance, be it of long-term (e.g., joint venture) or short-term (e.g., R&D agreement) duration.

In conclusion, a graph is presented (Fig. 4.6). The dimension of component modularity has not been the subject of discussion; however, as it has been treated before and is a vital aspect of the entire chapter, this dimension is also included in the graph.

4.4 Alternative to Modularization: The Formation of Material Groups

It might be the case, however, that circumstances restrict a company from modularizing its product range. This can be due to excessive efforts that would accompany modularization, or to structural conditions of the produced products that make modularization impossible.

In this case, the formation of material groups is an appropriate alternative. These groups are an integral part of the purchasing structure (Large 2009). Material groups are characterized by their homogeneity, i.e., the parts share similarity in terms of their characteristics, which in turn distinguish them from parts of other material groups. Material groups support a classification of the different parts included in a production process; thus, transparency increases and complexity is reduced. Moreover, an allocation of goods to purchasing markets is facilitated through material groups.

Production material, operating material, investment goods, trade goods and services are all included in a first, rough classification of material groups. However, a wide number of classification criteria can be applied with differing degrees of sophistication. Rather simple attributes such as price or demand are possible and feasible dimensions, just as more complex attributes can also be used such as, for example, the risk of supply or technical difficulties. For instance, an ABC analysis is a suitable basis for classification (Large 2009).

The decision about the outsourcing of material groups can be made analogously to that of component outsourcing, simply by substituting the material group for the product item. Thereafter, the material group is evaluated with regard to its strategic importance and its position compared to that of the competitors' products.

4.5 Manufacturing Strategies

It has been noted earlier in this analysis that the supply chain strategies presented stem from the manufacturing environment. The basic manufacturing concepts were then adopted and put into a broader, more general supply chain context by successively involving other functions and companies. Therefore, if supply chain processes are to be considered, a reversal of this generalization process is required. Consequently, for concretizing the strategic objectives of a supply chain on an operational level, it is essential to know beforehand what the various orientations of the manufacturing function can be like, and especially which role the customer plays in the manufacturing strategy (Stavrulaki and Davis 2010).

Olhager and Östlund (1990) were among the first to analyze the different strategies that a manufacturing section can apply. They recognized that there are two basic principles of how material and information flow through the production processes: **pushed** and **pulled**. Whereas **push** stands for a production-focused management that relies on long-term planning and stable demand forecasts, **pull** signifies an orientation directly responding to market demand. In addition to these pure orientations, a combination of them is also frequently applied.

This combination of oppositional strategic orientations has already been discussed in CM1, with regard to leagility. Central to this issue is the so-called

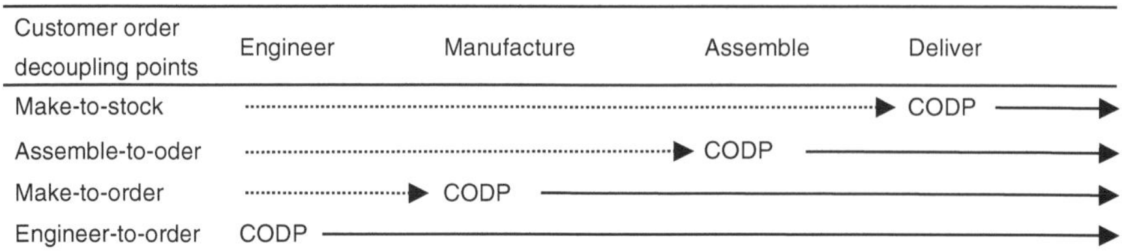

Fig. 4.7 Positions of the customer order decoupling point, after Olhager (2003) and Hallgren and Olhager (2006)

decoupling point (see for example Hoekstra et al. 1992; Naylor et al. 1999). On the strategic supply chain level, this is the point where lean is substituted for agile; on the operational level, the point is called the **customer order decoupling point** (CODP), indicating the impact that the customer has on the production process (Lee and Tang 1997). The CODP is chosen in accordance with the manufacturing strategy. Up to the CODP, the finishing of the product is deferred, enabling responsiveness to customer demand (see the concept of postponement in Chap. 2; Bucklin 1965; van Hoek 2001). Olhager (2003) has set up a mapping of manufacturing strategies onto the CODP (Fig. 4.7).

Various factors can be named that affect the choice of the most suitable manufacturing structure and hence the positioning of the CODP (Olhager 2003): market-related factors such as demand volatility, lead time or product differentiation expectations; product-related factors as, for example, product architecture (modularity); and production-related factors, such as production lead time or the flexibility of internal processes.

Olhager and Östlund (1990) define manufacturing strategies as being situated on a continuum, ranging from make-to-stock (MTS) to engineer-to-order (ETO). In total, Gosling and Naim (2009) count six different manufacturing strategies, namely: ship-to-stock (which they position before MTS on the continuum), make-to-stock (MTS), assemble-to-order (ATO), make-to-order (MTO), buy-to-order (BTO), and engineer-to-order (ETO). However, the four strategies included in Olhager (2003) (Fig. 4.7) are the most common ones, and will therefore be considered in the following.

4.5.1 Make-to-Stock

Following the classification of Olhager and Östlund (1990), Gunasekaran and Ngai (2005) define MTS (they term it traditional supply chain management) as a push manufacturing strategy. Stable production planning determines the manufacturing process, which is based on long-term demand forecasts, allowing for long delivery lead times; uncertainty is tackled by stocking finished goods in a buffer. In addition to long-term production planning, the relationships with buyers and suppliers are also of long duration (Gunasekaran and Ngai 2005).

The product is characterized by a high degree of standardization and is pushed into the market in high quantities (Skipworth and Harrison 2006). In general, the customer does not have a significant impact on the production process, as the position of the CODP indicates (Olhager 2003). On the contrary, the cost efficiency and productivity of the producing firm are the central targets of this manufacturing strategy (Olhager 2003).

4.5.2 Assemble-, Make- and Build-to-Order

It becomes apparent that ambiguity exists among scholars with respect to the usage of the "to-order" manufacturing strategies. Research by Olhager and Östlund (1990) indicated that BTO and MTO are similar. However, Gunasekaran and Ngai (2005) hold an alternative view; according to their definition, in an MTO strategy, the parts have to be manufactured before they are assembled. In contrast, in a BTO strategy, the parts are already prepared for assembly. The CODP is consequently positioned closer to the customer (Olhager 2003), and the lead times are shorter compared to MTO (Gunasekaran and Ngai 2005). By this definition, it seems to be appropriate to equate BTO with ATO. (It might be the case that BTO and ATO differ with regard to the ratio of in-house to out-house items produced. However, so as to reduce ambiguity, this option will be left aside; hence, ATO will be used in the following). As a final element of this conceptual distinction, one other difference between ATO and MTO can be mentioned: namely, that in the first strategy more parts and services are purchased from suppliers, whereas the latter is characterized by a higher degree of vertical integration (Gunasekaran and Ngai 2005).

As Olhager's (2003) mapping shows, MTO and ATO are manufacturing strategies that consist of both push and pull orientations. Their ideal is to manufacture "quality products or services based on the requirements of an individual customer or a group of customers at competitive prices" (Gunasekaran and Ngai 2005). Therefore, these strategies strive to combine high responsiveness and flexibility with high cost efficiency. As a result, costs inherent in the production process are reduced, as is the time for reacting to market forces (Lee and Tang 1997).

MTO and ATO are commonly implemented as a means to achieve a highly diversified product range, often termed as mass customization (cf. Rudberg and Wikner 2004), allowing a firm to satisfy multifaceted customer demands. This is normally realized through the introduction of a product architecture that permits the multiple usage of standard components. A range of basic, unfinished products can then be customized with relatively little effort according to a customer's specific requirements (Lee and Tang 1997). Due to this structural setup, it is possible to provide a great variety of product options. Moreover, despite the low volumes of individual end products, costs can be held down (Gunasekaran and Ngai 2005). All in all, the importance of the customer is obvious (Gunasekaran and

Ngai 2005). Nonetheless, the position of MTO and ATO in the mapping of Olhager (2003) shows that, on the other hand, production-related factors are also an integral part of these strategies.

4.5.3 Engineer-to-Order

Finally, an additional "to-order" manufacturing strategy is presented, where the CODP is positioned farthest upstream, meaning that customer impact is at its greatest (Olhager 2003). In the ETO strategy, customer requirements have a direct impact on the design and engineering stage of a product, pulling the product through the entire production process (Gosling and Naim 2009). Hence, a customer order is required to launch anew the design and production process. This strategy is thus traditionally applied in environments that are described by large, complex, and often singular projects, as are prevalent, for example, in the construction sector. In general, only small quantities of specialized products are demanded; by contrast, the product range is rather broad (Olhager 2003). The delivered products are typified by high complexity, resulting in an integral product architecture and thus a high degree of vertical integration (Hicks et al. 2001). Consequently, flexibility is regarded as crucial in an ETO environment (Gosling and Naim 2009).

4.6 Manufacturing Strategies and Supply Chain Strategies

It becomes evident that there is a striking congruence between manufacturing strategies and supply chain strategies. This is not surprising, as the latter strategies have emanated from the former. Apparently, the similarity appears most obvious when comparing competitive priorities according to Hill's (1993) concept. As stated in the literature review (CM1), generic supply chain strategies can be categorized in terms of their order winning criteria; more precisely, the factors that put them into a position to compete successfully in a market. In case of an agile supply chain strategy, flexibility serves as order winner. For lean supply chains, the order winner is costs; and for leagile supply chains, it is flexibility and costs (Christopher and Towill 2000; Bruce and Daly 2004).

These assignments perfectly match the orientations of the manufacturing strategies. As stated above, costs are the key criteria in an MTS environment (Olhager 2003). This manufacturing strategy can therefore be seen as part of a lean supply chain strategy (Stavrulaki and Davis 2010).

Following the definition of Gunasekaran and Ngai (2005), the MTO and ATO strategies are characterized by a striving for flexibility and cost efficiency. This corresponds directly to a leagile setup of the supply chain (Mason-Jones et al. 2000; Stavrulaki and Davis 2010). Differentiating between ATO and MTO, the

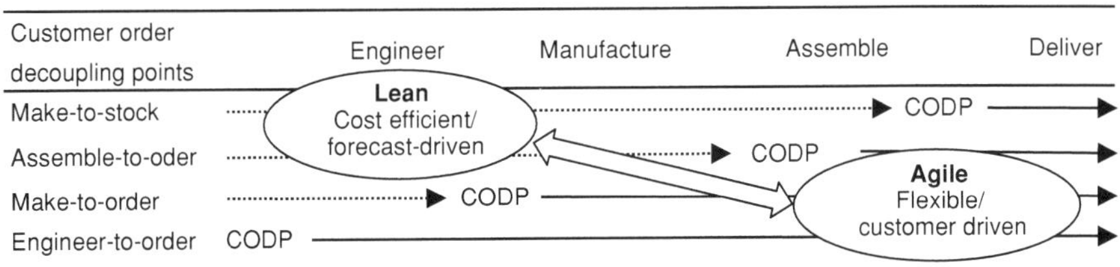

Fig. 4.8 Combining manufacturing and supply chain strategies, adopted from Olhager (2010)

first tends to be more cost efficient (lean), whereas the latter more strongly emphasizes flexibility (agile).

Finally, ETO is assessed with respect to a compatible supply chain strategy. Again, the assignment is obvious, as the focus on flexibility (Olhager 2003) entirely meets the objectives of the agile supply chain strategy concept (Gosling et al. 2007). However, Sanderson and Cox (2008) do not completely agree with this assignment; although they agree that flexibility is essential in an ETO environment, they point out that the role of costs is underestimated in this context, as, for example, ETO products or services can also have a functional design. Therefore, increasing costs, which are typically associated with an agile strategy, have to be avoided. Figure 4.8 graphically illustrates the correlations between manufacturing strategies and supply chain strategies.

The framework in Fig. 4.9, on the other hand, is a way of defining supply chain strategies with the help of their characteristics. The comparison illustrates supply chain characteristics, which are product-, manufacturing- and logistics-related in their performance. The figure indicates certain tendencies towards a given product line. Demand uncertainty, profit margin, and product variety, order lead time and labor skills are high, rather high, rather low or low. In this way one can derive a manufacturing strategy. The method makes it possible to analyze a supply chain and to define one's manufacturing strategy in this way.

The different manufacturing strategies MTS, ATO, MTO and ETO are defined according to their performance. One needs to recognize that these points form a continuum which ranges from MTS to ETO. MTS is a very cost efficient, lean strategy in which the CODP is positioned downstream in the supply chain. Here high volumes, low profit margins, and commodity products form the basis for the strategy. On the other hand, there is the ETO strategy in which the CODP is positioned upstream in the supply chain. Products are usually specialized and the supply chain is defined by high flexibility and agility since the manufacturer deals directly with the end customer order.

The framework helps to find the best possible strategy for coordinating a company's products and its supply chain, on the one hand, and its production and logistics processes, on the other (Stavrulaki and Davis 2010).

		Make-to-Stock	Assemble-to-Order	Make-to-Order	Engineer-to-Order
Product related characteristics	Demand uncertainty, profit margin, product variety, order lead time, labor skills	Low	→	←	High
	Product life cycle, Forecasting accuracy, volume	High			Low
Manufacturing related characteristics	Production process	Continuous, Large volume assembly/batch	Assembly line processes	Small batch Job shops	Job shops projects
	Product design	Cost conscious	Modular		Specialized
	Manufacturer has direct contact with end-user	Uncommon	←		Common
	Manufacturing processes focus	Efficiency	Customer contact point defines decoupling point, efficiency/flexibility focus		Flexibility
Logistics related characteristics	Number of intermediaries between manufacturer and end customer	Large			Small
	Bullwhip effect	Prominent			Less likely
	Supplier relationships	Collaborative, High information sharing			Opportunistic collaboration, more collaborative barriers
	Logistics processes focus	Efficiency			Flexibility
	Supply chain strategic capability	Lean	Leagility		Agility

Fig. 4.9 Comparison of supply chain characteristics with manufacturing strategies, according to Stavrulaki and Davis (2010)

4.7 Supply Chain Strategies and Customer Order Decoupling Point

The CODP is the point in the manufacturing value chain where the product is linked to a specific customer order (Olhager 2003). Its name indicates a direct connection with the customer order. The different manufacturing strategies such as MTS, MTO, ATO and ETO are the result of CODP positioning.

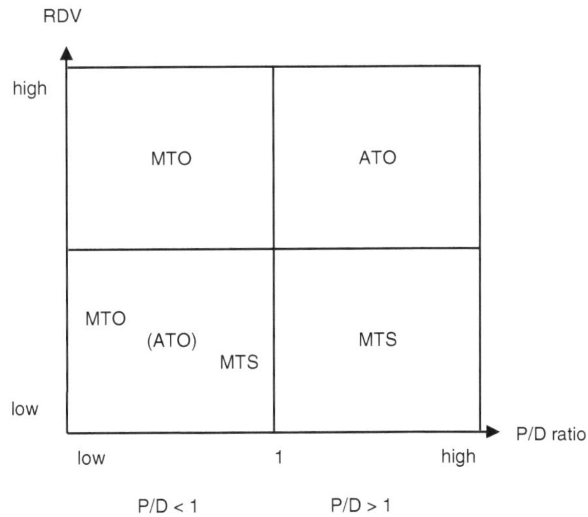

Fig. 4.10 Method to determine the position of the decoupling point and the manufacturing strategy in the supply chain, after Olhager (2003)

In the Olhager model the position of the CODP is determined by two variables: on one hand, the **production to delivery time ratio (P/D ratio)** and, on the other, the **relative demand volatility (RDV)**. If the two different factors are arranged as in Fig. 4.10, it is possible to choose one of the four different manufacturing strategies.

The P/D ratio is either less than one or greater than one. It indicates whether production can wait for the customer order or not. Both the P/D ratio and the RDV can be either high or low. In the case where the P/D ratio is <1, an MTO or MTS strategy can be considered. MTS is usually chosen when the company wants to increase its productivity. In case the P/D ratio is <1, an MTO strategy is advised.

A high RDV excludes the use of the MTS strategy, since this would lead to excessive inventory; therefore, one can either choose an MTO or ATO strategy. If the RDV is low, the company can choose between three different strategies, MTO, ATO and MTS.

The position of the CODP depends on the outcome of this method. The position of the CODP according to the strategy is illustrated in the previous figure, Fig. 4.7. The strategic importance of the CODP and its shifting forward and backwards helps to indicate the optimal delivery strategy. The model is an approach to determining the optimal delivery strategy.

Summary sheet

CM2: Manufacturing strategy and supply chain management

Goals of SCD Guide CM2

The aim of this SCD Guide CM2 is to apply the concept of product modularization. Individual components can be independently manufactured and thereby outsourced. An outsourcing decision framework as well as the subsequent outsourcing process is further outlined. In the following one can see analysis and methods of modularization, methods for making an outsourcing decision, and ways to determine supply chain strategies.

Methods and analysis for SCD Guide CM2

- Modularization framework
- Four-stage framework for evaluating the outsourcing decision
- Manufacturing strategy

Input per method for SCD Guide CM2

	Input from other CMs	Method	
Method for modularization	CM1	**Modularization framework** • Functional elements of a product • Cost of manufacturing and reusability • Convenience of assembly • Multiple usage of modules	
Methods for the outsourcing decision	CM1	**Outsourcing procedure** • Company's capabilities • Competitor's capabilities • Strategic importance of the item • Cost of producing the product	
Methods for determiningthe manufacturing strategy	CM1	**Manufacturing strategy selection** • Product characteristics, e.g., demand uncertainty, • Manufacturing-related characteristics, e.g., production process • Logistics-related characteristics, e.g., supplier relationships	**Positioning the decoupling point** • Relative demand volatility • Production to delivery time ratio

Output from SCD Guide CM2

- Modularized products
  Dimension in morphological box: Product modules
- Outsourcing decision variables in dimension "product modules" make (M) or buy (B)
- Positioning the customer order decoupling point
  Dimension in morphological box: Decoupling point

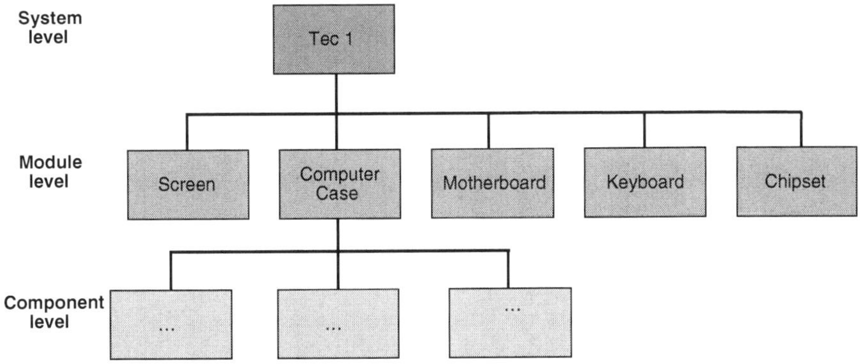

Fig. 4.11 Exemplary schematic product architecture of Tec 1, according to Mikkola (2006)

4.8 Application Example of SCD Guide CM2 and Possible Output

In the modularization process, the company plans to create a product architecture in order to split the different components of the product into subparts which can be manufactured individually. The product architecture and the different modules and components of the product play a crucial role in this process. In Fig. 4.11 the product Tec 1 has been split up into different separate modules of laptop production, namely, screen, computer case, motherboard, keyboard and chipset. In the further course of modularization, the module level could be further split up into the subparts of the component level.

If the product architecture is identified within this framework, the company is interested in the decision whether to outsource certain components or keep them in-house. The company applies the hierarchy of importance which identifies the level of specification needed for the production of the product. The pyramid shows the components of the production process which could possibly be outsourced. This method furthermore helps to determine whether the outsourcing process is applicable to the relevant product.

In Fig. 4.12 the different components have been characterized according to their importance. The specialized components are placed on top of the hierarchy. In our example the motherboard is a core element of the company and should therefore be kept in-house (make). The chipset is a strategic item with only a few specialized manufacturers on the market and therefore has to be outsourced (buy). The components which are placed underneath the core components in the hierarchy are not of strategic importance but are mainly specified components. Computer cases on the second level of the pyramid are therefore leverage items. The computer screen as well as the keyboard are noncritical items which are placed last on the hierarchy level. The components which are part of a mass

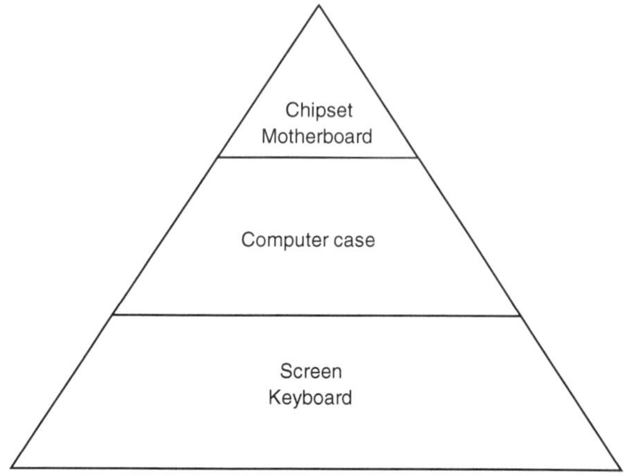

Fig. 4.12 Exemplary hierarchy of importance Tec 1

manufacturing process do not require the specific know-how that is only available within the company.

In the four steps of the decision of setting the value of the real net output ratio (level of non-outsourced production), the company decides whether it wants to outsource these products or whether to keep them in-house. In this case, the company decides to outsource the inferior parts of the hierarchy of importance pyramid, which are the screen, keyboard and computer case of the laptop. Furthermore, the chipset is sourced by another company, since the company does not have the necessary means and specialized knowledge to keep it in-house. In the morphological box, the make decision is indicated with a (M) and the buy decision with (B).

In order to find the correct manufacturing strategy, the company has to determine the position of the CODP. In CM1, we already discussed the importance of the positioning of the CODP. In this chapter, we have determined how to position the CODP with the help of Olhager's matrix (Olhager 2003) and the P/D ratio as well as the RDV. Different factors account for the position of the CODP. The closer the position of the decoupling point is to the manufacturer, the more cost efficient is the process. On the other hand, the closer it is to the customer, the more flexible and agile is the manufacturing process. With the help of the CODP, the applicable manufacturing strategy can be determined. By applying Olhager's (2003) method of determining the position of the CODP, it was determined that the company needs to apply the MTO strategy upstream in the supply chain due to the high RDV and the low P/D ratio (Fig. 4.13).

A MTO strategy as shown in Fig. 4.14 implies that the CODP is positioned upstream in the value adding process. This indicates a short lean part and a long agile part of the supply chain. Therefore, the supply chain reflects a high degree of

Customer order decoupling points	Engineer	Manufacture	Assemble	Deliver
Make-to-order	········▶	CODP	———————	———▶

Fig. 4.13 Exemplary positioning of the CODP for the private customer segment

Customer segment "private"

Manufacturing area						
	Tec 1 modules (MoB)	Screen (M)	Computer Case (M)	Motherboard (B)	Keyboard (M)	Chipset (B)
	Decoupling point	Engineer-to-order	Make-to-order	Assemble-to-order	Make-to-stock	

Fig. 4.14 Exemplary morphological box, Content Module 2

flexibility as opposed to MTS strategy, which is more cost efficient. The supply chain is thereby linked closely to the customer order. Note, this example and Table 3.4 only refer to the private customer segment.

References

Baldwin, C. Y., & Clark, K. B. (1997). Managing in an age of modularity. *Harvard Business Review, 75*(5), 84–93.

Barney, J. (1991). Firm resources and sustained competitive advantage. *Journal of Management, 17*(1), 99–120.

Bruce, M., & Daly, L. (2004). Lean or agile a solution for supply chain management in the textiles and clothing industry? *International Journal of Operations and Production Management, 24*(2), 151–170.

Bucklin, L. P. (1965). Postponement, speculation and the structure of distribution channels. *Journal of Marketing Research (JMR), 2*(1), 26–31.

Christopher, M. (2000). The agile supply chain. *Industrial Marketing Management, 29*(1), 37–44.

Christopher, M., & Towill, D.R. (2000). *Marrying lean and agile paradigms*. *Proceedings of EUROMA*. Ghent, Belgium, pp. 114–121.

Ernst, R., & Kamrad, B. (2000). Evaluation of supply chain structures through modularization and postponement. *European Journal of Operational Research, 124*(3), 495–510.

Gosling, J., & Naim, M. M. (2009). Engineer-to-order supply chain management: a literature review and research agenda. *International Journal of Production Economics, 122*(2), 741–754.

Gosling, J., Naim, M.M., Fowler, N., Fearne, A. (eds.) (2007). *Manufacturers' preparedness for agile construction*: *Agile Manufacturing*, 2007. ICAM 2007. IET International Conference on: IET.

Gunasekaran, A., & Ngai, E. W. T. (2005). Build-to-order supply chain management: a literature review and framework for development. *Journal of Operations Management, 23*(5), 423–451.

Hallgren, M., & Olhager, J. (2006). Differentiating manufacturing focus. *International Journal of Production Research, 44*(18/19), 3863–3878.

Halman, J. I., Hofer, A. P., & van Vuuren, W. (2003). Platform-driven development of product families: linking theory with practice. *Journal of Product Innovation Management, 20*(2), 149–162.

Henderson, R. M., & Clark, K. B. (1990). Architectual innovation: the reconfiguration of existing product technologies and the failure of established firms. *Administrative Science Quarterly, 35*(1), 9–30.

Hicks, C., McGovern, T., & Earl, C. F. (2001). A typology of UK engineer-to-order companies. *International Journal of Logistics: Research and Applications, 4*(1), 43–56.

Hill, T. (1993 [1st ed., 1985]). *Manufacturing strategy*: *Text and cases*. 2nd ed. Blue Ridge Ill.: Irwin Professional Publishing.

Hoekstra, S., Romme, J., & Argelo, S. M. (1992). *Integral logistic structures: developing customer-oriented goods flow*. New York: Industrial Press.

Kakabadse, A., & Kakabadse, N. (2002). Trends in outsourcing: contrasting USA Europe. *European Management Journal, 20*(2), 189–198.

Large, R. (2009). *Strategisches Beschaffungsmanagement: Eine praxisorientierte Einführung mit Fallstudien* (4th ed.). Wiesbaden: Gabler Verlag/GWV Fachverlage GmbH Wiesbaden.

Lee, H. L., & Tang, C. S. (1997). Modelling the costs and benefits of delayed product differentiation. *Management Science, 43*(1), 40.

Mason-Jones, R., Naylor, B., & Towill, D. R. (2000). Lean, agile or leagile? matching your supply chain to the marketplace. *International Journal of Production Research, 38*(17), 4061–4070.

McIvor, R. (2000). A practical framework for understanding the outsourcing process. *Supply Chain Management: An International Journal, 5*(1), 22–36.

McIvor, R., & Humphreys, P. K. (1997). A strategic model for the formulation of an effective make or buy decision. *Management Decision, 35*(2), 169–178.

Mikkola, J. H. (2003). Modularity, component outsourcing, and inter-firm learning. *R&D Management, 33*(4), 439–454.

Mikkola, J. H. (2006). Capturing the degree of modularity embedded in product architectures. *Journal of Product Innovation Management, 23*(2), 128–146.

Naylor, J. B., Naim, M. M., & Berry, D. (1999). Leagility: integrating the lean and agile manufacturing paradigms in the total supply chain. *International Journal of Production Economics, 62*(1–2), 107–118.

Olhager, J. (2003). Strategic positioning of the order penetration point. *International Journal of Production Economics, 85*(3), 319–329.

Olhager, J. (2010). The role of the customer order decoupling point in production and supply chain management. *Computers in Industry, 61*(9), 863–868.

Olhager, J., & Östlund, B. (1990). An integrated push-pull manufacturing strategy. *European Journal of Operational Research, 45*(2/3), 135–142.

Prahalad, C. K., & Hamel, G. (1990). The core competence of the corporation. *Harvard Business Review, 68*(3), 79–91.

Ro, Y. K., Liker, J. K., & Fixson, S. K. (2007). Modularity as a strategy for supply chain coordination: the case of U.S. auto. *IEEE Transactions on Engineering Management, 54*(1), 172–189.

Rudberg, M., & Wikner, J. (2004). Mass customization in terms of the customer order decoupling point. *Production Planning and Control, 15*(4), 445–458.

Sako, M. (2003). Modularity and outsourcing: The nature of co-evolution of product architecture and organization architecture in the global automotive industry. In A. Prencipe, A. Davies, & M. Hobday (Eds.), *The business of systems integration*. Oxford: Oxford University Press.

Sanderson, J., & Cox, A. (2008). The challenges of supply strategy selection in a project environment: evidence from UK naval shipbuilding. *Supply Chain Management, 13*(1), 16–25.

Shamsuzzoha, A. H. M. (2011). Modular product architecture for productivity enhancement. *Business Process Management Journal, 17*(1), 21–41.

Skipworth, H., & Harrison, A. (2006). Implications of form postponement to manufacturing a customized product. *International Journal of Production Research, 44*(8), 1627–1652.

Stavrulaki, E., & Davis, M. (2010). Aligning products with supply chain processes and strategy. *International Journal of Logistics Management, 21*(1), 127–151.

Ulrich, K. (1995). The role of product architecture in the manufacturing firm. *Research Policy, 24*(3), 419–440.

van Hoek, R. I. (2001). The rediscovery of postponement a literature review and directions for research. *Journal of Operations Management, 19*(2), 161–184.

von Hippel, E. (1994). Sticky information and the locus of problem solving: implications for innovation. *Management Science, 40*(4), 429–439.

Womack, J. P., Jones, D. T., & Roos, D. (1990). *The machine that changed the world: Based on the Massachusetts Institute of Technology 5 million dollar 5 year study on the future of the automobile*. New York: Rawson [u.a.].

Zsidisin, G. A. (2003). A grounded definition of supply risk. *Journal of Purchasing and Supply Management, 9*(5–6), 217–224.

CM3: Supplier Segmentation and Supply Strategy

5

5.1 Goals of Content Module 3

This chapter deals with the strategic role that suppliers and supply management play in a firm's considerations and planning. First, as a bridge to the previous chapter, a discussion of the different types of buyer–supplier relationships is conducted, particularly emphasizing the distinction between the traditional (competitive) and the modern (collaborative) approach (Park et al. 2010). This type of supplier segmentation is then complemented by adding the distribution of power among the market members as a further dimension. Thereafter, the model developed to this point is discussed with regard to Kraljic's categorization of procurement items and his purchasing portfolio matrix (Kraljic 1983). The perspective gained here is then compared to the different supply chain strategies. In conclusion, an alternative supplier segmentation tool (ABC analysis) is presented (Fig. 5.1).

5.2 Buyer–Supplier Relationships

Inter-firm relationships are central to the entire concept of supply chain management. Cox et al. (2001) highlight this issue in particular, when they define a supply chain as "the extended network of dyadic exchange relationships" (p. 28) designed for delivering a service or product to an end customer. Initially, Williamson (1985) claimed that there are two scenarios of governance, namely perfect competition and vertical integration; especially the latter was believed to be viable for coping with uncertain circumstances. More recently, Dyer and Singh (1998) have proposed an alternative view, declaring that the cooperation of firms in relationships or networks can provide them with a sustained competitive advantage. This change in perspective is supported by Chen and Paulraj (2004), who see the network as a concept positioned in between Williamson's (1985) two extreme positions: independent firms collaborate, while the vertical integration of the individual firm

E. Hofmann et al., *The Supply Chain Differentiation Guide*,
DOI: 10.1007/978-3-642-31936-5_5, © Springer-Verlag Berlin Heidelberg 2012

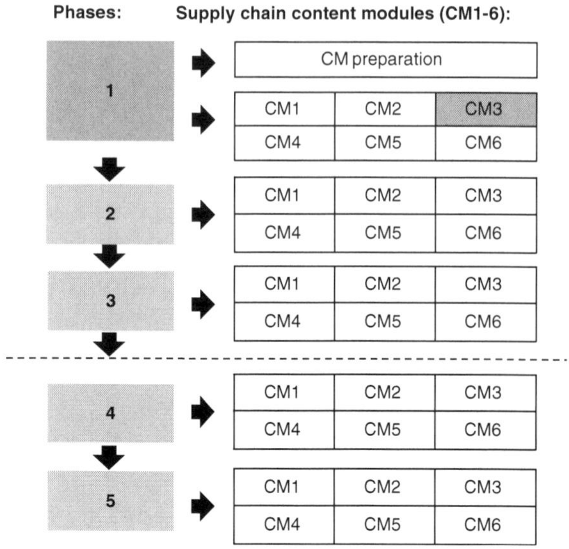

Fig. 5.1 Position of Chap. 5 in SCD Guide

remains low (Chen and Paulraj 2004). Consequently, the hierarchical structures have been substituted for by more cooperation (Williamson 1985).

Due to this development in management theory, the appreciation of inter-firm relationships has been supplemented considerably: besides the traditional **arm's length** management of suppliers, newer theories advocate the consideration of suppliers as **partners** (Dyer et al. 1998). Whereas the former view, which is still valid and frequently applied, is based on premises of minimal dependence and maximal bargaining power (Porter 1980), the latter view can be traced back to the successful** buyer-supplier buyer–supplier relationships prevalent in the Japanese car producing sector. We will take up the two different types of relationship, one after the other.

5.2.1 General Classification of Suppliers

Dyer et al. (1998) claim that the traditional **arm's length** supplier management is described by the following characteristic: the parts involved in the transaction do not play a strategically important role in the processes of the buying firm. More explicitly, this means that the sourced parts do not contribute to the differentiation and customization of the end product. The buyer–supplier relationship is therefore characterized by a low interdependence, a small need for coordination and relatively little value-adding through the transacted part (ibid.). According to Mikkola (2003), **commodity parts, supplier proprietary parts, detail-controlled parts** and **black box parts** (sorted by increasing buyer–supplier interdependence) can all be assigned to arm's length supplier management. Moreover, especially the previously discussed concept of modularization facilitates the effective management of arm's length relationships (Howard and Squire 2007).

Alternatively, Dyer et al. (1998) put forward the management of suppliers as **strategic partners**. Here, a linkage exists to the purchasing firm's core competencies; the sourced part has thus a direct impact on the quality and performance of the end product. This can be achieved through a high degree of cooperation, which usually results in co-developed parts. In this way interdependence increases (Dyer 1997). Therefore, the investments take place on a relationship-specific level, instead of on the transaction cost level (Mikkola 2003). Additionally for this type of supplier management, the effects of modularization are identifiable. Howard and Squire (2007) provide empirical evidence that modularization induces improved cooperation, due to the reduction of interface obstacles.

This integration of suppliers into the processes of the buyer has resulted in a generally decreased number of suppliers, accompanying a longer period of cooperation (Chen and Paulraj 2004). As a consequence, buyers attach greater importance to the qualifications of the suppliers, demanding a high degree of information transparency, including data about internal processes and costs. The benefits of this interconnectedness of buyer and supplier are shared risks and rewards for the partners.

However, Wynstra and ten Pierick (2000) recognize that neither project effectiveness (cost and quality of the product) nor project efficiency (cost and speed of process) will automatically improve through supplier involvement, due to the increased efforts of supplier coordination and management. Thus, the benefits of supplier involvement have to be assessed carefully.

5.2.2 Distribution of Power in Buyer–Supplier Relationships

Depending on the type of buyer–supplier relationship, the proportion of power can vary. (Cox et al. 2001) suggest focusing on the power dimension in supply chains in order to understand its characteristics and peculiarities. Although collaboration and integrated production to the benefit of all partners included is an essential aspect of supply chain management, Cox (2004) claims that all the companies involved are primarily pursuing their own goals and advantages, which puts the analysis of the buyer–supplier relationship and the distribution of dominance at the heart of the entire transaction.

As it has become obvious above, buyers have various options for sourcing parts from supplying firms. In order to find an appropriate solution, Cox (2004) emphasizes the focus on power and leverage dimensions. The combination allows for four possible power combinations (Fig. 5.2):

- **Interdependence** occurs if both, the buyer and the supplier, have a relatively high level of power. This is the case if there are only few available players on both sides, and the supplier is strongly dependent on the buyer. It must also hold

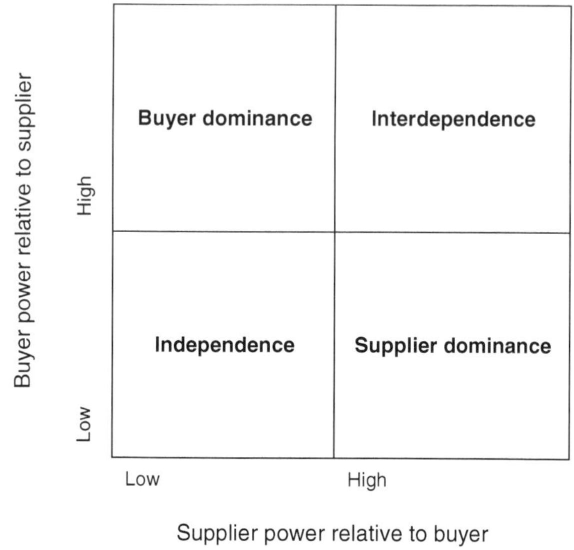

Fig. 5.2 The buyer–supplier power matrix, according to Cox (2004)

that switching costs are high (for both parties), the parts contributed by the supplier are relatively unique and there is little information asymmetry.

- **Buyer dominance** is given if the market accounts for fewer buyers than suppliers. The supplier's revenues are considerably dependent on the purchasing of the buyer. The supplier normally offers standardized commodity items, which makes switching easy for the buyer, but not for the supplier. Moreover, the supplier does not have any information advantages over the buyer.
- The opposite is the case if **supplier dominance** is prevalent. Here, a great number of buyers are purchasing from a small number of suppliers. Therefore, the dependency is also reversed; the buyer needs the supplier's part, which is relatively unique. In addition, costs for switching are now higher for the buyer than for the supplier. This scenario is completed by a significant information advantage of the supplier over the buyer.
- Finally, **independence** is presented as a possibility of power distribution in buyer–supplier relationships. This is characterized by an abundant number of firms from both sides, exchanging standard commodity products. As the name suggests, none of the parties is dependent on the other, nor are switching costs considerable. Furthermore, there is effectively no information advantage.

5.2.3 Combination of Buyer–Supplier Relationship Types with the Distribution of Power

With respect to the different options of power distribution between buyer and supplier as highlighted above (Fig. 5.2), Cox (2004) also identifies correlations between this distribution and the types of buyer–supplier relationships presented above. This means that, to obtain a successful supplier management at a given external condition (power distribution), one can assign the one of the types of buyer–supplier cooperation presented above.

- If a high degree of co-development and, thus **interdependence** between the buyer and supplier is characteristic of the relationship, a **collaborative** (formerly labeled partner) relationship is recommended, including its attributes such as long-term perspective and shared revenues (cf. Chen and Paulraj 2004). Here, the supplier in particular makes above-average returns (Cox 2004).
- If a **buyer's dominance** over its supplier(s) exists, the buying side can appropriate most of the gains, while the supplier has to accept an inferior role, which is connected with smaller margins. In general, two options of supplier management evolve: in an **arm's length** relationship, the duration of transaction remains normally rather short; cooperation is not very intensive. The second option assumes a long-term relationship with close *collaboration*.
- If the power distribution is reversed, and the **supplier** has **dominance** over the buyer(s), then the other circumstances of the previous paragraph are naturally also reversed; the supplier can dictate prices and margins, whilst the buyer has to accept the conditions set by the supplier. The relationships can be managed in a more (**collaborative**) or less (**arm's length**) closely cooperating mode.
- Finally, the last remaining power constellation, **independence,** is assigned to a buyer–supplier relationship type. Due to the fact that these transactions are normally undertaken in a short-term context with relatively loose cooperation, an **arm's length** approach is recommended. Both buyer and supplier (have to) accept the terms of the market.

The assignment of buyer–supplier relationship types to the power distribution matrix is depicted in Fig. 5.3.

5.3 Implications of Buyer–Supplier Relationships on the Sourcing Procedure

So far, the various combinations of buyer–supplier relationships and the dispersion of power have been presented. Next, implications for the actual sourcing are discussed.

Kraljic (1983) has presented a purchasing portfolio matrix, which has gained considerable attention from both scholars and practitioners. Up to now, a large number of scholars have worked with and extended his model; nevertheless, Gelderman and van Weele (2005) recognize that the modifications have been rather marginal and therefore the original matrix remains the standard approach. For example, Cox (2004) observed that, among practitioners, consultants in particular prefer this type of classification. In general, despite some critique from scholars who have questioned, for example, the appropriateness of the chosen

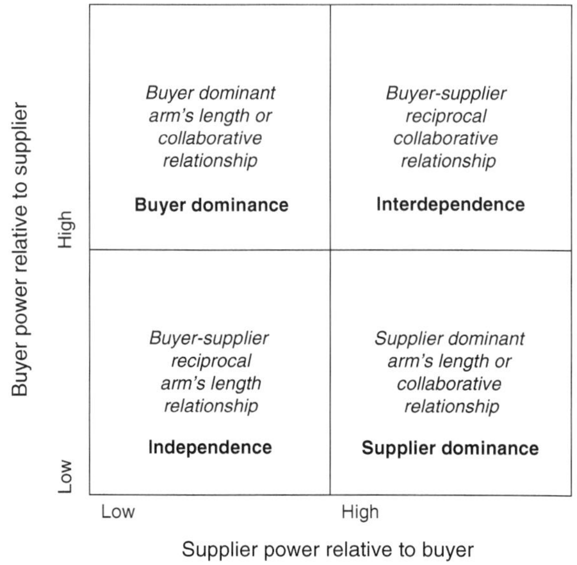

Fig. 5.3 Combining buyer–supplier relationship types with the power distribution matrix, after Cox (2004)

dimensions (Nellore and Söderquist 2000) or the inflexibility of the concept (Cox 1997); Gelderman and van Weele (2003) acknowledge that Kraljic's framework is still the dominant decision-making tool among purchasing managers. Due to the continuing relevancy of the model, in the following it is introduced and implemented within the context of the chapter. At a later stage, some small modifications are proposed, creating a bridge between the model and the buyer–supplier relationship.

Kraljic (1983) groups the procured items into four categories, which can be positioned alongside the two dimensions **profit impact** and **supply risk.** The following items are distinguished:

- **Strategic items** are characterized by high profit impact and high supply risk. Traditionally, the sourced items add high value to the purchasing firm's performance, which results in long-term contracts. Central criterion for these items is the assurance of availability.
- **Leverage items** stand for high profit at low supply risks. The transacted items can be commodities as well as more specialized items, and the time horizon of cooperation accounts for one to two years. Costs and material flow are the key criteria of the sourcing action.
- **Bottleneck items** are those which have low impact on a buyer's profit, but high supply risk. The purchased items are mainly specialized; the time frame can vary, depending on availability and flexibility. Costs and the reliability of the source function as the key criteria.

Fig. 5.4 Merging item categorization and the supplier relationship matrix

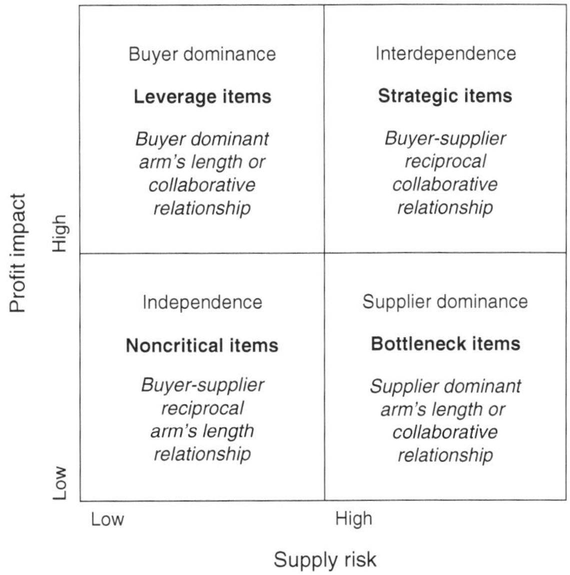

- Finally, the categorization is completed by mentioning **noncritical items**, which are typified by low profit and low supply risk. In this case, commodities are normally purchased; the duration of cooperation lasts at most one year. The central aspect of purchasing these items is functional efficiency.

5.3.1 The Merging of Item Categorization and Buyer–Supplier Relationship Types

In the following, one can merge the two dimensions item categorization and buyer–supplier relationship types into one matrix. This serves to give an overview of the relationship in accordance with product type.

5.3.1.1 Item Categorization (1/2)

It has become apparent that the dimensions chosen by Kraljic (1983) for the categorization of purchased items overlap to a great extent with the ones applied for assigning the diverse buyer–supplier relationships to the power distribution. On the one hand, profit impact strongly correlates with the power of the supplier; as it has been argued before, profit rises alongside of buyer's dominance (Cox 2004). On the other hand, increasing supply risk weakens the position of the buyer in favor of the supplier. Therefore, it is believed that the two different concepts can be combined and integrated into one matrix (Fig. 5.4).

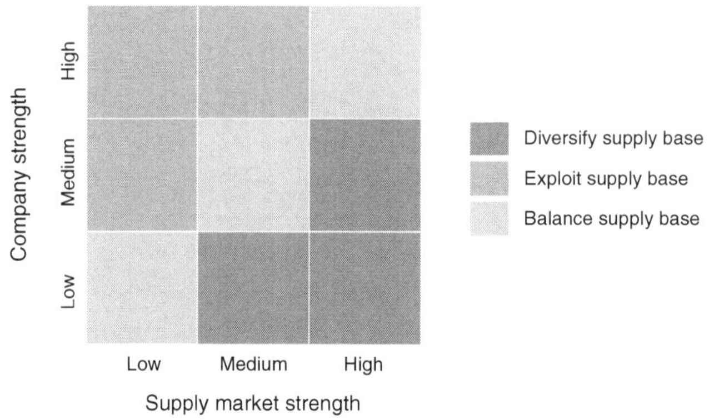

Fig. 5.5 The purchasing portfolio matrix (Kraljic 1983)

5.3.2 Purchasing Portfolio Matrix

5.3.2.1 Item Categorization (2/2)

Based on the previous categorization of items, Kraljic (1983) recommends three different strategies corresponding to the particular categories which are plotted in a buyer versus supplier strengths matrix (Fig. 5.4). This allows the highlighting of opportunities and weaknesses, as well as supply threats. Originally, these strategies were directed only at one of the four categories, strategic items. However, it is assumed that the strategies are more comprehensive if they are applied to the entirety of procured items.

If a company's position is considered as relatively strong compared to that of its supplier(s), an **exploitation** strategy is suggested, which means that the company can aggressively try to pursue high profit margins at the expense of the supplier. However, the firm also has to bear in mind the danger of placing excessive stress on the buyer–supplier relationship, impairing in this way long-term trust.

By contrast, if the purchasing company is in a weak position with regard to its supplier(s), it cannot stick to an aggressive negotiating position, but has to act more defensively, as it is dependent on the supplier. **Diversification** is said to be a viable opportunity, through substitution of material/parts or supplier. Furthermore, backward integration might be conceivable. In general, the sourcing firm cannot expect high gains.

Finally, if neither the buyer nor the supplier can attain an advantage over its counterpart, the logical consequence is a **balance** strategy.

A modification of the Kraljic matrix (that is believed to be a beneficial improvement) is made by Gelderman and van Weele (2003). Here, the balance strategy is developed in greater detail (while the other two are held constant). A distinction is made between the conditions depicted at the bottom left and the top right in Fig. 5.5. If the power of both parties is equal at a low level, **systems**

contracting is proposed; if both parties involved are characterized by a relatively high level of strength, **partnership** is recommended.

The assignment of strategies to market conditions closes the loop this section has gone through. Owing to the fact that for the purchasing portfolio matrix the distribution of power between buyer and supplier has once again been applied, there is a high degree of interoperability and interchangeability given. The choice of buyer–supplier relationship, the categorization of items and strategic considerations can thus be performed simultaneously. This integrated approach is in line with the proposal by Park et al. (2010), who call for a more holistic view of supplier management.

5.3.3 Integrated Supplier Relationship Management Procedure

Park et al. (2010) have developed a framework with an integrated approach to supplier relationship management. It manages to combine purchasing strategies, considerations for suppliers, collaboration in product development, production activities and suppliers assessments. In the following this framework is shown on the basis of a supplier assessment and development.

5.3.3.1 Integrated Supplier Relationship Management Framework

Supplier assessment and development aims to assess the supplier segments and to differentiate them. Supplier segmentation determines the strategic importance of materials to establish a functioning relationship and also evaluates the supplier.

Fig. 5.6, the framework for **supplier assessment and development** is presented. There are different factors influencing the assessment of suppliers.

First the **strategic material evaluation** is determined. The influencing factors are the strategic importance and the attractiveness of the relationship as shown in Fig. 5.6.

The strategic importance is shown through the classification of different purchasing items. These are, as already explained previously in this chapter, four different items –namely, strategic, leverage, bottleneck and noncritical items—as derived from the Kraljic matrix. The risks connected to these items can be derived from this model. Variables that impact these risks are availability, number of suppliers, competitive advantage, make-or-buy opportunities, storage risks and substitution possibilities (Kraljic 1983; Park et al. 2010).

Secondly, the attractiveness of the relationship is determined by the relative attractiveness of a given supplier and the relative relationship strength of supplier and buyer. The four different categories here are lack of attractiveness, buyer's attractiveness, supplier's attractiveness and mutual attractiveness.

In the last step the material evaluation is divided into three different relationship groups—strategic, collaborative and transnational relationships—which form the y-axis in Fig. 5.7. These relationships are influenced by the factors depicted in Fig. 5.7.

As seen in Fig. 5.6, the results from the **supplier evaluation** are then incorporated into the framework and classified according to bad, good or excellent

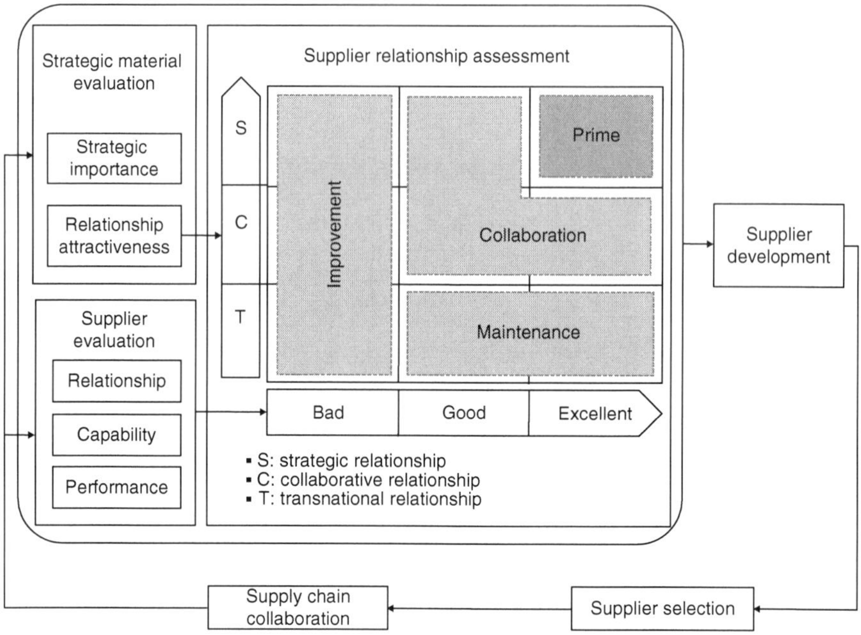

Fig. 5.6 Framework for supplier assessment and development, according to Park et al. (2010)

supplier groups. These factors form the x-axis in Fig. 5.6. The different factors are influenced by different variables:

Capabilities: quality systems, technological capability, financial capability, reputation, geographic location, organization, production capacity and open communication

Performance: quality, cost and delivery

Relationship: mutuality, cooperation, commitment, trust, conflict, conflict resolution and compliance

The next step as seen in Fig. 5.6 is the **supplier relationship assessment**. Here the supplier relationship is assessed via the matrix according to the two axes. **Supplier development** should improve supplier performance. At the end of this process, the firm reduces the supplier base in order to improve the supplier's performance. The suppliers are then divided into four different groups which are improvement, collaboration, maintenance and prime.

- **Improvement** refers to supplier inspections as well as improvement activities.
- The **collaboration** group aims to improve cooperation to increase mutual benefits.
- The **maintenance** group focuses on the maintenance of the status quo and pursuing mutual benefit.
- The **prime group** aims to create strong incentives and long-lasting relationships.

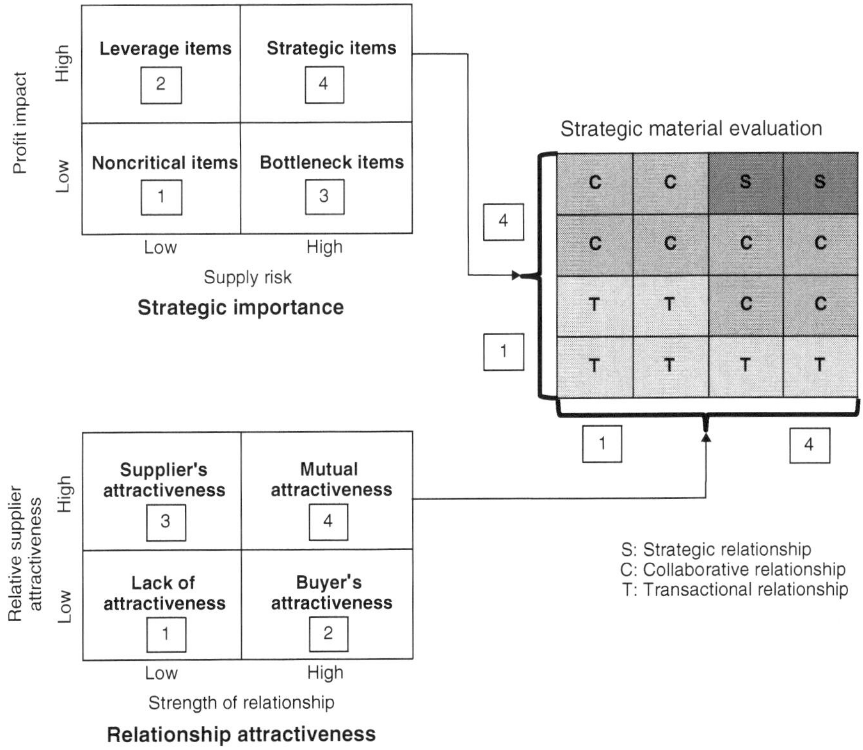

Fig. 5.7 Framework of a strategic material evaluation, according to Park et al. (2010)

In Fig. 5.8 an example is given in which the results of one product and the analysis of different companies are integrated into the framework. This makes it possible to assess the different supplier relationships for each individual product by evaluating and assessing the measures as explained above. Focusing on supplier relationship management within the company helps to differentiate supply chains and increase the efficiency of the purchasing process.

5.4 Supplier Management and Supply Chain Strategies

Just as with the assignment of outsourcing to supply chain strategies (see previous chapter), the connection of buyer–supplier relationships with respective supply chain strategies also remains somewhat vague. Cox (2004) notices that, despite their overall differences, both advocates of a lean strategy (cf. Womack et al. 1990) and of an agile strategy (cf. Christopher and Towill 2001) see long-term, trust-based buyer–supplier relationships as a driver of success. However, Cox (2004) claims that long-term partnerships in lean organizations are not based on the same preconditions as those of agile organizations: in the lean context, the buyer has dominance over the

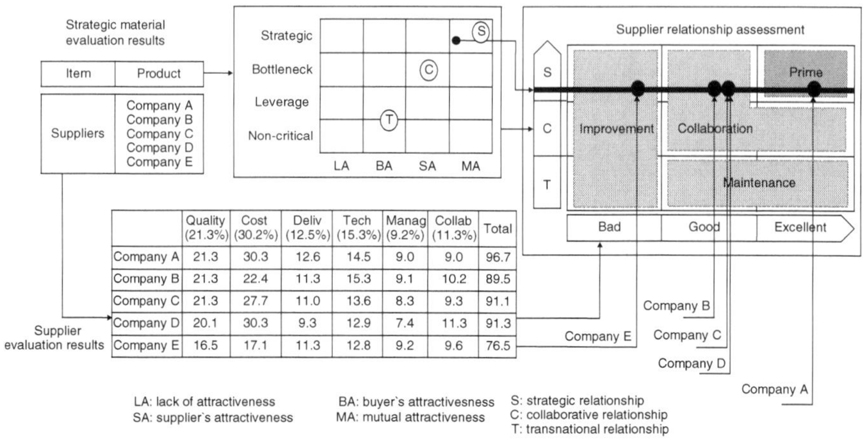

Fig. 5.8 Exemplary results of an integrated supplier relationship framework, in accordance with Park et al. (2010)

supplier, and the purchased item can be regarded as a leverage item. Therefore, the top left quadrant of the matrix (Fig. 5.5) can be assigned to a lean strategy. In general, it is assumed that the left side of the matrix, where the supply risk is low, is more likely to be dominated by the lean strategy. This means that the bottom left quadrant is, resultingly, also combined with a lean strategy: as the item is noncritical to the buyer's product, cost-orientation can be pursued; the buyer–supplier relationship remains at arm's length.

In contrast, on the right side of the matrix it can be more readily presumed that an agile supply chain strategy is prevalent, as the supply risk is more significant. Costs do not have such high importance, but an assured supply is crucial. For strategic items, Kraljic (1983) recommends long-term contracts to guarantee availability. A highly collaborative partnership is expected, handing over responsibility to the supplier. For bottleneck items, an agile strategy is also expected. The buyer does not possess any dominance over the supplier; instead, the converse is the case. Due to the dependency and the risk of supply, the buyer has to stay in a flexible mode. Moreover, Kraljic (1983) suggests backward integration as a solution, in order to enhance agility.

Again, liability has not explicitly been addressed in these considerations. However, according to Huang et al. (2002), the sourcing of components and modules for hybrid (legally managed) products consists of diverse streams, for which either a lean or an agile strategy is pursued. Consequently, the conclusion deduced above can be adopted.

Fig. 5.9 Exemplary supplier–buyer relationship for different modules of Tec 1

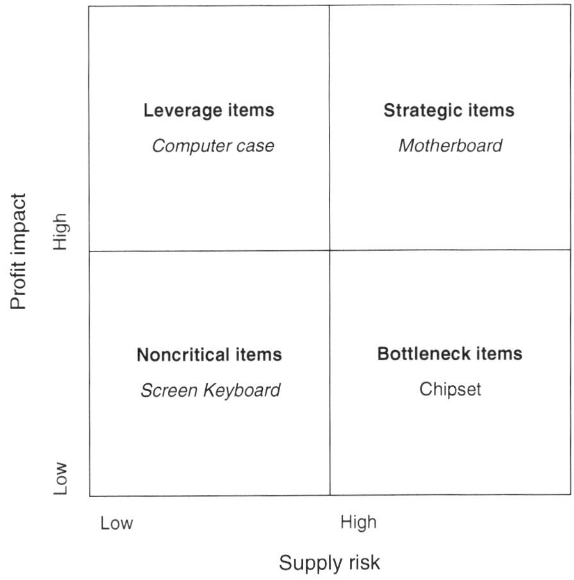

5.5 Alternative Approach to Managing Suppliers: The ABC Analysis

The ABC analysis has been described at length in CM1. In analogy to its use for segmentation, it is also commonly applied for the segmentation of suppliers. Gelderman and van Weele (2005) state that "for quite some time, ABC analysis (or Pareto analysis) was the only tool for differentiating between important and less important purchases" (p. 21). Regularly, due to its simplicity, ABC analysis is performed as an introduction to supplier categorization, in order to obtain a rough overview of the sample (Wagner and Johnson 2004).

The measurements classically used for an ABC analysis in this context are, for example, purchasing volume, the characteristics of the supplier with regard to technological, qualitative or financial matters, as well as the strategic importance of the supplier. However, Gelderman and van Weele (2005) criticize the fact that, due to the exclusive concentration on financial value, ABC analyses lack the treatment of costs associated with weak product performance.

Moreover, Gelderman and van Weele (2005) complain about the missing strategic directions provided by an ABC analysis. Nonetheless, this is contradicted by Wagner and Johnson's (2004) observation: the firms they have analyzed deduced strategic targets from segmentation via ABC analysis, as, for instance, tightening of cooperation with A suppliers.

The assignment to supply chain strategies yields the same conclusions as with the other types of supplier segmentation presented above: the more important the supplier is for the focal firm (A supplier), the more likely it is that it will be managed in an agile way. On the other hand, less important suppliers are attended to with a lean supply chain strategy.

Summary sheet

CM3: Supplier segmentation and strategy

Goals of SCD Guide CM3

The aim of SCD Guide CM3 is to emphasize the role that suppliers play in a firm's planning process. The different methods to analyze buyer–supplier relationships are implemented and methods to analyze the relationship with regard to the purchasing process are made known. Lastly alternative ways of managing suppliers with the ABC analysis are proposed.

Methods and analysis for SCD Guide CM3

- Buyer–supplier power distribution
- Purchasing portfolio matrix
- Integrated supplier relationship framework
- ABC analysis in managing suppliers

Input per method for SCD Guide CM3

	Input from other CMs	Method	Method
Method to identify buyer–supplier relationship	(None)	**Buyer–supplier power distribution** • Buyer power relative to supplier • Supplier power relative to buyer	
Purchasing portfolio matrix	CM2	**Purchasing portfolio matrix (1/2)** • Importance of purchasing E.g. cost of materials/total costs, value-added profile, profitability profile • Complexity of supply market E.g. supply monopoly or digopoly conditions, pace of technological advance, entry barriers	**Purchasing portfolio matrix (2/2)** • Supplier E.g. market size and growth, capacity utilization, competitive structure • Company E.g. purchasing volume, demand growth, capacity utilization
Method for managing suppliers	(None)	**Integrated supplier relationship framework** • Supplier assessment and development • Strategic material evaluation	**ABC analysis in managing suppliers** • Purchasing volume • Characteristics of the supplier with regard to technological, qualitative or financial matters • Strategic importance

Output from SCD Guide CM3

- Categorization of purchased modules (or components)
  Dimension in morphological box: Product (Module categorization)

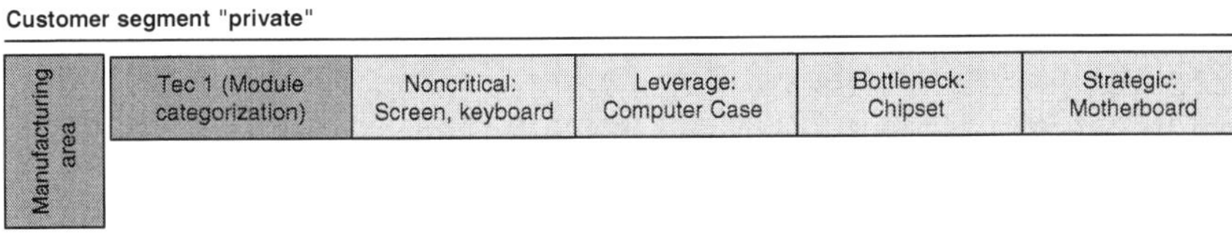

Fig. 5.10 Exemplary supplier–buyer relationship for different modules of Tec 1

5.6 Application Example of SCD Guide CM3 and Possible Output

In this example, the supplier–buyer relationship is analyzed according to the different modules of the exemplary product Tec 1 applied in the Kraljic matrix for the private customer segment. The supplier–buyer relationship is a relevant measure to analyze the power distribution between buyer and supplier. In Fig. 5.9 one can see the different components of Tec 1 in the matrix. The noncritical items such as the screen and the keyboard indicate that here there is not a strong dependence on the supplier and a low risk for the profit impact as well as the supply risk. The screen and keyboard do not contribute to the differentiation process of the product and therefore do not have strategic importance.

- The leverage items such as the computer case have a high profit impact but a small supply risk, since there are fewer buyers than suppliers. The computer case is a more or less standardized module in which the buyer does not have an advantage of information.
- The strategic items are the core items of the product which are manufactured in-house. In the matrix one can see that the supply risk is very high as is the profit risk. These modules, such as the motherboard in our example, have a high impact on the quality and performance of the product.
- These parts are usually co-developed by buyer and supplier and show a high interdependence between the two. Therefore, a high degree of cooperation and information sharing is necessary.
- The bottleneck items, such as the chipset as a module of Tec 1, have a high supply risk, but a low impact on profit. They are necessary for the manufacturing of the computer. In this case there are only very few suppliers of the chipset, thus making the company highly dependent on its supplier. The costs here are usually higher for the buyer than for the supplier.

Figure 5.9 only shows the first step of the Kraljic matrix. In a second step the balance of strategic items can be assessed with the help of the purchasing matrix.

The analysis has determined that the company has to focus on long-term trust-based supplier relationships, since the supply of modules such as the chipset are highly dependent on a long-term relationship between supplier and buyer. The analysis has shown that the supplier–buyer relationship is an important factor for the overall success of the product and the company itself

The morphological box in Fig. 5.10 shows the different modules according to their product categorization. For example, the screen and keyboard are two different product modules that are noncritical items, whereas the motherboard belongs to the strategic items.

References

Chen, I. J., & Paulraj, A. (2004). Towards a theory of supply chain management: the constructs and measurements. *Journal of Operations Management, 22*(2), 119.

Christopher, M., & Towill, D. R. (2001). An integrated model for the design of agile supply chains. *International Journal of Physical Distribution and Logistics Management, 31*(4), 235–246.

Cox, A. (1997). *Business success: A way of thinking about strategy, critical supply chain assets and operational best practice*. Stratford-upon-Avon: Earlsgate Press.

Cox, A. (2004). The art of the possible: Relationship management in power regimes and supply chains. *Supply Chain Management, 9*(5), 346–356.

Cox, A., Sanderson, J., & Watson, G. (2001). Supply chains and power regimes: Toward an analytic framework for managing extended networks of buyer and supplier relationships. *Journal of Supply Chain Management, 37*(2), 28–35.

Dyer, J. H. (1997). Effective interfirm collaboration: How firms minimize transaction costs and maximize transaction value. *Strategic Management Journal, 18*(7), 535–556.

Dyer, J. H., & Singh, H. (1998). The relational view: Cooperative strategy and sources of interorganizational competitive advantage. *Academy of Management Review, 23*(4), 660–679.

Dyer, J. H., Cho, D. S., & Chu, W. (1998). Strategic supplier segmentation: The next best practice in supply chain management. *California Management Review, 40*(2), 57–77.

Gelderman, C. J., & van Weele, A. J. (2003). Handling measurement issues and strategic directions in Kraljic's purchasing portfolio model. *Journal of Purchasing and Supply Management, 9*(5/6), 207.

Gelderman, C. J., & van Weele, A. J. (2005). Purchasing portfolio models: a critique and update. *Journal of Supply Chain Management: a Global Review of Purchasing and Supply, 41*(3), 19–28.

Howard, M., & Squire, B. (2007). Modularization and the impact on supply relationships. *International Journal of Operations and Production Management, 27*(11), 1192–1212.

Huang, S. H., Uppal, M., & Shi, J. (2002). A product driven approach to manufacturing supply chain selection. *Supply Chain Management: An International Journal, 7*(4), 189–199.

Kraljic, P. (1983). Purchasing must become supply management. *Harvard Business Review, 61*(5), 109–117.

Mikkola, J. H. (2003). Modularity, component outsourcing, and inter-firm learning. *R&D Management, 33*(4), 439–454.

Nellore, R., & Söderquist, K. (2000). Portfolio approaches to procurement analysing the missing link to specifications. *Long Range Planning, 33*(2), 245–267.

Park, J., Shin, K., Chang, T. W., & Park, J. (2010). An integrative framework for supplier relationship management. *Industrial Management and Data Systems., 110*(4), 495–515.

Porter, M. E. (1980). *Competitive strategy: Techniques for analyzing industries and competitors*. New York: Free Press.

Wagner, S. M., & Johnson, J. L. (2004). Configuring and managing strategic supplier portfolios. *Industrial Marketing Management, 33*(8), 717–730.

Williamson, O. E. (1985). *The economic institutions of capitalism: firms. Markets relational contracting*. New York: Free Press.

Womack, J. P., Jones, D. T., & Roos, D. (1990). *The machine that changed the world: Based on the Massachusetts Institute of Technology 5 million dollar 5 year study on the future of the automobile*. New York, NY: Rawson.

Wynstra, F., & ten Pierick, E. (2000). Managing supplier involvement in new product development: A portfolio approach. *European Journal of Purchasing and Supply Management, 6*(1), 49–57.

CM4: Activity Allocation and Supply Chain Process Definition

6

6.1 Goals of Content Module 4

The aim of CM4 is to give an overview of the factors which influence the decision-making process to produce internationally and show the implications of such a decision. The chapter outlines the different types of operations in an international context. These are developed further in terms of the different international strategies. The strategies are then aligned with the various supply chain strategies in a further step. In addition the implications that these strategies have on practice are determined (Fig. 6.1).

In the second part of this chapter the implications that manufacturing strategies have on supply chain processes are discussed. Here the SCOR model is introduced, which aims to standardize supply chain operations. The SCOR framework is then put into context in terms of both different manufacturing strategies and supply chain strategies. Furthermore, the different manufacturing strategies and the implications that these have on the production of products, the product itself and its procurement are discussed.

The third part of the chapter deals with a practical case, which explains the supply chain processes in a differentiated supply chain process in terms of the computer manufacturing company Dell. This example shows how companies manage to use the supply chain differentiation process successfully in today's business practice.

The last part of this chapter is a questionnaire which aims to find out whether the different allocation processes are related to specific geographic regions. It is aimed at showing tendencies towards an allocation process in different regions and not at imposing a code of practice, but rather offering a framework.

CM4 is meant to give an understanding of activities which are related to the allocation process in relation to supply chain processes and production in an international context.

E. Hofmann et al., *The Supply Chain Differentiation Guide*,
DOI: 10.1007/978-3-642-31936-5_6, © Springer-Verlag Berlin Heidelberg 2012

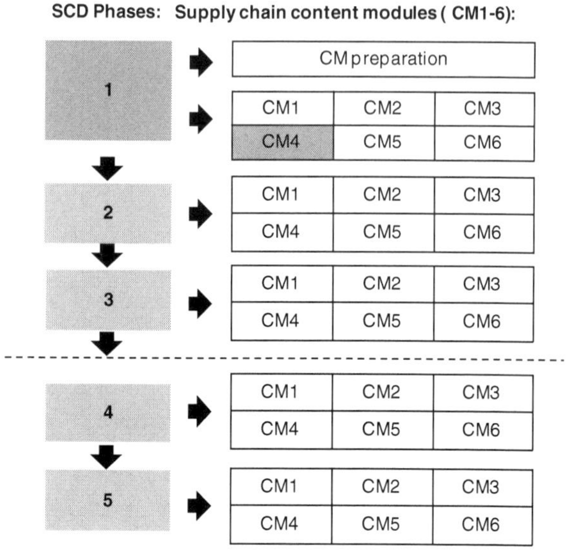

Fig. 6.1 Position of Chap. 6 in SCD Guide

6.2 Producing Internationally

Owing to the trend toward globalization, supply chains nowadays act on a highly international level. Rudberg and Olhager (2003) acknowledge that the focus has significantly changed, "from supplying domestic markets with products, via supplying international markets through export, to supply[ing] international markets through local manufacturing." (p. 29) Consequently, designing a supply chain no longer solely seeks out the most advantageous assignment of products to a specified number of facilities in a regional market; instead, an international dimension is added to the management of customers, facilities and strategic partners today (Chopra and Meindl 2007). The challenge that arises out of this development is to achieve an optimal alignment of the supply chain processes, pursuing cost efficiency on the one hand, while striving for high responsiveness to local markets' demands on the other (Delfmann and Albers 2000). Cohen and Mallik (1997) emphasize customer satisfaction as the overarching objective the supply chain activities have to serve: offering products at competitive costs and according to customer demand, as well as providing superior service and product availability. The main premise is therefore "to minimize the landed cost of products delivered to each market segment at each market location, while maintaining a high level of local customer service for product availability and system responsiveness, all of which lead to customer satisfaction throughout the life cycle of ownership" (Cohen and Mallik 1997).

This target coincides with the overall approach applied in this study. Throughout all of the elaborations of designing a differentiated supply chain, the customer is placed at the center. Therefore, the following discussion of organizing supply chains in an international context also has the purpose to fulfill the demand of different—internationally distributed—customer segments with regard to the customer criteria identified earlier. After this, strategic options for allocating resources internationally will be presented, and these will then be assigned to supply chain strategies and the corresponding customer priorities.

6.2.1 Different Ways of Operating in an International Context

Many scholars distinguish between two contrarian approaches for managing supply chains internationally.

- One option is to conduct a **globally concentrated production** (Dicken 1998), which is characterized by a centralized production of all products and their shipment to the various national or regional customer markets. The main point in favor of organizing in this way is the accomplishment of cost efficiencies through economies of scale (Dicken 1998). Moreover, the avoidance of uncertainties and problems associated with production in foreign countries, such as those arising from cultural differences or infrastructural deficiencies, can be a strong argument for home-country production (Meixell and Gargeya 2005). As a modification of this strategy, facilities can be erected abroad if the conditions are suitable; nevertheless, the focus remains on large-scale production for an international market (Delfmann and Albers 2000).
- Alternatively, in a **host-market production** approach, the manufacturing facilities are situated in the spatial region they serve (Dicken 1998). Moreover, Ferdows (1997) recognizes the trend for the R&D function to also move, alongside the production function, away from the home base of a company, due to the tight connections between these two functions. Compared to the global strategy, which focuses on the cost efficiencies in the production process, this strategy strives for reacting optimally to the characteristics of the particular market (Delfmann and Albers 2000). Clearly, the proximity to the customers' demands and requirements is a central advantage of this strategy (ibid.). In addition, Ferdows (1997) identifies, among others, tariff and trade considerations and labor cost advantages as criteria for this strategy. Cohen and Mallik (1997) add that the diversity of environments, which is a result of the placement of production facilities in different markets, yields exploitable contributions, such as different views on product and process engineering, for the entire corporation. By contrast, establishing production facilities offshore bears the risk that accompanies any non-home environment; cultural peculiarities might be unexpected and difficult to work with, and infrastructural shortcomings or insufficient workforce capabilities can significantly hamper the operation (Meixell and Gargeya 2005).

- In addition to these two oppositional approaches to serving an international market, a common third option combines characteristics of each of these types. Diverse names can be found for this type of strategy, all describing a relatively similar concept; however, it is believed that probably the term employed by Morash and Lynch (2002) **transnational strategy** best serves in the context of the perspective put forth in this guide. They claim that this strategy can be applied as a means of achieving the two singular targets, efficiency and responsiveness, at the same time. The key to success of this concept is a combination and configuration of the various aspects of international strategies to a global network. Consequently, a supply chain that is managed transnationally consists of centralized production in the home country, decentralized production in host countries, as well as an excentralized production of intermediate goods in third countries (for reasons, for instance, of labor costs), which are shipped to the other facilities for final assembly (Morash and Lynch 2002).

Obviously, as this strategy is made up of those previously presented, it also inherits their (dis)advantages. In addition, some additional appraisals can be put forward: for example, Cohen and Mallik (1997) note that such a strategy sustainably benefits a firm's business outcome, as it increases the competitiveness of the offered products by pursuing both cost and performance targets. As a drawback of this strategy, Meixell and Gargeya (2005) cite the risk accompanying long distances, which increases delivery time and can be a reason for delays or even losses. Moreover, they propose that currency exchange issues, political changes or environmental alterations can have a negative impact on a global network's performance.

6.2.2 Internationalization and Supply Chain Strategies

A topic that has not been directly addressed in the previous elaborations on international production strategies is the link that exists to the choice of an appropriate supply chain strategy. Nonetheless, because of the high degree of overlapping that exists between production strategy and supply chain strategy, the transfer can be easily made. The classification is conducted according to the ideas suggested by Morash and Lynch (2002) and is summarized in Table 6.1.

6.2.2.1 International Production Strategies

In the following the different international production strategies are explained. These production strategies can be used to align the overall supply chain strategies.

- For a **global strategy** (termed **globally concentrated production** above), an efficient (or lean) strategy is recommended, focusing on cost reduction through economies of scale and the elimination of waste. This strategy is highly production-driven, the product is normally characterized by high functionality and low individual specifications, and demand is rather stable and price-driven.

Table 6.1 Assignment of international production strategies to supply chain strategies

	Degree of centralization		
	Low	**Medium**	**High**
Internationalization	Global	Transnational	Multi-domestic
Description	Centralized production and shipment to the markets	Combination of centralized, decentralized and excentralized production into a global network	Decentralized production situated in the respective host markets
Main objectives	Cost-efficiencies (through size effects)	Cost-efficiencies and responsiveness (through mass customization/ Postponement)	Responsiveness to customer demands (through product differentiation)
Corresponding supply chain strategy	⬇ Lean	⬇ Leagile	⬇ Agile

- On the other hand, if a **multi-domestic strategy** (formerly termed **host-market production**) is implemented, the emphasis is put on the customer; normally, the peculiarities of the distinct markets and their customers' demands require an increased product differentiation and therefore a higher degree of responsiveness and flexibility, which results in an agile supply chain strategy. In addition, the smaller product quantities do not allow for large-scale, cost-efficient production.
- Following the logic of the assignment of international strategies to supply chain strategies, the **transnational strategy**, which lies in between the two polar strategies, corresponds with the leagile supply chain strategy, which is defined as a hybrid solution that combines the "best" of the lean and the agile strategy. As identified above, the main goals of a transnational strategy are cost efficiency and responsiveness, which are attained through a flexible management of the supplying network. Analogously, the corresponding drivers of a leagile organization are cost and flexibility, operationalized through mass customization and the concept of postponement.

6.2.3 Structuring the Network Design Decision

Chopra and Meindl (2007) published a framework (Fig. 6.2) that integrates the hitherto presented aspects of international network design into a decision-making procedure. The framework consists of four succeeding phases, of which only those phases not already elaborated above will be discussed in greater detail.

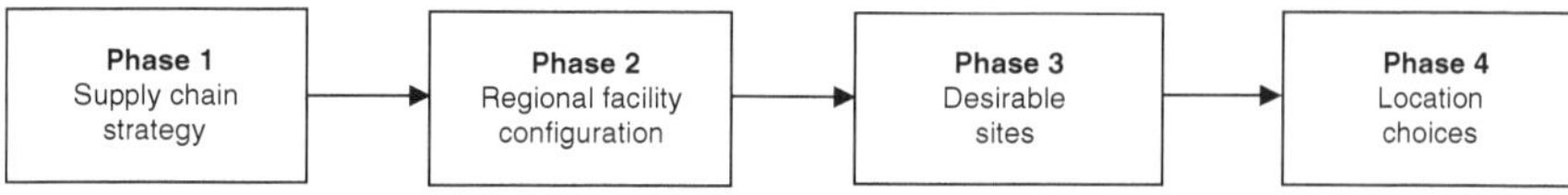

Fig. 6.2 Network design decision framework, adopted from Chopra and Meindl (2007)

6.2.3.1 Network Design Framework

First of all, the **supply chain strategy** has to be determined. This is followed by the **regional facility configuration**. For this phase, the factors presented above that determine the international production strategy, such as production technology, the potential for cost savings or local conditions, are included into the considerations. Next, **desirable sites** are identified. The main decision-making variable is the availability of suitable infrastructure. This can be divided into hard infrastructure, such as the presence of suppliers, transportation routes or resources, and soft infrastructure, which examines, for instance, the availability of a skilled workforce or the local community's mindset. Finally, the **location choice** is made. Naturally, the final solution is based on the previous phases, which means that the specified purpose of the new production site affects the evaluation and weighting of the relevant factors, and this in turn determines the definition of desirable sites. Out of the options generated here, the final location is determined.

On the basis of the presented categorization for managing the internationalization of a company, Ferdows (1997) refines the rather broad categories and puts forward six roles that a production facility abroad can take on within a corporation's planning.

- An **offshore factory** simply has the purpose of exploiting the advantageous conditions of a region, mostly caused by lower labor costs. Besides production, neither internal developments (such as product refinement) nor external developments (such as supplier integration) are involved.
- **Source factories** also aim at producing low costs. However, here the local management is endowed with more responsibility to organize and improve internal and external processes. Furthermore, the strategic importance of the produced goods is superior to those of the offshore factory, and their integration into their environment is more developed.
- A **server factory** is placed within the market it serves, in order to circumvent constraints such as taxes, logistics costs or exchange rate effects. However, it does not have the competencies for enhancing the product and adapting it to changed conditions.
- By contrast, **contributor factories** do not just deliver to the markets they are placed in, but also have the authority to become active in those markets. Therefore, functions such as R&D and procurement belong to company management.
- **Outpost factories** are situated in areas where superior knowledge capabilities are prevalent. Their main purpose is to absorb this knowledge and integrate it into the corporation. Therefore, strong exchange with the environment is

favored. As a producing site, these types of factories only play a secondary strategic role.

- Finally, **lead factories** take the approach of outpost factories further by acquiring local-area capabilities and directly implementing them into their own processes. Obviously, these factories are of the highest importance for the corporation and endow it with a significant knowledge gain.

6.2.4 Allocation of Supply Chain Processes to Respective Geographical Regions

The following set of questions can uncover tendencies for the process of allocating activities to specific geographical regions. The point here is not to outline a code of practice, but rather to frame a picture in which the process can be configured. It presents a questionnaire, which is not all-encompassing but aims instead to throw light on certain key dimensions. R&D and planning are not considered in the example that follows.

6.2.4.1 Process Allocation

Tendencies of process allocation can be identified with the following questionnaire. These questions are also helpful for improving process allocation.

General Question

1. Are there regions where the customers should be served mainly by means of an agile strategic supply chain orientation and at least one other region where the customers should be served mainly utilizing a lean strategic supply chain orientation?

YES: Consideration of an assignment of all processes to one region with agile orientation and one region with lean orientation.

NO: Assignment of all processes to one region may be sufficient.

Customer segment-related questions

2. Is delivery reliability important?

YES: Consideration of an assignment of source, make and deliver processes in respective regions.

NO: Assignment of source, make and deliver processes to one region may be sufficient.

3. Is product availability important?

YES: Consideration of an assignment of make or deliver processes in respective regions.

NO: Assignment of make and deliver processes to one region may be sufficient.

4. Is service quality important?

YES: Consideration of an assignment of deliver processes in respective regions.

NO: Assignment of deliver processes to one region may be sufficient.

5. Is product quality important?

YES: Consideration of an assignment of make, source and R&D processes in a high-wage region.

Complete allocation of functions in two regions? Yes ☐ No ☐

Functions / Region	Deliver [1,2,3,4]	Make [1,2,3,5,6]	Source [1,2,5,6]	Plan [1,7]	R&D [1,5,6,8]
Europe	☐	☐	☐	☐	☐
Asia	☐	☐	☐	☐	☐

Fig. 6.3 Process allocation to different geographical regions

NO: Assignment of make, source and R&D processes anywhere convenient.

Complementary questions for each customer segment

6. Is the price of the product important?

YES: Consideration of an assignment of make, source and R&D processes in a low-wage region.

NO: Assignment of make, source and R&D processes anywhere convenient.

7. Is it possible to centrally plan the supply chain and fulfill customer requirement in this region?

YES: Possibility to centralize plan processes in one region.

NO: Allocate R&D in this region if needed.

Results

In the following form (Fig. 6.3), the results for deliver, make, source, plan and R&D functions can be categorized according to region, either Europe or Asia (Fig. 6.3).

6.3 Implications of Manufacturing Strategies for Supply Chain Processes

For illustrating the different supply chain processes, the SCOR (Supply Chain Operations Reference), which was developed by the Supply Chain Council (SCC), is used. Discussion then turns to the implications that diverse manufacturing strategies have for supply chain processes.

6.3.1 The SCOR Framework

The Supply Chain Operations Reference (SCOR) model was introduced in 1996 as a tool to facilitate and standardize the planning and management of supply chain operations (Lambert et al. 2005). The model divides supply chain processes into five discrete subprocesses, each of which is treated with regard to four different levels of detail. However, owing to the character of the argument made here, we restrict ourselves to presenting only the five conceptual subprocesses.

The five subprocesses of supply chain processes are (Supply Chain Council 2008):

Manufacturing strategy	Core SCOR processes			Supply chain strategy
	Source	Make	Deliver	
Make-to stock (BTS)	High volumes; Costs and reliability as key factors	Highest volume; Continuous production	Large volume shipments; Costs and reliability as key factors	Lean
Assemble-to-order (ATO)		High volume; Batch production		Leagile
Make-to-order (MTO)	Low volumes; Quality and proximity as key factors	Low volume; Job shop production	Small volume shipments; In-time delivery as key factor	
Engineer-to-order (ETO)		One-of-a-kind; Project		Agile

Fig. 6.4 Aligning SCOR processes with manufacturing strategies, adopted from Stavrulaki and Davis (2010)

- Plan—specifies the course of action of the subsequent subprocesses according to the characteristics of supply and demand
- Source—manages the procurement of required goods and services
- Make—handles the organization of the manufacturing process
- Deliver—organizes the distribution of finished products to the customers
- Return—deals with after-sales service.

Different supply chain activities can be organized according to these five subprocesses. The following examines the implications that the identified manufacturing strategies have on the character of the subprocesses.

6.3.2 Aligning Supply Chain Processes With Manufacturing Strategies

Naturally, depending on the manufacturing strategy (CM2), the setup of the supply chain processes varies. Stavrulaki and Davis (2010) have implemented an alignment of the two concepts, which will briefly be discussed below. Since choosing a manufacturing strategy already includes the specification of the characteristics of supply and demand, the first of the five subprocesses (**plan**) can be considered dispensable and will therefore not be taken up. Moreover, the **return** process is assumed to be of no relevance for the purposes of our argument, and thus will also be excluded. Consequently, the three core processes **source, make** and **deliver** are the subject of consideration (Fig. 6.4).

6.3.2.1 Determining Supply Chain Process

It was shown previously in this chapter that both the MTS and the ATO manufacturing strategy focus on cost reductions, the former more than the latter. Since this target normally accompanies large-scale production, **sourcing** actions are also

Table 6.2 Combining manufacturing strategies with delivering processes (SCOR 10.0)

Deliver	Deliver stocked product (D1)	Deliver make-to-order product (D2)	Deliver engineer-to-order product (D3)
Product is…	Maintained in a finished goods state	Manufactured, assembled or configured from standard parts	Designed, manufactured and assembled from standard and custom parts
Production of product…	Prior customer order	After customer order	After customer order

characterized by high volumes, allowing for lower purchasing prices and high delivery reliability. By contrast, those strategies which focus on responsiveness to changes in customer demand procure in lower quantities, putting greatest value on quality and proximity.

With respect to the **make** process, the volume of production decreases continuously, the more the customer becomes the central determinant of production planning. In a MTS organization, large quantities are produced, achieved through continuous production. For an ATO strategy, batch production is most appropriate; for a MTO strategy, job shop production is very common. Finally, as the product is often of unique character in an ETO strategy, production is executed within a project organization.

In terms of the **delivery** process, Stavrulaki and Davis (2010) again distinguish between those strategies that are cost-oriented, and those where the customer has significant impact. In MTS and ATO strategies, finished goods are shipped in large quantities, focusing on low costs and stable procedure. MTO and ETO strategies, by contrast, normally deliver in small batches, with foremost emphasis on assuring in-time delivery.

In Table 6.2 one can see the outcome of combining manufacturing strategies with deliver strategy and their implications on the product itself and the production of the product. A lean strategic supply chain orientation is shown to deliver more make-to-stock products, whereas the agile strategy is shown to deliver more make-to-order products or engineer-to-order product.

Table 6.3 shows manufacturing strategies in combination with both the make decision and the time frame in which a product is completed and produced. Lean strategic supply chain orientation show more make-to-stock product processes, whereas the agile strategic supply chain shows more make-to-order product processes.

Table 6.4 shows the manufacturing strategy combined with the sourcing procedure in a table. The analysis of the table shows the impact that the strategy has on procurement and the product itself. Lean strategic supply chain orientation shows more

Table 6.3 Combining manufacturing strategies with making processes (SCOR reference manual 10.0)

Make	Make-to-stock (M1)	Make-to-order (M2)	Engineer-to-order (M3)
Product completed…	Prior to receipt of a customer order	After receipt of a customer order	After receipt of a customer order
Product produced according to…	Sales forecast ("off the shelf")	Customer order	Customer request
Production of…	Standard products	Standard and custom tailored product	Standard and custom tailored products (includes development and design)

Table 6.4 Combining manufacturing strategies with sourcing processes (SCOR 10.0)

Source	Source stocked product (S1)	Source make-to-order product (S2)	Source engineer-to-order product (S3)
Procurement of…	Product or service	Product	Product or service
Procurement based on…	Forecast	Customer order	Customer order
Product (or service)	Prefabricated	Designed or configured based on particular customer requirements	Designed or configured based on particular customer requirements

stocked product processes, whereas agile strategic supply chain orientation favors more source make-to-order product processes or engineer-to-order product processes.

6.4 Supply Chain Processes in a Differentiated Supply Chain Context—The case of Dell

For the purpose of illustrating the interconnection between manufacturing strategies, supply chain processes and the supply chain differentiation framework, a case is briefly introduced, showing the importance of a thorough consideration of the various aspects. These aspects have already been introduced in Part A above.

After its establishment in 1984, Dell Computer demonstrated an exceptional track record (Kraemer et al. 2000). This was to a large extent due to its business model: Dell chose a strategy of direct sales and build-to-order (BTO; similar to ATO, see discussion in CM2) management, benefiting from the result that this strategy yields, which is high flexibility at relatively low costs. For a successful implementation of this strategy, it was identified as crucial to have a comprehensive understanding of customer structure, breaking them down into segments (ibid).

However, as returns declined in recent years, Dell has decided to reexamine its business concept (Davis 2010). It turns out that customer structure has become even more complex, requiring increasingly divergent responses. Consequently, Dell decided to differentiate its supply chain. The previously defined customer segments were divided into two groups, each being served by a separate supply chain. One supply chain maintains previous strategy, that is, directly selling customized solutions in a rapid manner. This supply chain focuses mainly on business-to-business (B2B) customers. The newly launched supply chain addresses the requirements of private consumers, taking into account their demand for low-price options and multiple channel distribution. To achieve this, the customer order decoupling point was moved downstream; as a consequence, a make-to-stock (MTS) manufacturing strategy was introduced (Davis 2010).

If Dell's new business concept is analyzed with respect to its supply chain processes, it provides some practical evidence for the framework outlined above:

Delivery differs with regard to its volume: for private consumers, larger batches are distributed to the retailers and wholesalers. Depending on the character of the B2B customers' order, their products are also shipped in larger batches; however, for personalized solutions, small batches can also be expected. In general, it is worth considering an issue that has not yet received the attention it deserves: the distribution channel. In the case of Dell, two approaches have been implemented. While the initial supply chain strategy mainly incorporates direct distribution (Kraemer et al. 2000), the additional, more recently initiated supply chain relies significantly on indirect distribution through retailers and wholesaler (Davis 2010).

Since the new supply chain strategy with its MTS manufacturing strategy aims at the high-volume mass market, its make process is aligned accordingly; the production takes place on a continuous assembly line. The "old" supply chain is characterized by a batch manufacturing process, complemented by job shop production, if make-to-order (MTO) is required.

Finally, as described in the framework above, high-volume purchasing is the favored approach in both the MTS and the ATO strategy, driven by cost effects and stable supply. Moreover, if the customer's voice has a more significant impact (MTO), smaller volumes are purchased, with quality and proximity as key factors.

Summary sheet

CM4: Activity allocation and supply chain process definition

Goals of SCD Guide CM4

The aim of SCD Guide CM4 is to identify the possibilities of operating in an international context by choosing an international production strategy as well as a framework to implement the given strategy. The SCOR processes manufacturing strategies explain what impact supply chain strategies have on subprocesses. Furthermore the product processes are allocated according to different manufacturing strategies.

Methods and analysis for SCD Guide CM4

- International production strategies
- Network design framework
- Supply chain process determination
- Supply chain process allocation

Input per method for SCD Guide CM4

	Input from other CMs	International production strategies	Network design framework
Method for operating in an international context	(None)	• Cost of production • Customer's demand and requirements • Tariff and trade considerations • Labor costs • Cultural differences • Facilities • Delivery time • Infrastructural deficiencies • Political stability • Environmental situation • Currency exchange	• Conditions of a region • Costs • Taxes • Logistics costs • Exchange rate volatility • R&D procurement • Superior knowledge capabilities • Capabilities of the local area
	Input from other CMs	**Supply chain process determination**	**Supply chain process allocation**
Identifying manufacturing strategy implications	CM1 CM2	• Manufacturing strategy • Supply chain strategy • Product characteristics	• Questionnaire with general and customer-specific questions

Output from SCD Guide CM4

- Allocation of supply chain processes
  Dimension in morphological box: Process allocation
- Selection of appropriate supply chain processes
  Dimension in morphological box: Process type

6.5 Application Example of SCD Guide CM4 and Possible Output

This example is outlined to suit the customer segment "private" instead of other customer segments. PC Manufacturing Inc. determines the countries in which it produces its different modules and decides to opt for a global manufacturing

Table 6.5 Exemplary delivering and making process for Tec 1

Deliver	Make
Deliver make-to-order product (D2)	Make-to-order (M2)
Tec 1 is manufacturing assembled or configured from standard parts	Tec 1 is completed after receipt of a customer order
Production of Tec 1 after customer order	Tec 1 is produced according to customer order
	Production of standard and custom product

strategy. Following this, the company has to decide upon its deliver, make and source strategy within the supplier, deliver and manufacturing area.

In the following, it will be shown which one of the following manufacturing strategies the company chooses to deliver, make and source its products. The product Tec 1 is manufactured from standard parts which are produced after the customer order has come in.

The making process indicates that Tec 1 is completed right after the customer order and produced according to specified customer requirements. However, production can be standardized as well as custom-made. The procurement process is based on the customer order, and the product is designed or configured based on the requirements of the customer. Table 6.5 shows the analysis for the delivering and making process for the product Tec 1. The deliver make-to-order strategy as well as the make-to-order strategy have been identified for Tec 1 within the TO-BE analysis. The delivering process is fulfilled on all continents, i.e. in Asia, Europe, North America, South America, Africa and Australia. The making process on the other hand takes place only in Europe and North America as can be ascertained from morphological box below (Fig. 6.5).

For the different modules of the product there are different sourcing strategies which can be drawn from whether the product is a strategic, bottleneck, leverage or noncritical product module. The geographic distribution in the sourcing process involves Europe, Asia, North America and Australia.

In Table 6.6 the different sourcing strategies are shown in the different product modules. The sourcing process consists of different modules which can be produced individually.

All the different product modules are source stocked products, which are prefabricated instead of custom made. All of these modules are not highly customized but sourced beforehand. Tec 1 is a PC where all of its modules, whether they are strategic, bottleneck, leverage or noncritical items, are prefabricated, but customized in delivery and assembly. The customer order is very late in the process, but the demand for parts has been forecast.

In the exemplary morphological box, one can see the results of the TO-BE analysis of the customer, manufacturing and supplier areas. All of these results are only applied to the customer segment "private". In the customer area, it shows that

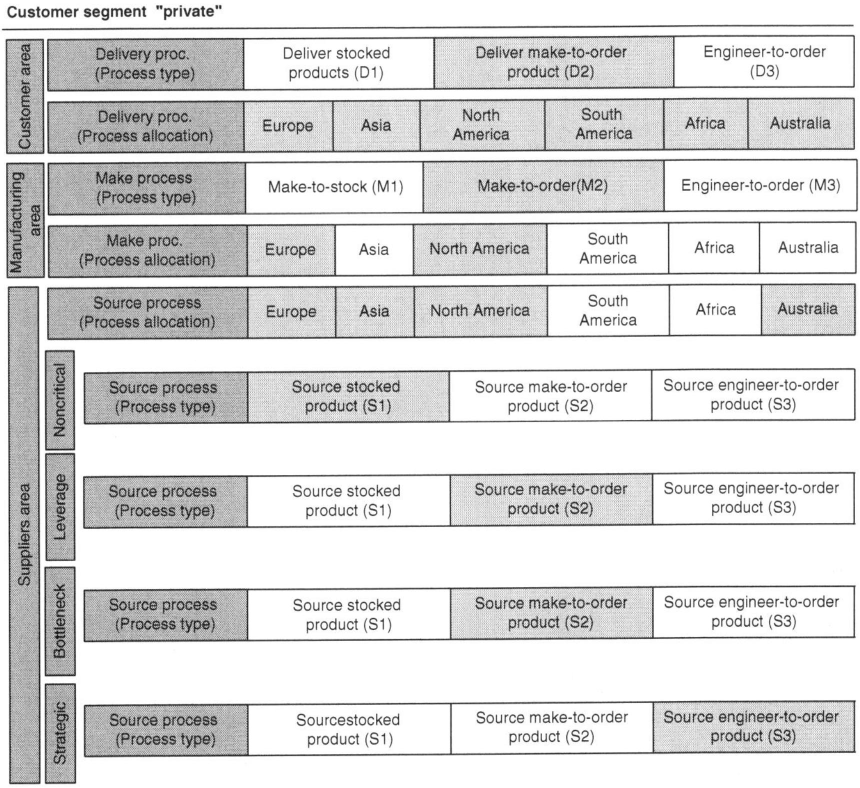

Fig. 6.5 Exemplary morphological box, Content Module 4

Table 6.6 Exemplary sourcing process for different modules of Tec 1

Product type	Strategic	Bottleneck	Leverage	Non-critical
Module	Motherboard	Chipset	Computer case	Screen and keyboard
Sourcing process	Source stocked product (S1)	Source stocked product (S1)	Source stocked product (S1)	Source stocked product (S1)

the deliver make-to-order product is the recommended delivery strategy for the private customer segment. Furthermore the delivery process should take place on all continents. In the manufacturing area it is presented that a make-to-order process should be adopted and allocated to Europe and Asia. The supplier area states the different types of items according to noncritical, leverage, bottleneck and strategic items and these, in turn, according to the recommended sourcing process.

References

Chopra, S., & Meindl, P. (2007). *Supply chain management: strategy, planning, and operation* (3rd ed.). Upper Saddle River: Pearson Prentice Hall.

Cohen, M. A., & Mallik, S. (1997). Global supply chains: research and applications. *Production and Operations Management, 6*(3), 193–210.

Davis, M. (2010). *Case study for supply chain leaders: Dell's transformative journey through supply chain segmentation*: Gartner Research ID Number: G00208603.

Delfmann, W., & Albers, S. (2000). *Supply chain management in the global context.* Working Paper No. 102, Dept. of General Management, Business Planning and Logistics of the University of Cologne, Cologne.

Dicken, P. (1998). *Global shift: transforming the world economy* (3rd ed.). New York and London: Guilford Press.

Ferdows, K. (1997). Making the most of foreign factories. *Harvard Business Review, 75*(2), 73–88.

Kraemer, K. L., Dedrick, J., & Yamashiro, S. (2000). Refining and extending the business model with information technology: Dell computer corporation. *Information Society, 16*(1), 5–21.

Lambert, D. M., García-Dastugue, S. J., & Croxton, K. L. (2005). An evaluation of process-oriented supply chain management frameworks. *Journal of Business Logistics, 26*(1), 25–51.

Meixell, M. J., & Gargeya, V. B. (2005). Global supply chain design: a literature review and critique. *Transportation Research: Part E: Logistics and Transportation Review, 41*(6), 531–550.

Morash, E. A., & Lynch, D. F. (2002). Public policy and global supply chain capabilities and performance: a resource-based view. *Journal of International Marketing, 10*(1), 25–51.

Rudberg, M., & Olhager, J. (2003). Manufacturing networks and supply chains: an operations strategy perspective. *Omega, 31*(1), 29–39.

Stavrulaki, E., & Davis, M. (2010). Aligning products with supply chain processes and strategy. *International Journal of Logistics Management, 21*(1), 127–151.

Supply Chain Council (SCC) (2008). Supply Chain Operations Reference (SCOR) Model, Version 9.0.

CM5: Supply Chain Governance 7

7.1 Goals of Content Module 5

The goal of this chapter is to identify the practical implications that accompany the supply chain topics previously presented. Just as the Chap. 6 (supply chain processes), it deals with the operationalization and implementation of strategic considerations, and presents the managerial implications of their execution. In particular, this chapter specifies the management of buyer–supplier relationships, which has already been discussed on a strategic level in Chap. 4 (Fig. 7.1).

The chapter commences with a presentation of different supply chain governance types. This is followed by a discussion of the actual management of the two singular types of supply chain partners: the customers and the suppliers. The chapter concludes with a discussion of information sharing between supply chain partners.

7.2 Supply Chain Governance Structure

It has been noted earlier (CM1, CM3) that there are various options for establishing relationships between buyers and suppliers. Analogically, Gereffi et al. (2005) propose a supply chain governance framework that attempts to capture the most relevant aspects of buyer–supplier interactions. This framework can be applied in order to support the management of buyer–supplier relationships; the outcome is then a combination and classification of the various relationship conditions which allows one to deduce managerial implications for relationship governance. Gereffi et al. (2005) discuss supply chain governance types with respect to three characteristic dimensions.

E. Hofmann et al., *The Supply Chain Differentiation Guide*,
DOI: 10.1007/978-3-642-31936-5_7, © Springer-Verlag Berlin Heidelberg 2012

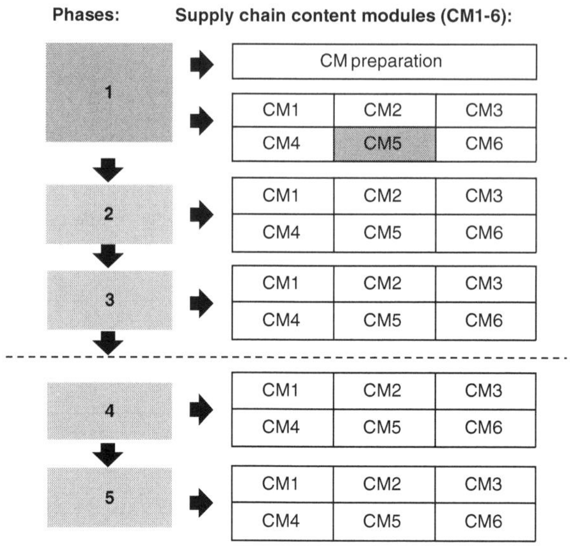

Fig. 7.1 Position of Chap. 7 in SCD guide

Table 7.1 Supply chain governance typology (Gereffi et al. 2005)

Governance type	Complexity of transactions	Ability to codify transaction	Capabilities in the supply -base	Degree of power asymmetry in the supply chain
Market	Low	High	High	Low
Modular	High	High	High	↑
Relational	High	Low	High	↕
Captive	High	High	Low	↓
Hierarchy	High	Low	Low	High

7.2.1 Supply Chain Governance Typology

The dimension **complexity** is employed to describe the difficulty in the transfer of information and knowledge accompanying interaction among firms. The **ability to codify** the transacted knowledge stands for the convenience of easily exchanging information. Finally, the **capabilities** of the supplier in fulfilling requirements are considered as a dimension.

Based on these three dimensions, five governance types are identified, as shown in Table 7.1.

It becomes apparent that the spectrum described by Gereffi et al. (2005) is based on transaction cost theory (Williamson 1985), ranking the governance types across the spectrum spanning between the two poles **perfect competition** (market) and **vertical integration** (CM2). As it can be seen in the outermost right-hand column of Table 7.1, the degree of power asymmetry constantly grows from the market to the hierarchy governance type.

Confronted with the buyer–supplier relationship matrix (CM3), remarkable correlations, but also partial contradictions, can be revealed, which probably can best be highlighted by investigating the degree of power distribution.

According to Gereffi et al. (2005), relatively low capabilities of the supplying side accompany a high degree of power asymmetry, endowing the buyer with dominance over the supplier; a **hierarchical** or **captive** governance type is the consequence. If the supplying side's capabilities are higher, the power asymmetry will decrease. Therefore, depending on the ability to codify the information, **relational** or **modular** governance types are recommended. However, at this point, the insights of Gereffi et al. (2005) seem to be incomplete. They lack the consideration that there might also be equality between buyer and supplier or even dominance by the supplier, as described in Chap. 4. For example, it was stated that particularly the tightest buyer–supplier relationship (strategic partnership) can be characterized by equal power. Finally, the power asymmetry is regarded as low, if the complexity of the transactions is also low. Buyer and supplier act independently of each other on the market.

This general classification of governance types will be explained in greater detail in the next few sections. The focus first turns to aspects of managing customers and suppliers. This is followed by a discussion of the exchange of information between supply chain partners.

7.2.2 Relationship Management Framework

Relationship governance issues are gaining considerable attention in the supply chain manager literature. The prevailing focus of existing research lies on individual dyadic relationships among firms like the relationship between a manufacturer and its customer or its supplier (Wathne and Heide 2004).

There are various options on how to establish a relationship between buyers and suppliers (Gereffi et al. 2005). Here, however, the focus lies on a **relationship management framework** depicted in Fig. 7.2 based on the work of Stuart (1997). The author stresses the importance of the suitable choice of the relationship to be developed between firms in order to achieve success within critical strategic elements. The framework is important in the context of supply chain management in order to identify and invest in the right relationships for the right partners.

The adapted framework allows one to classify relationships based on two main criteria: the first is represented by the **management intensity** of a firm involved to maintain the relationship and the second refers to the **attractiveness and importance** of the supplier or customer to a firm. The latter refers to the extent to which a material or service represents a high-value item to the firm. Another critical element, referring to the supplier relationship, represents the contribution that the supplier material or part makes regarding the perceived end user decision

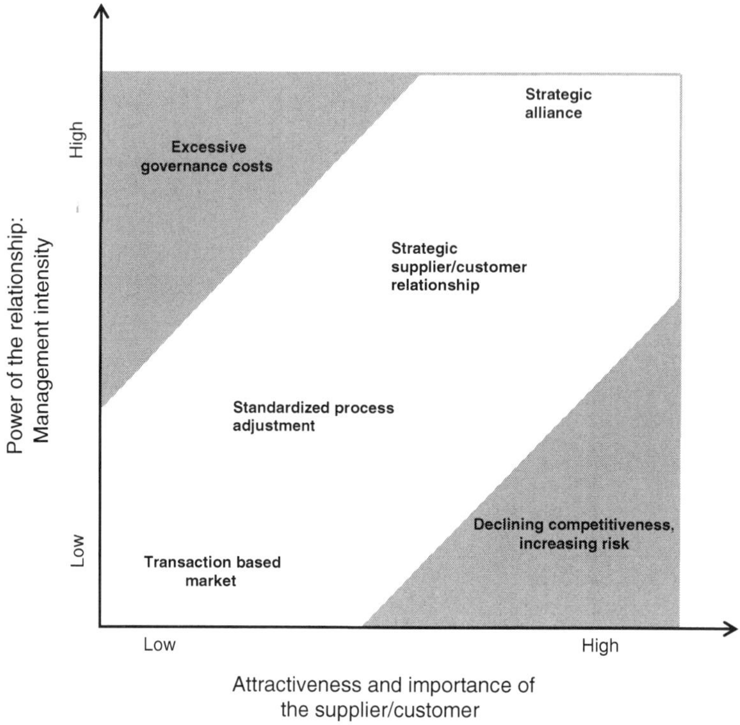

Fig. 7.2 Relationship management framework in supply chain management, after Stuart (1997)

to buy the product or service. However, choosing the suitable relationship for effective supply chain management demands consideration of both, governance costs as well as transaction costs and the possible risks involved (Stuart 1997).

Starting at the lower left side in Fig. 7.2, the four possible governance forms range from rather short-term relationships to strategic alliances (Stuart 1997). According to Stuart (1997), four generic buyer–supplier relationship types can be differentiated in supply chain management.

- A **transaction-based** market form of governance refers to a situation of low attractiveness of the contracting party to the firm as well as low management intensity invested into the relationship (Hoyt and Huq 2000). Characterize such relationships by little to no investments in assets and a minimal information flow. Moreover, the buyer can easily switch supplier if the resource is no longer needed or the supplier fails to meet obligations.
- The governance form of **standardized process adjustment** indicates a closer as well as generally a more long-term relationship compared to the previous one. The customer or supplier possesses a low to medium attractiveness to the firm and management intensity is low to medium as well.
- The **strategic supplier/customer relationship** is characterized by both, medium to high attractiveness of the contracting partner and management intensity.

This form of relationship is marked by trust, participation in processes, and a long-term relationship (Hoyt and Huq 2000).

- The **strategic alliance** represents a governance form applied when the partner possesses a high attractiveness and management intensity is high. This involves a pooling of resources and activities (Hoyt and Huq 2000) and a high level of information sharing. Hence, an example is the joint development of a new product.

7.2.3 Customer Relationship Management

The impact of customers on supply chain strategy and on the corresponding supply chain processes has been subject to extensive analysis in our study. Due to the general orientation of this framework, moving from the "customer backwards" (cf. Christopher et al. 2006), the role of customers, their characteristics, demands and requirements, as well as their implications for the setup of the entire supply chain have been widely considered.

However, what has been lacking so far in the deliberations undertaken is a method that actually supports the structured management of customers. For this reason, the concept of customer relationship management (CRM) is introduced. Nevertheless, owing to the fact that this topic traditionally belongs primarily to marketing research, it will only be addressed briefly here.

In a general context Payne and Frow (2005) note that there exists considerable ambiguity about the meaning and scope of CRM. This is to a large extent the result of its origins, which can be traced back to the emergence of IT-based customer management tools. By contrast, some scholars also see relationship marketing as synonymous with CRM (Parvatiyar and Sheth 2001). With the aim of including its different aspects, Payne and Frow (2005) define CRM as "a strategic approach that is concerned with creating improved shareholder value through the development of appropriate relationships with key customers and customer segments" (p. 168). This is achieved through the combination of relationship marketing strategies with IT systems.

Showing the relevance of CRM for the supply chain context, the Global Supply Chain Forum (GSCF) has set CRM as the first of eight identified key processes of supply chain management (Cooper et al. 1997). Here, CRM is seen as a means to provide a structure for the development and maintenance of the relationship with the customer (Croxton et al. 2001).

The CRM procedure proposed by the GSCF takes place on two different levels. On the strategic level, the preparations are performed, for example, the alignment of CRM with corporate strategy, or the definition of relevant criteria for customer categorization. The strategic subprocesses are then transferred to the operational level. On this level, the virtual analysis is carried out, including tasks such as the differentiation of customers, their arrangement in segments or the analyses and assessment of the segments. As a result, products and services are assigned to the

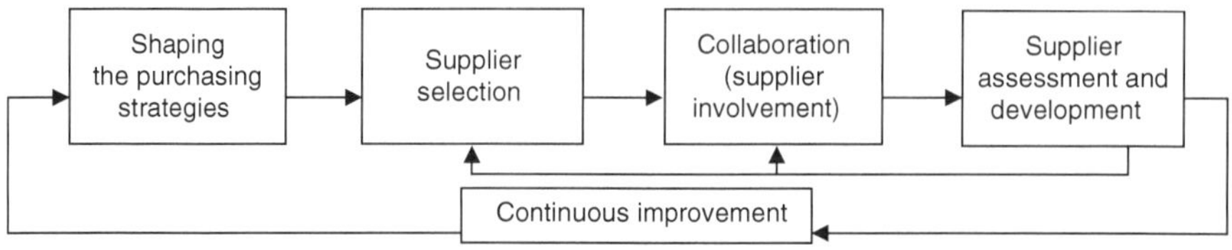

Fig. 7.3 Integrative supplier relationship management framework (Park et al. 2010)

various customer segments, as well as tasks for nurturing and maintaining the customer relationship (Croxton et al. 2001). Naturally, depending on the type of business and the structure of the customers, the efforts at CRM can vary. For example, in B2B markets the expenses for advertising and customer-retention actions can differ considerably from those in business-to-consumer (B2C) markets.

7.2.4 Supplier Relationship Management

The concepts previously presented also need to be discussed with respect to their application on the supplier's side of things. Normally, a firm possesses a wide number of suppliers, which form a portfolio. In the portfolio, close, value-generating, but costly strategic partnerships, as well as more ordinary, transaction-oriented relationships are organized (Bensaou 1999). Earlier in this argument (Chap. 4), the different types of buyer–supplier relationships were depicted, highlighting in particular the influence exerted by the relative distribution of power (Cox et al. 2001). In addition, the purchasing portfolio matrix and resulting strategies according to Kraljic (1983) were introduced.

Integrating these strategic aspects, Park et al. (2010) propose a framework that constitutes an SRM system (Fig. 7.3).

- The **purchasing strategy** is highly dependent on the character of demand and supply of a particular item, which in turn determines the distribution of power (see CM3). Often, the purchasing firm finds itself in a position that partly predefines the choice of a distinct type of relationship with the supplier, be it collaborative or at arm's length. In addition to the firm's position in the market, Cox et al. (2003) identify three more factors that affect the choice of buyer–supplier relationship: the **salience of the spend to the buyer** (its financial value and operational centrality), **the asset specificity of the spend** (the level of dedicated investments) and the **uncertainty of the spend** (the complexity of safe planning). The higher the prevalence of these factors, the more a purchasing firm is motivated to build a close, long-term cooperative relationship with the supplier (ibid.). In addition, it should be borne in mind that the type of buyer–supplier relationship has varying effects on the management of the relationship, as already pointed out in Chap. 5; if an asymmetry of bargaining power exists, one side can dictate the prices and thus the profits. Moreover, trust and commitment alternate according to the power distribution, as well as the supply risk (see for instance Kraljic (1983) and Cox et al. (2001). Furthermore, strategic intention plays a significant role.

- Next, **supplier selection** is performed. According to the identified purchasing strategy, this means either a more distant or a closer relationship. Obviously, if a closer cooperation is intended, the selection procedure considers other, additional factors compared to those of an ordinary transaction relationship; moreover, there is an expectation here that the decision will be more accurate and sound than in the latter case. However, circumstances might constrain the optimality of the selection; for instance, if the supplier has dominance over the buyer, the availability of options is curtailed (Bensaou 1999).
- In a subsequent step, the degree of **collaboration** is set. Again, the designated relationship type has a major impact. Collaboration can take place either in the production stage, in the product development stage, or in both stages. Popular examples for an integration of the supplier into the production process are just-in-time (JIT) delivery (Ballou 2004), vendor-managed inventory (VMI) (Chopra and Meindl 2007) and collaborative planning, forecasting and replenishment (CPFR) (Chopra and Meindl 2007).
- Finally, the SRM framework includes **supplier assessment and development**. The evaluation considers the supplier's capability, performance and collaboration. The development of the supplier's performance focuses on core suppliers, in order to reduce the supplier base in the long run.

The framework is complemented by the utilization of a continuous improvement system, containing a plan-do-check-act cycle. This steadily applied tool helps to achieve an improvement of the entire SRM process.

Excursus

A further development of customer/supplier relationship management is represented by customer interaction models (CIMs) and the supplier interaction models (SIMs). Besides the relationship that is aspired to with respect to a given customer/supplier segment CIMs and SIMs define:

- How to communicate with the customers/suppliers
- Which processes are carried out for a specific customer/supplier segment
- Which information is shared with each customer/supplier segment

In part there are IT systems accompanying such models (CIM/SIM systems) which replace previous CRM and SRM systems.

7.3 Information Sharing in Supply Chains

The management of information plays a crucial role in the successful management of supply chains. Information belongs, alongside of materials, to the two central flows that stream though a supply chain (see, for example, Stevens 1993). Throughout the argument made here, information has had a constant and significant impact on the topics discussed, first and foremost on the choice of a suitable supply chain strategy (for example, the speed and quality of demand information), but also, for example, on the customer segmentation procedure and supplier management.

Table 7.2 Different levels of information sharing in the supply chain

Supplier and customer relationship types	Level of information sharing
Strategic alliances	high
Strategic customer/supplier relationship	medium-high
Standardized process	medium-low
Transaction based	low

What has not yet been made subject of discussion to an adequate extent is the transfer of information between supply chain partners. This issue is closely related to the previous sections in which the diverse options of managing a firm's buyers and suppliers have been examined. As already indicated, the differences in the relationship types discussed in the previous sections do in fact also affect the character of the information exchange between the collaborating firms.

Therefore, in the following, **information sharing** between buyers and suppliers is discussed. Broadly defined, "information sharing refers to the extent to which critical and proprietary information is communicated to one's supply chain partner" (Li and Lin 2006). The purpose of exchanging information can be multiple; for example, in the product development process, the buyer discloses product specifications to a supplier, so that the supplier can design and deliver the fitting part (see Table 7.2 for different types of information sharing in the development process).

In the context of the present chapter, the sharing of information deals with the exchange of information that takes place during the actual production process. In order to keep the topic concise, information exchange between a supplying and a buying side is discussed in general, instead of considering both the upstream and the downstream information exchange of one focal firm. As a result, direct contact with consumers is not regarded as central for the purpose of this section; this type of information sharing is more concerned with the seller's making public of its product's features and its acquisition of information, as, for example, about its customer structure or its position vis-à-vis its competitors (Homburg and Krohmer 2006).

Nevertheless, there is a type of information that the final customer determines and that definitely must not be underestimated: demand. However, demand information in this context is only handled indirectly, as forwarded by retailers and wholesalers.

7.3.1 Characteristics of Information Sharing in the Supply Chain

The sharing of information can take place on various levels, ranging on a continuum from "no information shared" to "full information shared" (Sahin and Robinson 2002). More precisely, this means that the information a supplier can work with ranges from pure demand data to information about the point of sale

(POS) or the retailer's inventory levels all the way to projected future orders of the retailer (Chen and Lee 2009).

7.3.2 Different Levels of Information Sharing

In Table 7.2, one can see the different levels of information sharing according to the relationship type that exist between supplier and customer.

Here the strategic alliance is the strongest relationship between buyer and supplier as well as between supplier and customer, and it requires a high level of information sharing. Different methods to determine the relationships between customers or suppliers have already been discussed in detail in both CM1 and CM2. In this table, these relationship types are linked to the level of information sharing with customers and suppliers alike.

The **low level of information sharing** is transaction based. Here the only communication between buyer and supplier is the purchasing order. At the next higher level the **medium–low level of information sharing**, the buyer and supplier share slightly more information such as future planning and may have meetings on regular basis. But most of the information sharing at this stage is only operational. In the **medium–high level of information sharing** buyer and supplier have institutionalized meetings on a regular basis on a higher management level. More detailed plans are made which refer, for instance, to information about inventory. In the **high level of information sharing** buyer and supplier create strategic alliances and may share information about balance sheet totals and have regular meetings on a high management level.

7.3.3 Supplier and Customer Relationship and Information Sharing

The following method describes a way of determining the relationship level and thereby the information level within the supplier and customer relationship. In this way one can determine different factors, such as customer/supplier relationship, supply/demand risk and uncertainty, dynamic product innovation and technology, global operations and network and business process complexity according to the different customer and supplier segments and their relationship level:

- The **customer/supplier relationship** process is the level of integration according to the relationship level in the supply chain.
- **Supply/demand risk and uncertainty** describes the level of volatility in different aspects of the company's operations such as purchasing, where shortage risks are common.
- **Dynamic product innovation and technology** describe the length of innovation cycles of a specific product. Short cycles indicate a high level of innovation which leads to a close customer and supplier relationship. Products need to be

constantly invented or reinvented. Here more information needs to be exchanged or shared between suppliers as well as customers.

- The **global operations and network** indicate the level of global operations with suppliers and customers. Widespread global operations require a higher level of information sharing.
- **Business process complexity** describes the complexity of business operations, such as the manufacturing of products. Highly complex products require a high level of information sharing as opposed to standardized products.

In the Fig. 7.4, one can see the different supply chain factors on the y-axis. The different supplier and customer segments are aligned on the x-axis. It is now possible to scale these different factors and segments in the table as low, low–medium, medium–high and high. The results from this analysis are then put into the figure on the right according to total points. Here figures for each individual segment have to be added up and placed in the chart according to segment and level of information sharing (e.g. "low" equals one point).

This analysis helps to shows the connection between supplier and customer relationships and the level of information sharing. It is not thought to be all encompassing, but much rather to show an example on how to determine the level of information sharing between the different supplier and customer relationships.

7.3.4 Positive Effects of Information Sharing

The benefits of information sharing are multifaceted. The most frequently stated achievement is the reduction of the **bullwhip effect** (Lee and Tang 1997). According to Lee et al. (2000), "the bullwhip effect is essentially the phenomenon of demand variability amplification along a supply chain, from the retailers, distributors, manufacturer, and the manufacturers' suppliers, and so on." (p. 626) This effect appears especially in conjunction with high demand uncertainty. With the publication of POS data and a coordinated exchange of demand information upstream in the supply chain, this effect can be considerably diminished (Lee et al. 2000). As a result, production and replenishment are harmonized, which lowers costs and enhances the level of customer service (Zhao et al. 2002). In this way, a mismatch between supply and demand, which can become costly due, for instance, to stock-outs, higher inventories or obsolescence, is counteracted (Simatupang and Sridharan 2002). Moreover, risks associated with high uncertainty of customer, supplier and technology are lessened by a tight strategic cooperation (Li and Lin 2006). In addition, due to a better adjustment and integration of supply chain processes, information sharing leads to reduced lead times and faster order processing (Cachon and Fisher 2000). This allows a quicker response to changes in customer demand (Li and Lin 2006).

The effects of information sharing are particularly remarkable if demand is high, demand variability is high and if lead times are long (Lee et al. 2000).

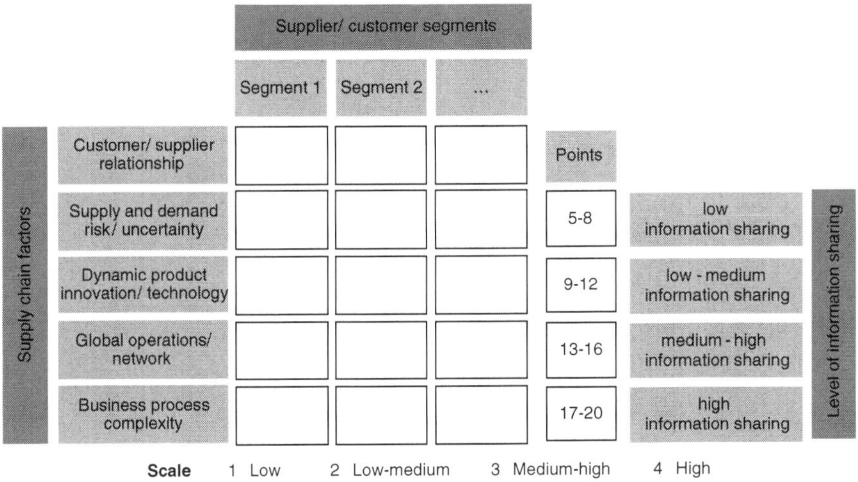

Fig. 7.4 Supply chain factors and information sharing according to different customer segments

Summing up, it can be stated that efficiency and effectiveness of a supply chain increase because of advanced information sharing, endowing the supply chain members with a long-term competitive advantage (Li and Lin 2006).

7.3.5 Negative Effects of Information Sharing

On the other hand, not all firms involved in a supply chain inevitably prefer a high degree of information sharing with the firms they are working together with. For instance, Zhao et al. (2002) claim that the effort and expenses that a retailer has in providing full information to the supplier can restrain it from cooperating, especially if its particular advantages are small. In this case, the supplier has to convince the retailer to cooperate by offering it incentives. In general, firms belonging to the same supply chain do not necessarily share the same motivations and thus the same view of information sharing; often, they pursue their own advantage first, regardless of the needs of the other supply chain members and the optimization opportunities inherent to the supply chain (Simatupang and Sridharan 2002). This individual focus regularly leads to poor supply chain performance.

Moreover, supply chain relationships are frequently characterized by distrust. The fear of appropriation of the shared information by partners and/or competitors is present in most collaborating firms (Lee and Whang 2000). Consequently, in order to prevent opportunistic behavior, many firms decide to reduce the amount of shared information (Li and Lin 2006). On top of this, firms often do not want to lose power due to the revelation of internal knowledge. However, the concern is not only directed at the immediate exploitation and publication of secrets, but also at indirect transfer, that is, the unintended leakage of information, via the partner, to direct competitors (for example, a retailer's information about the supplier to other retailers; Li 2002). Therefore, mutual trust, commitment and conforming visions of cooperation are valuable prerequisites for successful information sharing (Li and Lin 2006).

7.3.6 Enabling Information Sharing via IT Systems

As an additional factor that presupposes effective information sharing, Li and Lin (2006) name the application of intra- and inter-organizational IT systems. This is in line with the insights achieved by Sahin and Robinson (2002), stating that integrated data exchange systems facilitate the transfer of information, such as the POS, through the supply chain. Increasingly, the separate enterprise resource planning (ERP) systems are inter-organizationally connected by the use of the Internet, allowing for a more effective exchange of all data related to the production and delivery process (Christiansen et al. 2007). In the following, two examples of information sharing systems are briefly presented.

7.3.7 Information Sharing in Practice

If it is decided not to integrate the ERP systems of the individual supply chain partners, quick response (QR) is a commonly applied cooperation method (Sahin and Robinson 2002). This method is based on a reduction of the replenishment lead times, enabling the retailer to hold smaller stocks and refill inventory faster.

An often employed inter-organizational system in which the particular ERP systems are interconnected is vendor managed inventory (VMI; Sahin and Robinson 2002). Here, the supplying firm manages the inventory replenishment independently, based on the stock level at the buyer, without receiving an explicit order from the latter (Zhenxin et al. 2001).

Summary sheet

CM5: Supply chain governance

Goals of SCD Guide CM5

The aim of this SCD Guide CM5 is to propose a framework to capture the most relevant aspects of buyer–supplier interactions. Finding a method to managing customers and suppliers relations as well as the degree of information sharing in the actual production process is a further target of this chapter.

Methods and analysis for SCD Guide CM5

- Supply chain governance typology
- Relationship management framework
- Customer relationship management (CRM)
- Supplier relationship management (SRM)
- Supplier and customer relationship and information sharing

Input per method for SCD Guide CM5

	Input from other CMs	Method	Method
Method to identify buyer–supplier interactions	CM1 CM3	**Supply chain governance typology** • Complexity of transactions • Ability to codify transactions • Capabilities in the supply base • Degree of power asymmetry • Costs involved in coordinating activities	**Relationship management framework** • Relationship management intensity • Attractiveness and importance of the supplier/customer
Methods to manage customers and suppliers	CM1 CM3	**Customer relationship management (CRM)** • Relationship marketing strategies • IT-based customer management tools • Defined customer interaction models	**Supplier relationship management (SRM)** • Firm's position in the market • Financial value and operational centrality • Level of dedicated investment • The complexity of safe planning • Defined supplier interaction models
Method for information sharing in the supply chain	CM1 CM3	**Supplier and customer relationship and information sharing** • Customer and supplier relationship • Supply risk/uncertainty • Dynamic product innovation and technology • Global operations and network • Business process complexity	

Output from SCD Guide CM5

- Customer and supplier relationship
  Dimension in morphological box: Relationsh ip management (customers and suppliers)
- The degree of information sharing with different customers and suppliers
  Dimension in morphological box: information sharing

Table 7.3 Exemplary ABC analysis for customer segments (PC Manufacturing Inc.)

Customer segments	Business	Private	Public
ABC classification	A	C	B

7.4 Application Example of SCD Guide CM5 and Possible Output

The chapter has described the need for customer and supplier relationship management with regard to the supply chain differentiation process. In the following the PC Manufacturing Inc. aims to identify the hierarchy of different customer and supplier segments and align the CRM as well as SRM to this hierarchy.

Within **customer relationship management** the company has identified three different customer segments in CM1: business, private and public customers. The more important a customer segment is, the more important is the customer relationship management that is outlined in Table 7.3 with the help of ABC analysis.

The table shows the different customer segments, business, private and public customers, and their hierarchy. One can see that business customers are the most important customers for the PC Manufacturing Inc. This is due to the fact that businesses demand the largest number of PCs with the greatest regularity.

Public customers are B customers, since they demand large numbers of PCs with less regularity. The company can identify private customers as C customers, since the single customer does not demand large numbers of PCs and also does so with less regularity. A single private customer does not have the same economic weight as does breaking ties with one of one's business customers. PC Manufacturing Company has to put its emphasis on managing the A customers in order to establish a functioning customer relationship management.

Supplier relationship management follows the outline of the supplier–buyer relationship as identified in CM3. Here it is important to identify the most important suppliers versus those that are less important. In CM3, the suppliers are identified as leverage, strategic, noncritical or bottleneck suppliers.

The strategic suppliers are the most important suppliers here, since they are involved in the core competency of the company. The leverage item suppliers are the second-most important, followed by the bottleneck and noncritical suppliers.

The hierarchy of suppliers is of importance when evaluating supplier relationship management and the distribution of power between the supplier and buyer of PC Manufacturing Inc. (see CM3).

In the same way that high-priority customers have to be strongly tied to the company, suppliers also have to be managed according to their hierarchy within the supplier matrix. The company has to put strong emphasis on supplier relationship management of its important suppliers and less emphasis on its less important suppliers.

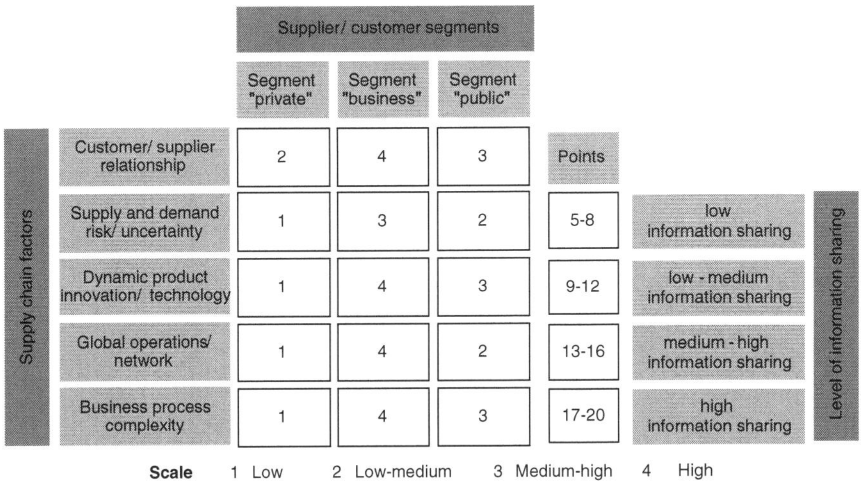

Fig. 7.5 Exemplary supply chain factors and information sharing according to different customer segments (PC Manufacturing Inc.)

The level of **information sharing** within customer and supplier relationship management is regarded differently according to the outcome of the information sharing analysis in Fig. 7.5. The segments are split into the three different identified customer segments, "private," "business" and "public". In the following they are rated as low, low–medium, medium–high and high according to five different factors. The sum of the numbers is then placed into the chart to detect the level of information sharing. Here it can be seen that private customers enjoy a low level of information sharing, whereas business customers garner a high level of information sharing and public customers enjoy a medium–high level of information sharing.

PC Manufacturing Inc. tries to focus on satisfying all customer and supplier needs. However, it is of utmost importance to put an emphasis on the level of information sharing according to the importance of each individual customer and supplier, in order to distribute the given resources in the most efficient manner.

In the following morphological box (Fig. 7.6), one can fill in the different levels of relationship management and information sharing according to the different suppliers and customer segments. It can be seen that relationship management is closely tied to the level of information sharing between supplier and buyer. Therefore noncritical suppliers display a low level of information sharing according to the previous analysis, which suggests a transaction-based relationship management between the supplier and PC Manufacturing Inc.

On the customer side, the segments are separated according to customer segment "private". In the same way customer relationships are connected to the level of information sharing, which means private customers have a low level of information sharing due to their transaction-based customer relationship.

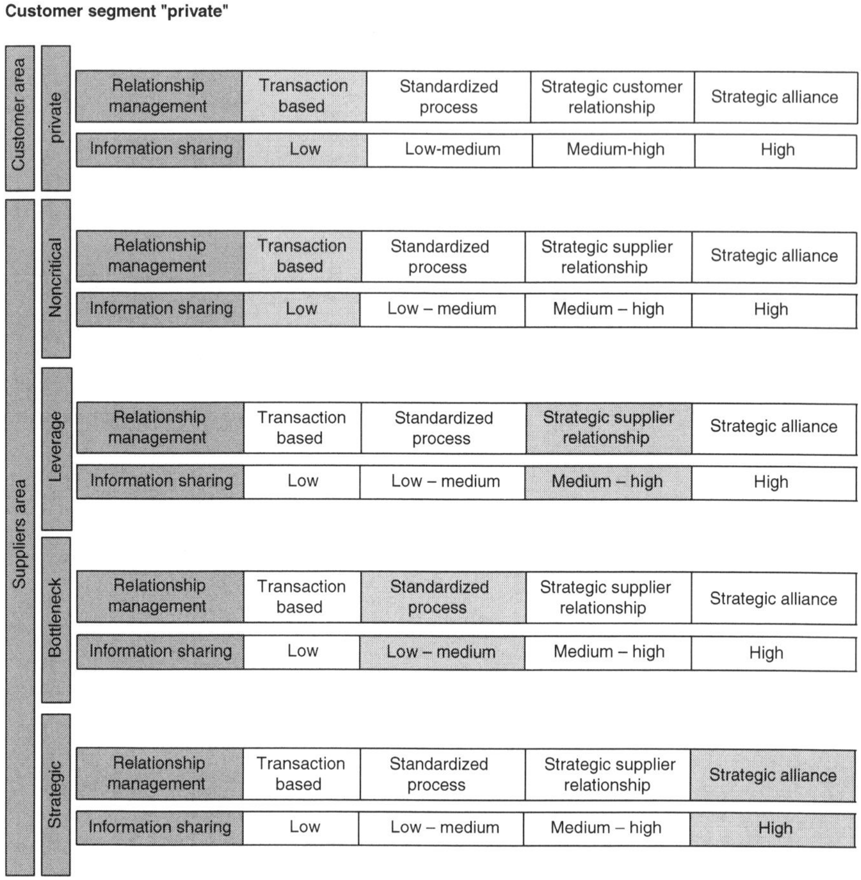

Fig. 7.6 Exemplary morphological box, Content Module 5

References

Ballou, R. H. (2004). *Business logistics/supply chain management: Planning, organizing, and controlling the supply chain* (5th ed.). Upper Saddle River, NJ: Pearson Prentice Hall.

Bensaou, M. (1999). Portfolios of buyer-supplier relationships. (Cover story). *Sloan Management Review, 40*(4), 35–44.

Cachon, G. P., & Fisher, M. (2000). Supply chain inventory management and the value of shared information. *Management Science, 46*(8), 1032–1048.

Chen, L., & Lee, H. L. (2009). Information sharing and order variability control under a generalized demand model. *Management Science, 55*(5), 781–797.

Chopra, S., & Meindl, P. (2007). *Supply chain management: Strategy, planning, and operation* (3rd ed.). Upper Saddle River, NJ: Pearson Prentice Hall.

Christiansen, P. E., Kotzab, H., & Mikkola, J. H. (2007). Coordination and sharing logistics information in leagile supply chains. *International Journal of Procurement Management, 1*(1), 79–96.

Christopher, M., Peck, H., & Towill, D. R. (2006). A taxonomy for selecting global supply chain strategies. *International Journal of Logistics Management, 17*(2), 277–287.

Cox, A., Lonsdale, C., Watson, G., & Qiao, H. (2003). Supplier relationship management: A framework for understanding managerial capacity and constraints. *European Business Journal, 15*(3), 135–145.

Cox, A., Sanderson, J., & Watson, G. (2001). Supply chains and power regimes: toward an analytic framework for managing extended networks of buyer and supplier relationships. *Journal of Supply Chain Management, 37*(2), 28–35.

Cooper, M. C., Lambert, D. M., & Pagh, J. D. (1997). Supply chain management: More than a new name for logistics. *International Journal of Logistics Management, 8*(1), 1–14.

Croxton, K. L., García-Dastugue, S. J., Lambert, D. M., & Rogers, D. S. (2001). The supply chain management processes. *International Journal of Logistics Management, 12*(2), 13–36.

Gereffi, G., Humphrey, J., & Sturgeon, T. (2005). The governance of global value chains. *Review of International Political Economy, 12*(1), 78–104.

Homburg, C., & Krohmer, H. (2006). *Marketingmanagement: strategie—instrumente—umsetzung—unternehmensführung* (2nd ed.). Wiesbaden: Gabler.

Hoyt, J., & Huq, F. (2000). From arms-length to collaborative relationships in the supply chain. *International Journal of Physical Distribution & Logistics Management., 30*(9), 750.

Kraljic, P. (1983). Purchasing must become supply management. *Harvard Business Review, 61*(5), 109–117.

Lee, H. L., & Tang, C. S. (1997). Modelling the costs and benefits of delayed product differentiation. *Management Science, 43*(1), 40.

Lee, H. L., So, K. C., & Tang, C. S. (2000). The value of information sharing in a two-level supply chain. *Management Science, 46*(5), 626.

Lee, H. L., & Whang, S. (2000). Information sharing in a supply chain. *International Journal of Manufacturing Technology and Management, 1*(1), 79–93.

Li, L. (2002). Information sharing in a supply chain with horizontal competition. *Management Science, 48*(9), 1196–1212.

Li, S., & Lin, B. (2006). Accessing information sharing and information quality in supply chain management. *Decision Support Systems, 42*(3), 1641–1656.

Parvatiyar, A., & Sheth, J. N. (2001). Customer relationship management: Emerging practice, process, and discipline. *Journal of Economic and Social Research, 3*(2), 1.

Park, J., Shin, K., Chang, T.-W., & Park, J. (2010). An integrative framework for supplier relationship management. *Industrial Management & Data Systems., 110*(4), 495–515.

Payne, A., & Frow, P. (2005). A strategic framework for customer relationship management. *Journal of Marketing, 69*(4), 167–176.

Sahin, F., & Robinson, E. P. (2002). Flow coordination and information sharing in supply chains: Review, implications, and directions for future research. *Decision Sciences, 33*(4), 505–536.

Simatupang, T. M., & Sridharan, R. (2002). The collaborative supply chain. *International Journal of Logistics Management, The, 13*(1), 15–30.

Stevens, G. C. (1993). Integrating the supply chain. *International Journal of Physical Distribution & Logistics Management., 19*(8), 3–8.

Stuart, F. I. (1997). Supply-chain strategy: Organizational influence through supplier alliances. *British Journal of Management, 8*(3), 223.

Wathne, K. H., & Heide, J. B. (2004). Relationship governance in a supply chain network. *Journal of Marketing, 68*(1), 73–89.

Williamson, O. E. (1985). *The economic institutions of capitalism: Firms*. New York: Markets Relational Contracting.

Zhao, X., Xie, J., & Zhang, W. J. (2002). The impact of information sharing and ordering coordination on supply chain performance. *Supply Chain Management: An International Journal, 7*(1), 24–40.

Zhenxin, Y., Yan, H., & Cheng, T. C. E. (2001). Benefits of information sharing with supply chain partnerships. *Industrial Management and data System, 101*(3/4), 114–119.

CM6: Supporting Activities—Project Management and Human Resources

8

8.1 Goals of Content Module 6

The goal of this chapter is to show the importance of positioning supply chain management within corporate management. In this context, organizational alignment of supply chain management is supported by three management methods. First, cooperation between different organizational functions is fostered if it is specifically appreciated and rewarded by upper management. Second, the installation of integrating personnel, such as project managers, facilitates the embedding of supply chain management in the corporation. Last, spatial proximity is traditionally conducive to organizational alignment, as communication and cooperation prove to be less complicated here (Fig. 8.1).

In the following, a framework is presented that shows what integration of supply chain management into a firm can look like, demonstrated through the utilization of a project management method. Moreover, the implications that the organizational alignment of supply chain management has for the management of human resources (HR) are considered.

8.2 Supply Chain Project Management

Ayers (2004) framework for describing the integration of a supply chain project into a corporation's structure is presented, which itself applied the project management maturity model (PMMM) developed by Kerzner (2001).

Ayers (2004) analyzes the five different stages of the PMMM model against the background of three organizational levels on which projects can take place: the **functional, company** and **supply chain** level. In addition, with respect to the character of projects, he distinguishes between **nonstrategic** and **strategic** projects. Nonstrategic projects are less important to a firm, as they are targeted at the fulfillment of short-term goals. Normally, these projects are evaluated by daily

E. Hofmann et al., *The Supply Chain Differentiation Guide*,
DOI: 10.1007/978-3-642-31936-5_8, © Springer-Verlag Berlin Heidelberg 2012

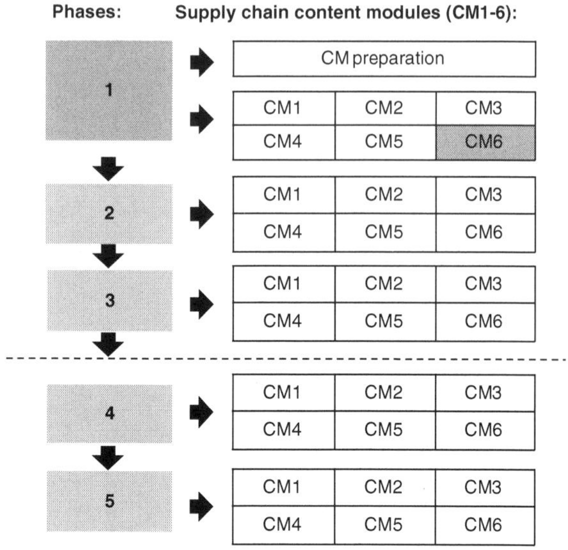

Fig. 8.1 Position of Chap. 8 in the SCD Guide

business measurements (such as profit). By contrast, strategic projects are of high importance, contributing to a firm's long-term success by shaping its competitive position.

8.2.1 The Project Management Maturity Model

The PMMM expresses "an organization's position on the maturity continuum" (Ayers 2004), judging the quality of a firm's project integration practice. Its five levels, which cover a spectrum ranging from **common language** to **continuous improvement**, are briefly introduced below:

(1) If a project management approach is characterized by a **common language**, some awareness of a need for project management exists; however, there is hardly any support by the upper management, the responsibility stays at the functional level. Moreover, tools of application are only used occasionally. Members of the organization are aware of the appreciation of project management, however, they are not competent in its execution. Project training and development are disregarded.

(2) On the next project management maturity level, **common processes**, basic understanding of project management techniques can be found, which are expressed in staff training efforts and the operation of project control methods. The increased importance of project management shows the significance of projects for the firm's success. Support increases on this level. Specialists are trained and the recognition of the need for processes and methodologies is recognized. Projects are tracked according to a cost accounting system and

necessary changes are made. The end of this phase is marked by the development of project life cycles, the formulation of a project management methodology accompanied by training, a commitment by executive management, resistance to scope changes (usually in the form of scope creep) and the implementation of project management software which covers costs and schedule.

(3) If project management achieves a level of **singular methodology**, "project mode" then becomes an inherent part of the corporate management culture. As projects are linked to the corporation's strategy, support is ensured throughout the entire firm. The performance of project management determines the success of the corporation. One of the implications of this can be that the organization adopts the best methodology and further develops it. Another aspect could be that the organization has a common process for use throughout the organization. There are several different components connected to this level. *Integrated process* means that there are no separate product development or change management projects. *Cultural support* implies that the entire organization supports the process. *Management support at all levels* refers to the support by all managers and project managers at the senior management level. Managers support their staff with joint accountability and alternative plans if needed. *Informal project management* is a methodology which can be adapted to each individual project. Informality furthermore strengthens communication within the project. The control tools include guidelines and checklists. *The return on investment from project management training and education* is an ongoing topic. *Behavioral excellence* refers to the recognition within the organization that this is not equal to day-to-day operation. This does not, however, guarantee success.

(4) The next stage on the PMMM scale is defined as **benchmarking**. In addition to an appreciation of project management as a determinant of a company's success, the need for constant improvement receives increasing attention. Designated efforts are undertaken to find improvement potentials. To do this, the perspective is broadened, going beyond corporate boundaries. Projects and their management are the core of the firm's strategy, often proceeding on a network (supply chain) level. Benchmarking is a prominent technique to identify ways to improve the project management culture. Thereby new software approaches can be identified. It is important that each project within the program has a similar format for tracking progress, including the use of variable milestones. A form of reporting using an easily accessed project management tool is also essential in providing transparency about progress.

(5) The most comprehensive level is termed **continuous improvement**. Here, improvement is obtained by a high degree of knowledge exchange between project teams. Consequently, project management practices and advancements are implemented corporation-wide. Similar to the benchmarking level, major projects are characteristic for the corporation. This fifth level requires "eternal" improvements. Examples of such measures include procedural documentation, organizationally tailored project management methodologies,

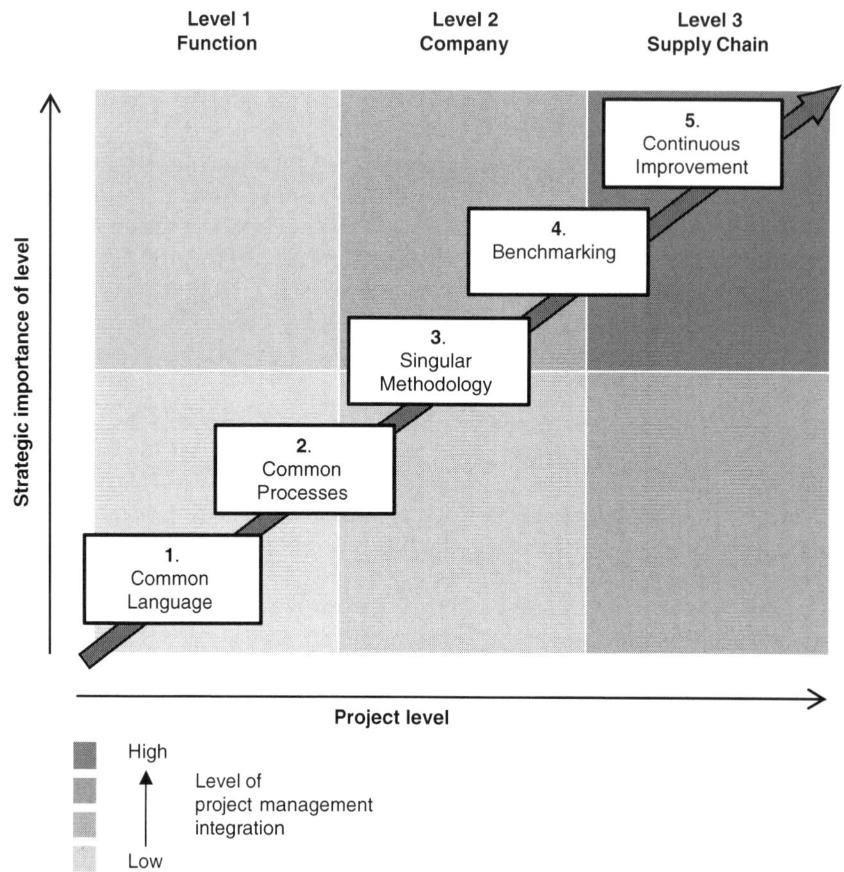

Fig. 8.2 A majority framework of supply chain project management, adopted from Ayers (2004)

capacity planning and capacity models. All of these categories represent a major effort. Project management skills are argued to be strategic assets.

There are two different types of projects, **strategic** and **nonstrategic**, seen on the y-axis of Fig. 8.2. Different types of strategic projects include changing the basis for competition, proprietary product and process technology, market-based justification and broad sponsorship. Different types of nonstrategic projects include fixing problems, nonproprietary technology, ROI, cash flow justification and functional sponsorship (Ayers 2004).

Next, the PMMM is set against the background of the previously introduced supply chain projects. The correlations are depicted in Fig. 8.2.

According to the ranking of various degrees of supply chain project management maturity, a corporation can assess its current position and set future goals for its supply chain project management performance.

Clearly, it can be postulated that not all types of corporations inevitably need the most sophisticated level of project management; as the respective characteristics of the various maturity levels indicate, project management is of pivotal importance if a firm's core businesses are primarily managed in projects. Bridging to the supply chain strategy context, this is the case if flexibility is the main driver, which means that an agile strategy is in operation. By contrast, if a firm's value generation is performed more in a continuous fashion than in a project fashion, high project management maturity is less relevant. This is the case if a lean strategy prevails.

8.2.2 Challenges of Supply Chain Management Projects

Projects in supply chain management often come with challenges, which arise from the complexity of supply chain management itself. Complexity in a supply chain management project arises from the number of participants in the project. Even if the project is "only" an intra-company project, several decision makers normally have to be involved, managers from purchasing, manufacturing and distribution. To bring consensus to a group of decision makers from different functional areas is a crucial task in a supply chain management project that requires sophisticated conflict resolution skills on the part of the project manager. Often whole projects in supply chain management fail due to a disagreement between functional managers.

A more difficult situation for the project leader arises in cases of inter-company projects in which not only the opinions of internal stakeholders have to be considered, but the opinions of stakeholders from associated companies as well. While the coordination of intra-company projects already consumes a lot of time, inter-company coordination becomes the main task of a project manager in supply chain projects. Furthermore, inter-company coordination requires a higher degree of sensitivity, since whole business relationships may be damaged by insufficient project manager skills. Inter-organizational boards represent one way of dealing with challenges arising from inter-company supply chain projects; they are described in the following subsection.

A further trigger of complexity in supply chain management projects is the number of flows influenced by such projects. Besides the physical flow, supply chain projects have to consider the flow of information and often even the financial flow. In most cases this results in an even higher number of involved stakeholders, since IT and finance managers have to be integrated into the project.

8.2.3 Inter-Organizational Boards

The higher the degree of integration in relationship management, the more it is advisable to have inter-organizational boards to coordinate the shared projects. Table 8.1 shows the different levels of implementation of inter-organizational boards in the supply chain management of a company. Thereby it can be seen that

Table 8.1 Level of implementation of inter-organizational board

Relationship level	Level of implementation
1 Strategic alliances	Implementation of organizational boards
2 Strategic supplier/ customer relationship	Implementation of organizational boards
3 Standardized process adjustment	Situational implementation of inter-organizational boards
4 Transaction based	No implementation of inter-organizational boards

strategic alliances and the strategic supplier and customer relationship implement inter-organizational boards, whereas in standardized process adjustments there is a situational implementation of inter-organizational boards depending on the level of cost reductions which can be expected from the cooperation. The transaction-based relationship does not include any implementation of inter-organizational boards. The level of strategic importance of the relationship to suppliers indicates that the level of implementation is aligned accordingly.

In Fig. 8.3, the supporting boards and committees of an industrial enterprise can be seen in a schematic overview. The boards are divided into four different boards which include the **executive governance council**, the **supplier advisory board**, the **customer advisory board** and the **senior-level supply chain executive**.

The goal of the **executive governance council** is to coordinate across the internal barriers in the supply chain activities of a company in order for the process to be success oriented.

The group of participants in the governance council largely consists of managers with divisional responsibilities, who have the power to allocate resources and thereby support the coordination of upstream and downstream companies as well as service providers. The interaction of managers reduces transactional costs, resources can be applied more efficiently and capacities fully utilized.

Through the harmonization of processes, the supply of better performance levels in service and quality can be guaranteed. The group can meet on a regular basis to align its processes and adapt newly proposed changes. With the establishment of this group it is possible to prepare the implementation phase of supply chain initiatives.

The **customer advisory board** creates a link between the company and the customer. Customers should be integrated into the development and optimization of supply chain processes in companies. The customer advisory board should have bi-annual meetings in order to talk about the performance of the company. The inviting company obtains insight into the most important interests and requirements of the downstream supply chain companies. Personal or behavioral aspects can make processes more efficient.

The **supplier advisory board** creates a link between the supplier and the company. The inter-disciplinary supplier advisory board functions on different

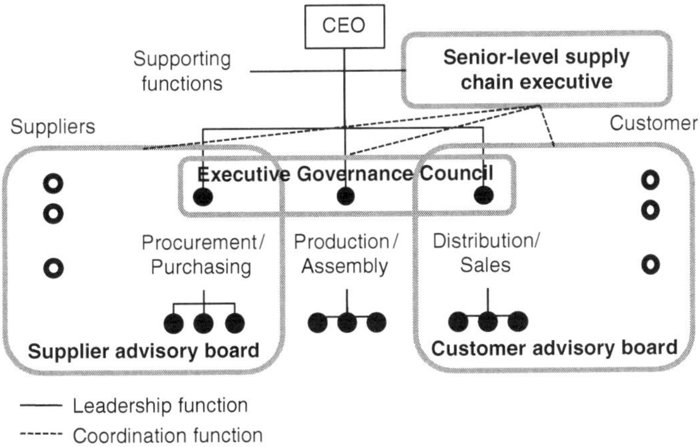

Fig. 8.3 Schematic overview of supporting boards and committees in an industrial enterprise

business levels within a company and creates decentralized purchasing and procurement structures.

Directly under the CEO is the **senior-level supply chain executive,** who coordinates the different supply chain areas of the company. One advantage of this institutionalization is that the whole process, from procurement and purchasing to the distribution of products and after sales service is subordinate to one person or one unit. Problems can be directly eliminated at the links between the different departments.

Table 8.2 shows a list of different alternatives which can be implemented in the development of a strategy or initiative in the supply chain context. It represents a selection of possibilities for institutionalizing supply chain management. In the table the boards and committees are listed on the action level with the relevant group of participants and their goals as well as possible results.

8.3 Human Resources in Supply Chain Management

8.3.1 The Role of Human Resource Management in Supply Chain Management

It has become apparent during the previous considerations that a successful integration of supply chain management into a corporation becomes increasingly important for the achievement of long-term strategic goals. As Christopher (2000) recognizes, it is especially of central relevance that the mindset of staff members supports the integration.

Table 8.2 Structural supporting mechanisms on the action level

	Participants	Objective	Result
Executive governance council	• Divisional leadership	• Overcoming internal barriers to supply chain initiatives • Harmonization of internal objectives with superior the supply chain initiatives	• Goal-oriented application of resources, optimal capacity utilization and strategic conform ratio of minimizing costs and maximizing flexibility • High performance level (degrees of service and quality) for the end customer
Customer advisory boards	• Representing the company from sales as well as marketing and if needed logistics • Significant downstream companies (customer)	• Insight over relevant requests and interests of other companies	• Commitment of resources and capacities according to the customer requirements • Less conflicts in the network
Supplier advisory board	• Representative of the company from the purchasing or production and if needed logistics • Significant upstream of the companies (suppliers)	• Insight into the relevant requests and interest other companies	• Application of resources and capacities according to the ability of suppliers • Less conflicts in the network
Senior level supply chain executive	• Position directly under the CEO	• Company internal processes, from the procurement to the production and distribution to the after sales, will be subordinate to a person or an organization	• Continuos process transparency and process steering on the action level • Support of the decision-making in the supply chain network

8.3.2 Human Resource Risks in Supply Chain Management

In line with this insight, Noe et al. (2006) name **motivational risk** as one out of four identified risks that human resource management (HRM) has to deal with. They acknowledge that a lack of acceptance and motivation from the employees' side considerably handicaps supply chain performance. In addition, **shortage risk, adaptation risk** and **risk of quitting** are spotted as major risks; shortage risk considers the deficiency of qualified personnel for enabling smooth supply chain processes; adaptation risk is concerned with the appropriate qualification of the appointed staff; risk of quitting deals with the efforts at retaining key supply chain personnel.

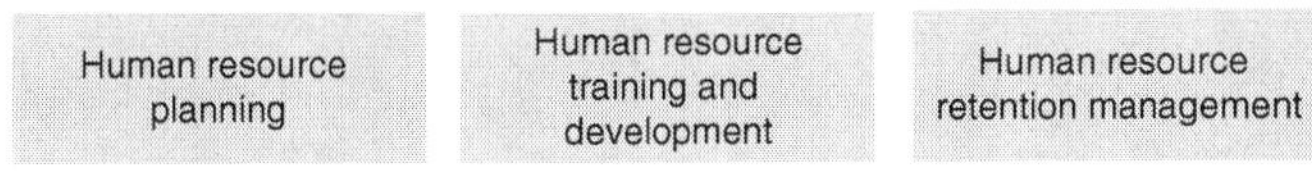

Fig. 8.4 Human resource risk prevention

Fig. 8.5 Steps to human resource planning in supply chain management, according to Noe et al. (2006)

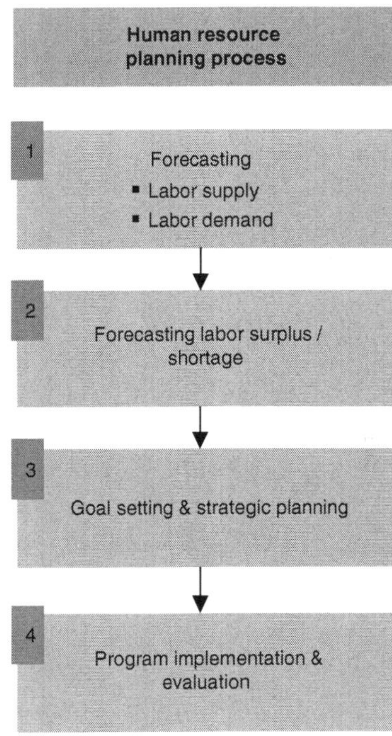

8.3.3 Prevention of Human Resource Risk in Supply Chain Management

According to Noe et al. (2006), these four major human resource risks can be addressed via the three aspects of HRM, which are strategic **human resource planning**, **human resource training and development** and **human resource retention** (Fig. 8.4).

Strategic **human resource planning** highlights the current and future human resource needs of supply chain management. Its main goal is to guarantee the maintenance of a qualified supply chain personnel base, in order to assure competitiveness. Human resource planning establishes long-term recruitment planning aiming at fulfilling organizational goals. In Fig. 8.5 one can see the implementation process of human resource planning. Reasons for human resource risks in this area can be the unawareness of future human resource needs as well as the lack of standardized procedures for identifying and recruiting personnel. Furthermore,

Fig. 8.6 Different human resource development levels in supply chain management

there are no methods available to systematically screen the labor market. Human resource planning is disconnected from overarching strategic goals and the effectiveness of human resource programs is not measured.

The human resource planning implementation process consists out of a four-step plan which involves forecasting of labor supply and demand, the forecasting of labor surplus or shortage, goal setting and strategic planning as well as program implementation and evaluation (Fig. 8.5). The long-term human resource planning processes prevent the risk of shortage within a company.

Human resource training and development deals with the maintenance and advancement of the skills and qualifications of the staff members. The main objective of this aspect is to adjust the employees' capabilities to the constant changes in the work environment, as well as refining their skills in order to achieve a better performance. Human resource development ensures ongoing employee training and support in light of the latest organizational and competitive needs.

The greater the change in the external environment, the greater is the need for internal training and development to prepare employees for altered job requirements. Guidelines for training and development include formal education (e.g. MBA programs), assessment (performance appraisal and feedback), job experience (on-the-job learning), and interpersonal relationships (e.g. mentoring). These measures enable and encourage continuous learning. The implementation process of human resource training and development with consideration for the different levels of human resource development (Fig. 8.6) prevent the aforementioned risk of adaptation.

Finally, **human resource retention** covers the challenge of motivating skilled supply chain employees to stay at the focal firm. This provides the firm with benefits in the long run, by assuring organizational stability, competitive advantage through skilled personnel and low human resource recruiting and employee turnover costs. Human resource retention management develops competitive compensation and development schemes to retain high-performing personnel and decreases employee turnover.

There are various different factors for successful retention: leadership, employee engagement and compensation.

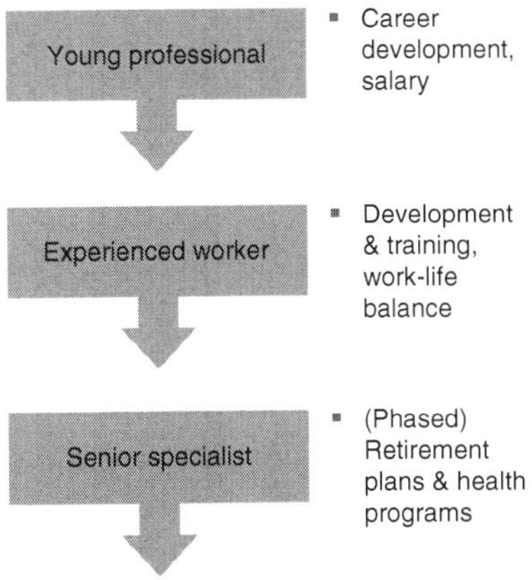

Fig. 8.7 Addressing changing employee interest with human resource retention management in supply chain management

Leadership has to keep employees updated about current organizational skills. **Employment engagement** improves the degree to which employees are committed to their jobs. **Compensation** implies a striving for fairness and transparency. Furthermore, each individual or team performance needs to be rewarded. This includes a balance of fixed and variable compensation.

By addressing changing employee interests, human resource retention management can manage to suit each employee (Fig. 8.7). Successful employee retention always presupposes awareness of employees' changing needs and desires during their tenure and appropriate measures to address them in order to prevent the risk of quitting.

All these measures can are developed in order to avoid the risks to human resources. In the TO-BE situation, these human resource risks should be avoided with the help of the different human resource measures. Furthermore, two different dimensions increase employee motivation significantly: are job content, on one hand, and the work environment, on the other.

- **Job content** should be structured in a way that employees perceive meaningfulness in their jobs, that they have responsibility and that they receive feedback and opportunities for improvement and performance-based compensation.
- On the other hand, the **work environment** needs to have positive effects on employee morale ensuring that the employee actively embraces corporate values and norms and can recognize and adhere to leadership guidelines. Furthermore, employee empowerment and participation should be encouraged.

8.3.4 Human Resource Planning in Supply Chain Management

Human resource planning in supply chain management is the basis for human resource activities. Here the human resource department detects the human resource demand in order to allocate capacities for the right department.

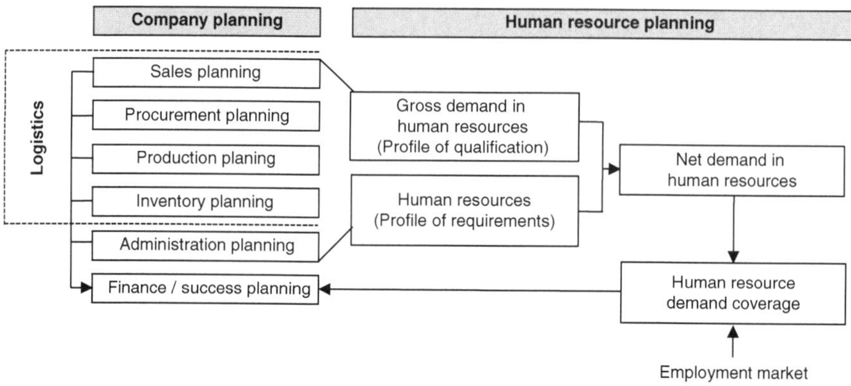

Fig. 8.8 Interdependencies between company and human resource planning in logistics systems (Pfohl 2009)

The main responsibility of human resource planning is the provision of human resources. In this section it is important to plan the short-, medium- and long-term demand for human resources. Human resources have to be allocated in the right time and quality. The human resource department therefore has to identify the demand for human resources according to the objectives of the supply chain (Fig. 8.8). Human resource planning is an integral part of company planning and therefore has to be aligned with the other departments such as production, procurement and inventory. Human resource planning mainly follows sales planning, since the latter provides information about the estimated volume and cost of products.

The gross demand for human resources can be derived by estimation. The difference between human resources and the gross demand for human resources represents the net demand for human resources. The supply of human resources then covers the human resource demand. Here it is important to sufficiently cover the human resource demand in the right quantity and quality. There is a significant difference between the internal and external recruitment process. Since the recruitment of new personnel from external sources proves to be extremely difficult, companies try to recruit personnel internally or train employees themselves. Another aspect is the outsourcing process within HRM, which has a wide relevance for supply chain management (Pfohl 2009).

8.3.5 Human Resource Development and Training

One of the responsibilities of supply chain managers is to deal with the qualification and training of personnel. In this way the right number of employees as well as the qualification of each individual employee can be guaranteed. In order to gain the best possible result, personnel has to receive training in professional, social as

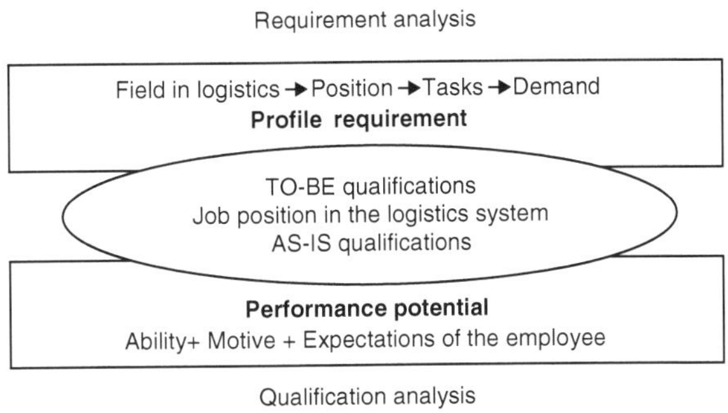

Fig. 8.9 TO-BE and AS-IS qualifications at the job position level in the logistics system (Pfohl 2009)

well as personal qualifications. In order to close the gaps between the demanded skills and qualifications, employees have a need for development and training which are performed during the course of work. Qualifications demand the coherence of performance potential of an employee, which is shown in Fig. 8.9.

The comparison between job requirements and performance potential shows the deficits of each individual employee. This gap can be closed with on-the-job training and development training. Oftentimes in logistics, training and development measures are limited to security training or introductory training. Here further emphasis needs to be put on training employees in order to further strengthen their professional qualifications.

8.3.6 Supply Chain Manager Development and Training

It is the task of a supply chain manager to manage current and future management tasks and to adopt the knowledge needed previously by managers in order to train future managers. In this way the company can secure the future management, selection and development of future managers. An increasing level of performance by supply chain managers and the improvement of internal communications can be secured through these measures (Pfohl 2009).

This helps to meet company goals and to train future managers in order to fulfill tasks more efficiently. Different measures can include the knowledge transfer of logistics-related subjects and logistics technology. Supply chain managers are trained by trainee programs, training courses, the exchange of experiences between current and future supply chain managers, case studies and role playing. Here the focus lies on the individual, who needs to be prepared for future challenges and responsibilities. This furthermore includes the frequent change of job positions, which deepens and widens the knowledge and the responsibilities of each manager. Moreover, the goal is to increase flexibility and develop a qualified team of supply chain managers. Managers need to be aware that the changing environment around them requires a willingness toward flexibility. Changes within the company can be much more easily dealt with (Pfohl 2009).

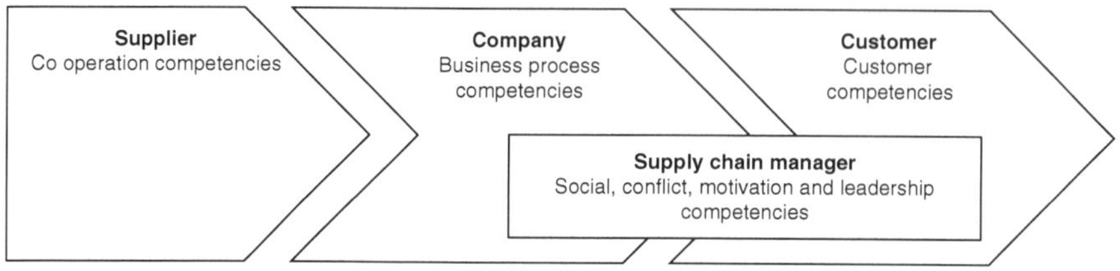

Fig. 8.10 Area of application of the basic competencies in supply chain management (Rudolph et al. 2007)

8.3.7 Employee Competencies in Supply Chain Management

Successful supply chain management only works through the collaboration of different fields of competencies. The competency approach outlines different important competencies which need to be in place in order to gain long-term success within the competition. They address problems and challenges within the supply chain. The most obvious barriers are problems in the flow of information, missing or contradictory success measurement factors, the mishandling of cooperation partners, missing vision, the fear of changing processes, lack of commitment on the part of employees, limited resources and an overall inability on the part of the employee to fulfill the tasks required (Rudolph et al. 2007).

The competencies are needed for different areas of the company. The most important aspect is the company itself, where internal synchronization and interdisciplinary transparency of processes can be reached with the help of business process competencies. Furthermore, there are suppliers, customers as well as the supply chain manager, who are all responsible for managing competencies, as seen in Fig. 8.10. Suppliers require co-operational competencies, as well as customer competencies. The supply chain manager needs to establish social, conflictual, motivational and leadership competencies in order to successfully lead the supply chain. The competencies are closely related to one another, which means that they cannot be developed independently of each other, but only in parallel. The systematic development of process supporting competencies is one of the core elements (Pfohl 2009).

The main competencies which are shown in Fig. 8.10 are described further in the following.

- The importance of **co-operational competencies** becomes apparent when looking at the vast changing market environment involved in competing with other supply chains. The selection of suppliers is thereby crucial for the success of the company. The efficiency and effectiveness of the supply chain can be increased through cooperation within the supplier-and-buyer relationship.
- Business process competencies represent the practical implementation of the market-related "core" activities of a company, which are directly related to customer requirements. Besides lowering process costs and procurement times, quality and performance need to be aligned to customer requirements. The

tendency to focus on the "core" competencies of the company often leads to an outsourcing process of part of the supply chain. The structure of network in the supply chain has thereby changed significantly and its scope has been further extended. Business process competencies demand that supply chain managers handle internal processes and supervise the supply chain and overall operations. Process and activity structures contribute to the fact that processes within the company follow a similar pattern, which leads to a process of standardization. The development and training of activity processes are the main tasks of process management. This requires an open mindset and the strong will to overcome existing barriers.

- The main goal of **customer competencies** is to know and understand customer requirements in depth. Procurement has to know and understand customer requirements and recognize consumer trends, because of the effect that they have on consumer behavior. The manager often has to overcome several different organizational and cultural barriers in order to come to know customer requirements.
- **Social competencies** describe the competencies that the supply chain manager needs in order to deal with supply chain partners. The establishment of a network and a relationship of trust with all parties involved demands social competencies on the part of the supply chain manager. These competencies help the supply chain manager to create strategic cooperation between the purchasing department and suppliers. Social competencies within procurement are important in the establishment of a network with strong business partners. Increasingly, the supply chain managers have to show social competencies in order to gain the trust and openness of their suppliers, which is the result of a diverse network and training.
- Leading teams and supply chains can lead to different conflict situations for the supply chain manager. **Conflictual competencies** are therefore important competencies which are needed by a supply chain manager. Conflicts need to be resolved in a constructive and solution-oriented manner. This requires a lot of experience on the part of the supply chain manager. Conflictual competencies are strongly intertwined with customer as well as business process competencies. In different departments, there is a demand for diplomacy as well as strong negotiating skills. Due to the differences in company cultures and structures between supplier and buyer, as well as the position in the supply chain, there is a higher potential for conflict. The conflictual competencies are related to the motivational and leadership competencies of an individual. Problems within interpersonal relationships cannot be eliminated completely, but are the symptoms of complex conversion processes.
- Motivational competencies and leadership competencies become increasingly important when talking about the competencies of a supply chain manager. Modern methods of global procurement lead to further international networks. There are more and more procurement departments which consist of international teams. The supply chain manager has to take the different backgrounds of teams and individuals into account and guarantee strong cohesion between the

members of the team. The team requires a coherent process of information sharing among all team members. Motivated employees thereby pass on their motivation to customers, which leads to increased customer satisfaction. The different cultural backgrounds within the team create barriers to the leadership style of the supply chain manager. The supply chain manager therefore has to carefully deal with the different academic and personal backgrounds of each individual employee (Rudolph et al. 2007).

Summary sheet

CM6: Supporting activities: Project management and human resources

Goals of SCD-Guide CM6

The aim of this SCD-Guide content module 6 is to judge a company's project integration practice by using the PMMM method. The integration of Human Resource Management (HRM) is becoming increasingly important. Different methods in human resource management can effectively help to prevent human resource risks.

Methods and analysis for SCD-Guide CM6

- The project management maturity model (PMMM)
- Human resource risks in supply chain management

Input per methods for SCD-Guide CM6

	Input from other CMs	Method	
Method in judging a project integration practice	(None)	**The project management maturity model (PMMM)** • Project level • Strategic importance	
Method preventing human resource risks	(None)	**Human resource risks in supply chain management** • Future human resource needs of supply chain management • Forecasting of labor supply and demand • Human resource development levels	
Supply chain competencies	(None)	**Supply chain manager competencies** • Social competencies • Conflict competencies • Motivation competencies • Leadership competencies	**Supply chain competencies** • Cooperation competencies • Business process competencies • Customer competencies

Output from SCD-Guide CM6

- Adequate level of project management identified
  Dimension in morphological box: Supply chain project management
- Prevention of human resource risks in supply chain management
  Dimension in morphological box: Supply chain process management (Human resources)

Table 8.3 Human resource risks for PC Manufacturing Inc

Human resource risks	Motivation risk	✔
	Shortage risk	✔
	Adaptation risk	✔
	Risk of quitting	✔

8.4 Application Example of SCD Guide CM6 and Possible Output

This chapter has outlined the supporting activities for companies including project management and human resource activities which should be implemented by PC Manufacturing Inc.

PC Manufacturing Inc. identifies in this context the importance of project management within its operations. In this way one is able to measure the quality of a firm's project integration practice. According to its framework of supply chain project management, the company is classified at the third level, that of **singular methodology**. "Project mode" is thus an integrated part of the corporate management culture at PC Manufacturing Inc. The performance of project management determines overall success here. By determining the level of project management integration, PC Manufacturing Inc. can determine its current position as well as determine its future project performance.

In the following the different measures for the role of HRM within PC Manufacturing Inc. are shown. Table 8.3 shows that human resource risks such as motivational risk, shortage risk, adaptation risk and risk of quitting are major threats to PC Manufacturing Inc. These can be prevented by making human resource measures such as human resource planning, human resource training and development and human resource retention an integral part of the human resource strategy. In this way PC Manufacturing Inc. tries to secure minimal human resource risks.

In the morphological box, it is possible to fill in the TO-BE situation of supply chain project management as well as the supply chain process management (human resources). The level of project management implemented can be identified and filled into the morphological box (Fig. 8.11).

Furthermore, the human resource risks such as shortage risk, risk of quitting, adaptation risk and motivational risk are within the morphological box. In the following, PC Manufacturing Inc. should focus on avoiding these risks by further implementing different human resource measures such as strategic human resource planning, human resource training and development and human resource retention. In a TO-BE situation, these risks have been avoided through the implementation of the human resource measures and therefore do not need to be filled in within the morphological box (Fig. 8.11).

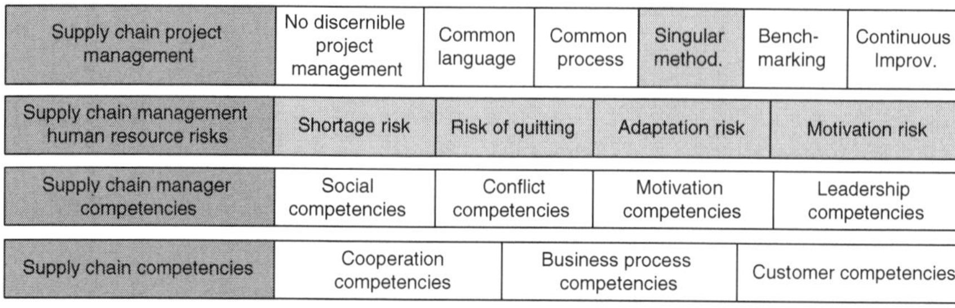

Fig. 8.11 Exemplary morphological box, Content Module 6

The supply chain competencies such as the co-operational, business process and customer competencies, as well as the supply chain manager competencies such as the social, conflictual, motivational and leadership competencies should be in place in order for the supply chain to function effectively.

References

Ayers, J. B. (2004). *Supply chain project management: a structured collaborative and measurable approach*. Boca Raton: St. Lucie Press.

Christopher, M. (2000). The agile supply chain. *Industrial Marketing Management, 29*(1), 37–44.

Kerzner, H. (2001). *Strategic planning for project management using a project management maturity model*. New York: John Wiley.

Noe, R. A., Hollenbeck, J. R., Gerhart, B. A., & Wright, P. M. (2006). *Human resource management: gaining a competitive advantage* (5th ed.). Boston: McGraw-Hill/Irwin.

Pfohl, H.-C. (2009). *Personalführung in der Logistik: Innovative Ansätze und praktische Lösungen* (2nd ed.). Hamburg: DVV Media Group Dt. Verkehrs-Verl.

Rudolph, T., Drenth, R., & Meise, N. (2007). *Kompetenzen für Supply Chain Manager* (1st ed.). s.l.: Springer.

Part III
Phases 2 to 5: From the AS-IS Analysis to the Selection and Implementation Preparation of Specific Corrective Actions

Phase 2: Identification of AS-IS Supply Chain and Analysis 9

9.1 Goals of SCD-Phase 2

This chapter aims at providing a semi-structured questionnaire to analyze the current AS-IS state of a supply chain by gathering information about its current configuration (Fig. 9.1).

In order to assess the AS-IS configuration of the supply chain holistically, aspects of customer and supplier segmentation, supply chain strategy, manufacturing-related aspects, supply chain processes, supply chain governance, and the efficiency of supply chain management integration are covered. The contents of these topics are briefly summarized below in Fig. 9.2.

The semi-structured questionnaire presents a guided approach which follows the structure of the morphological box within the SCD Guideline. Here, closed as well as open questions are presented and highlighted in boxes within the text. The open questions are intended to elicit additional information which is helpful when evaluating the AS-IS state of the supply chain, but will not be recorded explicitly in the morphological box.

Due to the fact that the supply chain differentiation approach possesses a consistent focus on customer requirements, the semi-structured questionnaire is constructed to map the current state for each single customer segment of the supply chain. Hence, if more customer segments are present, the questionnaire shall be applied proportionally for each customer segment. Nevertheless, the questionnaire is also applicable in cases where only one customer segment is present.

In addition to the semi-structured questionnaire analyzing the AS-IS configuration of the supply chain, the topic of **key performance indicator selection** is covered. Hence, an approach is presented on how to select appropriate performance metrics and how to reveal improvement areas by applying a process of **self-benchmarking**.

E. Hofmann et al., *The Supply Chain Differentiation Guide*,
DOI: 10.1007/978-3-642-31936-5_9, © Springer-Verlag Berlin Heidelberg 2012

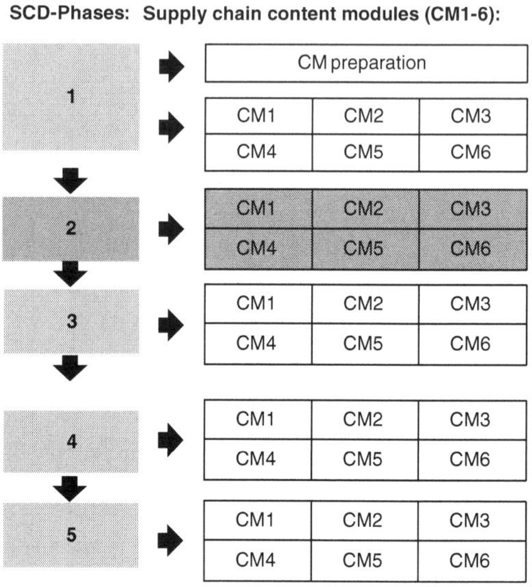

Fig. 9.1 Position of Chap. 9 in SCD Guide

9.2 Content Module 1a: Analyzing the Customers

The following section is concerned with the topic of customers within the supply chain. Hence, the section starts with the identification of the prevailing customers or customer segments and the derivation of implications resulting from the segments in a supply chain management view. Thereafter, characteristics of a customer segment are recorded and requirements allocated to a segment. Finally, aspects of distribution channels are considered.

9.2.1 Customer Segmentation

Since the introduction of the concept of market segmentation by Smith (1956), it has received considerable attention both in marketing theory and practice. Nowadays, market segmentation is a fundamental concept in marketing. Smith understood the existence of heterogeneity in the demand of customers and thus developed a market segmentation concept that aims at breaking down a heterogeneous market into a number of smaller and homogeneous markets each consisting of similar customer preferences (Wedel and Kamakura 2003).

Segmentation can be reached by two different approaches: either the product characteristics are adjusted to fit current customer segments, or new market segments are identified for current or newly developed products (Cooil et al. 2008; Ansoff 1957; McDonald and Dunbar 2009). By taking the first approach, a closely

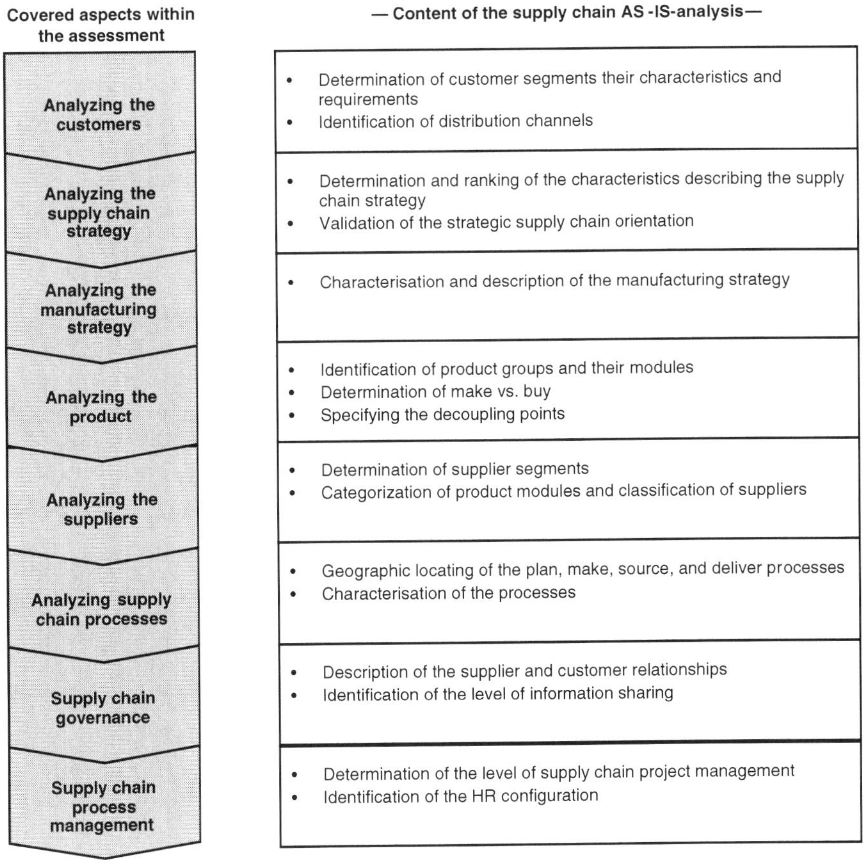

Fig. 9.2 Structure and content of the semi-structured questionnaire to analyze the supply chain AS-IS state

related concept to that of market segmentation emerges: the concept of customer segmentation with its explicit focus on customers and their needs (Marcus 1998).

The importance of segmenting customers into homogeneous groups is evident as firms have limited resources and therefore need to find a way to best serve their customers (Cooil et al. 2008). Furthermore, there is consensus about the fact that acquiring customers costs significantly more than keeping existing ones (Massnick 1997). By effectively segmenting customers, companies are able to detect which customer groups are potential customers for the company. In addition, segmentation allows one to best identify how to position the products and services for each group. Hence, segmentation presents an essential part of the development of a firm's objectives and strategies (Cooil et al. 2008).

However, in order to gain an overview of the customer structure of a firm, the number of potential customers first needs to be evaluated. Taking a supplier in the automotive industry as an example, possible customers are automobile manufacturers, such as Audi, BMW, or Porsche. Depending on the specific company and its industry, the **number of customers** can easily be in the thousands. However, today it is common to capture customer information electronically in order to be able to gain a deeper understanding of customers (Marcus 1998). Thus, such customer data should be easily retrievable.

What is the total number of your customers?

Furthermore, it is of interest whether any kind of **customer segmentation** already exists. Customer segmentation needs to be achieved before proceeding to the next step. The **number of segments** is of particular interest as Childerhouse et al. (2002) point out: segmentation ensures that design chains match customer requirements. Moreover, the number of segments indicates how many times the questionnaire should be run through ideally and thus, how many morphological boxes need to be completed in order to evaluate the AS-IS situation of the different supply chains.

Additional important information is the **criteria used to segment customers**. There is a possibility of evaluating customer's revenue or contribution to a company by using the ABC analysis, which is a classic tool of segmentation (Bruhn et al. 2008). This Pareto analysis categorizes a firm's customers into three categories: A, B, and C. Generally, the "80–20 rule" applies, assuming that 20 % of the customers (A customers) are responsible for 80 % of the revenue. Thus, A customers represent a significant category to the company, whereas C customers are marginally important (Cooper and Kaplan 1991; van Raaij et al. 2003).

Is a customer segmentation in place?
If yes, what is the total number of segments and which criteria is used to segment the customer?

Regarding the existing customer segments, the additional question arises whether or not **implications can be derived** if customer segmentation is viewed from a supply chain management perspective.

Which implications are derivable resulting from a customer segmentation seen from a supply chain management perspective?

Moreover, if there are such implications, which **criteria** should be considered for a supply chain management-relevant segmentation with regard to a specific customer segment? Childerhouse et al. (2002) identified **five possible key characteristics** to describe customer segments from a supply chain management perspective:

- The first characteristic is the **duration of the product life cycle**, which reveals significant information about a customer segment. During the life cycle stages of a product, criteria demanded by customers vary. Thus, at the beginning of the life cycle, design and capability play an important role, whereas at the saturation stage of a product, cost-related factors are most important.
- A second characteristic constitutes the **time window for delivery**, also called the delivery lead time. It represents the required speed of a demand chain. Thus, depending on the demand of a customer segment as well as on the specific product, the speed of delivery varies. The need for rapid response become evident when looking at different practical examples such as the replenishment of fashion goods.
- Taking the **demanded volume** of a product as a third criterion into account, a high-volume mass market allows for taking advantage of economies of scale, whereas a low-volume market requires a more flexible approach both in production and the demand chain.
- **Product variety** is a fourth characteristic. Hence, if a customer segment demands different varieties of a product, the supply chain's flexibility has to be aligned accordingly.
- A last criterion is represented by **demand variability**, which is seen as the most significant characteristic. The higher the variability in demand, the higher the risk of obsolescence and lost sales. In order to address such effects, forecasting (Fisher 1997) or collecting information (Mason-Jones and Towill 1997) are helpful methods.

Which criteria should be considered for a customer-oriented supply chain management segmentation?	
Possible answers	• Duration of product life cycle
	• Time window for delivery
	• Demand volume
	• Product variety
	• Demand variety

9.2.2 Customer Characteristics and Customer Requirements

Today, globalization is constantly progressing and creates new opportunities, whereas home markets are affected by saturation. Hence, firms are tending to expand their businesses internationally (Ter Hofstede et al. 2002). Consequently, this development has a clear impact on the design of supply chains as Steenkamp and Ter Hofstede (2002) point out. Different countries have different characteristics, such as language, culture, or lifestyle. Thus, different customer characteristics in different countries lead (among other things) to the differentiation of

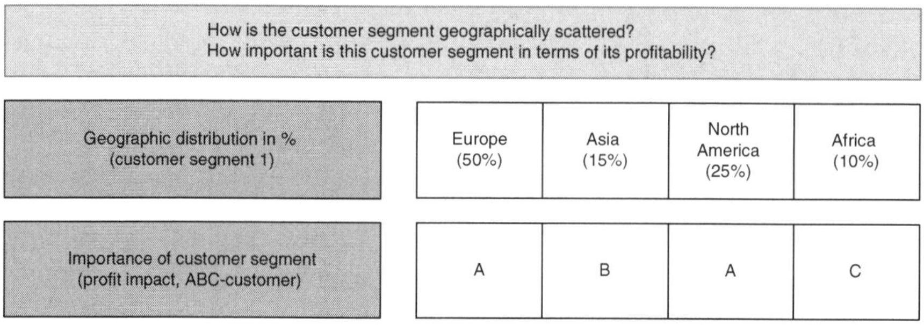

Fig. 9.3 Customer characteristics—geographic distribution and importance of a customer segment

product designs, brands, and packaging (Carpano et al. 1994). Moreover, especially logistics services are complex across national boundaries. On the one hand, distances are increasing and cost constraints arise, and, on the other, cultural conditions influence the utility of specific service offerings (Mentzer et al. 2004). Hence, it is crucial to characterize an identified customer segment with regard to its **geographical distribution**.

The **importance of a homogeneous customer segment** can be identified according to geographic distribution. The impact of a customer segment in a specific region can be taken as a reference when applying the ABC analysis as mentioned in the Section CM1. A fictional example is depicted in CM1 (Fig. 9.3). A customer segment which is buying blow molding machines from a manufacturer, for instance, is spread across Europe (the EU), Asia, North America, and Africa. The customers located in the EU, which account for 50 % of total customers, have been rated as A customers, thus making this customer segment highly important. The same applies for the customers in North America, representing 25 % of the total customers buying blow molding machines. The customers in Asia (15 %) are of average importance with regard to their profit impact, and the region Africa (15 %) is of least significance.

Aside from the closer description of customer characteristics through the geographical distribution of a specific customer segment and its importance in terms of its profit impact on the firm, it is crucial to describe the specific requirements of the customer.

Hence, it should next be clarified whether a company **systematically collects and analyzes data** on customer requirements. If yes, it might be interesting to record how the **data collection** is performed and which department is responsible. The data collection can, for example, be performed manually, IT-based or by means of enterprise resource planning (ERP) software. Departments generally responsible for data collection include Marketing and Sales, IT, as well as the SCM department or the Cash Collection Department if they exist.

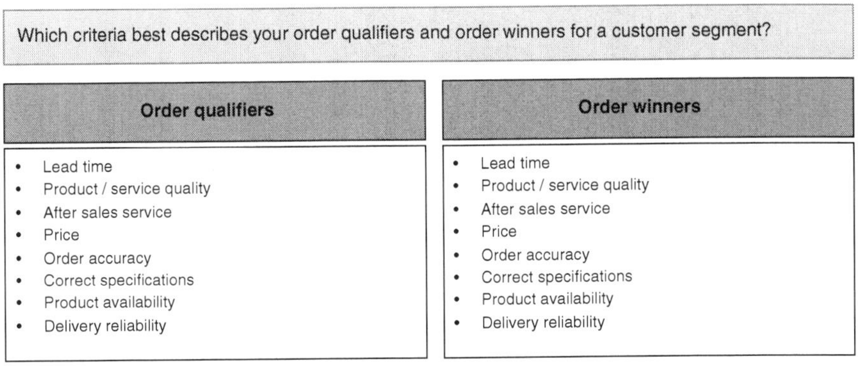

Fig. 9.4 Listing of criteria describing "order qualifiers" and "order winners", referring to Gilmour et al. (1994)

Is data on customer requirements systematically collected and evaluated?		
If yes, how is the data collected and which department is responsible?		
Possible answers:	Data collection	Departments
	• Manually, IT-based, or ERP	• Marketing and Sales, IT, or SCM
		• Cash Collection Department

However, the most important issues to be determined in this context with regard to the requirements of a specific customer segment are the "**order qualifiers**" and "**order winners**". This concept, initially developed by Hill in 1985 (Hill 1993), comes from the field of manufacturing theory. Christopher and Towill (2000), however, adapted it and developed a wider supply chain oriented concept.

- The "**order qualifiers**" represent the characteristics of a product or service required in order for a customer to consider purchasing it.
- The "**order winners**" by contrast are those characteristics that cause a firm's customer to choose the product or service over those of its competitors (Christopher and Towill 2000).

Based on a survey, Gilmour et al. (1994) generated a ranking of criteria which are important for satisfying the customers depicted in Fig. 9.4. Hence, it shall be **determined which criteria describe the "order qualifiers" and the "order winners" best** as requirements that a given customer segment possesses.

9.2.3 Distribution Channels

In order to analyze an AS-IS supply chain, it is necessary to take a closer look at the distribution channels used for a specific customer segment, as this topic represents a basic point in the field of logistics systems. Moreover, distribution

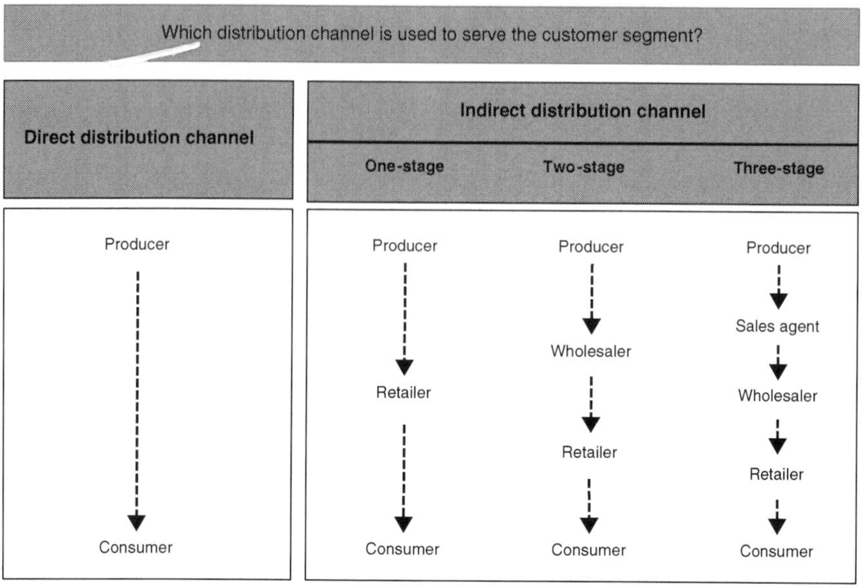

Fig. 9.5 Forms of direct and indirect distribution channels (Blythe 2005)

decisions may sometimes give a product a distinctive position in the market and affect customer satisfaction.

A **distribution channel** presents a way of selling a company's product either directly or via distributors (Bürli et al. 2008). Consequently, two basic types of distribution channels are distinguishable:

- The simplest and shortest channel is a **direct** one. Here, products are distributed directly to the end customers.
- Today, however, many producers are using **indirect** distribution channels to reach their customers. A semi-direct form of an indirect distribution channel is a one-stage channel using, for example, a retailer as an intermediary. If two intermediaries participate to deliver a product, a two-stage distribution channels is present. If three intermediaries act within the distribution channel, a three-stage distribution channel is present and so forth (Bürli et al. 2008).

An example is depicted in Fig. 9.5. Hence, it shall be stated **what kind of distribution channel** is used in order to serve a customer segment.

However, it must be stated that, given the fragmentation of markets and the advancements in technology, firms tend to no longer use one single distribution channel to supply a product, but rather multiple channels. Hence, a multiple channel is present when more than one channel is in use to sell the same product to the same target market. An example of this is the corporation General Electric, which uses both electrical distributors as well as category killers like home depots in order to supply its electrical products to medium-sized contractors (Frazier 1999).

Besides the type of distribution channel it is helpful for a holistic consideration of the AS-IS configuration of the supply chain to evaluate additional information on how the **transport strategy**, the **inventory strategy**, and the **location strategy** are organized for a customer segment (Ballou 1999):

- The **transportation strategy** states, for example, whether the transportation of goods is outsourced to a logistics service provider or performed by the firm itself. Moreover, it records the transportation mode such as trucking, railroads, air transportation, or water transportation.
- The **inventory strategy** deals with storage and handling of stock design, space layout, and material handling systems. Moreover, the level of inventory in the warehouses is considered, and whether or not the warehouses are company owned or managed by a contracting party.
- The **location strategy** covers the issue of facility locations throughout the network, which is an important aspect as it affects the entire logistics system. Aspects of this strategy include the location of a warehouse or the number of facilities.

What are the distribution channels in terms of transportation-, inventory-, and location strategy?

Possible answers:

Transportation strategy	Inventory strategy	Location strategy
• Logistics service provider	• Contract warehouse	• Location of warehouse
• Transport done by company itself	• Company owned warehouse	• Number of facilities

9.3 Content Module 1b: Analyzing the Supply Chain Strategy

This section aims at evaluating the current strategic supply chain orientation for a customer segment and, in a first step, some basic questions are presented to prepare the reader for the actual determination of the supply chain strategy. In a second step, the concept of "competitive priorities" is explained in order to describe the current supply chain strategy of a company. Finally, the strategic supply chain orientation is evaluated.

9.3.1 Fundamental Aspects of Strategic Supply Chain Orientation

Before starting to evaluate the current supply chain strategy, it is essential to determine whether **different supply chain strategies** are already in place for the customer segments. If this is the case, a supply chain strategy shall be recorded for each customer segment. If no differentiated supply chain strategy is present, the strategy will be documented once. The following section deals with the analysis of the supply chain strategy for each specific customer segment.

Are there different supply chain strategies for the customer segments?

For starters, some open-ended questions shall evaluate basic features about the supply chain strategy. Hence, it is important to identify what the supply chain strategy looks like for a customer segment, and specifically, what the **prior goals and the key characteristics** are. If, for instance, the overall goal of the supply chain strategy is the availability of fashion clothes, the key characteristics are a fast and reliable supply chain. Taking low prices of a product as the main goal of the supply chain strategy, the key characteristic can be described as cost efficiency.

What are the primary goals and key characteristics of the supply chain strategy for a customer segment?		
Possible answers:	Goals	Key characteristics
	• Availability	• Speed
	• Lead time	• Reliability
	• Product and service quality	
	• Price	

Another important aspect is the examination of how the strategy evolved. In specific, **when** was the strategy developed and **who** decided upon it. In addition, it is interesting to see **why** the strategy was developed in the first place and to what extent **external partners** were involved.

How did the strategy evolve, when was it developed, who decided upon it, why was it developed in the first place and to which extend were external partners involved?
• When:
• Who:
• Why:
• External partners:

9.3.2 Determining the Supply Chain Strategy

The fact that in present-day business supply chains rather than companies are competing with each other (Christopher 1992) highlights the importance of getting the right product, at the right time, and the right price to the customer as the key to

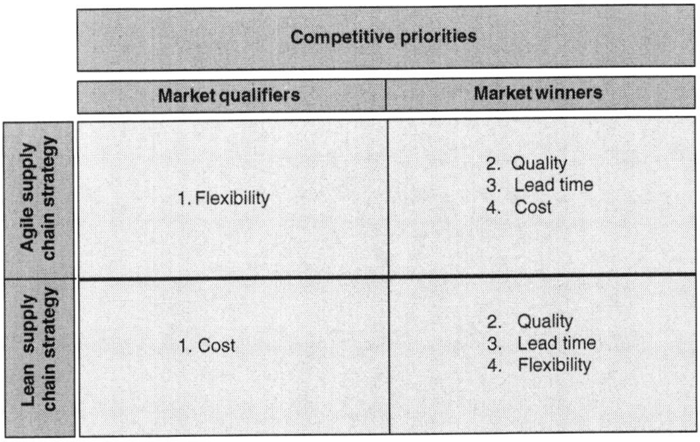

Fig. 9.6 "Competitive priorities" matrix for agile vs. lean supply chain strategy, referring to Mason-Jones et al. (2000)

survival. Hence, meeting customer requirements is crucial for a supply chain strategy (Christopher and Towill 2001). When focusing the supply chain on the end user, there are many measures that can be considered in order to describe and align the supply chain. However, the literature summarized four aggregated metrics named "**competitive priorities**" which best present the total value of a product to the end customer (Naylor et al. 1999): quality, cost, flexibility, and lead time (Hayes and Wheelwright 1984; Hult et al. 2006).

Due to the fact that many marketplaces are highly volatile and demand is difficult to predict, Fisher (1997) states that a responsive supply chain strategy is needed to meet the risk of uncertainty in demand. Based on this proposition a great number of scholars have addressed and extended Fisher's idea (ibid.); Christopher and Towill (2000) pick up the thread and refine the newly introduced supply chain strategy, which is called **agile**. However, not every demand is difficult to predict, which is true for commodity products, for example. Consequently, the focus here lies on minimizing physical costs, leading to a **lean** supply chain strategy (Fisher 1997). This approach has been based on the idea of lean manufacturing popularized by Womack et al. (1990). The focus lies on eliminating waste throughout the entire production process. Combined with scheduled process planning, it enables a firm to reduce production costs while guaranteeing high-quality products.

The connection between the idea of "competitive priorities" and lean and agile supply chain strategy is critical. Hence, generally speaking, if the main requirement is cost, the lean paradigm is most powerful. When flexibility is the prime requirement, the agile paradigm is likely to become the critical supply chain strategy, as depicted in Fig. 9.6 (Christopher and Towill 2001).

However, in order to determine which "competitive priority" best describes a supply chain, the four criteria quality, cost, flexibility, and lead time need to be traded-off against each other in order to **rank** them appropriately. The process is briefly described in the following.

Table 9.1 Examplary approach to weighting and ranking the "competitive priorities"

1

Factor 1		Factor 2	Weight
Quality	vs.	**Cost**	1/6
Quality	vs.	Flexibility	1/6
Quality	vs.	Lead Time	1/6
Cost	vs.	Flexibility	1/6
Cost	vs.	Lead Time	1/6
Flexibility	vs.	**Lead Time**	1/6

2

Competitive Priority	Strategic Importance (x/6 → % weight)
Quality	**1/3**→ 33.3%
Cost	**1/2**→ 50.0%
Flexibility	0
Lead Time	**1/6**→16.6%
	= 100 %

Assessing the relative importance of [these] four main "competitive priorities" helps to distinguish different strategic orientations

1. First, the **"competitive priorities" are traded-off against each other in pairs**, as indicated by Factors 1 and 2 in Table 9.1. Consequently, for each pair the "competitive priority" is indicated, which shows the focus of the company's current business strategy. Thus, taking the pair of quality and cost as an example: if the company business strategy aims at having a low price in the target market due to the fact that the firm faces price-sensitive customers, operating at low cost is a must. The quality must be stable and is an important attribute in order to be able to compete in the market. However, the "competitive priority" of cost will probably be ranked higher than quality. Therefore, cost is marked on the left-hand side in Fig. 9.6 and weighted with 1/6.
2. Second, the assigned weights to each of the "competitive priorities" in the first part of Table 9.2 are added up and the fraction is translated into a percentage as shown in the second part of the table, indicating the **strategic importance** of each of the "competitive priorities". In this specific example, cost at 50 % is ranked as the most important indicator to characterize the current supply chain strategy followed by quality, lead time and, finally, flexibility.

In the example in Table 9.1, the result of the ranking indicates a strategic focus on costs, which refers to a rather lean strategic supply chain orientation, as already outlined at the beginning of this part. In order to evaluate whether or not the

Table 9.2 Product groups and their modules—make (m) versus buy (b)

Which modules of a production group are produced in-house and which are sourced externally (make vs. buy)?

	Product group 1	m/b	Product group 2	m/b	Product group n	m/b
Module 1						
Module 2						
Module 3						
Module 4						
Module n						

strategic information collected so far is valid, different statements have been weighed against each other in Fig. 9.7. The main aim of these statements is to evaluate whether the strategic supply chain orientation is more lean or more agile. For each line in Fig. 9.7 the statement shall be marked which best describes the current supply chain strategy and business environment. Depending on the number of marked boxes on the left- and right-hand sides, the strategic supply chain orientation is indicated on a continuum from 1 to 10. Consequently, if more boxes are checked on the left-hand side, the supply chain strategy is leaner. Conversely, if more boxes are ticked on the right-hand side, the strategic supply chain orientation is more agile. However, if more or less the same number of boxes is marked on both sides, the supply chain strategy is mixed.

9.4 Content Module 2: Analyzing the Manufacturing Strategy

This section covers the characterization of current manufacturing strategy and thus will first focus on the description and characterization of this strategy or strategies. Second, a focus is put on the production groups and the modules a customer segment is willing to buy. In this context, it is evaluated which modules are produced in-house or sourced externally. Lastly, the concept of the decoupling point is described. This allows the customer order decoupling point to be positioned.

9.4.1 Fundamental Aspects of Manufacturing Strategy

In most industries today, optimizing internal structures based on business strategies is not enough. Hence, manufacturers try more and more to carefully link their internal processes to external suppliers and customers in unique supply chains in order to gain a competitive advantage (Frohlich and Westbrook 2001). Hence, for concretizing the strategic objectives of a supply chain on an operational level, it is essential to know what the various orientations of the manufacturing function are

☐	Statement 1	Statement 2	☐
☐	Production schedules are fix and adapting them is costly and time consuming.	Operations are built to allow for frequent change of production schedules.	☐
☐	Demand for your product is relatively stable and predictable.	Demand for your product is unstable (e.g., strong seasonality or life-cycle dependence).	☐
☐	You use the word "efficient" to describe your operations.	You use the words "innovative" or "responsive" to describe your operations.	☐
☐	Your products' life cycles tend to be long(ie., longer than six months).	Your products' life cycles tend to be short (ie., shorter than a year).	☐
☐	Shortening lead time is not a primary goal of your strategy.	Decreasing lead time is an ongoing concern.	☐
☐	Your customers' preferences and demanded products have been the same for many years.	Your customers' preferences have often changed in the past and can be expected to remain variable.	☐
☐	You have focused on establishing more cost-efficient operations (including procurement and delivery) lately.	You have lately worked on improving your operations' and supply chain's flexibility (e.g., move the decoupling point downwards the supply chain).	☐

Lean 1 ——————————————— 10 Agile

Fig. 9.7 Evaluating and verifying the strategic supply chain orientation strategic supply chain orientation

like, and especially which role the customer plays in the manufacturing strategy (Stavrulaki and Davis 2010).

However, the first step must be to answer the open question whether or not **different manufacturing strategies** are used in order to satisfy different customer segments. If this is the case, the manufacturing strategy shall be recorded for each existing customer segment. If one general manufacturing strategy exists for all customer segments, then this strategy shall be recorded once.

Are different manufacturing strategies used to satisfy the customer segment requirements?

To determine the present manufacturing strategy, a second question aims at evaluating whether it is possible to describe the manufacturing strategy in terms of **"competitive priorities"** such as quality, cost, flexibility, and lead time.

Is it possible to describe your manufacturing strategy/strategies in terms of "competitive priorities"?	
Possible answers:	• Quality
	• Cost
	• Flexibility
	• Lead Time

If these criteria are difficult to determine, try to **describe the present manufacturing strategy in general**.

Please describe your manufacturing strategy.

For companies utilizing different manufacturing strategies within their production processes, additional information on whether or not **different production lines** are in use would be of specific interest. A good example is provided by a company which is specialized in remanufacturing sealed torque converters for the automotive industry. In order to improve their flexibility in supplying, they operate three different production lines. One line is utilized primarily for General Motors units as well as some Ford converters. The second production line is operated for Ford and Chrysler. The third is aimed at handling everything else, such as low-volume runs where only a handful of units are requested (http://www.cvcconverters.com).

If different manufacturing strategies are used, are there also different production lines?

9.4.2 Product Modularization

Modularity is regarded as a general system concept: it describes the degree to which a system's components are separable and re-combinable (Schilling 2000). Hence, it represents the division of products or production groups into subsystems, so-called modules, with the target to increase the flexibility of the firm as well as that of its partners (Baldwin and Clark 1997).

The **level of modularity** is determined by the ability to disaggregate a product and re-combine its different components. The more independent the different components are from one another, the more likely is the option to utilize them separately, hence increasing the degree of modularity (Schilling 2000).

However, due to the excessive efforts accompanying modularization or structural conditions that make modularization impossible, as is the case in the process industry, a company might be restricted in modularizing its product range. In this case, an appropriate alternative is the formation of **material groups**. Material groups are characterized by their homogeneity. More precisely, parts of a product share similarity in terms of their characteristics, which in turn distinguish them from other parts of the material groups. As a rough classification of material groups, let us suggest product material, operating material, investment goods, trade goods, and services. However, a wide number of classification criteria can be applied, such as price and demand. More complex attributes are presented by risk of supply or technical difficulties (Large 2009).

In order to map the different modules, information is first needed about which specific **production group(s)** the selected customer segment is buying. Let us take

Dell, the computer manufacturer, as an example. Its products are structured into the following production groups: notebooks, desktop, server, and storage.

Which product group(s) is this customer segment buying?		
Possible answers:	• Notebook	Example
	• Desktop	
	• Server	
	• Storage	

The next question focuses on whether or not the product group(s) is (are) **modularized**. If this is not the case, maybe an alternative approach is used to modularize production groups. Hence, it shall be stated if a **category management system** is in use instead, and what the **material groups** are.

Are the product group(s) modularized?
If not, is a category management system used instead? What are the material groups?

9.4.3 Outsourcing

Following upon the investigation of the concept of modularization, this section is concerned with outsourcing, which is a self-evident consequence of the modularization make-or-buy decision.

The terminology outsourcing is described as "buying a part from another company rather than making it yourself" (Womack et al. 1990). Hence, a company starts a contractual agreement with a supplier in order to shift capacity to the supplier for something which has previously been performed in-house (Momme et al. 2000). If different knowledge is required to manufacture different components of a technical system, it is helpful to split the system into modules, which allows different members to manufacture these modules in a distributed manner (von Hippel 1994). In general, the increased utilization of a modular product structure has significantly facilitated outsourcing options (Mikkola 2003).

Now, based on the answers given in Sect. 9.4.2, for each identified product group of a customer segment, the corresponding modules shall be listed. Additionally, for each module a statement indicating whether the modules are **produced in-house (make) or sourced externally (buy)** is necessary.

9.4.4 Determining the Manufacturing Strategy and Decoupling Point

This part aims at determining the position of the decoupling point within the manufacturing process. Hence, in a first step, five different manufacturing strategies are briefly explained in order to determine the positioning of the decoupling point.

Olhager and Östlund (1990) first characterized the **manufacturing strategies** as being situated on a continuum ranging from make-to-stock to engineer-to-order. Since then, different manufacturing strategies have been adapted in numerous manufacturing enterprises such as: **make-to-stock (MTS)**, **assemble-to-order (ATO)**, **make-to-order (MTO)**, **source-to-order (STO)**, and **engineering-to-order (ETO)** (Olhager 2003; Hilletofth 2009; Amaro et al. 1999).

- **MTS** is defined as a push manufacturing strategy, meaning that management is production-focused, relying on long-term planning and stable demand forecasts which allow for long lead times. Furthermore, both production planning and relationships with buyers are of long duration. The product is mainly standardized and produced in high volumes (Olhager and Östlund 1990).
- **ATO** production allows for a certain degree of customization of the product. Hence, the final product is produced with standardized parts that can be assembled in different ways. The assembly of the particular finished product is initiated by the receipt of an order (Amaro et al. 1999).
- The **MTO** manufacturing strategies indicate that all operations needed to produce a specific product are undertaken as soon as a customer order is received. Compared to ATO production, the capability for a customer to have an impact on the customization of the product is greater here (Amaro et al. 1999).
- **STO** indicates that the materials and component parts of a product are ordered after obtaining the receipt of a customer order (SCOR 10.0).
- **ETO** allows for a direct impact of customer requirements on the design and engineering stage of a product. Hence, the product is pulled through the entire production process. This strategy is traditionally applied in environments defined by large, complex, often singular projects, as they are prevalent, for example, in the construction sector (Gosling and Naim 2009).

However, those five manufacturing situations are all related to different positions of the decoupling point. In recent decades the positioning of the decoupling point, sometimes also called the customer order decoupling point (CODP), has become a topic of strategic interest, since the concept highlights the involvement of customer orders.

Traditionally, the **decoupling point** is defined as “the point in the manufacturing value chain for a product where the product is linked to a specific customer order” (Olhager 2003). Hence, the decoupling point separates the supply chain into two parts: one part responds directly to the customer order and the other part of the supply chain is more planned in character and uses a strategic stock to buffer

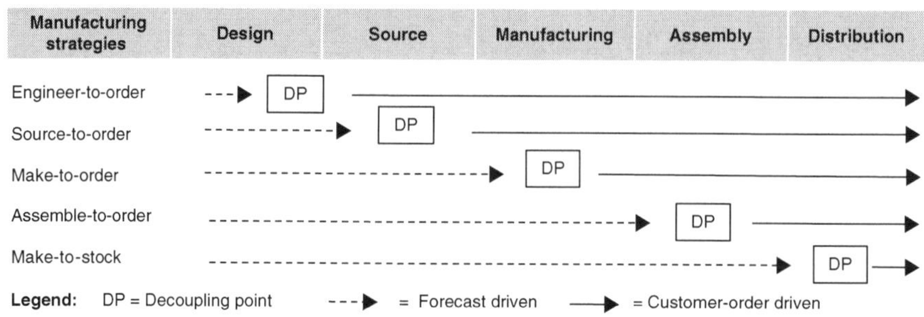

Fig. 9.8 Different manufacturing strategies related to different decoupling points, following Naylor et al. (1999)

against variability in demand. The products are market driven as they are pulled by the end customer, downstream from the decoupling point. However, upstream of the decoupling point, the supply chain is pushed by forecasts (Naylor et al. 1999).

The positioning of the decoupling point varies, depending on different factors such as the volatility of demand or modular product design to create a variety of choices for the customer. Hence, the different manufacturing situations are related to the different decoupling points as depicted in Fig. 9.8. The dotted lines illustrate those production activities which are forecast driven, whereas the straight lines depict customer order driven activities (Olhager 2003).

Figure 9.8 implies that companies delay ETO, STO, MTO, ATO, or MTS until after a customer order has been received. Hence, it can be decided which activities should be performed after an order is received and which activities should be performed before an order is received. Traditionally, companies applied the MTS approach. Such companies therefore performed all supply chain activities such as design, sourcing, manufacturing, assembly, and distributions based on forecast and before receiving a customer order (Hilletofth 2009) as illustrated in Fig. 9.8.

The positioning of the decoupling point separates the supply chain into two parts with different characteristics enabling the alignment of the paradigms of **lean** and **agile** (Naylor et al. 1999).

- The **lean** paradigm is applied upstream the decoupling point due to the fact that the demand is smooth and standardized products flow through a number of value chains.
- The **agile** paradigm in contrast is applied downstream the decoupling point as the demand varies significantly and the product variety per value stream has augmented.

Example:

Hewlett Packard, US-American technology company, faced a problem of variability in demand for their printers produced for the global market based on an aggregated demand. The position of inventories in the supply chain for market specific products was placed at the distribution centers. The printers were already customized for the individual markets. Thereby the problem arose, that

Table 9.3 Performance of supply chain activities depending on customer order customer order

For each product group it shall be stated whether the following activities are performed before or after a customer order has been received.

Activity	Product group 1		Product group 2		Product group n	
	before	after	before	after	before	after
Design / Engineering						
Sourcing						
Manufacturing						
Assembly						
Distribution						

despite the correct aggregated forecasts, an out of stock situation could occur in one country and another one would find itself in an overstocked situation due to the wrong national forecast. To solve this issue, the company decided to set the decoupling point for this product group at their distribution centers which ensured that the product differentiation took place at this point as well. This allowed to hold generic printers as the buffer stock and only differentiate them for the specific national markets when customer demand was present (Naylor et al. 1999). Thus, the company set the decoupling point at ATO which allowed the company to design, source, manufacture, and assemble generic printers without a specific order. In other words, the supply chain was no longer operated with only a lean structure since the agile structure was implemented downstream of the decoupling point.

In order to evaluate the decoupling point for the identified product groups in Part 1.4.2, it shall first be indicated whether the activities in Table 9.3: design/ engineering, sourcing, manufacturing, assembly, and distribution are **performed before or after a customer order has been received**.

In a second step, the given answers from Table 9.3 shall now be transferred to Fig. 9.9 in order to **position the decoupling point**. Hence, if for example the activities of design/engineering, sourcing, manufacturing, and assembly are carried out without a specific customer order and only the distribution is released when a customer order is present, the decoupling point for the specific production group is positioned at ATO. This implies that all activities before the decoupling point (left side) are carried out in the supply chain with a lean focus whereas after the decoupling point (right side), the supply chain is characterized by agility.

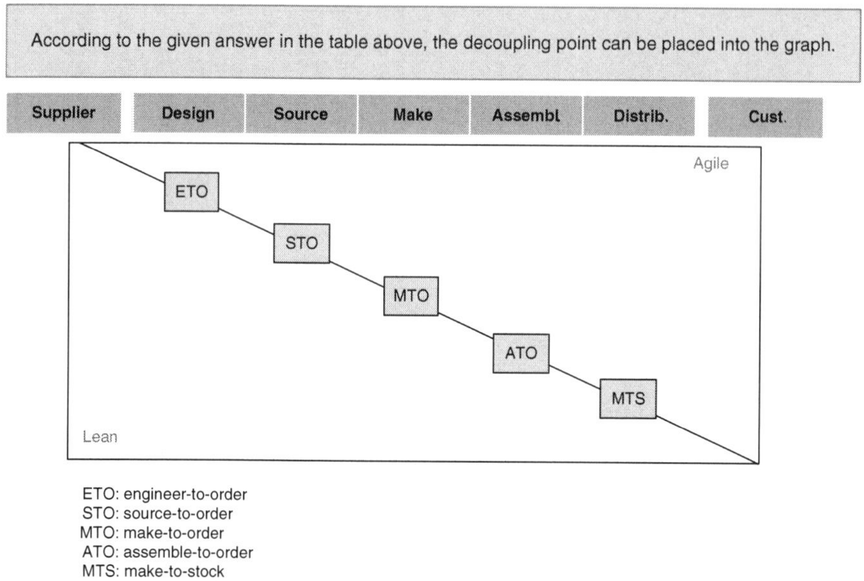

Fig. 9.9 Positioning of the decoupling point in the supply chain

9.5 Content Module 3: Analyzing the Suppliers

This section deals with the role different suppliers play within a firm. In a first step, the presents of different supplier bases is evaluated. Moreover, some general questions are presented about supplier segmentation. Second, a questionnaire is presented to classify a company's AS-IS suppliers based on a purchasing portfolio matrix developed by (Kraljic 1983).

9.5.1 Fundamental Aspects of Supplier Management

First of all, there is general information needed regarding the **overall number** of a company's present suppliers. Taking IKEA, a Swedish home furnishing retail company as an example, the firm possesses 31 trading service offices in 26 countries in order to monitor the production, test new ideas, and negotiate prices with about 1220 suppliers all over the world (http://www.ikea.com).

What is the overall number of the suppliers?	
Possible answer:	•1'220 (Example)

Moreover, it shall be determined whether **different supply bases** already exist for each of the identified customer segments. If this is the case, the questionnaire in this section should be applied to record the supplier segments for each customer segment. However, if a uniform supply base is applied on the different customer segments, the supplier segment shall be recorded once.

Are there different supply bases for different customer segments?	
Possible answer:	• Yes
	• No

The next step aims at determining specific information on supplier connected to one single customer segment. Hence, the **number of suppliers** present to satisfy a **specific customer segment** shall be determined.

How many suppliers are present to satisfy a specific customer segment?

Taking the topic of supplier segmentation into account, the question arises whether **suppliers are currently segmented**. If this is the case, additional information is useful about the present **number of supplier segments**.

Are the suppliers currently segmented?
How many supplier segments are present?

Moreover, it is of interest which **criteria** is used in order to segment the suppliers. One possibility is the ABC analysis which has already been addressed in Sect. 9.2.1 within the context of customer segmentation. This Pareto analysis is commonly applied to segment suppliers due to its simplicity. The ABC analysis is often performed as an introduction to supplier categorization to obtain a rough overview of the sample. Possible measurements to classify supplier segments are among others the purchasing volume, financial matters, or the strategic importance of the suppliers (Wagner and Johnson 2004).

Which criteria are used in order to segment the suppliers?	
Possible answer:	• ABC analysis

A last open question focuses on the use of a **differentiated supplier management**. The question arises whether different sourcing strategies can be applied to each individual supplier segment. Furthermore are there different relationship schemes present for the different supplier segments? In other words, some suppliers are managed at "arm's length" and other suppliers have a close relationship with the buying company. If this is the case, additional information such as **when** the differentiated supply management started and **why** as well as **who** was involved would be of particular interest.

Is there a differentiated supplier management approach in place?
If yes, when was the supplier management established and why? Who was involved?

9.5.2 Categorization of Modules and the Classification of Suppliers

Purchasing performance and supply chain management have gained significant importance as factors of a firm's competitiveness. In the past, two different and very well-known supplier management models have emerged describing how to optimally manage suppliers (Dyer et al. 1998). The traditional view known as the "arm's lengths model" endorse maximizing bargaining power and minimizing dependences on suppliers (Porter 1980). Hence, the main implication of this model for purchasing strategies is to avoid commitments and to deliberately keep suppliers at "arm's lengths". However, Japanese firms introduced in the past successfully a new model, a "partner model", which focused on closer supplier relationships. Different studies imply that the "partner model" compared to the "arm's length model" results in superior performance as more information is shared and better coordination of interdependencies is ensured. Moreover, investments are placed in relation-specific assets to lower costs and improved quality (Dyer et al. 1998). However, despite these economic benefits resulting from the Japanese model, a drawback is clearly the costs of setting up and maintaining relationships as well as increased dependencies (Helper 1991).

A key question for purchasing executives is which model is superior. Perhaps companies should think more strategically about their supplier management and choose more diversified approaches and not a "one size fits all" strategy (Dyer et al. 1998).

In this context, Kraljic introduced in 1983 the **purchasing portfolio matrix** which groups the procured items into four categories positioned alongside the two dimensions:

- Profit impact
- Supply risk

The approach allows categorizing purchased items or modules and thus, the suppliers delivering them. Hence, the purchased modules are first classified in term of profit impact and supplier risk. This allows to segment a company's AS-IS suppliers based due to the categorized modules the suppliers are delivering.

Table 9.4 Statements allowing to classify a company's modules and its suppliers, according to Kraljic (1983)

	Noncritical modules	Bottleneck modules	Leverage modules	Strategic modules
Items purchased	Commodities, some specified materials	Manly specified materials	Mix of commodities and specified materials	Scarce and/or high value materials
Key performance criteria	Functional efficiency	Cost management and reliableshort-term sourcing	Cost/price and material flow management	Long-term availability
Time horizon of relationship	Limited normally 12 month or less	Variable, depending on availability vs. short-term flexibility trade-offs	Variable, typically 12 to 24 months	Up to ten years, governed by long-termstrategic impact (risk and contract mix)
Typical sources	Established local suppliers	Global, predominately new suppliers with new technology	Multiple suppliers, mainly local	Established global suppliers
Count # of cells selected per column				

The two criteria sort out the purchased modules into the four categories, **noncritical modules**, **bottleneck modules**, **leverage modules**, and **strategic modules** as depicted in Table 9.4.

- **Noncritical modules** are characterized by a low profit impact as well as a low supply risk. Generally, the materials purchased are commodities or some specified materials such as steel rods, coal, or office supplies. The key criterion for sourcing such modules is functional efficiency.
- **Bottleneck modules** mainly consist of specified materials such as electric parts or catalyst material. The main reason for purchasing such modules described by low profit and high supply risk is cost management and a reliable short-term sourcing.
- **Leverage modules** denote a high profit impact and low supply risk consisting of mixed commodities and specified materials. Thereby, key performance criteria are cost and material flows.
- **Strategic modules** are characterized by both, high profit impact and high supply risk. The sourced items are generally scarce and of high value. Long-term availability is seen as the key criterion (Kraljic 1983).

Table 9.4 characterizes the four module categories by four central issues such as type of items purchased, key performance criteria, time horizon of the relationships with the supplier, and typical sources of each considered module of a product group. It shall be checked which statement best classifies **a company's AS-IS supplier segment**. The column which is most applicable to the strategy then classifies the module and thereby the supplier segments.

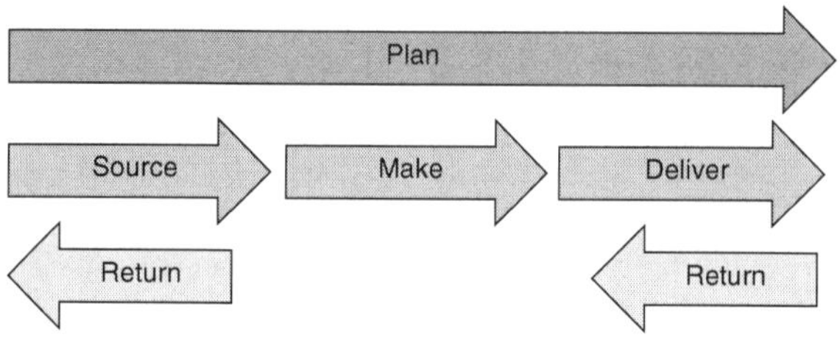

Fig. 9.10 Supply chain best practice management processes, referring to SCOR 10.0

This can be repeated for all modules of the product groups existing for the focused customer segment. If no categorization into product groups and their modules has been identified, the classification approach may also be applicable for material groups.

9.6 Content Module 4: Analyzing Supply Chain Processes

This section is concerned with the allocation and specification of the supply chain processes of a company. The first part aims at describing the basic supply chain processes and allocating their geographic locations. The second part focuses on those supply chain processes which change the state of material goods and determines the corresponding configuration of these processes.

9.6.1 Geographic Process Allocation

In order to reach a standard description of the process elements making up the internal supply chain, the processes **plan**, **source**, **make**, **deliver**, and **return** are considered as depicted in Fig. 9.10. These five categories are based on the supply chain operations reference model (SCOR). They identify the processes a supply chain requires to support the target of the customer orders (SCOR 10.0); (Stewart 1997).

- The **plan** process is associated with the planning activities required to operate the supply chain. This includes among others the make or buy decisions, long-term capacity and resource planning as well as aggregating and prioritizing demand requirements (Stewart 1997). However, in this context the plan process is located on a strategic level and thus, possesses a superior function regarding the other four processes.
- The **source** process outlines the ordering and obtaining of goods and services. This includes for example the scheduling of deliveries, shipment validation, and acceptance of supplier invoices (SCOR 10.0).
- The **make** process is describes by the Supply Chain Council (2010) as "[…] the activities associated with the conversion of materials or creation of the content

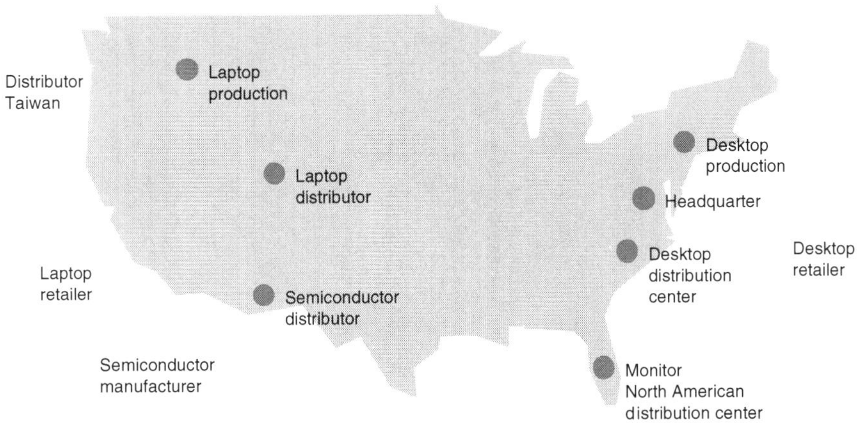

Fig. 9.11 Description and location of the supply chain processes—example of a laptop manufacturer

of services". Thereby, the make process refers to the transformation of materials rather than the manufacturing itself as this process represents all types of material conversion such as assembly, maintenance, repair, refurbishment or, remanufacturing to mention a few (SCOR 10.0).

- The **delivery** process covers the creation, maintenance, and fulfillment of customer orders (SCOR 10.0). This includes the reception and stocking of finished goods, management of delivery quantity, or orders maintenance (Stewart 1997).
- The **return** process represents in general activities that are concerned with the reverse flow of goods from the customer. This process includes the identification of a need to return, disposition decisions, and the shipment and receipt of the returned goods. However, repair or remanufacturing processes are not covered by the return process, they belong to the make process described above (SCOR 10.0). Moreover, the process return is listened in connection with the source and deliver processes. Hence, the activity **source return** documents the process of returning goods to suppliers as for example the return of unused material. The **deliver return** activity refers to the receipt of returned finished or defect goods (Poluha 2007).

As firms are tending to expand their businesses internationally due to the constant progression of globalization (Ter Hofstede et al. 2002) it seems evident to focus on the geographic location of the supply chain processes. In order to gain an overview of the geographic location of the supply chain processes plan, source, make, deliver, and return it is helpful to **pinpoint the processes on a map**.

Take for instance a computer manufacturer in North America, the location of its production facilities and distribution centers are indicated in Fig. 9.11. Regarding the sourcing activities, they are carried out in the laptop production as well as the desktop production which hold true for the production processes as well.

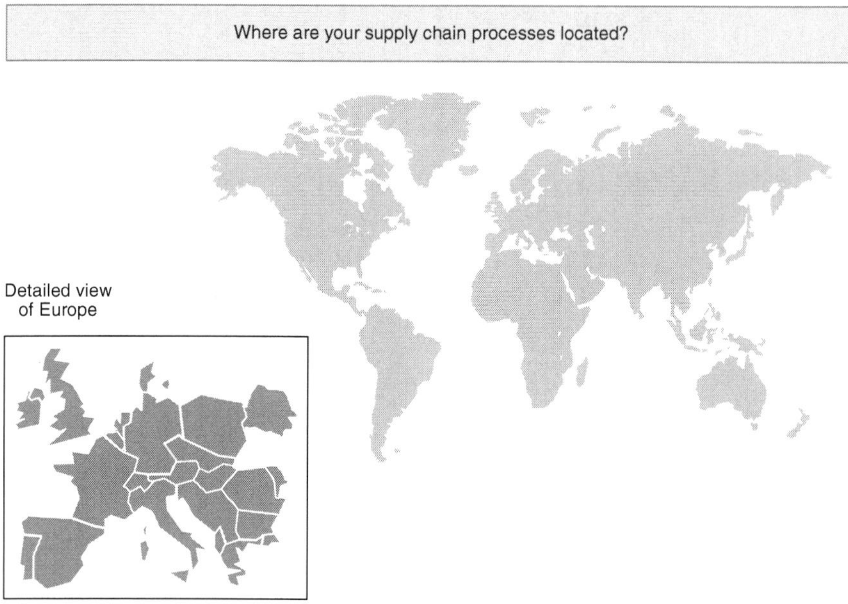

Fig. 9.12 World map and a detailed view of Europe

Moreover, sourcing processes are also carried out at the laptop distributors as well as at the desktop retailers place. Here, laptops and desktops are sourced for further distribution. Regarding the distribution processes, they are carried out at various places in this example. However, the desktop distribution center and the laptop distributor represent the assembly point for the worldwide distribution of the products. The plan process associated with the planning activities required to operate the supply chain are conducted at the headquarter. The source returns as well as the deliver return processes are not carried out in this specific example.

Sure, this is a simplified example as the focus lies restricted to the processes located in North America but it still outlines the intention of pinpointing the processes on a map. Hence, for a single customer segment the corresponding **supply chain processes plan, source, source return, make, deliver, and deliver return shall be located** in the world map depicted in Fig. 9.12. In order to gain a rough overview and to avoid complexity, it shall be stated in which part of the world a process is carried out. For example whether the make process is conducted in Europe, North America, South America, Australia, Africa, and/or Asia.

9.6.2 Configuration of Source, Make and Deliver Processes

The three processes source, make, and deliver, which all are processes triggered by the demand that changes the state of material goods, possess different **configurations**. All three processes have three different possible capabilities of

Table 9.5 Configuration of supply chain source process and the source return process

What are the appropriate supply chain source process configurations for the customer segment?

Source process configuration	Source stocked product (S1)	Source make-to-order (S2)	Source engineer-to-order (S3)
Characteristic	• Procurement of product or service based on forecast • Product is prefabricated	• Procurement of product based on customer order • Product is designed or configured based on particular customer requirements	• Procurement of products or services based on customer order • Product is designed or configured based on particular customer requirements

Supplier segments	Leverage	Noncritical	Bottleneck	Strategic
Source process				

Return process	Process implemented?
Characteristic	• A return process is performed for the sourced good or product

Table 9.6 Configuration of supply chain make process

What are the appropriate supply chain make processes configurations for the customer segment?

Make process configuration	Make-to-stock (M1)	Make-to-order (M2)	Engineer-to-order (M3)
Characteristic	• Product completed prior to entry of customer order • Production based on sales forecast	• Product completed after entry of customer order • Production based on customer order	• Product completed after entry of customer order • Production based on customer request

Production group	Group1	Group 2	Group 3	Group n
Make process				

representing as well as responding to the customer orders (see Tables 9.5, 9.6 and 9.7). These three different capabilities are represented by the categories, **stocked products (S1, M1, D1)**, **make-to-order (S2, M2, D2)**, and **engineer-to-order (S3, M3, D3)** depicted in Fig. 9.13. The categories refer to the manufacturing strategies mentioned in SCD-Phase 1.

Table 9.7 Configuration of supply chain deliver process and the deliver return process

What are the appropriate supply chain deliver/return processe configurations for the customer segment?

Deliver process configuration	Deliver-stocked product (D1)	Deliver make-to-order product (D2)	Deliver engineer-to-orderproduct (D3)
Characteristic	• Product is maintained in a finished goods state • Production prior to customer order	• Product is manufactured, assembled or configured form standard parts • Production after customer order	• Product is deigned, manufactured and assembled from standard and customer parts • Production after customer order

Customer segment	Segment 1	Segment 2	Segment 3	Segment n
Deliver process				

Return process	Process implemented?
Characteristic	• A return process is performed for the delivered product

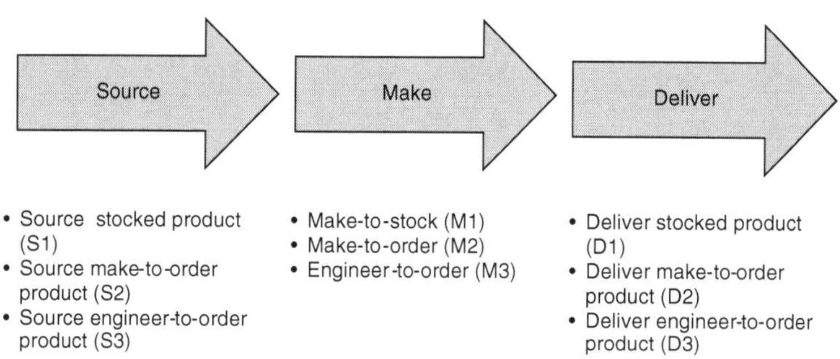

Fig. 9.13 Configurations of the main supply chain processes according to the SCOR model

The abbreviations represent the three different categories for each main process. Hence, the letter represents the initial of the process (S for source, M for make and D for delivery) and the number identifies the configuration of the process (S1 indicates sourced stocked product, S2 refers to source make-to-order product, and S3 to engineer-to-order product).

The three categories can be described as following:

- The category **stocked products (S1, M1, D1)** is clearly inventory driven and contains normally standard materials. Moreover, the category is characterizes by a short turnaround.

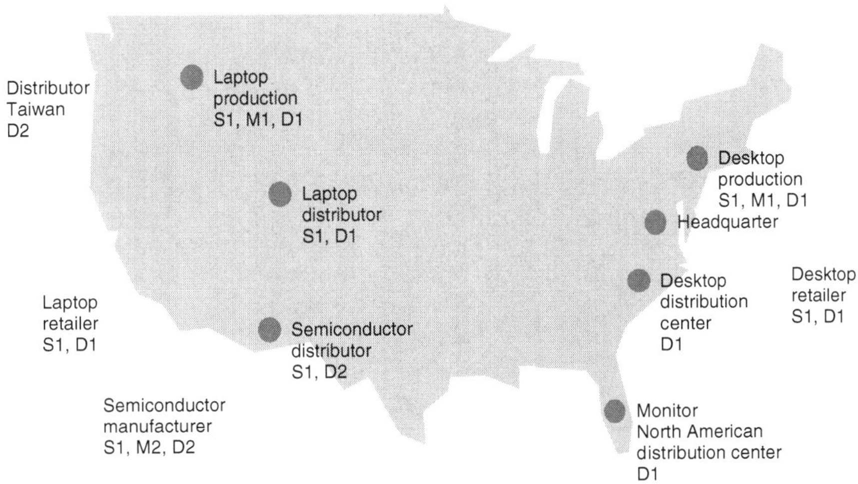

Fig. 9.14 Configuration of the supply chain processes—example of a laptop manufacturer

- The **make-to-order (S2, M2, D3)** category is customer order driven. Hence, the materials are configurable and the turn-around times are generally long.
- The third category, **engineer-to-order (S3, M3, D3)**, is customer requirement driven and as soon as a customer order is received, the design of the product starts. This category possesses the longest possible lead times of the three categories (SCOR 10.0).

A typical production location possesses generally a profile which is defined by the sourcing configuration S1 indicating procuring a prefabricated product or S2, procurement of production based on customer order. Moreover, the make process is specified by the configuration M1 indicating a make-to-stock fabrication. Last, the production location is defined by the D2 configuration regarding the delivery process indicating a supply of contract manufacturing product. However, not all facilities necessarily dispose over all three process types. A warehouse or distribution center may merely have the profile of D1 due to the fact that for example planed and delivered refilling orders steer the supply from the manufacturing side (Poluha 2007). Taking the example of the computer manufacturer in North America, the supply chain processes are configured as indicated in Fig. 9.14.

Now, it shall be stated which **supply chain source configuration** is appropriate for the regarded customer segment. This shall be determined for every supplier segment within the focused customer segment. The exact characteristics of the possible configurations S1, S2, and S3 are outlined in CM4.

In addition, it shall be stated whether a **return process is performed** in general in connection with the source process. Hence, whether defective, excess, or ageing products or inventory are returned (SCOR 10.0).

Next, it shall be stated which **configuration the make** process possess for the customer segment. Hence, for each identified production group of the specific customer segment, the corresponding configuration shall be determined. However, it would be equally possible to assign them regarding the different modules of a production group. The three configurations M1, M2, and M3 are characterized in detail in CM4.

The deliver process can be described in detail according to the configuration of customer segments. However, the delivery processes may vary within a customer segment regarding the distribution channels as outlined in Sect. 9.2.3.

In addition, it needs to be determined whether a **deliver return process** is performed in general such as the receipt and disposition determination of defective products or the receipt of maintenance or repair products (SCOR 10.0).

9.7 Content Module 5: Analyzing the Supply Chain Governance

This section is concerned with the determination of the buyer–supplier relationship regarding the customers as well as the suppliers. First, the topic of customer relationship as well as the level of information sharing is conducted. Subsequently, the same content is applied on the supplier side.

9.7.1 Relationship Management and Level of Information Sharing: Customers

In order to **describe the existing relationship between a firm and its customer segments** various factors can be consulted. Possible criteria are represented by the relationship strength or the importance of the customer segment to a company. Also the attractiveness of the customers in a financial context is a criterion to describe the relationship. Of course, these criteria are just a selection and others are suitable to describe the relationship.

Please describe the relationship between you and your customer segments	
Possible answers:	• Strong relationship
	• High attractiveness of the segment
	• High importance

However, to determine the precise governance form within the relationship management framework of (Stuart 1997) presented in SCD-Phase 1, Content Module 5, a questionnaire is presented to facilitate the allocation. Hence, for each customer segment the **relationship between a firm and its customer segments shall be described** by answering the questions in Table 9.8. The answers need to be summarized in the last box. If more answers are answered with yes, the level of relationship is rather intense and vice versa. A possible example is indicated for

Table 9.8 Questionnaire determining the level of customer relationship in supply chains

How would you describe the relationship between you and your customers?

Questions		Answer categories	Customer segment 1	Customer segment 2	Customer segment n
Do you have fixed personal contact on customer side (key accounts)?		yes / no	yes	no	
Do you consider your relationship to have a long-term or short-term focus?		long-term/ short-term	long-term	short-term	
Where higher management levels involved to build the relationship?		yes / no	no	no	
Are higher management levels involved to nurture the relationship?		yes / no	yes	no	
Does this relationship require higher investments compared to other customer relationships?		yes / no	yes	no	
How intensive is the level of relationship between you and your customers?	low(1) low-medium (4) medium-high (3) high (4)		medium-high	low	
Classification of relationships	transaction based standardized process adjustments strategic customer relationships strategic alliance		strategic customer relationships	transaction based	

Table 9.9 Questionnaire determining the level of information sharing between a company and its customer segmentscustomer segments

How would you describe the level of information sharing between you and your customers?

Questions		Answer categories	Customer segment 1	Customer segment 2	Customer segment n
How important is the customer segment?		A / B / C			
Do you invite your customers to "several" events?		yes /no			
Are there regular coordination meetings with your customers?		yes / no			
Do EDI linkages exist to share demand / supply data as well as for order placing and confirmation?		yes / no			
-If yes(1): Who paid for the investment of the connection?		you / customer or both			
-If yes (2): Who is responsible for the connection's maintenance?		you / customer or both			
How intensive is the level of information sharing between you and your customers?	low(1) low-medium (2,3) medium-high (3,4) high (5)				

Table 9.10 Questionnaire determining the level of supplier relationship in supply chains

How would you describe the level of information sharing between you and your suppliers?

Questions	Answer categories	Leverage	Non-critical	Bottle-neck	Strategic
Are there regular coordination meeting with your suppliers?	yes /no				
Do EDI linkages exist to share demand / supply data?	yes / no				
-If yes (1): who paid for the investment of the connection?	you / supplier or both				
-If yes (2): who is responsible for the connection's maintenance?	you/ supplier or both				
Dou you share information on inventory with your suppliers?	yes / no				
Do you share sales forecast information with your suppliers?	yes / no				
How intensive is the level of information sharing between you and your suppliers?	low (1) low-medium (2,3) medium-high (3,4) high (5)				

the customer segment 1 and 2. The question about the length of the relationship is an indication for the classification of the relationship.

Taking the example of the customer segment 1, the level of relationship is high, which indicates that the relationship form "strategic customer relationship" applies. In contrast, the evaluation of customer segment 2 refers clearly to a "transaction based" relationship form.

Besides determining the intensity of the relationship between a firm and its customer segments, the level of information sharing is of particular interest as well due to the fact that the management of information plays a crucial role in a successful management of supply chains. Broadly defined "information sharing refers to the extent to which critical and proprietary information is communicated to one's supply chain partner" (Li and Lin 2006). The sharing of information can take place on various levels, ranging on a continuum from "no information shared" to "full information shared" (Sahin and Robinson 2002). Hence, in order to **determine the level of information sharing** with the customer segments the questions in Table 9.9 shall be answered for each existing customer segment. The answers shall be summarized in the last box. Again, if more answers are answered with yes, the level of information sharing is rather high and vice versa. However, the questions which cannot be answered with yes or no and claims additional information regarding the process of information sharing.

9.7.2 Relationship Management and Level of Information Sharing: Supplier Side

Taking the connection to the supplier segments into account, the same procedure as in the previous section shall be applied in order to determine the level of relationship as well as the level of information sharing.

In a first step, the **relationship between a firm and its supplier segments shall be described** in general. Possible criteria are among others the relationship strength, the attractiveness of the supplier segments, and the importance of the segments to the buyer.

Please describe the relationship between you and your supplier segments.	
Possible answers:	• Strong relationship
	• High attractiveness of the segment
	• High importance

To **determine precisely the relationship** regarding the classified supplier segments: leverage, noncritical, bottleneck, and strategic of the regarded customer segment, the below questionnaire shall be completed (Table 9.10). By summarizing the answers in the last box, an indication arises whether the relationship is rather intense or not. Equally to the determination of the level of customer relationship, a very high level of relationship (indicated by the result of four positive answers) can be categorized as "strategic alliance". Vice versa, if the result of the questionnaire presents a rather low level of supplier relationship, the "category transaction based" applies.

Now, it shall be **described how intense the level of information sharing** is between a firm and its supplier segments. If there is a low level of information sharing, the demand data is the only information shared between the buyer and supplier. If a full information sharing level is prevalent, complete information is available on both sides. This may include data on transportation availability, inventory costs and level, demand data from the channel members etc. (Sahin and Robinson 2002).

The questions in Table 9.11 indicate the level of intensiveness of information sharing applied to yes or no answers. The answers then need to be summed up and thereby indicate the level of information sharing.

9.8 Content Module 6: Analyzing the Supporting Activities in the Supply Chain

This section addresses the issue of integrating the supply chain management discipline into the company. In succession, a simple framework is presented to measure an organization's competencies to exploit project management

Table 9.11 Questionnaire determining the level of information sharing between a company and its supplier segments

How would you describe the level of information sharing between you and your suppliers?

Questions	Answer categories	Leverage	Non-critical	Bottle-neck	Strategic
Are there regular coordination meeting with your suppliers?	yes /no				
Do EDI linkages exist to share demand / supply data ?	yes / no				
-If yes (1): who paid for the investment of the connection?	you / s. or both				
-If yes (2): who is responsible for the connection's maintenance?	you/ s.or both				
Dou you share information on inventory with your suppliers?	yes / no				
Do you share sales forecast information with your suppliers?	yes / no				
Are your suppliers involved into product development?	yes / no				
How intensive is the level of information sharing between you and your suppliers?	low (1) low-medium (2,3) medium-high (3,4) high (5)				

knowledge to improve supply chains. Furthermore, human resources management competencies within the context of supply chain management are considered.

9.8.1 Project Management Within the Supply Chain Context

Designing and enhancing supply chains calls for organized projects. The urgency of integrating the disciplines of supply chain management and project management is evident when considering supply chain changes. One driver for such changes is the ongoing need to improve processes such as lead time reduction programs or outsourcing activities. Another one is represented by collaborations, which are more and more necessary to meet mutual goals like the implementation of IT tool to exchange structured data. Hence, such activities require the coordination of resources, in other words, project management competencies are necessary to successfully implement a new strategy or an intended change (Ayers 2004).

However, in order to measure the project management maturity of a firm, a framework applied by Ayers (2004) based on Kerzner's (2001) **five-level Project Management Maturity Model** (PMMM) is presented.

The five levels of the PMMM starting with level 1 called "common language" and progressing to level 5 "continuous improvement" are explained below. The

Table 9.12 Assessment tool for evaluating the level of project management (Ayers, 2004)

Which cells best describe your company's AS-IS project management?

	Level 0	Level 1	Level 2	Level 3	Level 4	Level 5
Organization awareness	Unaware of the need for PM Functional orientation	Awareness exists of need for PM knowledge & language	Use of PM life cycles (phasing) Scope control. Use of software	Cultural barriers are eliminated Individuals can easily shift to "project mode"	Individuals are aware of the need for improving PM processes	Shared knowledge by project teams Cultivation of PM talent
Management support	None. Not on the mgmt. agenda	No investment in PM capability Little senior mgmt. support	Education provided in PM Willingness exists to address internal issues	Support for MP exists throughout the organization Projects are linked to strategy	Establishment of a Project Officer or Center of Excellence to pursue improvements	Recognition of continuous improvement as necessary
Process discipline	None.No PM processes exist	Occasional use of PM methodology initiated at lower levels	Concerted effort to use PM Cost and schedule controls are used	Single, informal approach used on all types of projects	Company looks outside for upgrading PM processes	Changes are made to company's own PM processes
Motivation	Ignorance. No apparent motivators PM not considered important	Insufficient motivation to take authority away from functional managers	Company must under take major important projects in order to survive	PM efficiency perceived to be closely linked to company success	The company strategy depends on projects (internal development of new products)	The company strategy is heavily dependent on projects (offering/ product is a project itself like plant construction and building
Count #of cells selected per column						

ranking of the degrees of the project maturity allows a company to assess its current position and define improvement areas within project management.

- **Level 1 "common language"** indicates an occasional use of project management. There is an awareness of the need for project management but no competence in execution exists. Moreover, top management support is not consistently provided or even lacking and there is little project management training and development provided. The projects have mainly a functional and non-strategic scope.
- At the next stage, **level 2 "common process"**, the support for project management broadens. There is an awareness of the need for processes and

methodology. Moreover, support exists from top to bottom and training of specialists and other employees involved is provided.

- The next project maturity level, **level 3 "singular methodology"**, indicates that an organization adopts one suitable project management methodology and applies it on all projects. Support of the management is existent throughout the firm.
- If the project management achieves **level 4 "benchmarking"**, a permanent support structure like a center of excellence for project management is existent. Moreover, the need for identifying ways to improve the project management culture is receiving attention within the firm. Hence, the idea of benchmarking is applied to search for enhancements form the outside to upgrade project management processes.
- The last stage is represented by **level 5 "continuous improvement"**. Here, a company actually applies benchmarking information for continuous process improvements and project management teams share valuable knowledge. Hence, changes are made to a company's own project management processes (Ayers 2004).

However, there is an addition level existing to describe the maturity of project management indicated by Ayers (2004) as **level 0 "no project management perspective"**. This level simply declares that a company completely ignores the need for project management.

In order to be able to determine the corresponding level of project management maturity **the cell in a row describing best the AS-IS situation of project management** can be selected (Table 9.12). In the end, the level which contains the selected cells represents the corresponding level of project maturity.

9.8.2 Human Resource Perspective

The relationship between human resources management (HRM) and supply chain performance has been examined by few researchers so fare. Nonetheless, past research focusing on best practices of "leading-edge firms" declared that human resource management may improve the possibility of maximizing a firm's supply chain management performance. An early study conducted by Gowen and Tallon (2003) determined that the need for training the workforce increases as the rate of environmental change enhances. Moreover, best practice companies see training and human resource development as a strategic requirement. Another study by (Novack et al. 1995) examined that the more supply chains evolve with an enhancing number of organizations and greater complexity, the more employees will be required to improve their ability to communicate across several organizational functions and entities. Hence, in order to outperform in such an environment, organizations need a strong commitment to human resource management.

It has become apparent that successful integration of human resource management and supply chain management becomes increasingly important for achieving high performance within the supply chain. In line with this insight Noe et al. (2006) state **four risks** human resource management has to deal with: adaption risk, motivational risk, shortage risk, and risk of quitting. The authors state that a lack of acceptance and motivation from the employees affects the performance of a supply chain (Noe et al. 2006):

- **Adaptation risk** is concerned with appropriate qualification of the appointed staff.
- **Motivational risk** refers to a lack of acceptance and motivation from the employees' side which considerably handicaps the supply chain performance.
- **Shortage risk** considers the deficiency of qualified personnel for enabling smooth supply chain processes.
- The last of the four risks, the **risk of quitting**, deals with the efforts of retaining key supply chain personnel.

Based on this four risk categories is facing, is shall now be determine how the **human resource management of a company is configured** in order to face those risks. Hence, it shall be indicated for each statement depicted in Table 9.13 to which degree it applies on a scale of one to five: one indicating a total disagreement and five a full affirmation of the statement. The statements are categorized in **regions** and **supply chain processes**. The regions may vary depending on the area of activity of a company. For firms acting in the European region, only the first column needs to be considered. If a firm is acting in an international environment, the statements shall be considered for each geographic region accordingly. Moreover, referring to the SCOR model, the supply chain processes consist of four main processes such as plan, source, make, and deliver as indicated in Section CM4. Thereby, the plan process is located on a strategic level whereas the other three processes refer to an operative level. Hence, the statements shall be evaluated for each process within a region.

9.9 Approach for Key Performance Indicators Selection

In addition to the described AS-IS supply chain mapping, the topic of performance metrics is considered in this section. Hence, an approach is presented on how to select key performance indicators (KPIs) of the supply chain in order to measure the right things at the right time with reasonable accuracy. In addition, a self-benchmarking approach is introduced to reveal improvement areas.

The selection of performance metrics is seen as a very critical step in the evaluation of any system. A large number of performance metrics are available in order to characterize systems such as production, distribution, and inventory which increasingly make the selection of measurements more difficult (Beamon 1999). However, as Gunasekaran et al. (2001) state in the context of supply chain management: "[…] metrics are needed to test and reveal the viability of strategies

Table 9.13 Statements determining the risks within human resource management in supply chains

To what extend does the statements describe a company's human resource configuration in accordance to the supply chain?

	Europe				Asia				...				
	P	S	M	D	P	S	M	D	P	S	M	D	
Employees have personal development plans (created via personal feedback sessions).													Adaption risk
The organization assesses employee performance regularly and systematically.													Adaption risk
The organization supports development of skills exceeding the standard job requirements.													Adaption risk
The organization embraces explicit corporate values and norms (such as a clear mission or vision).													Motivation risk
The organization states clear leadership guidelines.													Motivation risk
Employee empowerment and participation are desired and supported.													Motivation risk
Employees perceive to have a satisfying work-life balance.													Motivation risk
Employees are aware of their own contribution to overall company success.													Motivation risk

	Europe				Asia				...				
	P	S	M	D	P	S	M	D	P	S	M	D	
A strategic HR planning process is in place (aligned with overall strategic planning).													Shortage risk
The organization uses measures to systematically screen the labor market.													Shortage risk
The organization uses a systematic selection procedure to assess applicants' qualifications.													Shortage risk
Effectiveness of HR programs is measured (if present).													Risk of quitting
The compensation package contains variable components.													Risk of quitting
Management regularly informs employees about the organization's current situation and goals.													Risk of quitting
HRM recognizes employees' changing capabilities and needs over their tenure and addresses them.													Risk of quitting

Key:

P: Plan (strategic) S: Source M: Make D: Deliver HR: Human resource

Degree of affirmation:

1: Fully disagree 2: Partly disagree 3: Undecided 4: Partly agree 5: Fully agree

without which a clear direction for improvements and realization of goals would be highly difficult".

However, to ensure that only relevant metrics are measured, the following approach derives possible metrics based on two main factors: the **desired supply**

Table 9.14 Competitive ranking of a fictive manufacturing firm

1. Flexibility	2. Quality	3. Cost	4.Lead time

Table 9.15 Six possible strategic supply chain orientations

Strategic supply chain orientation	Corresponding competitive priority
Agile	Flexibility
Agile	Quality
Agile	Lead time
Strategic supply chain orientation	**Corresponding competitive priority**
Lean	Cost
Lean	Quality
Lean	Lead time

chain strategy and the most important **competitive priorities** resulting from the TO-BE supply chain analysis conducted in SCD-Phase 1. The analysis of the strategic TO-BE supply chain orientation resulted in determining whether the desired supply chain should have a lean or agile orientation. Furthermore, by applying the AHP approach, a ranking of the competitive priorities (flexibility, quality, cost, and lead time) was reached. Taking into account an example of a fictive manufacturing firm, the company aims at having ideally an agile supply chain orientation with a competitive ranking depicted in Table 9.14.

In general, the results from the two analyses conducted in the CM1 deliver six possible strategic supply chain orientations presented in Table 9.15. Regarding the fictive example, the desired supply chain orientation and the corresponding competitive priorities are marked in bold. Only the two first competitive priorities of the ranking are marked due to the fact that those are the most important to be considered.

Based on the strategic supply chain orientation, suitable performance metrics may be selected from Table 9.16 matching the desired supply chain strategy and the corresponding competitive priorities. There are various other ways to select and categorize metrics, but the advantage of this alignment is the positioning of the metrics in a strategic context which is seen by Neely et al. (1995) as a prerequisite due to the fact that performance measures influence what people do. Furthermore, the table shows for which processes the KPIs are appropriate (columns 1–5), gives a short description of the KPIs and lines out, which corrective actions are

Table 9.16 Key performance indicators with respect to different strategic supply chain orientations (1/3)

Plan	Source	Make	Deliver	Return (S)	Return (D)	KPI	Description	Lean-lead time	Lean-quality	Lean-cost	Agile-lead time	Agile-quality	Agile-flexibility	Suitable corrective actions in case of insufficient performance (Phase 3)
x						Average lead time	Average time needed from the first to the last timestamp a company defines in its supply chain (in days)	x			x		x	1–8; 14–16;19; 21–23;25;27; 29–30; 40–43
x	x	x	x			Average throughput time	Productivity of a process over a unit period (e.g. output per hour, number of orders shipped)	x			x		x	1–3; 5;11; 18;22;29;32–33; 39–41; 45
x	x	x				Manufacturing lead time	Total amount of time required to produce a particular item or batch	x			x		x	1–3;5;11;29;32–36
		x			x	Quality level	Percentage of defects of products produced or differently defined quality indicator		x			x		1–3
x	x	x	x			Inventory holding cost	Cost of carrying inventory (per unit); can be split up into work-in-progress (WIP) inventories, finished goods inventories etc.			x				3;8;21;26;27;29; 31–36;40–42
x	x	x				Obsolescence cost/Scrap cost	Cost of obsolete inventory, sometimes includes spoilage			x				1–8;10–14;17–21;23–26; 28–36;48

(continued)

Table 9.16 (continued)

Plan	Source	Make	Deliver	Return (S)	Return (D)	KPI	Description	Lean-lead time	Lean-quality	Lean-cost	Agile-lead time	Agile-quality	Agile-flexibility	Suitable corrective actions in case of insufficient performance (Phase 3)
		x				Machine breakdown time	Average time machinery is unusable due to breakdowns or maintenance and repair activities		x	x		x	x	–
			x	x	x	Distribution costs	Total cost of distribution, including transportation and handling costs			x				37–46
		x				Manufacturing costs	Total cost of manufacturing, including labor, maintenance, and re-work costs			x				2; 14;18;20–23; 26–36;38
x						ROI (Return on investment) or Return on supply chain fixed assets	Usually measured by the ratio of net profit to total assets; measures the profitability of an organization/return on "supply chain fixed assets" uses supply chain revenue and fixed asset values of supply chain assets			x				1–8;14–16; 32–36
x	x	x	x			Fill rate (target fill rate, average item fill rate)	Proportion of orders filled immediately (e.g. the % of of ship-from-stock orders shipped within 24 h of order receipt)	x			x		x	8;11;17;22–23; 27–28;30; 32–34;38

(continued)

Table 9.16 (continued)

Plan	Source	Make	Deliver	Return (S)	Return (D)	KPI	Description	Lean-lead time	Lean-quality	Lean-cost	Agile-lead time	Agile-quality	Agile-flexibility	Suitable corrective actions in case of insufficient performance (Phase 3)
x		x	x		x	On-time delivery	Measures item, order, or product delivery performance; possible metrics: product lateness (delivery date minus due date); average lateness or earliness of orders; percent on-time deliveries (percent of orders delivered on or before the due date)	x			x		x	1–8;10–12;14; 17–18;21–31; 34–35;27–43; 45–46
x		x	x		x	Perfect condition	% of orders delivered in an undamaged state that meet the specifications, have the correct configuration, are faultlessly installed (if applicable), and accepted by the customer		x			x		1–8;10–14; 20–28;34;37–38
x		x	x		x	On-time deliver in full (OTIF)	Measures the success at delivering exactly what the customer ordered on the day (/at the time) it was supposed to be delivered	x	x		x	x	x	1–8;10–12; 14;17–18; 21–31;34–35; 27–46

(continued)

Table 9.16 (continued)

Plan	Source	Make	Deliver	Return (S)	Return (D)	KPI	Description	Lean-lead time	Lean-quality	Lean-cost	Agile-lead time	Agile-quality	Agile-flexibility	Suitable corrective actions in case of insufficient performance (Phase 3)
x	x	x	x	x		Backorder/ Stockout	Measures item, order, or product availability performance; possible metrics: number of backorders (items backordered due to stockout); number of stockouts (number of requested items that are out of stock); average backorder level (number of items backordered divided by the number of items)	x	x		x	x	x	1–8;10–12; 20–31;34;36
x	x	x	x			Customer response time	Amount of time between an order and its corresponding delivery	x			x		x	3–4;6–8;10–14; 17;20–21; 23–28;30; 34;36;38
x	x	x	x		x	Customer complaints	Number of customer complaints registered	x	x	x	x	x	x	10;13

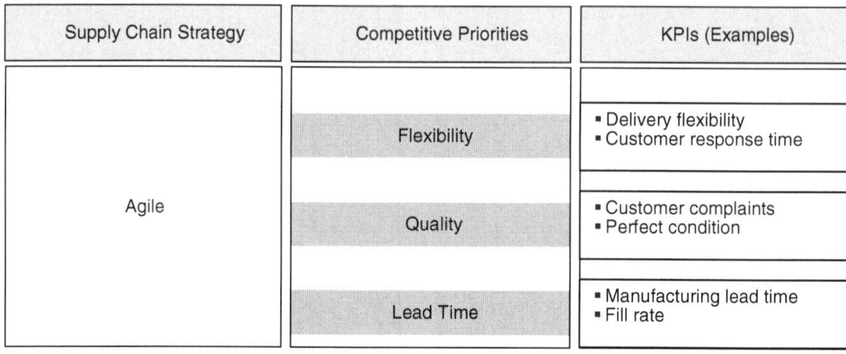

Fig. 9.15 Example for KPI selection

convenient in case of underperformance regarding the specific KPI. The corrective actions are found in Chap. 10 (Phase 3).

In a next step, the table checks to detect performance metrics especially relevant to the operations of the company which are not covered by the supply chain strategy and the corresponding competitive priorities filters. If there are additional performance metrics which need to be taken into account, they should be added to the existing list.

So far, the approach on how to filter relevant performance metrics has been explained. However, a metric aims at quantifying the efficiency and or the effectiveness of an action but (Neely et al. 1995) the numbers alone do not permit to determine the competitive performance of a firm. Hence, a **self-benchmarking** is conducted in order to identify improvement opportunities to reach the desired TO-BE state.

Given the fictive example of the manufacturing company desiring an agile strategy with a focus on both flexibility and quality as criteria for the selection of KPIs, Fig. 9.15 gives an example for suitable KPIs.

Benchmarking in general is a very popular tool used for continuous improvements in organizations' performances and competitiveness or in other words, for identifying improvement opportunities (Beamon 1999); (Soni and Kodali 2010). The approach was made popular by Xerox, a leading company for business processes and document management, in the 1980s as the company successfully applied the tool in order to regain market share (Soni and Kodali 2010; http://www.xerox.com). Hence, the tool has been proven to be valuable by providing opportunities to learn from other organizations (Meybodi 2009). However, Hyland and Beckett (2002) state that a high rate of internal learning which both refines current practices and adopts new ones is essential in order to stay competitive. To reach internal learning, one of the most appropriate tools is

Table 9.17 Self-benchmarking of the supply chain—assessing the performance of the KPIs

Key performance indicator	TO-BE performance	AS-IS performance
Machine breakdown time	8	8
On-time delivery in full (OTIF)	8	6
Back order/Stockout	7	3
Customer complaints	9	8
Distribution costs	8	9
Forecasting accuracy	...	...
Inventory turnover	...	...

represented by internal benchmarking due to the fact that it is often cited as a method to study organizational learning and knowledge transfer (Southard and Parente 2007). Self-benchmarking or internal benchmarking is defined as "[...] the process of identifying, sharing, and using the knowledge and practice inside one's own organization" (O'Dell and Grayson 1998). The tool possesses different advantages such as:

Downsizing the problem of data and access confidential information (Neely et al. 1995)

Simple access of data and information required

Presenting a "stepping stone" towards external benchmarking (Soni and Kodali 2010)

However, in order to conduct a self-benchmarking within the presented approach, for each selected and listed **KPI its performance shall be stated** on a scale from 1 to 10. 1 indicates the worst and 10 represent the best possible performance for the given KPIs. This needs to be conducted for both, the desired TO-BE state and the current AS-IS state of the KPIs. Through this approach, a comparison of the desired and the actual performance of the selected KPI are reached. A possible example is depicted in Table 9.17.

The self-benchmarking reveals, by the comparison of the TO-BE and the AS-IS performance of the KPIs, which areas need to be improved in order to reach the desired TO-BE state. Taking the example depicted in Table 9.17 as a reference, it shows that the processes measured by the OTIF indicating the success at delivering exactly what the customer ordered at the right time. (http//:www.kpilibrary.com) The self-benchmarking indicates however that distribution costs are too high and thereby revealing another area where improvement is needed. Hence, the examples show clearly that the self-benchmarking approach successfully helps to disclose improvement areas.

Summary sheet

SCD-Phase 2: Identification of AS-IS supply chain and analysis

Goals of SCD-Guide Phase 2

The goal of Phase 2 is to give a guideline to analyze the AS-IS situation of a company. Thereby different measures are used in order to determine the current situation of a company.

Methods and analysis for SCD-Guide Phase 2

- Customer segmentation
- Supplier segmentation
- Product modularization
- Activity allocation
- Supply chain governance
- Supporting activities

Input per methods for SCD-Guide Phase 2

	Input from other phases		
Customer and supplier segmentation		**Customer segmentation**	**Supplier segmentation**
	(None)	• Importance of customer segmentation • Customer requirement evaluation	• Classification of current supplier segments
Product modularization and activity allocation		**Product modularization**	**Activity allocation**
	(None)	• Modularization of product groups • Identifying the customer order decoupling point	• Configuration of supply chain sourcing, making and delivering process
Method for supplier buyer relationships and supporting activities		**Supply chain governance**	**Supporting activities**
	(None)	• Determining the customer and supplier relationship and the level of information sharing	• Determining the level of project management • Determining the human resource management risks

Output from SCD-Guide Phase 2

- Completely filled in morphological box for supply chain AS-IS situation

9.10 Application Example of SCD-Guide SCD-Phase 2 and Possible Output

In SCD-Phase 2, the supply chain AS-IS situation is described for a later comparison of the current state to the TO-BE state in SCD-Phase 3. The morphological box is an effective way of highlighting the AS-IS situation of a company state of the supply chain.

As already described in the previous sections, the dimension (rows) and the characteristics (columns) of the morphological box depend on the chosen analyses within the content modules. By means of a decision with respect to certain analyses the intended, structure of a possible supply chain is determined.

The PC Manufacturing Inc. has analyzed the current situation according to the different content modules 1–6. Thereby it became apparent that the PC Manufacturing Inc.'s supply chain is currently not completely tangible by means of the morphological box, since the structure of its current supply chain does not correspond to the structure of the chosen analyses and thereby to the structure of the morphological box. For example, the company operates in the moment only one supply chain. This leads to fact that only one morphological box may be filled in. The entire morphological box is presented in Fig. 9.16 and 9.17.

The **descriptive part** of the morphological box includes different categories such as the geographic distribution, demanded products, requirements ranking and distribution channel. The geographic distributions are illustrated in percentages according to the different continents. Furthermore the different products Tec 1, Tec 2 and Tec 3 are shown, whereas the morphological box is filled in for product Tec 1 and all customer segments. In the requirements ranking the first requirement is quality followed by price, product availability, delivery reliability and service quality. The distribution channels are direct distribution as well as retailers.

The **customer area** includes competitive priorities, strategic supply chain orientation, relationship management, information sharing, delivery process (process type and allocation). The competitive priorities ranking including first cost, quality, flexibility and then lead time. The strategic supply chain orientation of Tec 1 follows a lean strategy. The relationship management is transaction based and the level of information sharing thereby low. The process type of the delivery process are stocked products and the process allocation is on all continents.

In the **manufacturing area** there are the different product modules as well as their categorization according to the make process (process type and process allocation) as well as the positioning of the customer order decoupling point. The different modules of Tec 1 are screen, computer case, motherboard, keyboard and chipset. The keyboard and screen are noncritical items, the computer case is a leverage item, the chipset is a bottleneck item and the motherboard is a strategic item. The making process is make-to-stock and is being done in Europe, Asia, North America and Australia. Furthermore the positioning of the customer order decoupling point is make-to-stock within the AS-IS analysis.

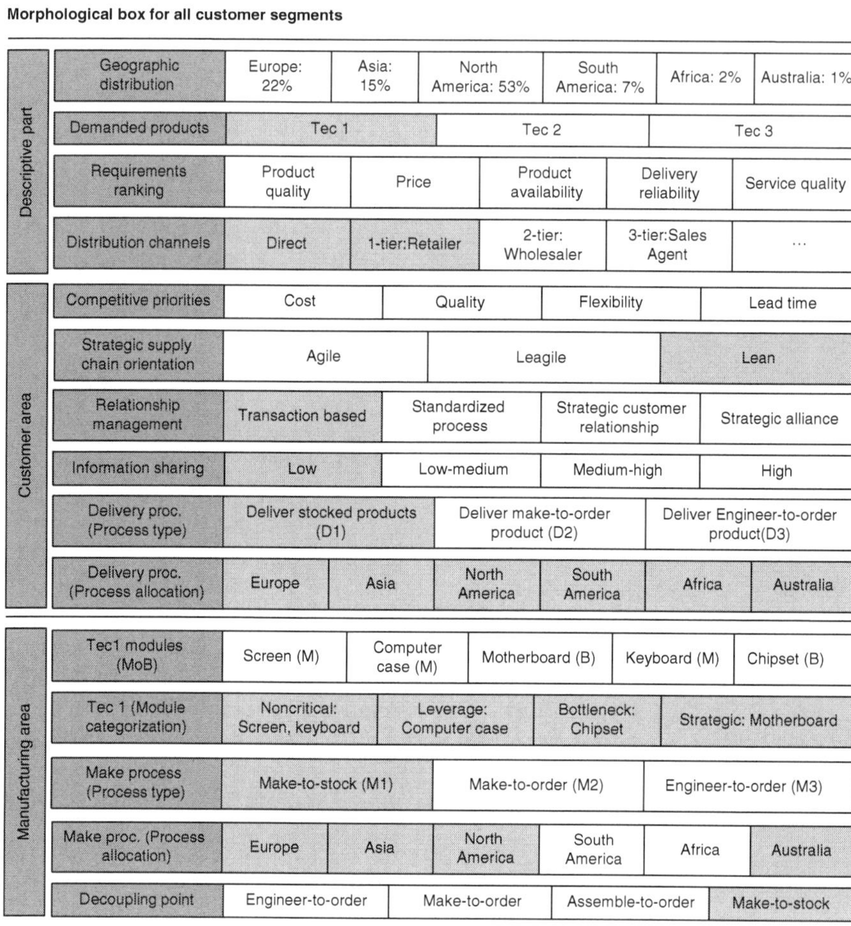

Fig. 9.16 Exemplary morphological box AS-IS of PC manufacturing Inc

In the **suppliers area** of the AS-IS analysis there are the different sourcing processes according to whether the items are noncritical, leverage, bottleneck or strategic. The overall sourcing process takes place in Europe, Asia, North America and Australia. The suppliers of noncritical items have a transaction based relationship management and therefore a low level of information sharing. The sourcing process is thereby source stocked products. The suppliers of leverage items have standardized process relationship management and therefore a low-medium level of information sharing. The sourcing process is source stocked products. The suppliers of bottleneck items are transaction based and have a low level of information sharing and are source stocked products. The suppliers of strategic items have a strategic alliance with the buyer and thereby a high level of

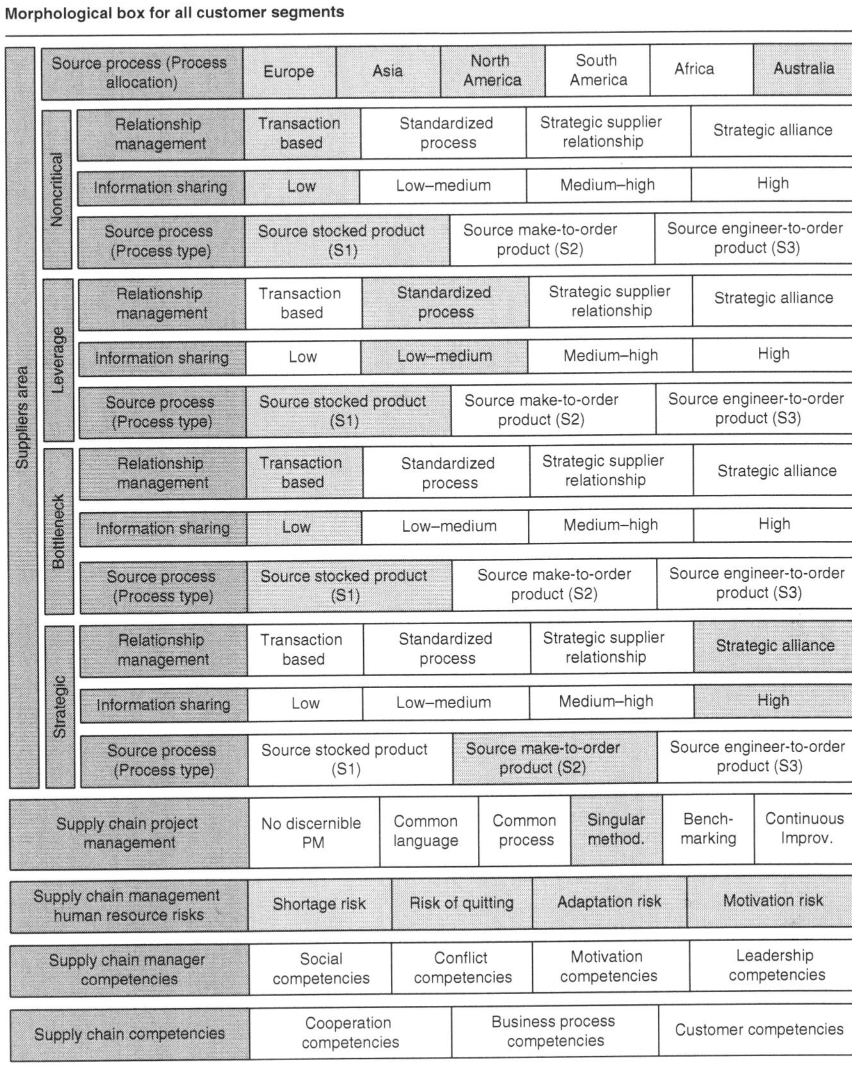

Fig. 9.17 Exemplary morphological box AS-IS of PC manufacturing Inc

information sharing. The sourcing process of strategic items is hereby source make-to-order.

The **supporting parts** such as the supply chain project management and the supply chain management human resource risks are the last part in the morphological box. The supply chain project management is on the level of singular methodology and the supply chain management human resource risks are shortage risks, risk of quitting, adaptation risk and motivational risk. The competencies which a supply chain manager needs to have are social, conflict, motivation and leadership competencies. The general competencies of a supply chain are cooperation, business process and customer competencies.

The AS-IS analysis shows the analysis for all customer segments of PC Manufacturing Inc. and is not supposed to be all-encompassing but rather shows how to effectively fill in the morphological box to show the current state of the supply chain.

References

Amaro, G., Hendry, L., & Kingsman, B. (1999). Competitive advantage, customisation and a new taxonomy for non make-to-stock companies. *International Journal of Operations & Production Management, 19*(3/4), 349–371.

Ansoff, I. (1957). Strategies for diversification. *Harvard Business Review, 35*(5), 113–124.

Ayers, J. B. (2004). *Supply chain project management: A structured collaborative and measurable approach*. Boca Raton: St. Lucie Press.

Baldwin, C. Y., & Clark, K. B. (1997). Managing in an age of modularity. *Harvard Business Review, 75*(5), 84–93.

Ballou, R. H. (1999). *Business logistics management: Planning, organizing, and controlling the supply chain*. London: Prentice-Hall Internat.

Beamon, B. M. (1999). Measuring supply chain performance. *International Journal of Operations & Production Management, 19*(3/4), 275–292.

Blythe, J. (2005). *Essentials of marketing* (3rd ed.). Harlow, Essex: Financial Times/Prentice Hall.

Bruhn, M., Georgi, D., & Hadwich, K. (2008). Customer equity management as formative second-order construct. *Journal of Business Research, 61*(12), 1292–1301.

Bürli, R., Friebe, P., & Pifko, C. (2008). Distribution: Grundlagen mit zahlreichen Beispielen, Repetitionsfragen mit Lösungen und Glossar: Compendio Bildungsmedien AG.

Carpano, C., Chrisman, J. J., & Roth, K. (1994). International strategy and environment: An assessment of the performance relationship. *Journal of International Business Studies, 25*(3), 639–656.

Childerhouse, P., Aitken, J., & Towill, D. R. (2002). Analysis and design of focused demand chains. *Journal of Operations Management, 20*(6), 675–689.

Christopher, M. (1992). *Logistics and supply chain management: Strategies for reducing costs and improving services*. London: Pitman Publ.

Christopher, M., & Towill, D. R. (2000). Marrying lean and agile paradigms. *Proceedings of EUROMA*, (pp.114–121). Ghent, Belgium.

Christopher, M., & Towill, D. R. (2001). An integrated model for the design of agile supply chains. *International Journal of Physical Distribution & Logistics Management, 31*(4), 235–246.

Christopher, M., & Towill, D. R. (2002). Developing market specific supply chain strategies. *International Journal of Logistics Management, 13*(1), 1–14.

Cooil, B., Aksoy, L., & Keiningham, T. L. (2008). Approaches to customer segmentation. *Journal of Relationship Marketing, 6*(3/4), 9–39.

Cooper, R., & Kaplan, R. S. (1991). Profit priorities from activity-based costing. *Harvard Business Review, 69*(3), 130–135.

Dyer, J. H., & Singh, H. (1998). The relational view: Cooperative strategy and sources of interorganizational competitive advantage. *Academy of Management Review, 23*(4), 660–679.

Fisher, M. L. (1997). What is the right supply chain for your product? *Harvard Business Review, 75*(2), 105–116.

Frazier, G. L. (1999). Organizing and managing channels of distribution. *Journal of the Academy of Marketing Science, 27*(2), 226–240.

Frohlich, M. T., & Westbrook, R. (2001). Arcs of integration: An international study of supply chain strategies. *Journal of Operations Management, 19*(2), 185–200.

Gilmour, P., Borg, G., Duffy, P. A., Johnston, N. D., Limbek, B. E., & Shaw, M. R. (1994). Customer service: Differentiating by market segment. *Journal of Physical Distribution & Logistics Management, 24*(4), 18–23.

Gosling, J., & Naim, M. M. (2009). Engineer-to-order supply chain management: A literature review and research agenda. *International Journal of Production Economics, 122*(2), 741–754.

Gowen, C. R., 3rd, & Tallon, W. J. (2003). Enhancing supply chain practices through human resource management. *Journal of Management Development, 22*(1), 32.

Gunasekaran, A., Patel, C., & Tirtiroglu, E. (2001). Performance measures and metrics in a supply chain environment. *International Journal of Operations & Production Management, 21*(1/2), 71–87.

Hayes, R. H., & Wheelwright, S. C. (1984). *Restoring our competitive edge: Competing through manufacturing*. New York: Wiley.

Helper, S. (1991). How much has really changed between US automakers and their suppliers. *Sloan Management Review, 32*(4), 15–28.

Hill, T. (1993 [1st ed. 1985]). *Manufacturing strategy: Text and cases* (2nd ed.) Blue Ridge Ill.: Irwin Professional Publishing.

Hilletofth, P. (2009). How to develop a differentiated supply chain strategy. *Industrial Management & Data Systems., 109*(1), 16–33.

Hult, G. T. M., Ketchen, D. J., Cavusgil, S. T., & Calantone, R. J. (2006). Knowledge as a strategic resource in supply chains. *Journal of Operations Management, 24*(5), 458–475.

Kerzner, H. (2001). *Strategic planning for project management using a project management maturity model*. New York: Wiley.

Kraljic, P. (1983). Purchasing must become supply management. *Harvard Business Review, 61*(5), 109–117.

Large, R. (2009). *Strategisches beschaffungsmanagement: Eine praxisorientierte Einführung mit Fallstudien* (4th ed.). Wiesbaden: Gabler Verlag/GWV Fachverlage GmbH Wiesbaden.

Li, S., & Lin, B. (2006). Accessing information sharing and information quality in supply chain management. *Decision Support Systems, 42*(3), 1641–1656.

Marcus, C. (1998). A practical yet meaningful approach to customer segmentation. *Journal of Consumer Marketing, 15*(5), 494.

Mason-Jones, R., & Towill, D. R. (1997). Information enrichment: Designing the supply chain for competitive advantage. *Supply Chain Management, 2*(4), 137–148.

Mason-Jones, R., Naylor, B., & Towill, D. R. (2000). Lean, agile or leagile? matching your supply chain to the marketplace. *International Journal of Production Research, 38*(17), 4061–4070.

Massnick, F. (1997). *The customer is CEO: How to measure what your customers want–and make sure they get it*. New York: AMACOM.

McDonald, M., & Dunbar, I. (2009). *Market segmentation: How to do it, how to profit from it*. Oxford: Butterworth-Heinemann.

Mentzer, J. T., Myers, M. B., & Cheung, M.-S. (2004). Global market segmentation for logistics services. *Industrial Marketing Management, 33*(1), 16–20.

Meybodi, M. Z. (2009). Benchmarking performance measures in traditional and just-in-time companies. *Benchmarking: An International Journal, 16*(1), 88–102.

Mikkola, J. H. (2003). Modularity, component outsourcing, and inter-firm learning. *R&D Management, 33*(4), 439–454.

Momme, J., Moeller, M. M., & Hvolby, H.-H. (2000). Linking modular product architecture to the strategic sourcing process: Case studies of two Danish industrial enterprises. *International Journal of Logistics: Research & Applications, 3*(2), 127–146.

Naylor, J. B., Naim, M. M., & Berry, D. (1999). Leagility: Integrating the lean and agile manufacturing paradigms in the total supply chain. *International Journal of Production Economics, 62*(1–2), 107–118.

Neely, A., Gregory, M., & Platts, K. (1995). Performance measurement system design: A literature review and research agenda. *International Journal of Operations & Production Management, 15*(4), 80–116.

Noe, R. A., Hollenbeck, J. R., Gerhart, B. A., & Wright, P. M. (2006). *Human resource management: Gaining a competitive advantage* (5th ed.). Boston, Mass: McGraw-Hill/Irwin.

Novack, R. A., Langley, C. J., and Rinehart, L. M. (1995). Creating logistics value: Themes for the future. Council of Logistics Management: Oak Brook.

O'Dell, C., & Grayson, C. J. (1998). If only we knew what we know: Identification and transfer of internal best practices. *California Management Review, 40*(3), 154–174.

Olhager, J. (2003). Strategic positioning of the order penetration point. *International Journal of Production Economics, 85*(3), 319–329.

Olhager, J., & Östlund, B. (1990). An integrated push-pull manufacturing strategy. *European Journal of Operational Research, 45*(2/3), 135–142.

Poluha, R. G. (2007). *Application of the SCOR model in supply chain management*. Youngstown: Cambria Press.

Porter, M. E. (1980). *Competitive strategy: Techniques for analyzing industries and competitors*. New York: Free Press.

Sahin, F., & Robinson, E. P. (2002). Flow coordination and information sharing in supply chains: Review, implications, and directions for future research. *Decision Sciences, 33*(4), 505–536.

Schilling, M. A. (2000). Toward a general modular systems theory and its application to interfirm product modularity. *Academy of Management Review, 25*(2), 312–334.

Smith, W. (1956). Product differentiation and market segmentation as alternative marketing strategies. *Journal of Marketing, 21*(1), 3–8.

Soni, G., & Kodali, R. (2010). Internal benchmarking for assessment of supply chain performance. *Benchmarking: An International Journal, 17*(1), 44–76.

Southard, P. B., & Parente, D. H. (2007). A model for internal benchmarking: When and how? *Benchmarking: An International Journal, 14*(2), 161–171.

Stavrulaki, E., & Davis, M. (2010). Aligning products with supply chain processes and strategy. *International Journal of Logistics Management, 21*(1), 127–151.

Steenkamp, J.-B. E. M., & Ter Hofstede, F. (2002). International market segmentation: Issues and perspectives. *International Journal of Research in Marketing, 19*(3), 185–213.

Stewart, G. (1997). Supply-chain operations reference model (SCOR): The first cross-industry framework for integrated supply-chain management. *Logistics Information Management, 10*(2), 62–67.

Stuart, F. I. (1997). Supply-chain strategy: Organizational influence through supplier alliances. *British Journal of Management, 8*(3), 223.

Ter Hofstede, F., Wedel, M., & Steenkamp, J.-B. E. M. (2002). Identifying spatial segments in international markets. *Marketing Science, 21*(2), 160–177.

van Raaij, E. M., Vernooij, M. J. A., & van Triest, S. (2003). The implementation of customer profitability analysis: A case study. *Industrial Marketing Management, 32*(7), 573.

von Hippel, E. (1994). Sticky information and the locus of problem solving: Implications for innovation. *Management Science, 40*(4), 429–439.

Wagner, S. M., & Johnson, J. L. (2004). Configuring and managing strategic supplier portfolios. *Industrial Marketing Management, 33*(8), 717–730.

Wedel, M., & Kamakura, W. A. (2003). *Market segmentation: Conceptual and methodological foundations* (2nd ed.). Boston, Mass.: Kluwer Acad. Publ.

Womack, J. P., Jones, D. T., & Roos, D. (1990). *The machine that changed the world: Based on the Massachusetts Institute of Technology 5 million dollar 5 year study on the future of the automobile*. New York: Rawson [u.a.].

Phase 3: Supply Chain Gap Analysis in the SCD-Guide

10

10.1 Goals of SCD-Phase 3

The aim of this analysis is to generate a long list of possible corrective actions, which can be applied to the different modules of the supply chain segmentation framework (Fig. 10.1). After the identification of the TO-BE and AS-IS configurations (designs) for all supply chain modules, a gap analysis is conducted (see Fig. 10.2).

For overcoming the deviations that are recognized in the different modules, the corrective actions listed in this document can be used. An alternative option for realizing need for action is the validation of adequate KPIs. Since a difference between AS-IS and TO-BE states is always assumed in this document, the AS-IS situation is only specified in select cases, when it adds to the matter's understanding. Situations where TO-BE corresponds to AS-IS and thus no need for action is identified are disregarded.

Table 10.1 serves as a guideline to lead through the contents of SCD-Phase 3. It lists all process steps toward a strategy-oriented supply chain that have been introduced so far in their proposed order. This guideline does not only refer back to the contents of SCD-Phase 2, which explain how to define the desired TO-BE states, but primarily leads the user's way to appropriate corrective actions after the gap analysis has been performed. In the fifth column step's configuration equal to TO-BE state, the answer can either be yes or no which indicates which steps still need to be performed.

(1) Firstly, it is possible that the collection of corrective actions is not comprehensive enough yet or that the actions are not appropriate to achieve an organization's specific goals. In this case, it might be helpful to turn to alternative specialized literature or to draw on expert advice.

(2) A second possibility for the inability to choose corrective actions might be an erroneous execution of the prerequisite steps, especially the TO-BE state definition and the AS-IS analysis. Although it is tempting to stick closely to the familiar situation, the derivation of the TO-BE state requires consequent solution orientation. Otherwise the gaps between AS-IS and TO-BE might be

E. Hofmann et al., *The Supply Chain Differentiation Guide*,
DOI: 10.1007/978-3-642-31936-5_10, © Springer-Verlag Berlin Heidelberg 2012

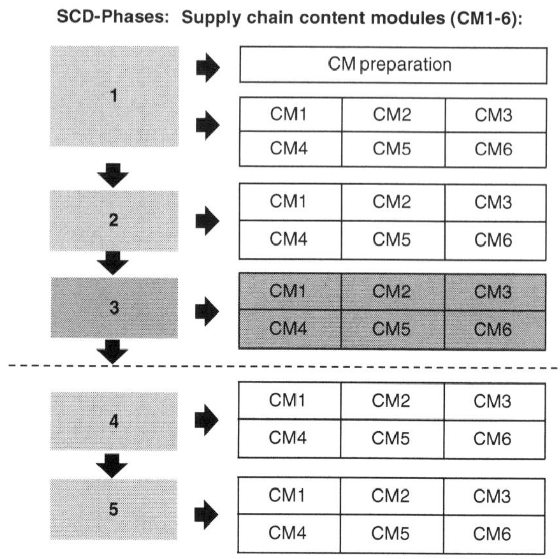

Fig. 10.1 Position of chapter 10 in SCD-Guide

negligibly small. Additionally, the analysis of the AS-IS state requires honesty regarding the current situation (and its possible flaws), since otherwise the results of the gap analysis will not be meaningful either.

10.2 CM1: Customer Segmentation and Supply Chain Strategy

The customer segmentation is starting point of the entire following procedure. The main aim is to configure the different supply chain segments based on customer requirements. For complexity reduction not every single customer is considered. Instead a homogeneous customer segment is the unit of analysis for identifying crucial customer requirements.

10.2.1 Customer Segmentation and Customer Requirements

Customer segmentation should be conducted along certain criteria, which may be found in the guideline concerning the derivation of a TO-BE supply chain. If the current customer segmentation does not satisfy these criteria, a new segmentation should be set up. The issues cited here all refer to the business unit level.

TO-BE	Corrective action
1. Customer segmentation exists on business unit level	Segmentation of customers with respect to adequate criteria (e.g. ABC-analysis, XYZ-analysis)

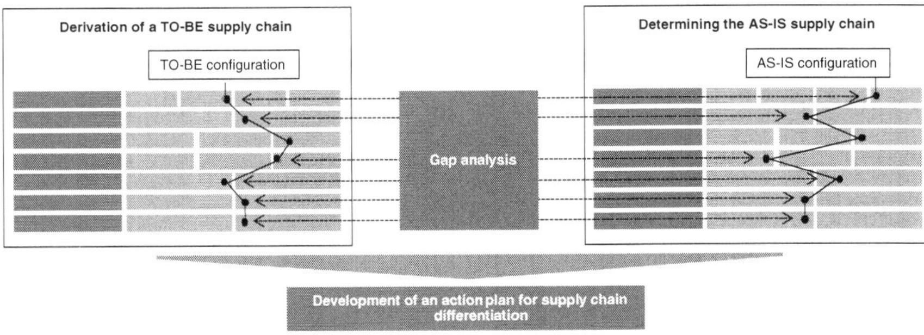

Fig. 10.2 Gap analysis for comparing TO-BE and AS-IS configurations of supply chains

10.2.2 Derivation of the Supply Chain Strategy

After the customer requirements have been identified, a supply chain strategy is derived. To keep the generic framework simple, only two generic supply chain strategies are considered. Every company applying the framework can define its own supply chain strategies, which should always be based on the customers' requirements.

	TO-BE	Corrective action
1.	Agile strategy	Change supply chain configuration (following sections)
2.	Lean strategy	Change supply chain configuration (following sections)

10.3 CM2: Modularization and Vertical Range of Manufacture

10.3.1 Service Offerings Per Customer Segment

For each customer segment and each product sold to this segment the type and degree of additional services to be offered should be defined. They can include different kinds of services for all phases of the customer relationship, ranging from the selection of the right product over installation and commissioning services to after sales services such as maintenance and repair. For example, a high-value customer segment should get an 8 h service in case of a machine breakdown, whereas a low-value customer segment might only get a 24 h service. The after sales service decision is discussed further in Sect. 10.6.5 about the return process.

	TO-BE	Corrective action
1.	Service offering per customer segment and product is defined	Analyze importance of the customer (segment), customer requirements and the desired relationship strength, as well as the products served to define service offerings

Table 10.1 Process guideline for SCD-Phase 3 and the selection of corrective actions

No.	Process step	Chapter	Instruction how to perform step in Chapter	Step's configuration equal to TO-BE state (yes/no)? If yes, proceed to next step	If not: Check if all prerequisite steps been performed and redo them if necessary	If prerequisite steps have been performed: select corrective actions
1	Customer segmentation	10.2.1	3.2		/	10.2
2	Supply chain strategy selection	10.2.2	3.3		1	10.2
3	Service offerings	10.3.1	10.3.1		1–2	10.3
4	Product modularization	10.3.2	4.2, 4.4		1–3	10.3
5	Make-or-buy decisions (per module)	10.3.3	4.3		1–4	10.3
6	Supplier segmentation (per product/module)	10.4	52, 5.2		1–5	10.4
7	Supply strategy selection	10.4	5.4		1–6	10.4
8	Allocation of SC activities	10.5	6.2		1–7	10.5
9	"Plan" process selection (per product/module)	10.6.1	10.6.1		1–5, 8	10.6
10	"Deliver" process selection (per product/module)	10.6.2	6.3		1–5, 8–9	10.6
11	"Make" process selection (per product/module)	10.6.3	6.3		1–8	10.6
12	"Source" process selection (per product/module)	10.6.4	6.3		1-8, 11	10.6
13	"Return" process selection (per product/module)	10.6.5	10.6.5		1–12	10.6

(continued)

Table 10.1 (continued)

No.	Process step	Chapter	Instruction how to perform step in Chapter	Step's configuration equal to TO-BE state (yes/no)? If yes, proceed to next step	If not: Check if all prerequisite steps been performed and redo them if necessary	If prerequisite steps have been performed: select corrective actions
14	Governance: CRM selection per customer segment	10.7.1	7.2, 7.3		1–13	10.7
15	Governance: selection of information sharing level per customer segment	10.7.1	7.2, 7.3		1–14	10.7
16	Governance: supplier relationship management selection per supplier segment	10.7.2	7.2, 7.3		1–15	10.7
17	Governance: selection of information sharing level per supplier segment	10.7.2	7.2, 7.3		1–16	10.7
18	Project management maturity level selection	10.8.1	8.2		1–17	10.8
19	Human resource actions selection	10.8.2	8.3		1–17	10.8
20	Corrective action selection	10.9	10.9		1–17	/
21	Resource availability check	10.10	10.10		1–17, 20	/
22	Corrective action implementation preparation	12	12		1–17, 20–21	/

10.3.2 Specification of the Different Modules Within a Product

To ensure consistent planning along the whole supply chain, products have to be broken down into units, which are either produced in-house or sourced from external suppliers. A first step therefore is the modularization of the products, if possible. If a modularization is not possible, another option is to build material groups (categories), which may be analyzed in the following steps.

	TO-BE	Corrective action
1.	Modularization of products conducted	Identify component categories or "modules" for each product based on material groups or by breaking down their component—end item relationships

10.3.3 Make-Or-Buy Decision Per Module and the Vertical Range of Manufacture

The following corrective actions are applicable whenever a gap is identified concerning the make-or-buy decision of a module.

	AS-IS	TO-BE	Corrective action
1.	Module bought	Module made	Reintegrate module
2.	Module mixed	Module bought	Outsource whole module
3.	Module mixed	Module made	Reintegrate whole module
4.	Module made	Module bought	Outsource module (and following activities like sourcing (possible integration of service provider))
5.	Module bought	Module mixed	Outsource a part, rest keep in-house
6.	Module made	Module mixed	Reintegrate a part, rest keep in-house

10.4 CM3: Supplier Segmentation and Supply Strategy

The modules or categories identified before are now classified by their importance for the manufactured products. Based on this classification and an adequate segmentation framework, the correct number of supplier segments can be identified. Subsequently, supply strategies for each segment and the right number of suppliers have to be identified. Concrete corrective actions can be derived according to the model which is used. In the presented case the (Kraljic 1983) matrix is applied.

	AS-IS check	TO-BE	Corrective action
1.	Has an adequate number of supplier segments been identified?	Homogeneous supplier segments available	Segmentation of suppliers with respect to adequate criteria (e.g. ABC-analysis, XYZ-analysis)
2.		Low number of segments	New supplier segmentation with respect to adequate criteria (e.g. ABC-analysis, XYZ-analysis)
3.		High number of segments	New supplier segmentation with respect to adequate criteria (e.g. ABC-analysis, XYZ-analysis)
4.	Has a differentiated supply strategy been chosen based on module classifications?	Differentiated supply strategy per supplier segments	Introduce differentiated supply strategy per supplier segment
5.		Certain module is categorized as "noncritical item"	Change module categorization and supply strategy accordingly (i.e. local suppliers; short term contracts)
6.		Certain module is categorized as "leverage item"	Change module categorization and supply strategy accordingly (i.e. multiple sourcing mainly local; short to medium term contracts)
7.		Certain module is categorized as "bottleneck item"	Change module categorization and supply strategy accordingly (i.e. global, majorly new suppliers with new technology; variable term contracts, depending on availability and flexibility of supply base)
8.		Certain module is categorized as "strategic item"; supply strategy advice "diversify"	Change module categorization and supply strategy accordingly (i.e. spread volumes, buy on spot markets with focus on low prices, consider backward integration)
9.		Certain module is categorized as "strategic item"; supply strategy advice "balance"	Change module categorization and supply strategy accordingly (i.e. keep volumes at same supplier or shift carefully, balance contracts and purchasing on spot markets)
10.		Certain module is categorized as "strategic item"; supply strategy advice "exploit"	Change module categorization and supply strategy accordingly (i.e. centralize volumes, build up long term contracts, use favorable bargaining position)
11.	Has an adequate number of suppliers been selected?	Single sourcing (one supplier)	Supplier reduction and prioritization
12.		Dual sourcing (two suppliers)	Supplier diversification and development
13		Multiple sourcing (many suppliers)	Supplier diversification and development

10.5 CM4: Allocation of Supply Chain Activities

In this step it is decided where (geographical regions) which activities (processes) should be performed. The strategy used for penetrating geographical markets and customer segments in these geographical regions was derived in step one. The perspective with respect to the size of the geographical region that is targeted in this step is scalable to fit company-specific needs. For instance, a perspective as narrow as a regional one may be taken, or one as large as a continental or even global view.

TO-BE	Corrective action
1. Plan activities for specific customer segment(s) located in considered region	Relocate plan, source, make, deliver, or R&D activities to this region, hire respective capacities or reallocate them from other geographical region
2. Source activities for specific customer segment(s) located in considered region	
3. Make activity for specific customer segment(s) located in considered region	
4. Deliver activity for specific customer segment(s) located in considered region	
5. R&D activity for specific customer segment(s) located in considered region	

10.6 Functional Supply Chain Processes

10.6.1 Plan Process

The planning process spans all supply chain activities dealing with balancing resources and expected demand requirements. Planning in supply chain management is often still performed without comprehensive coordination between different departments. A preferable state, however, is an integrated intra-firm planning process allowing for information sharing and joint decision making. Closer relationships with some supplier and customer segments may even require integrated planning processes between supply chain companies.

AS-IS	TO-BE	Corrective action
1. Single planning process (departments or process owners plan independent from each other)	Integrated (intra-firm) supply chain planning	Implement coordination between departments with respect to supply chain planning
2. Integrated intra-firm supply chain planning	Integrated inter-firm supply chain planning	Enable information sharing of relevant supply, demand, and/or production data, for example by establishing electronic data interchange (EDI) linkages

10.6.2 Deliver Process

For every customer segment an adequate deliver process is selected from the SCOR systematic (SCOR 10.0).

TO-BE	Corrective action
1. Deliver process is "deliver stocked product"	Change deliver process to deliver stocked product (e.g. warehousing of finished products)
2. Deliver process is "deliver make-to-order product"	Change deliver process to deliver make-to-order product (e.g. warehousing of unfinished products and components for fast assembly; postponement)
3. Deliver process is "deliver engineer-to-order product"	Change deliver process to deliver engineer-to-order product (e.g. use of CAD/CAE applications to simulate design, cost and manufacturing process)

10.6.3 Make Process

For every product (or module, if necessary), an adequate make process is selected from the SCOR systematic (SCOR 10.0).

TO-BE	Corrective action
1. Make process is "make-to-stock"	Change make process to make-to-stock (e.g. accurate and approved work instructions/process plans)
2. Make process is "make-to-order"	Change make process to make-to-order (e.g. build subassemblies/products to forecast at highest generic level to minimize make cycle time)
3. Make process is "engineer-to-order"	Change make process to engineer-to-order (e.g. cellular manufacturing)

10.6.4 Source Process

For every supplier segment, an adequate source process is selected from the SCOR systematic (SCOR 10.0).

TO-BE	Corrective action
1. Source process is "source stocked product"	Change source process to source stocked product (e.g. consignment agreements)
2. Source process is "source make-to-order product"	Change source process to source make-to-order product (e.g. electronic kanban support)
3. Source process is "source engineer-to-order product"	Change source process to source engineer-to-order product (e.g. concurrent engineering or implementation of EDI)

10.6.5 Return Process

The SCOR systematic places return processes both upstream and downstream of the supply chain. The "source return" processes refer to the return of raw material or components to suppliers, whereas the "deliver return" processes address the receipt of returned finished goods from customers. Furthermore there is the return of empty containers. For all situations, three different return processes are defined (for defective products, MRO (maintenance, repair, and overhaul) products, and excess products). They are not mutually exclusive and can (or even should) be exercised simultaneously, depending on the chosen supply chain strategy and other factors such as product complexity and service level offered to the customer.

TO-BE	Corrective action
1. Source return process is "return excess product"	Change source return process to "return excess product" (allow source suppliers visibility to current return status, give advanced shipping notice)
2. Source return process is "return defective product"	Change source deliver process to "return defective product" (implement metrics to detect defective products, specify return conditions)
3. Source return process is "return MRO product"	Change source return process to "return MRO product" (consolidate MRO return shipments, establish continuous updates about authorized repair sites)
4. Deliver return process is "return excess product"	Change deliver return process to "return excess product" (maybe outsource excess materials return process, communicate with customers to set conditions for return)
5. Deliver return process is "return defective product"	Change deliver return process to "return defective product" (standardize return procedure, e.g. set up electronic or pre-authorized returns)
6. Deliver return process is "return MRO product"	Change deliver return process to "return MRO product" (develop local receiving process close to repair, electronic reminders of scheduled maintenance)

10.7 CM5: Supply Chain Governance

10.7.1 Customer Relationship Management and Information Sharing

In this step an adequate relationship model for dealing with a respective customer segment is selected. Considering the selected relationship model, information sharing schemes are discussed as well.

Depending on the relationship intensity and the customer's importance, four basic relationship schemes are "transaction based", "standardized process adjustment", "strategic customer relationship", and "strategic alliance" (ordered by increasing relationship intensity and importance). Levels of information sharing range from "low" to "high" depending on an assessment of different elements which affect information sharing between the organization and its customer(s).

TO-BE	Corrective action
1. Customer relationship management is "transaction based"	Change relationship management to transaction based (design customer interfaces very lean and prevent any kind of customer integration, e.g. minimize customer service to complaint handling)
2. Customer relationship management is "standardized process adjustment"	Change relationship management to standardized process adjustment (design customer interfaces lean and standardized, possibly some kind of IT-integration, inter-organizational planning of material flows)
3. Customer relationship management is "strategic customer relationship"	Change relationship management to strategic customer relationship (design customer interfaces with focus on integration, emphasize joint projects e.g. for R&D, CPFR, CRM-system, inter-organizational planning of material flows)
4. Customer relationship management is "strategic alliance"	Change relationship management to strategic alliance (design customer interfaces with focus on strong integration, emphasize joint projects e.g. for R&D, offer further services like JIT and JIS, CPFR, CRM-system, inter-organizational planning of material flows)
5. Information sharing is "low"	Change information sharing to low, e.g. do not deliver any capacity planning or investments plans, only accept placement of orders
6. Information sharing is "low–medium"	Change information sharing to low–medium, e.g. possibly communication of capacity planning on low detail degree, possible IT-integration of the customer for placement of orders, ask customer for short term planning if convenient
7. Information sharing is "medium–high"	Change information sharing to medium–high, e.g. communicate capacity planning, IT-integration of customer, ask customer short and middle term plan if convenient, digital links among supply chain partners, CRM-system, inter-organizational planning of material flows
8. Information sharing is "high"	Change information sharing to high, e.g. communicate capacity planning on high detail level, IT-integration of customer, ask customer short, middle and long term plan if convenient, digital links among supply chain partners, CRM-system, inter-organizational planning of material flows

10.7.2 Supplier Relationship Management and Information Sharing

Like in the previous step for customers, similar considerations with respect to relationship models and information sharing schemes are performed for the supplier segments.

TO-BE	Corrective action
1. Supplier relationship management is "transaction based"	Change relationship management to transaction based (design supplier interfaces very lean and prevent any kind of supplier integration)
2. Supplier relationship management is "standardized process adjustment"	Change relationship management to standardized process adjustment (design supplier interfaces lean and standardized, possibly some kind of IT-integration, inter-organizational planning of material flows)
3. Supplier relationship management is "strategic supplier relationship"	Change relationship management to strategic supplier relationship (design supplier interfaces with focus on integration, emphasize joint projects e.g. for R&D, CPFR, inter-organizational planning of material flows)
4. Supplier relationship management is "strategic alliance"	Change relationship management to strategic alliance (design supplier interfaces with focus on strong integration, emphasize joint projects e.g. for R&D, offer further services like JIT and JIS, CPFR, inter-organizational planning of material flows)
5. Information sharing is "low"	Change information sharing to low, e.g. do not deliver any capacity planning or investments plans, only accept placement of orders
6. Information sharing is "low–medium"	Change information sharing to low–medium, e.g. possibly communication of capacity planning on low detail degree, possible IT-integration of the supplier for placement of orders, ask supplier for short term planning if convenient
7. Information sharing is "medium–high"	Change information sharing to medium–high, e.g. communicate capacity planning, IT-integration of supplier, ask supplier for short and middle term plan if convenient, digital links among supply chain partners
8. Information sharing is "high"	Change information sharing to high, e.g. communicate capacity planning on high detail level, IT-integration of supplier, ask supplier for short, middle and long term plan if convenient, digital links among supply chain partners

10.8 CM6: Supply Chain Project Management and Human Resources Perspective

10.8.1 Supply Chain Project Management

In case of project management, a maturity model is applied. In this model it is hardly possible to implement a higher maturity level before the predecessor level has been mastered. E.g. maturity level two should be implemented before level three. The five levels after the base level "no discernible project management" are "common language", "common processes", "singular methodology", "benchmarking", and "continuous improvement" (Ayers 2004).

AS-IS	TO-BE	Corrective Action
1. Supply chain project management maturity is "no discernible project management"	Supply chain project management maturity is "common language"	Change supply chain project management to "common language" (e.g. create awareness of need for project management)
2. Supply chain project management maturity is "common language"	Supply chain project management maturity is "common processes"	Change supply chain project management to "common process" (e.g. use software to improve project management, educate employees in project management skills)
3. Supply chain project management maturity is "common processes"	Supply chain project management maturity is "singular methodology"	Change supply chain project management to "singular methodology" (e.g. eliminate cultural barriers, implement support for project management throughout the company)
4. Supply chain project management maturity is "singular methodology"	Supply chain project management maturity is "benchmarking"	Change supply chain project management to "Benchmarking" (e.g. establish a project office or a center of excellence to pursue improvements)
5. Supply chain project management maturity is "benchmarking"	Supply chain project management maturity is "continuous improvement"	Change supply chain project management to "continuous improvement" (e.g. cultivate project management talent and share knowledge of project teams (knowledge management concerning conducted projects))

10.8.2 Supply Chain Process Management: Human Resources Perspective

In CM6, "human resources" are considered in the sense of capabilities of human resource management. Therefore, the TO-BE state assumes certain capabilities in treatment with human resources as a prerequisite. If a company's capabilities are not sufficient for an implementation of the proposed corrective actions, consulting firms specialized in human resources may be hired for support (e.g. Mercuri Urval).

TO-BE	Corrective action
1. Strategic HR planning implemented	Implement strategic HR planning (establish long term recruitment planning aiming at fulfilling organizational goals)
2. HR development and training implemented	Implement HR development and training (ensure ongoing employee training and support considering organizational and competitive needs)
3. HR retention management implemented	Implement HR retention management (develop competitive compensation and development schemes to retain high performing personnel and decrease employee turnover)

In order to facilitate the implementation of these measures, the following table presents some typical HR problems and ways to address them.

AS-IS	TO-BE	Corrective action
1. Lack of qualified personnel (shortage risk)	Having the right people with appropriate characteristics and skills available	Improve recruiting and strategic HR planning: forecast the organization's HR needs and plan for how those needs can be met (state objectives, develop and implement programs, evaluate programs' outcomes; e.g. by staffing, appraising, compensating, and training)
2. Personnel is insufficiently trained (adaptation risk)	Employees are prepared for the changing requirements of their jobs	Implement HR development programs for all levels of hierarchy: develop personal development plans, assess employees' potential and personal ambitions, employ on-the-job and off-the-job learning
3. High employee turnover (retention risk)	Talent is nurtured and retained	Carry out HR retention techniques: take care of employees' changing needs and desires during their tenure, ensure fair and adequate compensation (including variable components), acknowledge people's desire for a sound work-life balance
4 Low employee morale and underperformance (motivation risk)	High employee motivation and morale	Apply job design methods to enrich and/or enlarge employees' tasks, foster employee empowerment, make use of (multicultural) teams

10.9 Collection of Corrective Actions

The following corrective actions are sorted to the five management processes defined by the SCOR model and can be used to address gaps which became apparent during one of the previous sections. They are presented along with an explanation and their result, a reference to one of the previous sections of this paper, and an overview of all affected SCOR processes. An "o" indicates the action's primary classification to one of the SCOR processes and an "x" other secondary relations. For instance, the corrective action CPFR (collaborative planning, forecasting and replenishment) is simultaneously affecting plan, source, make, and deliver operations. It shall be noted, however, that the corrective actions' classifications are subjective to a certain degree and can be adjusted to fit a company's unique needs and processes. The introductory paragraphs before each table summarize for which purposes the corrective actions are useful, i.e. which operational goals they can help to achieve.

10.9.1 Corrective Actions: Plan Process

The first collection of corrective actions depicted below is assigned to the SCOR model's first management process, "plan". Actions taken from this list can be especially effective to improve an organization's general supply chain coordination, the integration of supply chain management in its organization, its service portfolio or its relationship with logistics service providers. Furthermore, these corrective actions can help to improve several of an organization's sub-processes such as inventory or distribution management, or support optimizations of lead time and forecasting.

10.9.2 Corrective Actions: Source and Make Processes

The following table presents corrective actions suitable for the management processes "source" and "make". Regarding "source" processes, the corrective actions selected here aim at enhancing the organization's supplier and customer linkages to meet forecasting and planning challenges, as well as to improve supply chain coordination. In the transition zone between "source" and "make" processes, the selected corrective actions can also be helpful if the organization strives for effective forecasting methods, for improving its inventory management, and/or for implementing sound coordination with service providers regarding capacity-related issues. Measures from the "make" section are especially appropriate to address any issues related to inventory management, such as effective inventory management, appropriate inventory segmentation and sufficient visibility, sufficient production capacities as well as capacity utilization.

Corrective action	Description and result	Reference to CMs	Plan	Source	Make	Deliver	Return
Integrated process modeling and software reconfiguration tools	Responsiveness and flexibility are emphasized by developing expertise in making business processes re-programmable, re-configurable and continuously changeable	1–Customer segmentation and supply chain strategy	o				
Inter-organizational planning of material flows	Software that provides multiple data models including the business rules and metrics for the entire supply chain planning process. Algorithms use the business rules and metrics as the drivers for the planning engine	6–Functional supply chain processes (plan)	o		x		
Integrated supply chain planning system with interfaces to all supply/demand data sources through digitally enabled supply networks	Tools support balanced decision making (e.g., trade-off between service level and inventory investment)	6–Functional supply chain processes (plan)	o	x	x	x	x
EDI/connection (e.g. XML-based) among supply chain members	Real-time exchange of supply chain information between supply chain members collaborative planning systems, internet trading exchanges, B2B integration and application server systems	5–Supply Chain Governance	o	x	x	x	x
Supply chain advance planning system	Collaboration among supply chain partners extends outwards to customers, spanning the supply chain. Planning re-planning business rules plan changes	5–Supply chain governance	o	x	x	x	
Supply chain event management systems (supply chain integration)	All key participants in the supply chain, including strategic partners, have full visibility of the demand/supply plan	5–Supply chain governance	o	x	x		

(continued)

(continued)

Corrective action	Description and result	Reference to CMs	Plan	Source	Make	Deliver	Return
B2B integration and application server systems	Forecasts are replaced with actual customer replenishment signals and orders where possible	5–Supply chain governance	o	x	x		
Rules-based distribution planning system	Demand priorities reflecting strategic customer relationships as business policies are automatically followed in allocating resources; first-in-first-out (FIFO) is utilized as the default scheduling priority	1–Customer segmentation and supply chain strategy	o	x	x	x	
Activity based costing	Value pricing based on "cost to serve"; ever day low pricing (EDLP); cost plus pricing	2–Modularization and vertical range of value creation	o				
Proactive education of customers to set expectations and encourage close working relationships	Knowledge of long-lead items, visibility to supply resources, agreement on levels of flexibility	5–Supply chain governance	o				x
Available-to-promise (ATP) check	Available-to-promise (ATP) provides an availability and feasibility check concerning a customer request or a customer order	5–Supply Chain Governance	o	x	x		
Integrate customer-focused marketing plans with the management of the supply chain	Comprehensive S&OP (sales and operations planning)	1–Customer segmentation and supply chain strategy	o	x	x	x	
Customer relationship management system (CRM)	Software that provides customer input and keeps the customer informed about the planning of the production and delivery process by managing all contacts and communication with the customer thorough all channels including internet and traditional sales and customer service channels	5–Supply chain governance	o	x	x	x	x

(continued)

(continued)

Corrective action	Description and result	Reference to CMs	Plan	Source	Make	Deliver	Return
Business intelligence (BI) software	A data warehouse and data mart is the source of all planning (master) data, business rules and transaction data. Analytical tools enable the ongoing maintenance and improvement of the business rules based on actual data	6–Functional supply chain processes (plan)	o	x			
Joint service agreements (JSAs) between buyers and suppliers	Define the levels of “flexibility” or resource upside available within stated lead times and agreed upon conditions	3–Supplier segmentation and supply strategy	o	x	x	x	
Collaborative planning tools with source suppliers	Joint service agreements to document acceptable service levels in terms of installation costs, installation cycle time, etc.	3–Supplier segmentation and supply strategy	o	x	x	x	x

“o” = primary “x” = secondary

Corrective action	Description and result	Reference to CMs	Plan	Source	Make	Deliver	Return
Frequent review and adjustments of the demand plan	To reflect actual consumption or customer forecast information	1–Customer segmentation and supply chain strategy	x	o			x
Inter-company resource planning with EDI/Internet communication	EDI links integrate supplier resource information (inventory, capacity availability, etc.) with own resources	5–Supply chain governance	x	o			
Digital linkage to supplier quoting, planning, configuration and customer service applications	Consideration of supplier's material availability in company's supply resources (including supplier's production plans and capability, inventory, and delivery plans)	5–Supply chain governance	x	o			
Integrated software systems for matching shelf stock to expectations	A software-based system that corrects shelf inventory levels based on actual product present (possible RFID solution). Identifies stock-outs from shrinkage or item misplacement.	6–Functional supply chain processes (source and make)	x	o	o		
Collaborative planning, forecasting, replenishment (CPFR)	Collaborative planning, forecasting and replenishment is a concept that allows collaborative processes across the supply chain, using a set of process and technology models	6–Functional supply chain processes (source and make)	x	o	o	x	
Dynamic deployment based on constraint-based planning and optimal scheduling	Advanced planning and scheduling logic with constraint, cost, and resource optimization	6–Functional supply chain processes (Source and Make)	x	o	o		
Exception management (e.g.: unplanned orders are accepted and scheduled only when there is no detrimental impact on overall product delivery plan)	Digital linkages using XML standards (Rosettanet, eBXML, OAGI) to automatically query production capacity and ATP and schedule unplanned orders	1–Customer segmentation and supply chain strategy		o	o		

(continued)

(continued)

Corrective action	Description and result	Reference to CMs	Plan	Source	Make	Deliver	Return
Bi-directional digital links (XML, EDI, etc.) or internet procurement networks to customer service linkage	Distinct and consistent linkages exist to ensure disruptions and opportunities in material resources are quickly and accurately communicated and acted upon	5–Supply chain governance		o	o		
Enterprise-wide planning system for re-balancing of full-stream supply/demand	Re-balancing of full-stream supply/demand on a daily basis, including source-make-deliver resources and requirements from "customers' customer to suppliers' supplier"	5–Supply chain governance	x	o	o	x	
Integrated supply chain or demand planning with point of sale and customer inventory systems	Customer relationship and digital linkages (XML, EDI, Etc.) provide accurate visibility into actual demand via customer forecasts, product plans, production plans, and inventory positions	5–Supply chain governance	x	o	o		x
Eliminate "special deals" to improve forecast accuracy	Reduces uncertainty, lowers safety stock requirements, cheaper to administer	1–Customer segmentation and supply chain strategy	x	o	o		
Enterprise resource planning System (ERP)	On-line visibility of all supply chain demand requirements and resources, both currently available and committed (pegged)	6–Functional supply chain processes (plan)	x	o	o		
Vendor managed inventory (VMI)	VMI is a concept for planning and control of inventory, in which the supplier has access to the customer's inventory data and is responsible for maintaining the inventory level required by the customer. Re-supply is performed by the vendor through regularly scheduled reviews of the on-site inventory. The on-site inventory is counted, damaged or outdated goods are removed, and the inventory is restocked to predefined levels	5–Supply chain governance	x	o	o		x

(continued)

(continued)

Corrective action	Description and result	Reference to CMs	Plan	Source	Make	Deliver	Return
Integrated demand planning driven by POS; customer movement data	Continuous replenishment programs; vendor managed inventory, telemetry to automatically communicate replenishment of chemicals	5–Supply chain governance	o	o			x
Frequent review and adjustments of inventory targets	Digital Linkages using XML standards (RosettaNet, eBXML, OAGI) to automatically query inventory levels	1–Customer segmentation and supply chain strategy		o			
ABC-analysis	Classification of products by value	1 and 3–Customer segmentation and supplier segmentation	x	o		x	
XYZ-analysis	Classification of products by re-ordering frequency	1 and 3–Customer segmentation and supplier segmentation		o			
Categorize 100 % of total inventory (active, usable, excess, obsolete) for appropriate action	Classification of inventory with respect to different criteria	2–Modularization and vertical range of value creation		o			
Integrated load planning and building with warehouse management	Consolidate oders by customer, source, traffic lane, carrier, etc.	2–Modularization and vertical range of value creation	x	o			
Real time inventory control, stock locator, and rules based picking logic	Dynamic location assignment including lot control, zoned picking, quality assurance	2–Modularization and vertical range of value creation		o			

"o" = primary "x" = secondary

10.9.3 Corrective Actions: Deliver Processes

The final collection of corrective actions has been compiled to improve an organization's "deliver" processes. On the edge of "make" and "deliver", the corrective actions can be useful to optimize supply chain coordination, distribution management, as well as inventory management. Corrective actions assigned to the "deliver" process are grouped around potential for optimization of an organization's distribution processes. This includes better coordination with logistics service providers, shorter lead time, enhanced distribution planning, effective utilization of different transportation modes, and even an appropriate service portfolio. The table's last two corrective actions are process-spanning and can directly be related to all three preceding categories ("source", "make", and "deliver"), and therefore affect lead and transit time, capacity utilization and distribution planning.

Corrective action	Description and result	Reference to CMs	Plan	Source	Make	Deliver	Return
Advanced shipping notices, e.g. container labeling	Bar coding; EDI; integrated transportation/warehouse management	6–Functional supply chain processes (deliver)			o	o	
Automatic identification	Bar coding and radio frequency communications (RFID and other tagging)	6–Functional supply chain processes (make and deliver)	x		o	o	x
Consolidation of carriers	Transportation modeling and rate analysis	4–Allocation of supply chain activities		x		o	
Merge-in-Transit/Hub consolidation	Merge-in-Transit is a practice to combine items from multiple sources into a single customer shipment. This includes items on stock in the distribution center, from which the shipment is sent, items on stock in other distribution centers, items on stock elsewhere (e.g. at a plant or a supplier) as well as make-to-order items. The items to be merged are cross-docked from inbound receipt to outbound shipping. Merging is usually performed in a shipper's distribution center (DC) or in a carrier's terminal	6–Functional supply chain processes (source and deliver)		x		o	
Cross docking	Used in many distribution centers (DC) to increase inventory velocity while maintaining shipping efficiency. In a traditional DC, the receiving process is disjointed from the shipping process and storage acts as an intermediary between the two processes. Cross docking actively links the receiving and shipping processes. In a DC, both cross docking (no storage) and traditional (with storage) operations might take place	6–Functional supply chain processes (source/deliver)		x		o	x
Route scheduling, carrier selection, and rating	Carrier/route optimization based on continuous movement and consolidation or pooling	4–Allocation of supply chain activities		x		o	

(continued)

(continued)

Corrective action	Description and result	Reference to CMs	Plan	Source	Make	Deliver	Return
Rules-based carrier selection and actual rate database	Select carriers by (for ex.): least cost per shipment and rate using actual rates prior to release to billing; lead or response time; reliability	6–Functional supply chain processes (source/deliver)		x		o	
Shipment tracking and tracing	Satellite communications, GPS, RFID	6–Functional supply chain processes (source/deliver)		x		o	x
Integrated inbound/outbound transportation planning	Consolidation of inbound and outbound requirements	4–Allocation of supply chain activities	x	x		o	x
Carrier agreement	Carrier agreements are agreements between a company and its domestic and global carriers (for both, inbound raw materials and outbound finished goods) specifying service levels, payment terms, and other conditions	6–Functional supply chain processes (source/deliver)	x			o	x
Event-driven supply chain re-planning	Change in the demand signal instantaneously "reconfigures" the production and supply plans	1–Customer segmentation and supply chain strategy		x	x	x	
Supply chain modeling and visualization system	Capability to run "simulated" full-stream supply/demand balancing for "what-if" scenarios	6–Functional supply chain processes (plan)		x	x	x	

"o" = primary "x" = secondary

10.10 Supply Chain Resources

The feasibility of implementing one or more of the corrective actions presented in Sect. 10.9 depends on whether enough organizational resources are available or not. The following table depicts a framework for categorizing different resources in an organization along with examples for such resources.

Category	Resource examples
Financial resources	**Cash**: Cash flows or accruals for supply chain-specific investments
Physical resources	**Infrastructure**: Warehouse and production facilities
	Vehicles: Transportation vehicles, network etc.
	Machines: Specific production machines
Organizational resources and capabilities	**Systems, tools and processes**: Information systems, management and incentive systems, demand planning, supplier selection, new product introduction tools and procedures, supply chain project management and cooperation procedures
	Structure: Alignment of R&D, supply chain management and other departments, interdisciplinary project team capacity
	Culture: Learning capabilities, cooperation attitudes and communication level, etc.
Human resources and capabilities	**Knowledge**: Specialists for supply chain function areas such as planning, sourcing, manufacturing, distribution or internal logistics
	Capabilities: Process-specific know-how, etc.

If a mismatch between the resources required and the resources available to implement a certain corrective action is recognized, appropriate measures have to be taken. Examples for such measures can be found in the following table, which addresses specific resource-related problems and suiting remedies.

	TO-BE	Corrective action	Resource category
1.	IT infrastructure and systems are sufficient to support selected corrective actions	Implement needed IT infrastructure and systems	Organizational resources and capabilities
2.	Capabilities of staff with respect to R&D, market research, product and process management are sufficient to support selected corrective actions	Train staff or hire new staff	Human resources and capabilities
3.	Production capacities are sufficient to support selected corrective actions	Invest in production capacities	Physical resources

(continued)

(continued)

	TO-BE	Corrective action	Resource category
4.	Warehousing capacities are sufficient to support selected corrective actions	Invest in warehousing capacities	Physical resources
5.	Transport capacities and modal split are sufficient to support selected corrective actions	Invest in transport capacities or outsource transport, investigate modal split in transport	Physical resources and Organizational resources and capabilities

Summary Sheet

SCD-Phase 3: Supply chain gap analysis and identification of courses of action

Goals of SCD-Guide Phase 3

The goal of Phase 3 is to show the existing gaps between the AS-IS and the TO-BE situation of the supply chain differentiation analysis. This chapter aims to find the existing gaps and corrective actions and focus on the most relevant aspects of the supply chain differentiation process.

Methods and analysis for SCD-Guide Phase 3

- Comparing the AS-IS analysis with the TO-BE analysis

Input per methods for SCD-Guide Phase 3

Corrective actions for the implementation of the supply chain differentiation process

Input from other phases	Customer segmentation	Product modularization
Phase 1 Phase 2	• Customer segmentation • Supply chain configuration	• Reintegrating or outsourcing decision of product modules

Input from other phases	Supplier segmentation	Activity allocation
Phase 1 Phase 2	• Change module categorization • New supplier segmentation • Segmentation of suppliers • Supplier reduction/prioritization • Supplier diversification/development	• Relocate plan, source, make, deliver, and/or R&D activities to this region, hire respective capacities or reallocate them from other geographical region

Input from other phases	Supply chain governance	Supporting activities
Phase 1 Phase 2	• Change relationship management • Change level of information sharing	• Change supply chain project management • Implement HR measures (HR planning, training and development and retention)

Output from SCD-Guide Phase 3

- Identification of gaps and corrective actions for the implementation of the supply chain differentiation process

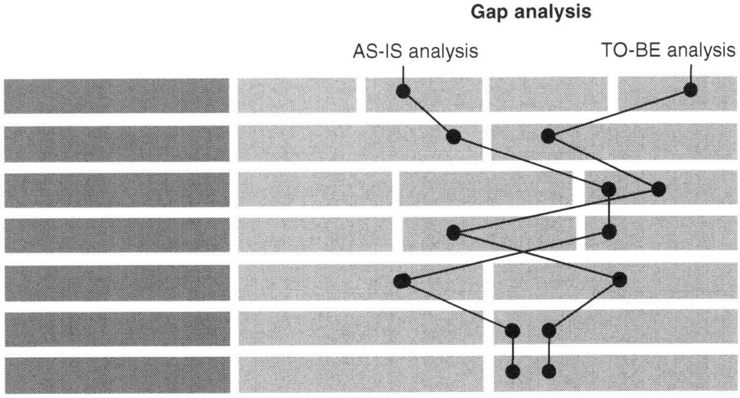

Fig. 10.3 Schematic overview of the gap analysis for SCD-Phase 3 of the supply chain differentiation process

10.11 Application Example of SCD-Guide SCD-Phase 3 and Possible Output

In SCD-Phase 3, PC Manufacturing Inc. tries to find the existing gaps between the AS-IS supply chain and the TO-BE supply chain of SCD-Phase 1 and 2. In order to find the differences between the two, it is necessary to match the different content modules with one another as shown in the morphological box and find the gaps respectively.

Content Module 1 describes that there has not been any significant customer segmentation done for the supply chain differentiation process. The customer segmentation has not fully taken place within the current situation of PC Manufacturing Inc. The biggest gap and focus of this supply chain gap analysis lies thereby within the customer segmentation. The customer segmentation is one of the core aspects of a successful implementation of the supply chain differentiation process, since it is the basis for the supply chain segmentation.

The descriptive part of the morphological box serves only for the characterization of the regarded customer segment. Therefore it does not need to be considered for the gap analysis. The following gaps have been identified with the gap analysis.

- In the TO-BE analysis, PC Manufacturing Inc. has identified three different **customers segments** which are business, private and public. The AS-IS analysis has thereby only found two different customers segments which are private and business due to the fact that they have different distribution channels but not yet aligned to the supply chain.

  Corrective action: Implementation of supply chain segmentation according to customer segmentation.

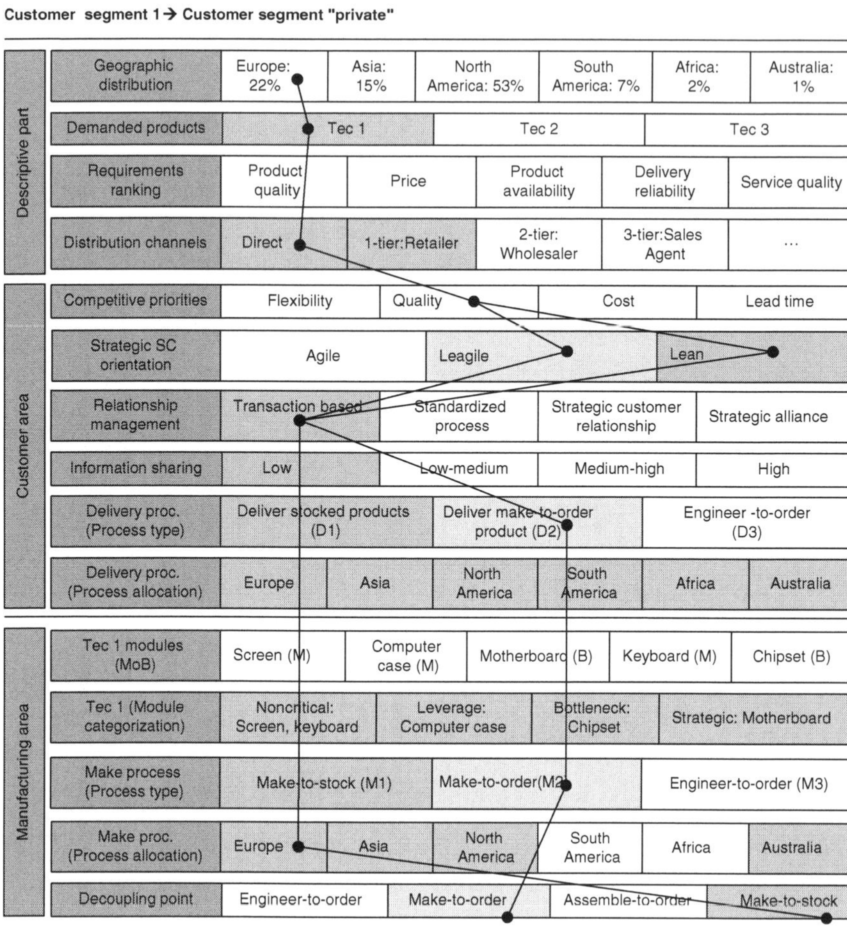

Fig. 10.4 Exemplary morphological box of PC Manufacturing Inc. (1/2)

- The analysis of the **manufacturing area** has shown that the supply chain is currently lean without taken customer requirements into further consideration and the making process is currently make-to-stock. The TO-BE analysis suggested a leagile supply chain due to the fact that it takes customer requirements into consideration. Furthermore the make process needs to be shifted from make-to-stock to a make-to-order process.
  Corrective action: *Change strategic supply chain orientation to leagile-.*
- Gaps can furthermore be seen within the **supplier area**, where bottleneck and noncritical item and their buyer–supplier relationships are rather transaction based. Leverage items are standardized processed and information sharing is medium–low. The strategic items and their buyer–supplier relationship is based on a strategic alliance and their level of information sharing is high. The gap

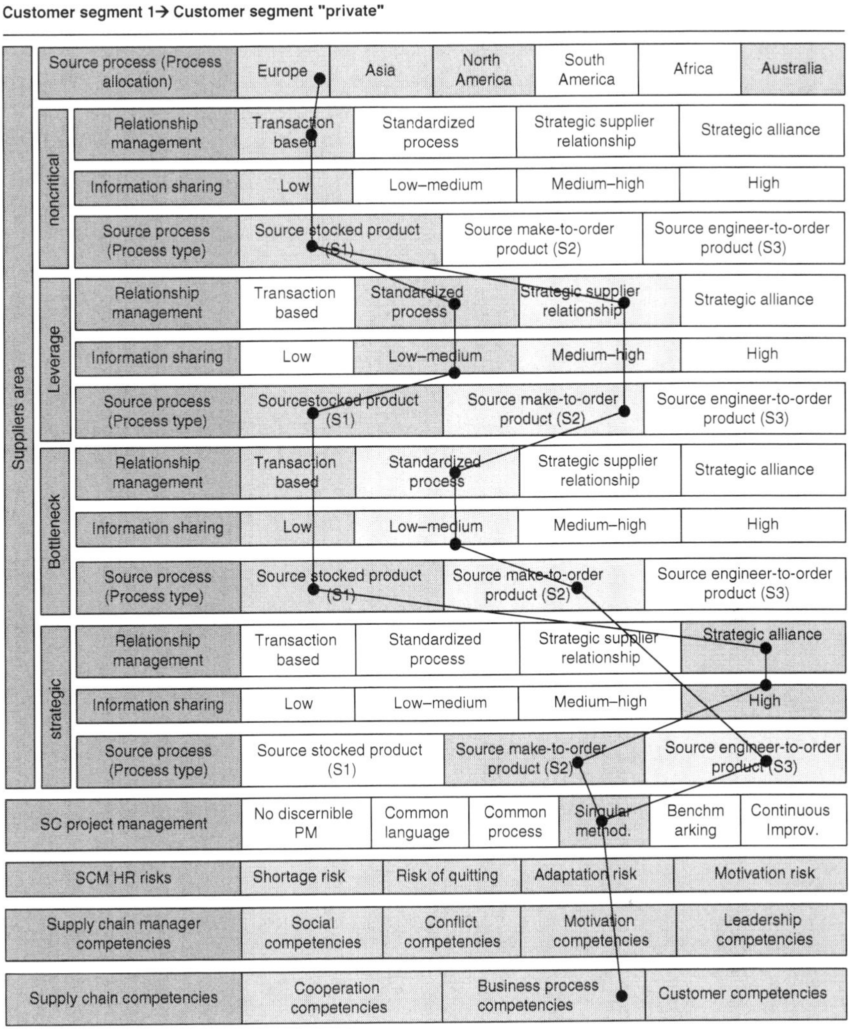

Fig. 10.5 Exemplary morphological box of PC Manufacturing Inc. (2/2)

analysis shows however, that leverage as well as bottleneck items should have another level of buyer–supplier relationship and thereby a higher level of information sharing. Leverage items are therefore based on a strategic supplier relationship and a medium–high information sharing. Bottleneck items are based on standardized processes and therefore have a low-medium level of information sharing.

Corrective action: Changing the relationship management and information sharing of suppliers of leverage and bottleneck items.

- Further gaps between the two analyses are within the **supporting activities**. In the AS-IS analysis it has shown that the human resource risks exist due to the missing implementation of human resource measures as seen in the TO-BE analysis. It is therefore important for PC Manufacturing Inc. to implement the different human resource measures such as human resource planning, training and development and retention. Furthermore the supply chain manager competencies and supply chain competencies need to be consolidated. This will help to prevent human resource risks which could occur in the future.
  Corrective action: Improvement to the next project management level, implementation of human resource planning, training and development and retention as well as supply chain competencies.

In Fig. 10.3 there is a schematic overview of the two different analyses put into one morphological box. It shows the gaps between the analyses and the corrective actions which need to be closed by the company within the supply chain differentiation process.

The gap analysis has shown that especially within CM1, CM3, CM4 and CM6, there are significant gaps and a strong need for corrective actions in order to close the gaps between the AS-IS and TO-BE situation of PC Manufacturing Inc. The morphological box shows the AS-IS analysis as well as the TO-BE analysis. It can be seen that the AS-IS analysis has been marked in darker grey shaded, whereas the TO-BE analysis is marked into lighter grey shaded. The parts of the morphological box which are only shaded into one color show the parts of the morphological box, where there are no existing gaps (Figs. 10.4 and 10.5).

References

Ayers, J. B. (2004). *Supply chain project management: a structured collaborative and measurable approach*. Boca Raton: St. Lucie Press.

Kraljic, P. (1983). Purchasing must become supply management. *Harvard Business Review, 61*(5), 109–117.

Phase 4: Supply Chain Prioritization and Selection of Corrective Actions

11

11.1 Goals for SCD-Phase 4

SCD-Phase 4 aims to identify a limited number of corrective actions which can help to change an organization's supply chain management toward the optimal supply chain as identified in SCD-Phase 1. Prerequisite steps for the procedure outlined in this guideline are a gap analysis that compares TO-BE and AS-IS supply chains and a self-benchmarking on adequate KPIs. Gaps revealed by these analyses can then lead to the most appropriate corrective actions if the proposed four steps are performed. This document proceeds as follows: after an introductory section about the four-step approach and the derivation of corrective actions the remaining sections provide a more detailed description of all necessary steps to be taken, illustrated by practical examples. A final paragraph gives an outlook on the following content module, which deals with preparing the implementation of the selected corrective actions (Fig. 11.1).

11.2 Prioritization Procedure for Corrective Actions

Two separate paths lead to the identification of corrective actions in the differentiation approach, one being more strategic, the other one being more operative. Prerequisite to both paths is the derivation of a TO-BE supply chain and the identification of the current AS-IS supply chain (Fig. 11.2). Once this groundwork has been done, decision makers in charge of the supply chain optimization procedure can decide to pursue either one of the two paths, or both, since they should be considered as complementary approaches.

In case of the strategic path, the completed morphological boxes from SCD-Phase 1 and 2 are used to perform a gap analysis, which compares desired and actual supply chains and thereby helps to uncover differences between these two supply chain designs. The operative path provides that based on an organization's competitive priorities adequate key performance indicators (KPIs) are selected. Decision makers can use these KPIs to conduct a self-benchmarking of their

E. Hofmann et al., *The Supply Chain Differentiation Guide*,
DOI: 10.1007/978-3-642-31936-5_11, © Springer-Verlag Berlin Heidelberg 2012

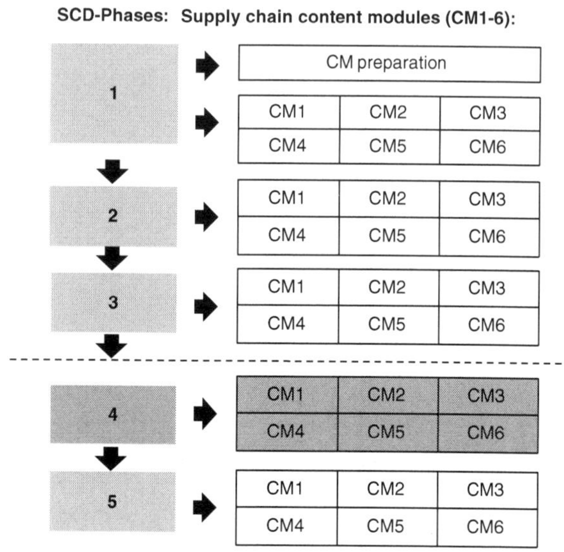

Fig. 11.1 Position of chapter 11 in SCD-Guide

organization's performance on these dimensions. Just like the gap analysis, the self-benchmarking reveals differences between optimal and actual states. It is the goal of all following steps to identify corrective actions appropriate to overcome the differences and approach the desired TO-BE supply chain as closely as possible.

The following four-step procedure is applicable to both paths:

1) **Goal prioritization**: determine most urgent gaps
2) **Identification of corrective actions**: compile a preliminary list of possible actions
3) **Pre-selection of corrective actions**: reduce the number of actions to a manageable size
4) **Evaluation and prioritization of remaining corrective actions**: select the ones that can realistically be implemented and will help to achieve the desired TO-BE supply chain states

11.3 Step 1: Goal Prioritization

The preliminary step of prioritizing an supply chain organization's gaps or "goals" which need to be addressed in the following steps is necessary because it is likely that the gap analysis reveals several fields requiring improvement, which cannot be optimized simultaneously. It follows logically from this project's structure that gaps discovered in one of the earlier steps such as supply chain strategy, customer segmentation or product modularization will have effects on later processes, making additional gaps in later modules more likely. In order to economically

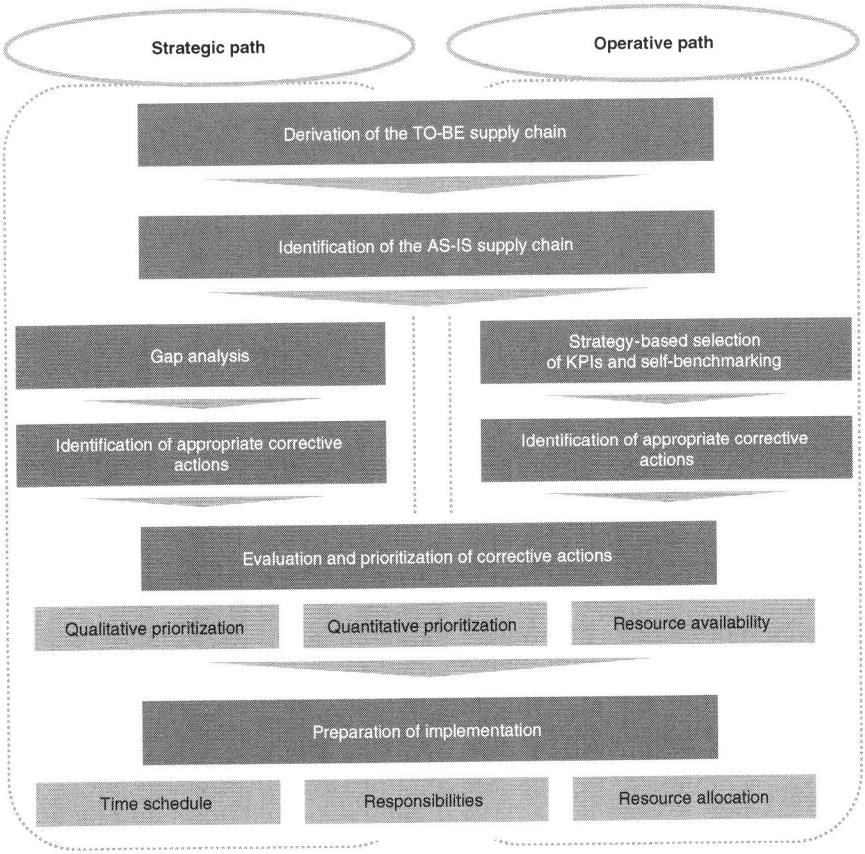

Fig. 11.2 Procedure for identifying and prioritizing corrective actions in supply chain differentiation

employ their resources, companies should therefore prioritize the numerous identified gaps and begin with addressing the most critical ones. It shall be noted that prioritization should not mean to ignore other deficient areas, but merely to postpone its solution as long as other problems are more pressing. While in the previous stages the different topics, gaps, and opportunities discussed may have been confusing, an advantage of this step it that the data to be analyzed is graphically organized by the morphological boxes or by the tables summarizing the KPI (self-) benchmarking.

(a) In order to rank gaps by urgency, three considerations are proposed:
The individual gap's criticality for the organization's competitiveness should be assessed. Deviations from the desired states in categories such as strategic supply chain orientation are more vital to an organization's performance than differences in areas like the information sharing level with customer and suppliers, and should therefore be addressed first (which is not to mean that the

latter does not contribute to an organization's overall health as well). Likewise, for the KPI path, some key performance indicators are more direct measures of the chosen strategic orientation than others and can thus be considered to be more important. "Average lead time" or "manufacturing lead time", for instance, are more direct measures of lead time than is "capacity utilization".

(b) A second method for sorting gaps by criticality is to consider their respective magnitude. In all categories with ordinal scales and in the case of KPI benchmarking, a greater difference indicates a greater need for action. It may thus be reasonable to start addressing those gaps, in which the greatest leap forward is necessary to achieve the intended TO-BE supply chain state. This advice is more difficult to apply in categories without clear internal scales, such as decisions concerning the type of distribution, make, and source processes, or those dealing with locating supply chain processes. In these cases a relevance ranking is more promising. To determine the interdependence between different modules, the checklist introduced at the beginning of SCD-Phase 3 can be used. It describes the logical order of the framework's steps and highlights which steps are prerequisite for others.

(c) The third method acknowledges the importance of managerial experience and industry knowledge. At this stage of the supply chain differentiation project, decision makers have undergone all the analytic steps from derivation of the TO-BE supply chain states to identifying and categorizing the AS-IS situation by the proposed framework. They presumably always spent most time discussing exactly those areas which should now be addressed first. Paired with their knowledge of the company traditional strengths and weaknesses as well as of important market trends, this experience is indispensable for the decision to address gaps in the most relevant areas. The outcome of this pre-selection should be the definition of a limited number of gaps, ordered by their importance. Then appropriate corrective actions for addressing the gaps can be identified.

The three different decisions can be examined and a decision on which of the following approaches is most appropriate, can be made.

11.4 Step 2: Identification of Corrective Actions

The next step following the definition of the most important supply chain management goals is the identification of appropriate corrective actions. The framework provides a "long list of corrective actions" as the main tool for this identification. Since the process toward the corrective actions differs slightly between the strategic path and the operative path, the two will be explained separately.

	Mgmt. process according to SCOR model	Corrective action	Description and result	Reference to CMs	Plan	Source	Make	Deliver	Return
40	Deliver	Merge-in-Transit / Hub consolidation	Merge-in-Transit is a practice to combine items from multiple sources into a single customer shipment. This includes items on stock in the distribution center, from which the shipment is sent, items on stock in other distribution centers, items on stock elsewhere (e.g. at a plant or a supplier) as well as make-to-order items. The items to be merged are cross-docked from inbound receipt to outbound shipping. Merging is usually performed in a shipper's distribution center (DC) or in a carrier's terminal.	6 - Functional Supply Chain Processes (Source/Deliver)		x		o	
41	Deliver	Cross -docking	Used in many distribution centers (DC) to increase inventory velocity while maintaining shipping efficiency. In a traditional DC, the receiving process is disjointed from the shipping process and storage acts as an intermediary between the two processes. Cross docking actively links the receiving and shipping processes. In a DC, both cross docking (no storage) and traditional (with storage) operations might take place.	6 - Functional Supply Chain Processes (Source/Deliver)		x		o	x

"o" = primary ; "x" = secondary

Filter options

1	2	3	4
Supply chain modules	SCOR processes	Organizational goal	Allocation from KPIs

Fig. 11.3 Illustration of two of the filter options in the "long list of corrective actions" (full tables can be found in Chap. 10)

As for the **strategic path**, three complementary ways lead to the identification of corrective actions, all using different filters that have been worked into the Fig. (11.3). The first method follows most intuitively from the preceding steps, since it considers the different modules of the framework (such as "customer segmentation" or "functional supply chain processes"). Decision makers can thus simply look up their most important gaps obvious from the morphological box and identify possible corrective actions. This approach is especially useful if an entire process step of the framework needs improvement, but it is advisable to use the other filtering methods as well. The second option uses a categorization by the SCOR processes. Since an unambiguous classification of all corrective actions to only one of the SCOR processes is neither practical nor reasonable, all corrective actions have a primary and, if applicable, several secondary classifications with respect to the SCOR processes. The primary classification is indicated by a circle ("o") and the secondary classification(s) by a cross ("x"). The last filtering

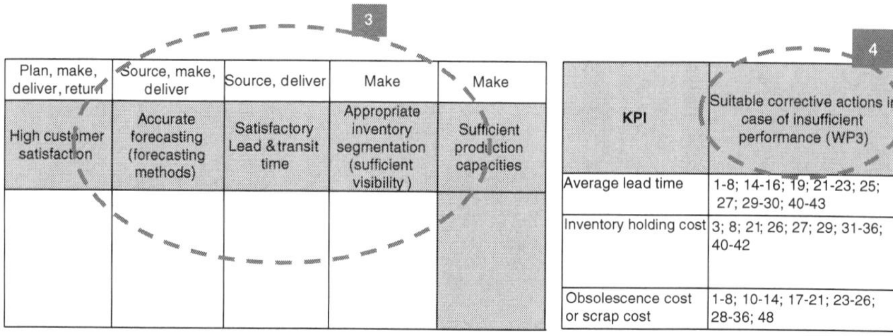

Fig. 11.4 Illustration of the third and fourth filter option (Full tables for filter 3 can be found in the Appendix, for filter 4 in Chap. 9)

possibility covers more specific organizational goals such as "efficient production capacity utilization" or "effective cooperation and coordination with 3PLs".

Moreover, the filter method mentioned last is equally well suited for the **operational path** coming from the KPI self-benchmarking. In this case the connection between the area requiring a corrective action and the company goals as listed in Fig. (11.3) is even more straightforward. Sometimes even the wording of the KPI and the organizational goal in the "corrective actions" figure is identical, in other cases a little derivation is necessary (for example from all cost-related KPIs to organizational goals dealing with "efficiency"). The other option for deriving corrective actions from the KPI benchmarking is via the suggestions in the Figs. (11.3) and (11.4). The numbers listed behind each KPI refer to different corrective actions. Since this list aims to provide an extensive pool of possible corrective actions, some of the proposed actions are more closely related to the respective KPIs and some more remotely. The different filter options are illustrated in Figs. (11.3) and (11.4).

11.5 Step 3: Pre-Selection of Corrective Actions

Since Step 2 is likely to help identify several possible corrective actions, of which not all may be attainable and even desired, the final two steps suggest a structured procedure how corrective actions can be evaluated and selected. The goal of the third step is to pre-select the most promising corrective actions from the original sample to ensure that companies do not waste time and money with unfeasible or inappropriate actions. Decision makers therefore have to delete irrelevant measures from the list and determine a hierarchy among the remaining corrective actions indicating their preferred sequence of implementation. Table 11.1 shows five criteria which aid in this decision.

The pre-selection can be conducted with a short questionnaire (see Table 11.2). It suggests one assessment question for each of the above mentioned decision criteria. A simple ordinal scale with qualitative criteria helps to screen the range of

Table 11.1 Decision criteria for evaluating corrective actions for supply chain differentiation

Decision criteria	Explanatory questions
1. Utility	How likely is this corrective action to lead to the desired target (in comparison with the other alternatives or in absolute terms)?
2. Feasibility of implementation	How likely is the implementation to succeed? Are sufficient financial resources financial resources and expertise available (e.g. to cover implementation and maintenance cost)?
3. Time to implementation	How long will it take to get this measure up and running?
4. Usability	Are employees sufficiently qualified to execute the measure (especially if IT is concerned?)
5. Risk of scope creep and budget overrun	How reliable are your previous estimates concerning cost, time, and expertise?

Table 11.2 Questionnaire for pre-selecting corrective actions for supply chain differentiation

Criteria	Answer options	Measure 1	Measure 2	Measure 3	Measure 4	Measure 5
In your opinion, how appropriate is the measure to address the gap?	(1) Not appropriate (2) Medium appropriateness and undecided (3) Perfectly appropriate					
How likely is this measure's implementation to succeed (consider resource availability)?	(1) Very unlikely (2) Equal probability of failure versus success (3) Very likely					
Do you believe the projected timeframe to implementation is attainable?	(1) Unattainable (2) Medium attai-nability/ undecided (3) Attainable					
Is sufficient expertise available to execute the measure now and in the long run?	(1) No (2) Probably yes; if not yet available it can be obtained (3) Yes					
How high is the risk that the limits of time and money will be exceeded?	(1) High (2) Medium (3) Low					

corrective actions quickly to derive a final list of the most promising ones. Every measure rated with at least one "(1)" in the questionnaire should be disregarded for implementation. Of course, the managers applying this questionnaire retain all discretion with respect to this decision, since this strict rule may—in the worst case—lead to all corrective actions being separated out. It may then be necessary to lower the rule for eliminating alternatives or to use different questions.

11.6 Step 4: Evaluation and Prioritization of Corrective Actions

The corrective actions remaining after the pre-selection in step 4 now undergo a final, more detailed analysis. Its goal is to clarify the measures' strengths and weaknesses and to define their rank order. Two decision making methods are suggested, which differ in scope and level of complexity. As a general rule, decision makers representing all different affected functions should participate in any of the techniques. They should bear in mind, however, that a healthy balance between the decision procedure itself and the following implementation process is advisable. That is, the decision process for determining the measures' ranking should not need more time and effort than the implementation itself. Before the alternative methods are explained, some general remarks about this decision shall be provided.

In addition to the questions directly related to the five decision criteria presented in Table 11.2, some additional factors impact the decision for or against certain corrective actions as well. To raise awareness of such ancillary considerations, three of them are shortly explained in the following paragraphs.

11.6.1 Existence of Prior Experience

The first thing managers have to ask is whether any prior experience exists in the company with measures similar or equal to the ones under discussion. If so, it is recommendable to discuss which specific experiences were made in order to facilitate the implementation. It might be necessary to contact former managers or employees who have left the company by now, or to use external contacts to gather more information. Even managers unfamiliar with such actions are then able to obtain a realistic picture of common fallacies or success factors and to avoid unpleasant surprises. Possibly external support may be necessary for conducting the whole evaluation and selection procedure if an objective decision making cannot be guaranteed otherwise.

11.6.2 Extent of Intra- and Inter-Organizational Implementation

Secondly, managers should discuss if the selected measure(s) will be implemented by the organization alone of jointly in cooperation with partners from the supply chain. Whereas in some cases it may simply be an attractive way to share the cost and risk attached to implementation, other cases will even require close cooperation (for example most IT projects). Besides the positive effects collaboration may have on project management, managers should be aware that it may bring along conflict potential and higher cost for coordination as well.

11.6.3 Interdependencies and Logical Hierarchies

Finally, if this has not yet been done in the previous step, decision makers should pay attention to a possible logical hierarchy among the corrective actions, since this needs to be taken into account when the measures are to be implemented. It is possible that one measure should be realized before another because it establishes necessary infrastructure the second measure needs as well, or because this order creates synergy effects. Such a hierarchy may not be detected by the application of the decision methods, which are explained in the following sections and should thus be determined beforehand.

11.6.4 Weighted Score Method

The first decision making technique discussed here is the "weighted score method". It is a relatively simple and sufficiently objective method to make a decision in a multi-criteria decision situation. In this decision model, managers first have to decide about the relative importance of each of the five criteria (utility, feasibility of implementation, time to implementation, usability, and risk of scope creep and budget overrun) and assign weights to them, which have to add up to 100 %. For example, the criterion "utility" could be seen as the most important one, followed by "time to implementation". These two criteria would then receive the weights 40 and 30 %, respectively, while the remaining 30 % have to be allocated to the other three criteria, again depending on their relative importance.

In the next step decision makers rate each alternative's performance on different categories, which describe the criteria more closely, on a 5-point Likert scale (Table 11.3). The criterion "utility" could for instance be described by the sub-categories "appropriateness" (of the measure for reaching the goal) and "sustainability" (of the actions' outcome). Depending on their performance, the different measures receive values between 1 and 5 for each sub-category. In order to determine the final score of each corrective action, the averages of the different sub-category scores are calculated to describe one criterion, which are then multiplied by the weight assigned to this criterion. The five values for each corrective action derived by this method are then summed up to achieve the final scores, of which the highest one indicates the preferred corrective action.

Table 11.4 shows an example of the sub-category assessment questions that have to be answered for all corrective actions. Although the answer options are phrased in words ("not appropriate"; "hardly appropriate"), answers should be

Table 11.3 Questionnaire to derive category ratings for the corrective actions

Criteria	Assessment questions	Scale				
		1	2	3	4	5
A)	In your opinion, how appropriate is the measure to address the gap?	Not appropriate	Hardly appropriate	Undecided	Appropriate	Perfectly appropriate
	Do you believe the improvement achieved by the measure is sustainable?	No	Hardly	Undecided	Mostly	Yes
B)	Do you believe that enough financial resources are available (or obtainable) to finance the implementation?	No	Hardly	Undecided	Mostly	Yes
	Do you believe that enough financial resources are available (or obtainable) to finance the maintenance cost (if applicable)?	No	Hardly	Undecided	Mostly	Yes
	Please provide an estimate of the total investment necessary (including equipment, maintenance, software, and personnel cost, both immediate and on-going)					
	Do your own managers/employees possess sufficient knowledge and capabilities to guide through the implementation phase?	No	Hardly	Undecided	Mostly	Yes
	Do you believe that enough physical resources (infrastructure, vehicles, machines) are available (or obtainable) for the corrective action?	No	Hardly	Undecided	Mostly	Yes
	Do you believe that enough organizational resources and capabilities (systems, processes, structure, and culture) are available (or obtainable)?	No	Hardly	Undecided	Mostly	Yes
C)	How long will it take to implement the measure?	> 8 months	7–8 months	5–6 months	3–4 months	1–2 months
	Do you think this timeframe is attainable?	No	Hardly	Undecided	Mostly	Yes

(continued)

Table 11.3 (continued)

Criteria	Assessment questions	Scale				
		1	2	3	4	5
D)	Are specific skills/human resources required to run the measure once implemented?	Not at all	Hardly	Undecided	Mostly	Significantly
	Are these skills/human resources already available in-house?	No	Hardly	Undecided	Mostly	Fully
	If not: How can they be acquired?	New hires	Training of current staff	Other:		
E)	How high is the risk that your budget limit will be exceeded?	High	Relatively high	Medium	Relatively low	Low
	How high is the risk that the time frame will be exceeded?	High	Relatively high	Medium	Relatively low	Low
	How high is the risk that unforeseen external events impede the implementation?	High	Relatively high	Medium	Relatively low	Low

written down in their numerical values ("1";"2") to allow for the following calculations. These sub-items for each criterion are only suggestions and should be adapted to fit a unique organization's needs, if necessary. The open questions for the criteria B and D can be used to note down additional information on the decision, if desired. Please see the example case presented in Sect. 11.7 for a practical demonstration of the entire weighted score method.

The weighted score method has both strengths and weaknesses. On one hand, it is easy to comprehend and relatively fast to execute; on the other hand, the result obviously depends strongly on the chosen importance weightings of the five criteria. If the number of assessed corrective actions is higher and if the decision is very important (be it due to its potential impact on the organization's processes or because of the investments), it may be advisable to conduct sensitivity analyses with respect to the importance weights. Such analyses test how the final scores behave if the importance weights are changed. In situations where a slight modification in the allocation of the importance weights is sufficient to change the recommendation from one corrective action to another, the robustness of this decision method decreases. Managers may then wish to consider a supplemental method to verify the result.

11.6.5 Analytic Hierarchy Process

Another method for solving multi-criteria decision problems is the analytic hierarchy process (AHP), which has already been used to derive a competitive priorities ranking in SCD-Phase 1. Especially the first steps of this method are similar to the simpler weighted score method, but the two differ significantly in the way how important ratings and overall scores are calculated. Just like the weighted score method, the AHP organizes problems into a hierarchy, with an overall goal at the top (in our situation, the goal to identify a ranking of different corrective actions), alternative methods of reaching the goal (the different corrective actions), and several criteria against which the alternatives have to be measured (utility, feasibility, etc.).

The most creative way in the decision making process is prioritizing the hierarchy. There are different steps in elaborating a hierarchy according to (Saaty 1996):

(1) Identifying the overall goal. What are you trying to accomplish? What is the main question?
(2) Identify the subgoals of the overall goal. If relevant, identify time horizons that affect the decision.
(3) Identify criteria that must be satisfied to fulfill the subgoals of the overall goal.
(4) Identify subcriteria under each criterion. Note that criteria or subcriteria may be specified in terms of ranges of values of parameters or in terms of verbal intensities such as high, medium, low.
(5) Identify the actors involved.
(6) Identify the actors' goals.

Table 11.4 The fundamental scale is a scale of absolute numbers used to assign numerical values to judgments made by comparing two elements with the smallest element used as the unit and the larger one assigned a value from this scale as a multiple of that unit. (Saaty 1996)

Intensity of importance	Definition	Explanation
1	Equal importance	Two activities contribute equally to the objective
3	Moderate importance	Experience and judgements lightly favor one activity over another
5	Strong importance	Experience and judgment strongly favor one activity over another
7	Very strong or demonstrated importance	An activity is favored very strongly over another, its dominance demonstrated in practice
9	Extreme importance	The evidence favoring one activity over another is of the highest possible order of affirmation
2,4,6,8	For compromise between the above values	Sometimes one needs to interpolate a compromise judgment numerically because there is no good word to describe it
Reciprocals of above value	If activity i has one or the above non zero numbers assigned to it when compared with activity j, then j has the reciprocal value when compared with i	A comparison man dated by choosing the smaller element as the unit to estimate the larger one as a multiple of that unit
Rationals	Ratios arising from the scale	If consistency were to be forced by obtaining n numerical values to span the matrix

Table 11.4 shows a comparison of the relationships between two elements that share a common parent. The set of the judgments can be shown in a square matrix in which the set of elements are compared with itself. There are two questions which are considered: Which of the two elements is more important with respect to a higher level criterion, and how strongly, using the 1–9 scale for the element at the top matrix? (Saaty 1996) (Table 11.4).

The criteria can each be described more closely by several sub-categories. Such a hierarchy is depicted in Fig. (11.5).

Contrary to what is done in the weighted score method, alternatives are assessed by means of pairwise comparisons against one criterion at a time. Likewise, the relative importance of the criteria among themselves with respect to reaching the goal is found by pairwise comparisons. For example, utility is compared to feasibility of implementation, to time, and so on, until all possible pairs of these five criteria have been assessed. According to the AHP, the "losing" criterion of every comparison always receives the rating "1", whereas the other one is assigned a

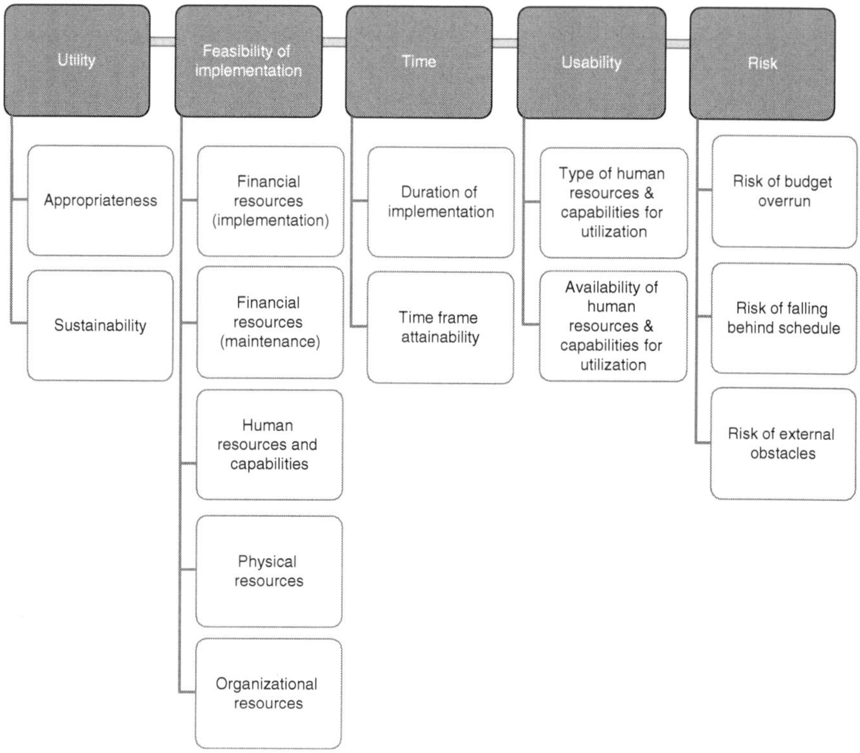

Fig. 11.5 Example of the hierarchical organization of criteria and categories for the selection of corrective actions

rating between 2 and 9, depending on how much more important the decision maker considers it to be. In a similar way, decision makers evaluate the alternative corrective actions with respect to their strength in meeting the criteria. The results of each set of comparisons are summarized in a matrix. A detailed description of the exact calculation is beyond the scope of this guideline, but it shall be noted here that priorities of all alternatives and criteria are mathematically represented by the matrices' principal right eigenvectors. Every alternative thereby receives a rating of its relative importance with respect to each criterion. These ratings are finally multiplied by the different relative importance weightings of the different criteria to obtain a final score for each alternative. As in the weighted score method, the "best" corrective action is the one with the highest final score.

The AHP's strength is that it is a proven and practically useful method, which leads to relatively objective results. Although the intermediate steps to be performed by the decision makers are simple (since one alternative is only compared to one other at a time), the following calculations are sophisticated enough that the final results cannot be intuitively foreseen. This advantage is especially visible in comparison to the weighted score method, where the criteria's rankings are determined by the decision makers and their relevance for the final result is clear to everyone. The AHP is also well suited for decision problems with a greater number of alternatives and criteria as the individual decisions do not become more difficult. On the other hand, the AHP naturally is quantitatively more complicated and more time-consuming.

Summary sheet

Phase 4: Supply chain prioritization and selection of corrective actions

Goals of SCD-Guide Phase 4

The goal of SCD-Phase 4 is to analyze the corrective measures of the gap analysis in SCD-Phase 3 and to prioritize them given different steps of the process. Thereby the most important actions are evaluated and selected in order to be implemented for the supply chain differentiation process.

Methods and analysis for SCD-Guide Phase 4

- Pre-selection of corrective actions
- Weighted score method
- Analytical hierarchy process (AHP)

Input per methods for SCD-Guide Phase 4

	Input from other phases	Method	Method
Method to pre-select the corrective actions	(None)	**Pre-selection of corrective actions** • Questionnaire for pre-selecting corrective actions	
Methods to evaluate and prioritize of corrective actions	(None)	**Weighted score method** • Assessment questionnaire to derive category ratings	**Analytic hierarchy process** • Utility • Feasibility of implementation • Time • Usability • Risk

Output from SCD-Guide Phase 4

- The prioritization and selection of corrective actions which create the outline for the implementation of the supply chain differentiation process

11.7 Application Example of SCD-Guide SCD-Phase 4 and Possible Output

To illustrate the entire procedure of SCD-Phase 4 and 5, this section presents an example application of all four steps. For the sake of simplification, only the "strategic path" via the gap analysis is explained.

The company PC Manufacturing Inc. analyzed its customer requirements and defined an optimal TO-BE supply chain strategy and processes. Afterwards the current supply chain was recorded and compared with the optimal one. This gap analysis showed that PC Manufacturing Inc. already had a satisfactory congruity between the two designs in many areas. However, four greater gaps were identified:

1) **Level of information sharing**: With suppliers of bottleneck as well as leverage items information sharing levels were found to be too low.
2) **Customer segmentation:** There is still just one customer segment, the TO-BE analysis suggests to divide the customers into several different segments such as private, public and business.
3) **Strategic supply chain orientation:** Changing the supply chain orientation from lean to leagile.
4) **Project management maturity level**: The gap analysis revealed that the company's project management is still at the singular methodology.

The supply chain management team agreed to narrow down the number of gaps to at most two different ones in order to focus their effort and resources. They used mainly three factors to evaluate the topics:

- Criticality of the gap
- Size of the gap
- Insider and market knowledge

Table 11.5 shows the decision criteria and the project teams' comments:

Following reflections, PC Manufacturing Inc's managers decided to address the insufficient level of information sharing and the make process gap. These gaps are more important than the other ones and the need for action is even more pressing due to the size of the gaps. Furthermore, the managers saw competitive pressures for both of them.

11.7.1 Identification of Corrective Actions

Depending on the nature of the gaps, corrective actions should either be selected for each one individually or jointly. PC Manufacturing Inc. decided to pursue the goal of improving the level of information sharing between its supply chain partners. If possible, however, actions should be found which can have a supporting effect on the supply chain orientation as well.

They first chose to filter Fig. (11.6) with the "long list of corrective actions" for "Supply Chain Governance". Thereby they identified 14 different corrective actions which could all be helpful to improve their level of information sharing,

Table 11.5 Exemplary outcome of the goal prioritization of PC Manufacturing Inc

Gaps	Criticality of gap	Size of gap	Additional comments
Level of information sharing	Very critical since a close relationship with our core customers and suppliers is an essential element of our strategy	Significant: momentary level for suppliers of leverage and bottleneck items was assessed with "low", but a level of at least "medium–high" is strongly recommended	General trend toward IT integration; the company somewhat lags behind
Customer segmentation	Critical since different customer segmentation lead to an optimization in processes and customer requirements	Significant: So far there is only of customer group and thereby no difference between the different customer segments	Resource intensive corrective, thereby more difficult to implement
Strategic supply chain orientation	Important; the strategy is central to satisfying a customer segment	Relatively large; a switch to a leagile supply chain strategy would improve supply chain processes	Could help to reduce inventory levels
Project management maturity level	Although projects are part of the day-to-day business, Project management skills are not yet as crucial for our competitive situation	Significant: current level is estimated to be "singular methodology", whereas a "benchmarking" situation is desired	Resources could better be spent elsewhere

which is part of supply chain governance. The screenshot below (Fig. 11.6) shows the first corrective actions identified by this filter.

A second filter was set for "source and make processes", leading to three additional potential measures (see Fig. 11.7). The managers checked the applicability of these measures by using different columns, which contain references to relevant organizational goals. Most of the measures found by this method had already been identified in the previous steps. They therefore decided to stay with these 17 measures.

11.7.2 Pre-Selection of Corrective Actions

In the next step, PC Manufacturing Inc. had to choose the most promising ones from the identified 17 actions. As mentioned before, they mainly focused on the information sharing gap. They used the short questionnaire introduced in Sect. 11.5, which is presented in Fig. 11.8.

At the end of pre-selection process, PC Manufacturing Inc.'s managers narrowed down the number of possible corrective actions to the four most promising ones. The following four corrective actions were believed to be most adequate to achieve the desired TO-BE states:

	Management process according to SCOR model	Corrective action	Description / Result	Reference to CMs	Plan	Source	Make	Deliver	Return
4	Plan	EDI connection (e.g. XML-based) among supply chain members	Real-time exchange of supply chain information between supply chain members collaborative planning systems, internet trading exchanges, B2B integration and application server systems	5 - Supply Chain Governance	o	x	x	x	x
5	Plan	Supply chain advance planning system	Collaboration among supply chain partners extends outwards to customers, spanning the supply chain.	5 - Supply Chain Governance	o	x	x	x	
6	Plan	Supply chain event management systems (Supply chain integration)	All key participants in the supply chain, including strategic partners, have full visibility of the demand/supply plan	5 - Supply Chain Governance	o	x	x		
7	Plan	B2B Integration and application server systems	Forecasts are replaced with actual customer replenishment signals and orders where possible	5 - Supply Chain Governance	o	x	x		
10	Plan	Proactive education of customers to set expectations and encourage close working relationships	Knowledge of long-lead items, visibility to supply resources, agreement on levels of flexibility	5 - Supply Chain Governance	o				x
11	Plan	Available-to-promise (ATP) check	Available-to-Promise (ATP) provides an availability and feasibility check concerning a customer request or a customer order	5 - Supply Chain Governance	o	x	x		

Fig. 11.6 Screenshot from the "long list of corrective actions" for PC Manufacturing Inc (1)

	Management process according to SCOR model	Corrective action	Description and result	Reference to CMs	Plan	Source	Make	Deliver	Return
20	Source, Make	Integrated software systems for matching shelf stock to expectations	A software-based system that corrects shelf inventory levels based on actual product present (possible RFIDsolution). Identifies stock-outs from shrinkage or item misplacement.	6 - Functional Supply Chain Processes (Source & Make)	x	o	o		
21	Source, Make	Collaborative planning, forecasting, replenishment (CPFR)	Collaborative planning, forecasting and replenishment is a concept that allows collaborative processes across the supply chain, using a set of process and technology models	6 - Functional Supply Chain Processes (Source & Make)	x	o	o	x	
22	Source, Make	Dynamic deployment based on constraint-based planning and optimal scheduling	Advanced planning and scheduling logic with constraint, cost, and resource optimization	6 - Functional Supply Chain Processes (Source & Make)	x	o	o		

Fig. 11.7 Screenshot from the "long list of corrective actions" for PC Manufacturing Inc (2)

	Criteria	Answer options	Integrated software systems for matching shelf stock to expectations	Collaborative planning, forecasting, replenishment (CPFR)	EDI connection (e.g. XML-based) among supply chain members	Supply chain advance planning system	Supply chain event management systems (Supply chain integration)	Customer relationship management system (CRM)
A	In your opinion, how appropriate is the measure to address the gap?	1) not appropriate 2) medium appropriateness/ undecided 3) perfectly appropriate	2	3	3	2	2	3
B	How likely is this measure's implementation to succeed (consider resource availability)?	1) very unlikely 2) equal probability of failure vs. success 3) very likely	1	2	3	2	3	2
C	Do you believe the projected timeframe to implementation is attainable?	1) unattainable 2) medium attainability/ undecided 3) attainable	3	3	2	1	2	2
D	Is sufficient expertise available to execute the measure now and in the long run?	1) no 2) probably yes; if not yet available it can be obtained 3) yes	2	2	2	3	1	3
E	How high is the risk that the limits of time and money will be exceeded?	1) high 2) medium 3) low	2	2	2	1	3	3
		Outcome	rejected	put on shortlist	put on shortlist	rejected	rejected	put on shortlist

Fig. 11.8 Exemplary pre-selection outcome for PC Manufacturing Inc

1) An EDI connection among all supply chain partners (EDI)
2) A customer relationship management system (CRM)
3) Vendor managed inventory (VMI)
4) Collaborative planning, forecasting, and replenishment (CPFR)

In the supply chain prioritization and selection of corrective actions, PC Manufacturing Inc. tries to prioritize the goals and corrective actions. Thereby the company determines the most important gaps between the AS-IS and TO-BE analysis. These have already been identified during SCD-Phase 3 in the gap analysis.

PC Manufacturing Inc.'s managers decided to use the weighted-score method for their decision problem. Therefore, they now had to decide about the relative importance of the five assessment criteria. Later in this step, these importance weights are necessary to calculate the final scores of each method. After an intense discussion on the company's priorities and its current situation, they agreed on the importance weighting shown in Table 11.6.

Table 11.6 Possible importance weights for the decision criteria for PC Manufacturing Inc

Decision criteria for corrective actions		Importance weight (%)	Sum
A)	Utility	50	
B)	Feasibility of implementation	30	
C)	Time	10	
D)	Usability	5	
E)	Risk	5	100 %

Questions \ Options	EDI	CRM	CPFR
a1	4	5	4
a2	4	3	4
average A)	4.00	4.00	4.00
b1	2	4	4
b2	4	3	3
b3	1	2	4
b4	2	3	5
b5	3	2	1
average B)	2.40	2.80	3.40
c1	3	4	1
c2	1	3	5
average C)	2.00	3.50	3.00
d1	3	2	5
d2	1	2	4
average D)	2.00	2.00	4.50
e1	3	4	4
e2	5	2	4
e3	2	3	1
average E)	3.33	3.00	3.00

Decision criteria for corrective actions	Importance weight
A) Utility	50%
B) Feasibility of implementation	30%
C) Time	10%
D) Usability	5%
E) Risk	5%
	100%

Options		Final Score
1	EDI	3.19
2	CRM	3.44
3	CPFR	3.7

Fig. 11.9 Example of a calculation with the weighted score method for PC Manufacturing Inc

The next, more time-consuming step was to rate the remaining four alternatives on all sub-categories of the five main criteria. The result of the whole rating of all corrective measures in the different categories is depicted in Fig. (11.9). As can be seen, average ratings were calculated for the five criteria (A to E).

The managers then multiplied the averages by each criterion's importance weighting and summed up the results to derive the final scores, which are shown in the small table at the bottom right of Fig. (11.9). In the example at hand, "collaborative planning, forecasting, and replenishment" is the most favorable solution within this set of decision criteria and importance weightings. But as this measure is closely followed by the corrective action "customer relationship management", the latter option may be viable as well. PC Manufacturing Inc. therefore initialized first actions for the implementation of a CPFR system. The whole procedure could now be repeated for the second-most important gap.

In SCD-Phase 5, it shows how to select, evaluate, and prioritize possible corrective actions for addressing gaps that were identified during the preceding gap analysis. A practical four-step approach with the goal of deriving a clear hierarchy among different promising and feasible corrective actions was suggested. Core to this approach is the incremental procedure, which narrows down an initially large number of options to the "best", preferable one. Although this approach aims to be implementable by a large number of companies, sufficient discretion remains with the managers in charge of this decision process, since many pieces of this process can be tailored to company-specific needs.

The final Phase of the differentiation approach deals with preparing the implementation of the previously chosen corrective methods. It will arouse attention of common fallacies and highlight practical issues relevant to the implementation of improvement methods of different scopes. The most important gaps and corrective actions are in the illustrative case. The following:

- PC Manufacturing Inc. has identified information sharing as the most important gap within the analysis. This concerns mainly the suppliers of leverage as well as bottleneck items which need to have a higher level of information sharing.
- Furthermore PC Manufacturing Inc. has identified customer segmentation as an important gap. The TO-BE analysis of PC Manufacturing Inc. has shown that the identification of three different segments business, private and public need to be classified in order to meet the customer requirements.
- Furthermore the supply chain needs to be aligned to a more leagile approach, since the decoupling point is at a less advantageous point in the supply chain.
- Furthermore the project management maturity level needs to be improved from its current state singular methodology to a higher level.

Then PC Manufacturing Inc. has multiplied the average of the results with the weighted score of the different criteria and therefore identified customer relationship management system as the most pressing corrective action. PC Manufacturing Inc. has identified the need for customer segmentation according to the three different segments business, private and public, which have already been identified in the TO-BE analysis of the company in SCD-Phase 1. The same method has been conducted for the other corrective actions.

Reference

Saaty, T. L. (1996). *Multicriteria decision making: planning, priority setting, resource allocation* (2nd ed.). PA: University of Pittsburg.

Phase 5: Preparation of Implementation of Supply Chain Differentiation

12

12.1 Goals for SCD-Phase 5

The following guideline functions as a preparation for the actual implementation process. Since the TO-BE supply chain and the AS-IS supply chain have been analyzed, the gap analysis has been conducted and the supply chain gap analysis and identification of courses of actions has been determined, it is now necessary to take the preparatory steps to implement the supply chain differentiation process into the company. The implementation process demands a high level of knowledge within project management (Fig. 12.1).

Project management is gaining more and more importance not only as a corporate discipline but also as an area of responsibility in companies. In many industries, projects have become the prevailing working form and this process is accelerating due to shortening life cycles of products and fastening technology changes of environmental and competitive conditions (Zimmermann et al. 2010).

The basis for project management already exists in many organizations nowadays. However, too often it lingers in a latent state awaiting management acknowledgement. It is crucial to recognize the business contribution of project management and thus, to assure that a maximum return on project management investment is achieved. An essential component to reach an effective project management process constitutes the introduction of the right methodology within the company (Barratt 2004).

Each project passes from its initiation until the execution different life cycles, described as phases. Regarding the project management literature, manifold specialized life cycle models exist. In the following section, a rather generic phase model is presented as depicted in Fig. 12.2. Although the model consists of four phases, only the first three phases shall be considered within the guideline as these phases cover the preparation of the project before its realization.

E. Hofmann et al., *The Supply Chain Differentiation Guide*,
DOI: 10.1007/978-3-642-31936-5_12, © Springer-Verlag Berlin Heidelberg 2012

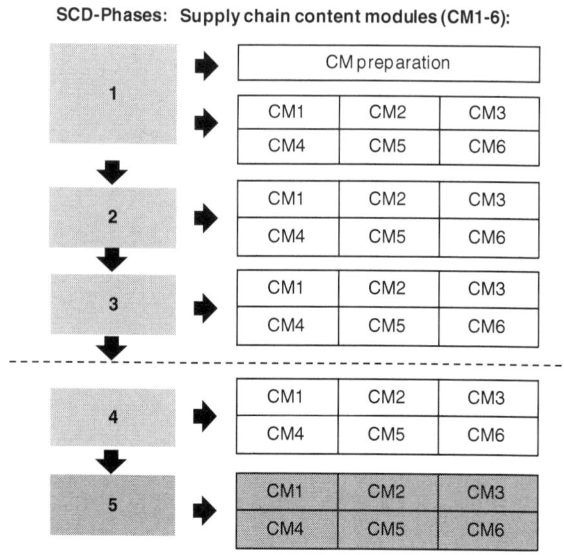

Fig. 12.1 Position of Chap.12 in SCD-Guide

12.2 Step 1: Project Conception

12.2.1 Description and Content of the Phase

Generally, only vague information is available at the beginning of a project and thus, as a first step, the project charter is formulated and defined. Frequently, specifications covering aspects of project planning and implementation are included. Moreover, problems and tasks are defined, targets of the project are recorded, and a description of the service to be rendered is created. These requirement specifications built the basis for the formulation of the project charter. Besides, a feasibility study, an effort estimation, a profitability analysis, and a risk analysis is covered in this starting phase.

The **feasibility study** evaluates whether the resources required for the realization of the project such as qualified personnel, necessary technology, or financial resources are present and timely profitable. Within the scope of the **effort estimation**, the effort required for the execution of the project regarding its quantity and value is defined. The **profitability analysis** provides information about the expectable profit which is especially for internal projects of significance, as they include no contractual agreement concerning the revenue. Regarding the **risk analysis**, potential risks factors are identified which are obstructive for a proper project closure. In order to minimize the identified risks, suitable countermeasures are developed.

However, different possibilities exist on how to fulfill the project charter. Hence, each version of the project should be evaluated with regard to its feasibility, required effort, profitability, and its possible risks. Based on this

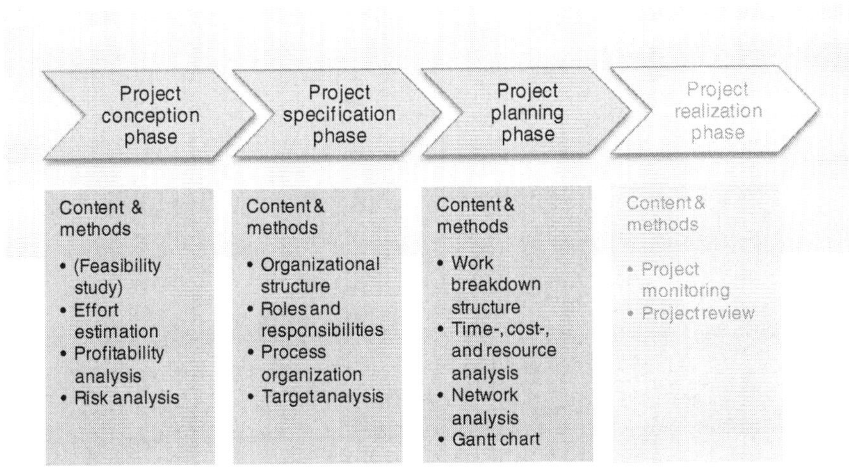

Fig. 12.2 Phases, content, and methods of the project life cycle (Zimmermann et al. 2010)

information, it is generally decided whether a project and which alternative is most suitable (Zimmermann et al. 2010).

However, due to the fact that SCD-Phase 4 of the guideline covers the selection and prioritization of corrective actions, certain decisions regarding the project conception phase of the implementation are already considered. The suggested analytical hierarchy process method to select corrective actions implies the consideration of criteria such as time, usability, risk, utility, and feasibility of implementation. Hence, the content of the project conception phase is already covered in this section and therefore, only the effort estimation, the profitability analysis, and the risk analysis are evaluated on a superficial level.

12.2.2 Methods

12.2.2.1 Effort Estimation

The effort estimation constitutes the basis for the calculation of the project duration and its costs. A company determined whether the project is realizable, if resources are available within the time frame, and if the project is profitable. Thus, the decision is based on the quality and accuracy of the effort estimation. In order to be able conduct a usable effort estimation, experience and preparation are required. Generally, tree possible methods arise:

- The **function point analysis** is based on an analogy- and weighting procedure. Thus, the analysis determines requirements from the users perspective without decomposing the project. Number and complexity of business transactions such as inputs, expenses, database, and reference data are determined in order to deliver the function points.

- **Multiplier method**: Tasks are decomposed into small and clear units for which the effort is known. Hence, summarizing the effort times the number of units results in the total expenditure.
- **The percentage method** provides values for each phase, based on experiences, to evaluate the percentage of the total effort. Thus, a phase is estimated and realized in detail and after the completion of the phase, the estimation is taken as a basis for the remaining phases. This method is suitable for a plausibility check to evaluate estimated values evaluated by another method (Kuster et al. 2008).

12.2.2.2 Profitability Analysis

The aim of the profitability analysis is to consider the project from an economic point of view. Before the profitability analysis can be performed payments, outputs, and costs indirectly or directly resulting from the project execution need to be considered (Zimmermann et al. 2010). The profitability calculation contains statistical as well as dynamic procedures. Statistical methods merely take into account on phase and the results are then assumed to be true for the remaining phases (Kuster et al. 2008):

- The **cost comparison method** determines the costs of one or two investment projects and compares them.
- The **profit comparison method** chooses from several investment opportunities one version, which accounts for the highest profit.

Regarding dynamic procedures, they try to record the occurring payment flows during the whole life span of the project (Kuster et al. 2008):

- The **net present value (NPV)** is a common method and calculates the net present value based on the difference between the discounted incoming and outgoing payments. The higher the NPV, the better is the profitability of the project.
- The **internal rate of return (IRR)** method evaluates which project version accounts for the higher internal interest rate. Thereby, the internal interest rate is the rate where the net present value is equal to zero.

12.2.2.3 Risk Analysis

Every project includes different risks which are obstructive for a successful project termination. Different kinds of risks are distinguishable into factual risks, economical risks, and risks regarding the dates. The risk analysis passes three steps (Zimmermann et al. 2010):

- First, for each defined sub-system of the project potential risks are identified and analyzed. Normally, qualitative techniques are applied such as expert surveys or brainstorming in order to determine factual risks. For risks regarding dates, stochastic methods such as the PERT method are applied. Economical risks can be evaluated in the context of the profitability analysis.
- A second step includes the evaluation of the identified risks. The scope of the risks depends on the probability of occurrence and the resulting consequence for the project. The probability of occurrence can be determined by experts by the network plan technique PERT (program evaluation and review technique)

form the first step (Zhong and Zhang 2003). This technique quantifies the probability of a not timely termination of the project. The consequences, if a risk occurs, are normally expressed in a monetary unit. An exact estimation of risks is in practice often impossible and thus, they are divided into A, B, or C risks whereas A risks possess a relatively high economic consequence.

- The third step accounts for the evaluation of possible measurements to prevent the identified risks or to minimize their impact on the project.

Summary sheet

Phase 5, Step 1: Preparation of implementation of supply chain differentiation (conception)

Goals of SCD-Guide Phase 5, Step 1

Phase 5, Step 1 aims to identify problems and tasks within the preparation and implementation process. Furthermore it specifies aspects of project planning and project implementation.

Methods and analysis for SCD-Guide Phase 5, Step 1

- Effort estimation
- Profitability analysis
- Risk analysis

Input per methods for SCD-Guide Phase 5, Step 1

Methods to prepare and implement the supply chain differentiation process

Input from other phases	Effort estimation
(None)	• Inputs • Expenses • Database • Reference data

Profitability analysis
• Output and costs directly or indirectly resulting from project execution

Input from other phases	Risk analysis
(None)	• Factual risks • Economical risks • Risks regarding the dates

Output from SCD-Guide Phase 5, Step 1

- Identification of problems, risks and tasks for implementation
- Identification of targets for project planning

12.3 Step 2: Project Specification

12.3.1 Description and Content of the Phase

As soon as the realization of the project is decided the next step, the project specification phase, follows. Firstly, it is mandatory to determine the **organizational structure** of the project. Thus, is must be decided which employee from which department shall be involved and how the project management and project team is integrated into the organizational structure (Zimmermann et al. 2010). Moreover, it is crucial to define **roles and responsibilities**. These aspects are essential as vague distribution of tasks and a lack of comprehension of roles makes it impossible for the group to exploit fully their performance capacity (Kuster et al. 2008).

Secondly, the determination of an appropriate **process organization** specifying the further proceeding of the project. For this purpose, central milestones and their relation are identified. Milestones represent a special occasion such as the completion of an important sub-project.

Based on the project charter and its related specified requirements evaluated in the project conception phase, the identified goals are broken down into sub-goals. Thus, within a **target analysis** the pursued goals regarding the realization of the project are systematically structured, formulated, and recorded bindingly for every party involved. Thereby, it is essential to formulate the goals in an operative way in order to be able to determine the degree to which the goals are achieved. This is a mandatory requirement regarding an effective project controlling and management. Furthermore, targets are identified regarding the timing of the project progress. Hence, topics like minimizing the project duration or the uniform utilization of determined resources are considered (Zimmermann et al. 2010).

12.3.2 Detailed Descriptions and Methods

12.3.2.1 Organizational Structure

There exists no "cookbook" solution to successfully integrate project management into the organizational structure. However, the basic rule applies that well defined responsibilities and roles are more critical for the success of a project than the structure. If the employees within the structure know their responsibilities and their job, the structure is of less importance (Barney 1991). However, it is worthwhile to think about the organizational structure. Three main forms of organization regarding the involvement of project management exists which each have their advantages and drawbacks:

- A **pure project organization** allocates the project management division equally important to the other organizational units. The project management thereby presents an autonomous organizational unit and thus, all involved employees are allocated exclusively to the project management during the realization of the project. This organization structure is suitable for complex projects or projects which are time sensitive. Thus, a main advantage is the concentration on the realization of the projects due to short communication channels and clear allocation of responsibilities. However, a drawback is the inflexibility of the personnel and the difficulty to reintegrate the employees into the company after finishing the project.

- The **staff unit project organization** sub-divides the project organization directly to the management as a staff unit. Hence, only minor changes regarding the organizational structure are required. The project manager has no authority; he is responsible for the right approach or the timely information of the line. The staff unit project organization is widely spread in practice and is suitable for projects with a scope similar to conventional tasks within the company such as a project for a simple product development. Beneficial is the high flexibility regarding the employment of staff and the responsibility of the project stays within the line. However, the reaction rate is relatively low and often, nobody feels directly responsible for the project.
- A hybrid form of the two above mentioned organization forms is the **matrix project organization**. On the one hand, the project organization is like the staff unit project organization sub-divided to the management. On the other hand, the project members are subordinated to the department head of the respective division. This is the most frequent organization form in practice as often, only imitated resources are available. The matrix project organization is characterized by its flexible employment of staff and the project management. Moreover, the team feels responsible for the project. However, this organizational form is vulnerable to conflicts between the project work and the daily business and has relatively high requirements regarding communications skills of the employees' involved (Kuster et al. 2008).

12.3.2.2 Roles and Responsibilities

The roles and committees should be formed suitable to the project and corporate culture in order to effectively reach the target of the project. Furthermore, the project must be clearly embedded in the management level and the decision process must be transparent (Kuster et al. 2008). A possibility to define roles and responsibilities, which follows the classic models, is presented in. However, it is more important to clearly define roles rather than matching this model within the organization (Barney 1991) (Fig. 12.3).

- The **principal** is in most cases the decision maker. However, sometimes it is possible to divide the decision making competence for example between the management and the board of directors. Generally, the role of the principal covers tasks such as defining the strategic basic conditions, prioritizes project, define milestones and assure resources (Kuster et al. 2008).
- The **sponsor** of a project belongs to the executive level and represents three key roles. First, the sponsor has control and authority over the project budget. Second, it is important to champion the project at the executive level in order to

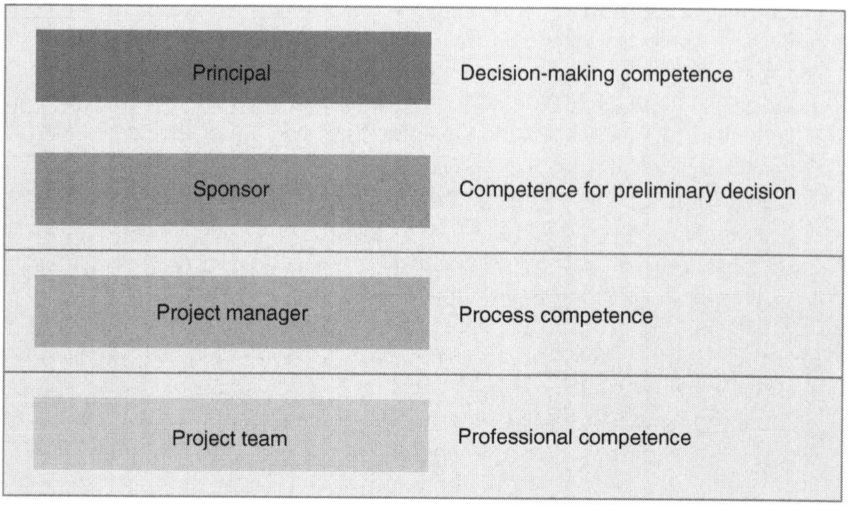

Fig. 12.3 Institutional project organs and level of competences (Kuster et al. 2008)

get attention, high priority and secure resources. Third, the sponsor should have authority to overcome political issues. Thus, for internal projects, he acts as a mediator between the project manager and the client.

- The primary task of the **project manager** is to manage the team. He does not actually do the work regarding the project (Kuster et al. 2008) and thus, is responsible for the operative handling of the project.
- The **project team** has generally the task to work on the project regarding its content. Hence, the project team consists of specialized tasks performers who concentrate on one item to ensure it meets its quality specifications (Barney 1991).

12.3.2.3 Process Organization

In order to be able to specify the further process of the project **milestones** should be defined. Milestones represent the process of the project in a rough manner with regard to its chronology. In order to be able to constantly verify the progress of the project, major projects are sub-divided into different phases with controllable intermediate results (Kuster et al. 2008). Thereby, the sub-divisions of the project may be built on the effort estimation evaluated in the project conception phase (Zimmermann et al. 2010). Regarding major projects or high insecurity within the project, it is advisable to define several milestones on critical points as depicted in Fig. 12.4.

12.3.2.4 Target Analysis

The target analysis aims on the one hand to systematically structure and formulate targets within a project and on the other hand to record them in a binding manner.

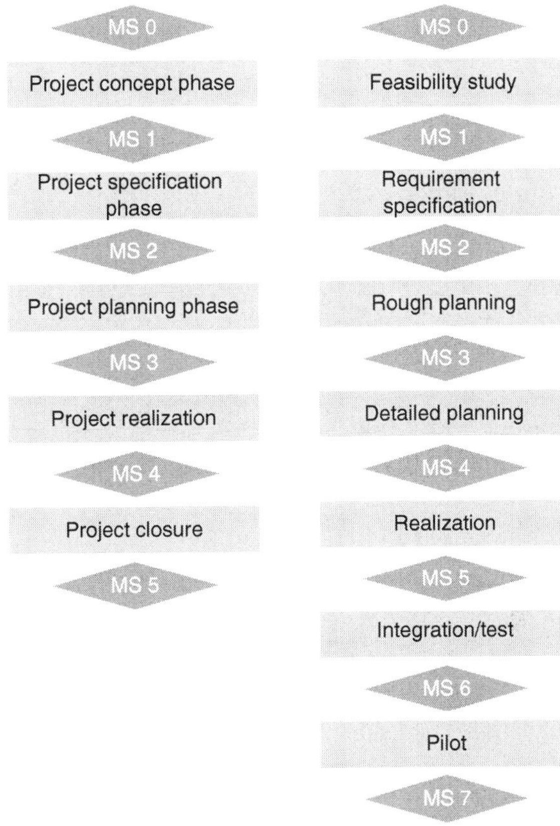

Fig. 12.4 Milestone plans for easier and more complex projects (Kuster et al. 2008)

Besides the necessity to define targets in an operative manner for an effective project controlling and management, project targets are embedded in the target agreements for each project responsible. Basically, to two different targets are distinguishable:

- **Product related targets** are associated to an object of a project such as a product considering a product development project. These kinds of targets are derivable from the specification made in the project charter containing a detailed description of requirements regarding the achievements of the project. After having identified product related targets, they are divided into sub- and detailed targets. Such a systematical division supports the project management by identifying synergies and conflicts regarding the identified goals.
- **Project related targets** are indirectly or directly linked to the timely chronology of the project. Thus, depending on the planning horizon of the project, different targets are considered. Regarding for instance a medium term project with a planning horizon of several months to few years, besides key resources such as experts or special machines also resources provided by the market on a middle term or short term horizon are considered. An example for such

resources is qualified personnel or a vehicle fleet. If a long term project planning horizon of several years is considered, mainly key resources are taken into account and other resources which are, under strategic viewpoint, not regarded as scarce resources, can be neglected (Zimmermann et al. 2010).

Summary sheet

Phase 5, Step 2: Preparation of implementation of supply chain differentiation (specification)

Goals of SCD-Guide Phase 5, Step 2

Phase 5, Step 2 aims at identifying and determining the roles and responsibilities within the process organization. The goals are furthermore broken up into sub-goals.

Methods and analysis for SCD-Guide Phase 5, Step 2

- Process organization
- Target analysis

Input per methods for SCD-Guide Phase 5, Step 2

Methods to prepare and implement the supply chain differentiation process	Input from other phases	Process organization	Target analysis
	(None)	• Sub-division of project into different phases with controllable intermediate results	• Product related targets • Project related targets

Output from SCD-Guide Phase 5, Step 2

- Identification of targets regarding the timing and the project progress.
- Adequate process/project organization

12.4 Step 3: Project Planning

12.4.1 Description and Content of the Phase

The project planning phase aims for a detailed planning of the project progress. Thus, the project is first systematically decomposed into sub-projects and work packages presented in a **work breakdown structure (WBS)**. Furthermore, a **time-, cost-, and resource analysis** evaluates first the duration of the execution regarding the individual project activities as well as the timely relation of the activities within the project. In addition, the required resourced for the execution of the project such as personnel or material is determined in detail. Last, costs are evaluated and defined for the individual project activities.

Thus, after having identified and quantified all structural elements of the project, a **network analysis** is conducted in order to extract information regarding the time flow of the project such as the earliest or latest possible starting point of the project activities. From this type of analysis, time intervals for each activity are resulting. In order to evaluate a binding plan for the project progress, each activity requires an exact starting point within its time interval. Hence, each activity must be scheduled. This scheduling takes place under the consideration of the prevailing resource capacities and the timely dependency of the processes. Moreover, the individual activities are set in order to fulfill the specified target criteria deducted by the target analysis. In practice, activities are frequently scheduled to reach an early termination of the project or to maximize the net present value resulting from the project execution (Zimmermann et al. 2010).

A network plan is a suitable method to indicate the dependencies between the individual activities. However, the extensiveness of the method and its unhandiness is a clear drawback and thus, the more common **Gantt chart** illustrating the sequence of activities in the form of a bar chart on a time axis is presented in the next paragraph. The bar chart includes equivalent data as the network plan but presents them differently. Advantages such as a compact form of presentation, increased readability, and the visualization of the timely relation are resulting from a Gantt chart (Kuster et al. 2008).

12.4.2 Methods

12.4.2.1 Work Breakdown Structure

The work breakdown structure (WBS) is widely considered to be the most essential construct required for effective project management. The tool decomposes or breaks down project activities and tasks into the smallest possible unit of work. After the construction of the WBS, it becomes the core of the center of the project plan and the primary driver for the remaining project. Thus, resource planning, estimates, tracking, or risk management are all based on the WBS.

Several possibilities exist to break down the project as the work can be decomposed by departments, components, regions, cost centers, or by every other method which fits the project management team. A common WBS consists of phases at the highest level. The second level of the WBS is called deliverables, followed by work packages on the third level. This type of model, depicted in Fig. 12.5, is what the Project Management Institute (PMI) refers to as deliverable-based WBS (Barratt 2004; Barney 1991).

The project phases depicted in Fig. 12.5 are not typically a WBS construct but they arrange the work to improve executive and project management oversight. Thus, the executive management has the ability to examine the progress of the project and to determine whether the project reached maturity to continue to the

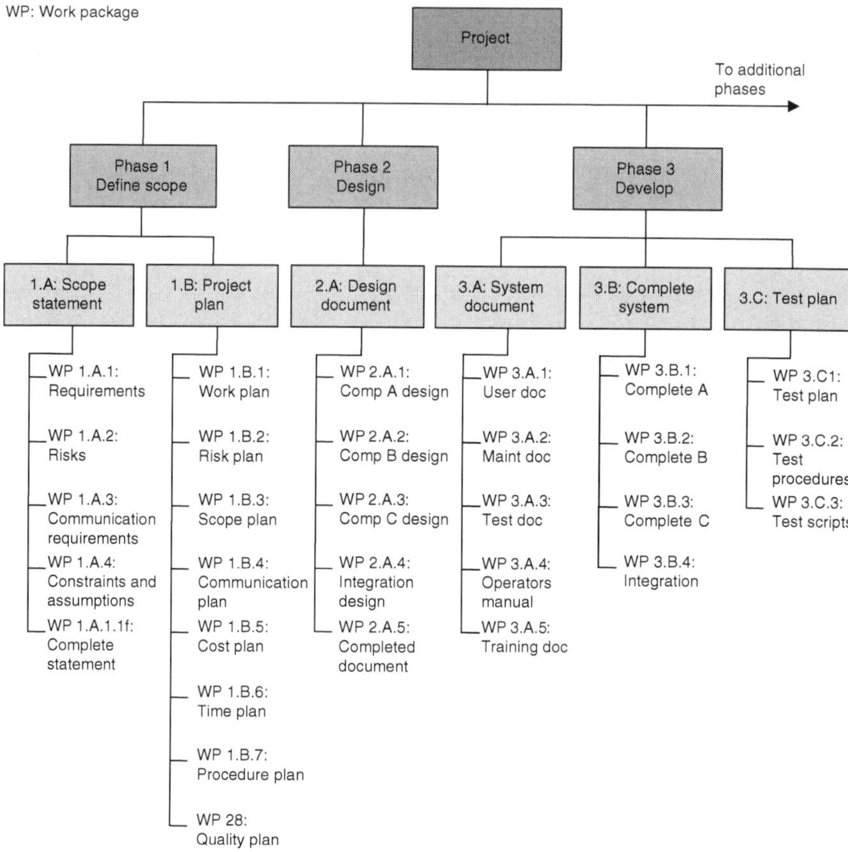

Fig. 12.5 Sample deliverables based work breakdown structure (Barney 1991)

next phase. Moreover, the deliverables assist managers in justifying the work and affirm that items and topics are not forgotten. Regarding the work package levels, the definition can be slightly difficult in practice. Representing the task required to fulfill the superior deliverable, the work packages must have requirements which are clear, measurable, and verifiable (Barney 1991).

12.4.2.2 Time Analysis

Regarding the **time analysis**, the duration and the minimum and maximum distance between activities is quantified. The duration of the processes can be determined by different approaches depending on the individual project and its processes:

- In major projects, single activities and sub-projects are often from external parties performed such as suppliers or subcontractors. Thus, the duration of **activities can be estimated** based on delivery-times or agreed deadlines. For internal- as well as external activities, the estimation can be based on experiences of the planner. However, this approach is only suitable if the planner dispose over experiences from comparable preceding projects.

- Different factors make it difficult for the duration to be estimated. Historical information of **expert judgement** can often help to better estimate time frames.
- **Analogous estimating** is also called "top-down estimating", which means that the duration of previous activities is the basis for similar future activities.
- Quantities for individual work categories can be multiplied by the productivity unit rate in order to estimate **quantitatively based durations**.
- Additional time frames called **reserve time** are incorporated into the estimation. They represent a percentage of the estimated duration and can be adjusted in a later point in time (Project Management Institute 2000).
- Another possibility to determine the working time is provided by **synthetic methods**. The Methods Time Measurement (MTM) for example disaggregate process into simple sequences rated with a suitable time (Kerbosh and Schell 1975).

The most common method to estimate durations of activities, the network plan, is explained in more detail in this section.

12.4.2.3 Cost Analysis

The **cost analysis** determined costs which occur during the execution of the project. Thereby, different types of project costs exist. The following costs should be considered for the inclusion in the estimates accruing at the work package level:

- **Labor costs** estimates are normally entered at the work package level. The costs are aggregated successively at the higher WBS levels to provide the total project labor costs in the end.
- **Direct costs** are also entered at the work package level for items acquired by direct purchases. Direct costs include normally different types of cost items such as material, equipment, or contract workers.
- Project **indirect costs** such as computer hardware, software applications, or training and education cannot be directly allocated to specific work packages. Regarding major projects, costs associating with project managing and planning become indirect costs. However, also these costs should be covered by the project budget.
- **Contingency funds** are project costs dealing with uncertainty in the future such as labor extension or modified requirements.
- The **management reserves** are set aside to in order to be able to deal with unknown future circumstances.

Across organizations, different methods exist to estimate project costs. The following list covers briefly some of the more common techniques (Barratt 2004):

- The **bottom-up estimating** method determine costs for each work package in the WBS. This requires a comprehensive WBS. The accuracy of the method is driven by the size of the single work packages.

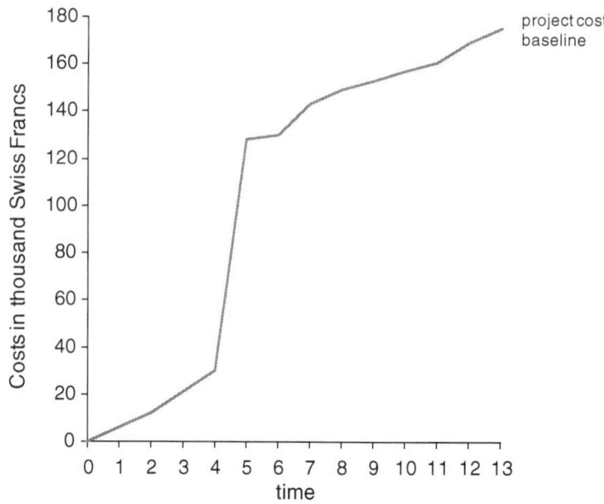

Fig. 12.6 Project cost baseline (Kuster et al. 2008)

- The **delphi technique** is normally used by different experts working as a team in order to derive independent cost estimates. Thus, they resolve any discrepancies to deliver estimates usable for the project. Here, the estimates depend on the experts' experiences and the technique is rather ponderous.
- The **parametric modeling** applies project characteristics in a mathematical model. The so called parametric models are normally oriented towards a specific industry or type of work effort such as construction costs per square foot. Obtained are such models generally through an internal development or vendors. However, the accuracy of the commercially available models differ.

Upon completion of the cost analysis for a project, a **project cost baseline** is established. Normally, the project cost baseline is prepared in conjunction with the identified data from the resource- and time analysis. The curve depicts the development of the cumulated total costs of the project over the project life time (Barratt 2004). The cumulated cost-line graph depicted in Fig. 12.6 is alternatively known as the "S" curve due to its typical shape (Barney 1991).

12.4.2.4 Resource Analysis

In order to specify project resource requirements, it is helpful to examine each work package element in the project work break down structure (WBS) depicted in Fig. 12.7. The elements of the work package level are considered to determine the resource and the effort required to fulfill specified project work. Project planners start here by attaching different names to the project work packages, specify a resource type, and level of resource qualification required. In order to realize this, three steps are required:

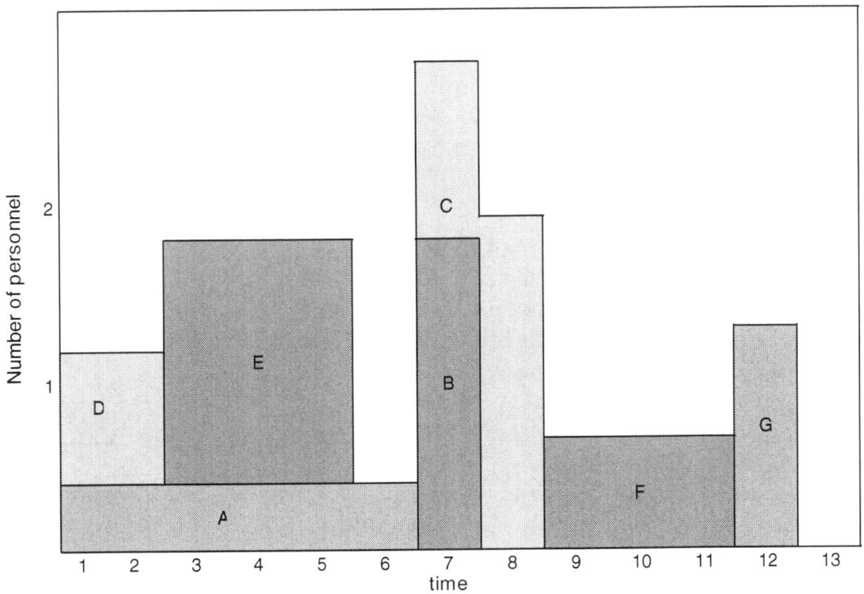

Fig. 12.7 Profile of a resource plan (Kuster et al. 2008)

- First, it is essential to review each WBS work element at the project work package level. This is realizable by determining the type of work required to be accomplished and align a competent resource with the effort. At this level, work efforts are generally separate and distinctive. Afterwards, any resource specified at the work package level is accounted for upwards throughout the project. This first step results in a preliminary resource requirement matrix.
- Second, resource qualification requirements are refined. Here, every resource assigned to work elements is examined in order to evaluate whether the qualification of each resource are appropriate.
- Third, the individual resources requested to participate on the project shall be named, if possible. The named resources should be consistent with position qualification.

Upon completion of project resource utilization, the resources are finally entered into the WBS at the work package level. This compilation enables the specification of the total project staff strength for all project elements and activities. Therefore, the number of resources are represented which are requested for the staffing allocation (Barratt 2004).

Another possibility to determine the required resources for a project is presented by a resource plan. The resource plan include at least all resources which are available at a defined point in time. Thus, external parties, specialists, machines, facilities, or every other not exchangeable resource are included. An example is depicted in Fig. 12.7 (Kuster et al. 2008). The numbers in Fig. 12.7

represent the different resources, in this case the different employees involved in the project, which are deployed in the project over the time.

12.4.2.5 Network analysis and Gantt Chart

The network analysis, conducted in order to extract information regarding the time flow of the project, can be performed by different methods. The most known network analysis is the **critical path method (CPM)** which is a mathematical model of scheduling. Each project diagram has at least one series of activity which defines the length of the project. If the case may be that along this path a task is delayed, an equivalent delay occurs at the end of the project. However, certain activities do not affect the defined project schedule as they can accept a specific delay. Thus, an activity can "float" a certain amount of time without impacting the end date of the project (Barney 1991). The critical path is characterized as the path with the shortest time to complete the project. Thus, it is the path with zero float (Barratt 2004). If for example task has a low day float, meaning the task has a duration of two days but the deliverable is only needed after four days, the project manager can reassign the person assigned to this task for emergencies or for other non-project activities (Barney 1991). In order to be able to early initiate necessary measures, activities on the critical path must be reviewed in reasonable intervals.

Another form to present chronology of activities is the **metra potential method (MPM)** which also belongs to the deterministic network techniques like the CPM (Kuster et al. 2008). However, this method shall only be mentioned here. For further information see (Kerbosh and Schell 1975; Zimmermann et al. 2010). Regarding the CPM, its resulting network plan is rather bulky. Thus, the bulk chart (Gantt chart) is represented here as the content is the same but the presented form is more compact and with a higher readability.

A **Gantt chart** is a one page document including milestones which are attempted to be reached. Milestones are events which certainly defines at which stage the project is situated. Completing a result is equivalent to a milestone and indicates the start of the consecutive stage (Barney 1991). They are embedded in the work break down structure in order to visualize progress without indicating every work element (Barratt 2004). The Gantt chart illustrates the sequence of activities in the form of a bar chart on a time axis. If a phase is terminated, a milestone is indicated as depicted in Fig. 12.8.

In order to be able to reach an effective project management, it is important to choose the right methodology. Within the three described phases, several elements and methods have been presented to support effective project management. Thereby, a crucial element is clearly the assignment of roles and responsibilities in order allow the group to fully exploit their performance capacity. Furthermore, within the project planning phase, the work breakdown structure is a highly useful construct for effective project management as it specifies all project work and

ID	Name	Duration	Start
1	**Phase 1**	**24 dys**	**Thu 07.04.11**
2	Activity 1	4 dys	Thu 07.04.11
3	Activity 2	5 dys	Wed 13.04.11
4	Activity 3	10 dys	Wed 20.04.11
5	Activity 4	3 dys	Wed 04.05.11
6	Activity 5	2 dys	Mon 09.05.11
7	**Phase 2**	**31 dys**	**Wed 11.05.11**
8	Activity 6	5 dys	Tue 10.05.11
9	Activity 7	10 dys	Tue 17.05.11
10	Activity 8	8 dys	Wed 01.06.11
11	Activity 9	7 dys	Mon 13.06.11
12	**Phase 3**	**13 dys**	**Wed 22.06.11**
13	Activity 10	6 dys	Tue 21.06.11
14	Activity 11	8 dys	Wed 29.06.11
15	**Porject closure**	**2 dys**	**Mon 11.07.11**

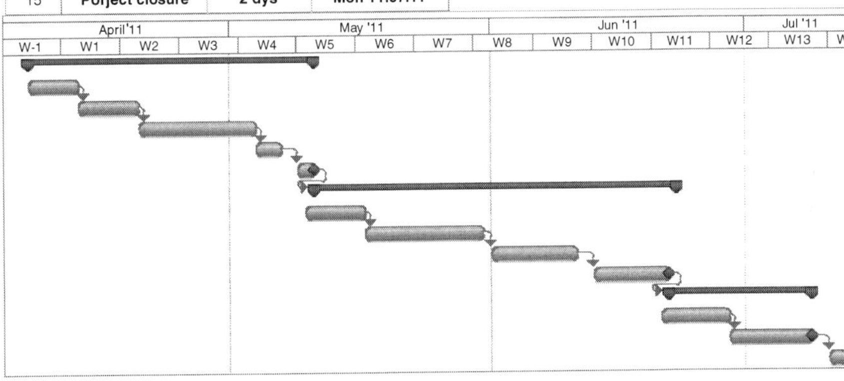

Fig. 12.8 Exemplary sample Gantt chart created by Microsoft® Project

aligns factors of costs, schedule and resource utilization to each planned work element. In order to have an overview over the assigned cost, the project cost baseline offers an useful visualization of the cumulated total costs of the project over its life time as a result of the cost analysis. A last tool to be mentioned is the Gantt chart offering a one page document illustrating the progress of the project. Clearly, manifold other methods exist in order to manage projects efficiently but this rough summary shall give an overview of possible methods applicable regarding the different phases of the project before its realization.

Summary sheet

Phase 5, Step 3: Preparation of implementation of supply chain differentiation (planning)

Goals of SCD-Guide Phase 5, Step 3

Phase 5, Step 3 aims at systematically decomposing the project into sub-projects and work packages according the timely relation of activities.

Methods and analysis for SCD-Guide Phase 5, Step 3

- Work breakdown structure
- Time analysis
- Cost analysis
- Resource analysis
- Network analysis and Gantt chart

Input per methods for SCD-Guide Phase 5, Step 3

Methods for prepare and implementation

Input from other phases	Work breakdown structure	Time analysis
(None)	• Breaking down project activities into the smallest possible unit	• The duration of the minimum and maximum distance between activities

Input from other phases	Cost analysis	Resource analysis
(None)	• Labor costs • Direct costs • Indirect costs • Contingency funds • Management reserves	• Work break down structure • Resource plan

Input from other phases	Network analysis and Gantt chart
(None)	• Activities which define the length of the project

Output from SCD-Guide Phase 5, Step 3

- Identification and quantification of all structural elements of a project
- Compact presentation of the relation between different project activities

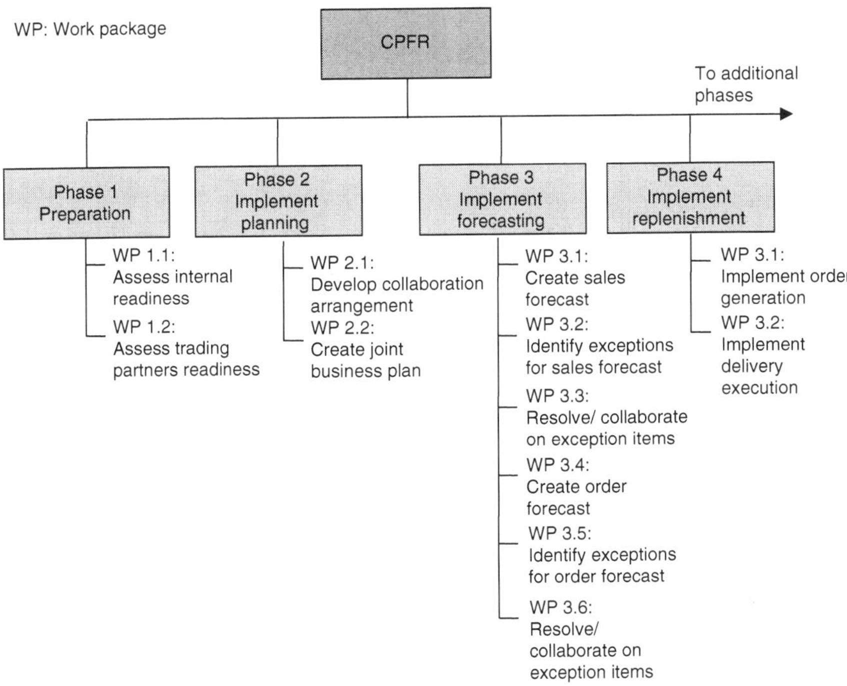

Fig. 12.9 Exemplary work breakdown structure to implement CPFR by PC Manufacturing Inc

12.5 Application Example of SCD-Guide SCD-Phase 5 and Possible Output

PC Manufacturing Inc. has now identified the most important steps of the process for the different corrective actions which need to be taken. A further task is to prepare and implement these different measures. Project management is hereby one of the key aspects for the implementation process within the supply chain differentiation process.

Thereby the company can use different methods which vary from the work breakdown structure, time analysis, cost analysis, resource analysis to the network analysis and Gantt chart. These different analysis help to outline the steps which need to be taken in order to implement the differentiation process.

First of all PC Manufacturing Inc. fulfilled the work-breakdown structure for the most pressing corrective action in order to break down the project activities into the smallest possible units. The work breakdown structure is an essential construct required for successful project management. This step is important in order to plan and structure the project more effectively.

ID	Name	Duration	Beginning	End
1	**Phase 1: Preparation**	**7 dys**	**Wed 01.06.11**	**Thu 09.06.11**
2	WP 1.1: Assess internal readiness	3 dys	Wed 01.06.11	Fri 03.06.11
3	WP 1.2: Assess trading partner readiness	4 dys	Mon 06.06.11	Thu 09.06.11
4	**Phase 2: Implement planning**	**7 dys**	**Fri 10.06.11**	**Mon 20.06.11**
5	WP 2.1: Develop collaboration arrangement	2 dys	Fri 10.06.11	Mon 13.06.11
6	WP 2.2: Create joint business plan	5 dys	Tue 14.06.11	Mon 20.06.11
7	**Phase 3: Implement forecasting**	**20 dys**	**Tue 21.06.11**	**Mon 18.07.11**
8	WP 3.1: Create sales forecast	4 dys	Tue 21.06.11	Fri 24.06.11
9	WP 3.2: Identify exceptions for sales forecast	5 dys	Tue 28.06.11	Mon 04.07.11
10	WP 3.3: Resolve/ collaborate on exception items	2 dys	Tue 05.07.11	Wed 06.07.11
11	WP 3.4: Create order forecast	3 dys	Thu 07.07.11	Mon 11.07.11
12	WP 3.5: Identify exceptions for order forecast	4 dys	Tue 12.07.11	Fri 15.07.11
13	WP 3.6: Resolve/ collaborate on exception items	2 dys	Mon 18.07.11	Tue 19.07.11
14	**Phase 4: Implement Replenishment**	**8 dys**	**Wed 20.07.11**	**Fri 29.07.11**
15	WP 3.1: Implement order generation	3 dys	Wed 20.07.11	Fri 22.07.11
16	WP 3.2: Implement delivery execution	5 dys	Mon 25.07.11	Fri 29.07.11

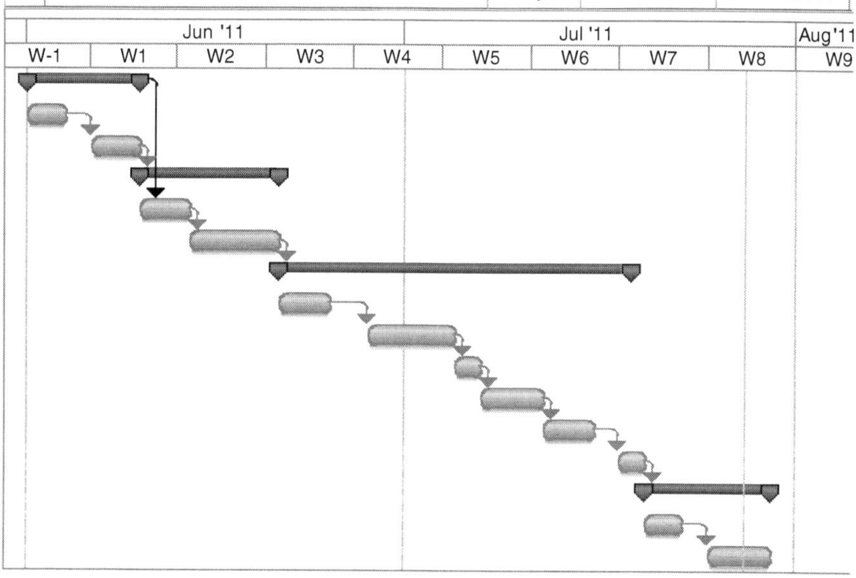

Fig. 12.10 Exemplary Gantt chart for the project to implement CPFR by PC Manufacturing Inc

CPFR has been identified in SCD-Phase 4 as an important corrective action in order to improve the information sharing between buyer and suppliers. In Fig. 12.9 the work breakdown structure for the corrective action CPFR has been identified. The four different phases preparation, implement planning, implement forecasting and implement replenishment have been identified and split into various different phases which represent the smallest possible unit in the structure.

In a second step, PC Manufacturing Inc. needs to identify the time frame, resource and cost framework of the project. The minimum and maximum distance between activities is hereby determined. This can be done with different methods mentioned in chapter 12-Phase 5. There are different costs which need to be taken into consideration, which are labor costs, direct costs, indirect costs, contingency funds and management reserves. The resource analysis examines and reviews each phase and integrates the resources with the help of the resource plan.

In a third step, PC Manufacturing Inc. uses the Gantt chart in order to consider the flow of information within the project. The Gantt chart uses the work breakdown structure in order to indicate milestones of the project. It is a document which attempts to show the start and end of each stage within the project progress. Each one of the phases which have been identified during the work breakdown structure are now put into a time frame. Thereby it is easier to have an overview of the whole project from project beginning to the end (Fig. 12.10). The whole project duration thereby determines the scope of the project.

The different measures help to improve and further strengthen the supply chain differentiation process and to create preconditions for the smooth transition into multiply supply chains. PC Manufacturing Inc. has to fulfill these measures in order to introduce the supply chain differentiation process. Next to the outlined methods, there are manifold ways of conducting project management in this context. These methods are meant to create an understanding of the implications of preparing and implementing the supply chain differentiation process.

References

Barney, J. (1991). Firm resources and sustained competitive advantage. *Journal of Management, 17*(1), 99–120.

Barratt, M. (2004). Understanding the meaning of collaboration in the supply chain. *Supply Chain Management, 9*(1), 30–42.

Kerbosh, J., & Schell, H.J. (1975). *Network planning by the extended metra potential method*. Report KS-1.1, Eindhoven: University of Technology, Department of Industrial Engineering.

Kuster, J., Huber, E., Lippmann, R., Schmid, A., Schneider, E., Witschi, U., et al. (2008). *Handbuch Projektmanagement*. Berlin Heidelberg: Springer.

Zhong, D. H., & Zhang, J. S. (2003). New method for calculating path float in program evaluation and review technique (PERT). *Journal of Construction Engineering and Management, 129*(5), 501.

Zimmermann, J., Stark, C., & Rieck, J. (2010). *Projektplanung: Modelle, Methoden, Management*. Berlin: Springer.

Appendix

The description of corrective actions is shown in Tables A.1, A.2, A.3, A.4, A.5, A.6, A.7, A.8, A.9, A.10 and A.11.

E. Hofmann et al., *The Supply Chain Differentiation Guide*,
DOI: 10.1007/978-3-642-31936-5, © Springer-Verlag Berlin Heidelberg 2012

Table A.1 Description of corrective actions (1/5)

	Mgmt. process according to SCOR model	Corrective action	Description / result	Reference to CMs	Affected processes (SCOR methodology)				
					Plan	Source	Make	Deliver	Return
1	Plan	Integrated process modeling and software reconfiguration tools	Responsiveness and flexibility are emphasized by developing expertise in making business processes re-programmable, re-configurable and continuously changeable	1 - Customer segmentation and supply chain strategy	o				
2	Plan	Inter-organizational planning of material flows	Software that provides multiple data models including the business rules and metrics for the entire supply chain planning process. Algorithms use the business rules and metrics as the drivers for the planning engine.	6 - Functional supply chain processes (plan)	o		x		
3	Plan	Integrated supply chain planning system with interfaces to all supply/demand data sources through digitally enabled supply networks	Tools support balanced decision making (e.g., trade-off between service level and inventory investment)	6 - Functional supply chain processes (plan)	o	x	x	x	x
4	Plan	EDI connection (e.g. XML-based) among supply chain members	Real-time exchange of supply chain information between supply chain members collaborative planning systems, internet trading exchanges, B2B integration and application server systems	5 - Supply chain governance	o	x	x	x	x

(continued)

Table A.1 (continued)

	Mgmt. process according to SCOR model	Corrective action	Description / result	Reference to CMs	Affected processes (SCOR methodology)				
					Plan	Source	Make	Deliver	Return
5	Plan	Supply chain advance planning system	Collaboration among supply chain partners extends outwards to customers, spanning the supply chain. planning re-planning business rules plan changes	5 - Supply chain governance	o	x	x	x	
6	Plan	Supply chain event management systems (SC integration)	All key participants in the supply chain, including strategic partners, have full visibility of the demand/supply plan	5 - Supply chain governance	o	x	x		
7	Plan	B2B Integration and Application Server Systems	Forecasts are replaced with actual customer replenishment signals and orders where possible	5 - Supply chain governance	o	x	x		
8	Plan	Rules-based distribution planning system	Demand priorities reflecting strategic customer relationships as business policies are automatically followed in allocating resources; first-in-first-out (FIFO) is utilized as the default scheduling priority	1 - Customer segmentation and supply chain strategy	o	x	x	x	
9	Plan	Activity based costing	Value pricing based on "Cost to Serve"; EDLP; cost plus pricing	2 - Modularization and vertical range of value creation	o				
10	Plan	Proactive education of customers to set expectations and encourage close working relationships	Knowledge of long-lead items, visibility to supply resources, agreement on levels of flexibility	5 - Supply chain governance	o				x

"o" = Primary "x" = Secondary

Table A.2 Description of corrective actions (2/5)

	Mgmt. process according to SCOR model	Corrective action	Description / result	Reference to CMs	Affected processes (SCOR methodology)				
					Plan	Source	Make	Deliver	Return
11	Plan	Available-to-promise (ATP) check	Available-to-Promise (ATP) provides an availability and feasibility check concerning a customer request or a customer order	5 - Supply chain governance	o	x	x		
12	Plan	Integrate customer-focused marketing plans with the management of the supply chain	Comprehensive S&OP (sales and operations planning)	1 - Customer segmentation and supply chain strategy	o	x	x	x	
13	Plan	Customer relationship management system (CRM)	Software that provides customer input and keeps the customer informed about the planning of the production and delivery process by managing all contacts and communication with the customer thorough all channels including internet and traditional sales and customer service channels	5 - Supply chain governance	o	x	x	x	x
14	Plan	Business intelligence (BI) software	A data warehouse / data mart is the source of all planning (master) data, business rules and transaction data. Analytical tools enable the ongoing maintenance and improvement of the business rules based on actual data	6 - Functional supply chain processes (Plan)	o	x			

(continued)

Table A.2 (continued)

	Mgmt. process according to SCOR model	Corrective action	Description / result	Reference to CMs	Affected processes (SCOR methodology)				
					Plan	Source	Make	Deliver	Return
15	Plan	Joint service agreements (JSAs) between buyers and suppliers	Define the levels of "flexibility" or resource upside available within stated lead times and agreed upon conditions	3 - Supplier segmentation and supply strategy	o	x	x	x	
16	Plan	Collaborative planning tools with source suppliers	Joint service agreements to document acceptable service levels in terms of installation costs, installation cycle time, etc.	3 - Supplier segmentation and supply strategy	o	x			x
17	Source	Frequent review and adjustments of the demand plan	To reflect actual consumption or customer forecast information	1 - Customer segmentation and supply chain strategy	x	o			x
18	Source	Inter-company resource planning with EDI/Internet communication	EDI links integrate supplier resource information (inventory, capacity availability, etc.) with own resources	5 - Supply chain governance	x	o			
19	Source	Digital linkage to supplier quoting, planning, configuration and customer service applications	Consideration of supplier's material availability in company's supply resources (including supplier's production plans & capability, inventory, and delivery plans)	5 - Supply chain governance	x	o			
20	Source, make	Integrated software systems for matching shelf stock to expectations	A software-based system that corrects shelf inventory levels based on actual product present (possible RFID solution). Identifies stock-outs from shrinkage or item misplacement	6 - Functional supply chain processes (source and make)	x	o	o		

(continued)

Table A.2 (continued)

	Mgmt. process according to SCOR model	Corrective action	Description / result	Reference to CMs	Affected processes (SCOR methodology)				
					Plan	Source	Make	Deliver	Return
21	Source, make	Collaborative planning, forecasting, replenishment (CPFR)	Collaborative planning, forecasting and replenishment is a concept that allows collaborative processes across the supply chain, using a set of process and technology models	6 - Functional supply chain processes (source and make)	x	o	o	x	

“o” = Primary “x” = Secondary

Table A.3 Description of corrective actions (3/5)

	Mgmt. process according to SCOR model	Corrective action	Description / result	Reference to CMs	Affected processes (SCOR methodology)				
					Plan	Source	Make	Deliver	Return
22	Source, make	Dynamic deployment based on constraint-based planning and optimal scheduling	Advanced planning and scheduling logic with constraint, cost, and resource optimization	6 - Functional supply chain processes (source and make)	x	o	o		
23	Source, make	Exception management (e.g.: unplanned orders are accepted and scheduled only when there is no detrimental impact on overall product delivery plan)	Digital linkages using XML standards (Rosettanet, eBXML, OAGI) to automatically query production capacity and ATP and schedule unplanned orders	1 - Customer Segmentation and supply chain strategy		o	o		
24	Source, make	Bi-directional digital links (XML, EDI, etc) or internet procurement networks to customer service linkage	Distinct and consistent linkages exist to ensure disruptions and opportunities in material resources are quickly and accurately communicated and acted upon	5 - Supply chain governance		o	o		
25	Source, Make	Enterprise-wide planning system for re-balancing of full- stream supply/demand	Re-balancing of full-stream supply/demand on a daily basis, including source-make-deliver resources and requirements from "customers' customer to suppliers' supplier"	5 - Supply chain governance	x	o	o	x	

(continued)

Table A.3 (continued)

	Mgmt. process according to SCOR model	Corrective action	Description / result	Reference to CMs	Affected processes (SCOR methodology)				
					Plan	Source	Make	Deliver	Return
26	Source, make	Integrated supply chain or demand planning with point of sale and customer inventory systems	Customer relationship and digital linkages (XML, EDI, Etc.) provide accurate visibility into actual demand via customer forecasts, product plans, production plans, and inventory positions	5 - Supply chain governance	x	o	o		x
27	Source, make	Eliminate "special deals" (for example to improve forecast accuracy)	Reduces uncertainty, lowers safety stock requirements, cheaper to administer	1 - Customer segmentation and supply chain strategy	x	o	o		
28	Source, make	Enterprise resource planning system (ERP)	On-line visibility of all supply-chain demand requirements and resources, both currently available and committed (pegged)	6 - Functional supply chain processes (plan)	x	o	o		
29	Source, make	Vendor managed inventory (VMI)	VMI is a concept for planning and control of inventory, in which the supplier has access to the customer's inventory data and is responsible for maintaining the inventory level required by the customer. Re-supply is performed by the vendor through regularly scheduled reviews of the on-site inventory. The on-site inventory is counted, damaged or outdated goods are removed, and the inventory is restocked to predefined levels	5 - Supply chain governance	x	o	o		x

(continued)

Table A.3 (continued)

	Mgmt. process according to SCOR model	Corrective action	Description / result	Reference to CMs	Affected processes (SCOR methodology)				
					Plan	Source	Make	Deliver	Return
30	Source, make	Integrated demand planning driven by POS; customer movement data	Continuous Replenishment Programs; Vendor Managed Inventory, telemetry to automatically communicate replenishment of supplies	5 - Supply chain governance		o	o		x
31	Make	Frequent review and adjustments of inventory targets	Digital Linkages using XML standards (RosettaNet, eBXML, OAGI) to automatically query inventory levels	1 - Customer segmentation and supply chain strategy			o		

"o" = Primary "x" = Secondary

Table A.4 Description of corrective actions (4/5)

	Mgmt. process according to SCOR model	Corrective action	Description / result	Reference to CMs	Affected processes (SCOR methodology)				
					Plan	Source	Make	Deliver	Return
32	Make	ABC analysis	Classification of products by value	1 and 3 - Customer segmentation and supplier segmentation		x	o	x	
33	Make	XYZ analysis	Classification of products by re-ordering frequency	1 & 3 - Customer segmentation and supplier segmentation			o		
34	Make	Categorize 100% of total inventory (Active, usable, excess, Obsolete) for appropriate Action		2 - Modularization and vertical range of value creation			o		
35	Make	Integrated load planning and building with warehouse management	Consolidate oders by customer, source, traffic lane, carrier, etc.	2 - Modularization and vertical range of value creation	x		o		
36	Make	Real time inventory control, stock locator, and rules based picking logic	Dynamic location assignment including lot control, zoned picking, quality assurance	2 - Modularization and vertical range of value creation			o		
37	Make, deliver	Advanced shipping notices, e.g. container labeling	Bar coding; EDI; integrated transportation/warehouse management	6 - Functional supply chain processes (deliver)			o	o	
38	Make, deliver	Automatic identification	Bar coding and radio frequency communications (RFID and other tagging)	6 - Functional supply chain processes (make and deliver)	x		o	o	x
39	Deliver	Consolidation of carriers	Transportation modeling and rate analysis	4 - Allocation of supply chain activities		x		o	

(continued)

Table A.4 (continued)

	Mgmt. process according to SCOR model	Corrective action	Description / result	Reference to CMs	Affected processes (SCOR methodology)				
					Plan	Source	Make	Deliver	Return
40	Deliver	Merge-in-transit / hub consolidation	Merge-in-Transit is a practice to combine items from multiple sources into a single customer shipment. This includes items on stock in the distribution center, from which the shipment is sent, items on stock in other distribution centers, items on stock elsewhere (e.g. at a plant or a supplier) as well as make-to-order items. The items to be merged are cross-docked from inbound receipt to outbound shipping. Merging is usually performed in a shipper's distribution center (DC) or in a carrier's terminal	6 - Functional supply chain processes (source/deliver)		x		o	

"o" = Primary "x" = Secondary

Table A.5 Description of corrective actions (5/5)

	Mgmt. process according to SCOR model	Corrective action	Description / result	Reference to CMs	Affected processes (SCOR methodology)				
					Plan	Source	Make	Deliver	Return
41	Deliver	Cross-docking	Used in many distribution centers (DC) to increase inventory velocity while maintaining shipping efficiency. In a traditional DC, the receiving process is disjointed from the shipping process and storage acts as an intermediary between the two processes. Cross docking actively links the receiving and shipping processes. In a DC, both cross docking (no storage) and traditional (with storage) operations might take place.	6 - Functional supply chain processes (source/deliver)		x		o	x
42	Deliver	Route scheduling, carrier selection, and rating	Carrier/route optimization based on continuous movement and consolidation/pooling	4 - Allocation of supply chain activities		x		o	
43	Deliver	Rules-based carrier selection and actual rate database	Select carriers by (for ex.): least cost per shipment and rate using actual rates prior to release to billing; lead or response time; reliability	6 - Functional supply chain processes (source/deliver)		x		o	
44	Deliver	Shipment tracking and tracing	Satellite communications, GPS, RFID	6 - Functional supply chain processes (source/deliver)		x		o	x
45	Deliver	Integrated inbound/outbound transportation planning	Consolidation of inbound and outbound requirements	4 - Allocation of supply chain activities	x	x		o	x

(continued)

Table A.5 (continued)

	Mgmt. process according to SCOR model	Corrective action	Description / result	Reference to CMs	Affected processes (SCOR methodology)				
					Plan	Source	Make	Deliver	Return
46	Deliver	Carrier agreement	Carrier agreements are agreements between a company and its domestic and global carriers (for both, inbound raw materials and outbound finished goods) specifying service levels, payment terms, and other conditions	6 - Functional supply chain processes (source/deliver)	x			o	x
47	Source, make, deliver	Event-driven supply chain re-planning	Change in the demand signal instantaneously "reconfigures" the production and supply plans	1 - Custo mer segmentation and supply chain strategy	x	x	x	x	
48	Source, make, deliver	Supply chain modeling and visualization system	Capability to run "simulated" full-stream supply/demand balancing for "what-if" scenarios	6 - Functional supply chain processes (plan)	x	x	x	x	

"o" = Primary; "x" = Secondary

Table A.6 Assignment of corrective actions to specific objectives (1/6)

		Plan	Plan	Plan	Plan, source, deliver	Plan, make, deliver, return	Source, make, deliver	Source, deliver
	Corrective action	Effective integration of SCM in the organization	Proper supply chain coordination	Efficient interfaces	Effective cooperation and coordination with 3PLs	High customer satisfaction	Accurate forecasting	Satisfactory lead and transit time
1	Integrated process modeling and software reconfiguration tools	x	x	x				x
2	Inter-organizational planning of material flows	x	x		x			x
3	Integrated supply chain planning system with interfaces to all supply/ demand data sources through digitally enabled supply networks	x	x				x	x
4	EDI connection (e.g. XML-based) among supply chain members	x	x	x	x			
5	Supply chain advance planning system				x		x	x

(continued)

Table A.6 (continued)

		Plan	Plan	Plan	Plan, source, deliver	Plan, make, deliver, return	Source, make, deliver	Source, deliver
	Corrective action	Effective integration of SCM in the organization	Proper supply chain coordination	Efficient interfaces	Effective cooperation and coordination with 3PLs	High customer satisfaction	Accurate forecasting	Satisfactory lead and transit time
6	Supply chain event management systems (SC integration)	x	x					
7	B2B integration and application server systems	x	x	x				
8	Rules-based distribution planning system	x						x
9	Activity based costing		x					
10	proactive education of customers to set expectations and encourage close working relationships					x	x	
11	Available-to-promise (ATP) check							
12	Integrate customer-focused marketing plans with the management of the supply chain		x	x		x		
13	Customer relationship management system (CRM)					x	x	

(continued)

Table A.6 (continued)

		Plan	Plan	Plan	Plan, source, deliver	Plan, make, deliver, return	Source, make, deliver	Source, deliver
	Corrective action	Effective integration of SCM in the organization	Proper supply chain coordination	Efficient interfaces	Effective cooperation and coordination with 3PLs	High customer satisfaction	Accurate forecasting	Satisfactory lead and transit time
14	Business intelligence (BI) software					x	x	
15	Joint service agreements (JSAs) between buyers and suppliers					x	x	
16	Collaborative planning tools with source suppliers	x	x					
	Sum of assigned corrective actions	**8**	**9**	**4**	**3**	**5**	**6**	**5**
17	Frequent review and adjustments of the demand plan						x	
18	Inter-company resource planning with EDI/internet communication		x		x			
19	Digital linkage to supplier quoting, planning, configuration and customer service applications	x	x	x		x	x	
	Sum of assigned corrective actions	**1**	**2**	**1**	**1**	**1**	**2**	**0**

Table A.7 Assignment of corrective actions to specific objectives (2/6)

		Plan	Plan	Plan	Plan, source, deliver	Plan, make, deliver, return	Source, make, deliver	Source, deliver
	Corrective action	Effective integration of SCM in the organization	Proper supply chain coordination	Efficient interfaces	Effective cooperation and coordination with 3PLs	High customer satisfaction	Accurate forecasting	Satisfactory lead and transit time
20	Integrated software systems for matching shelf stock to expectations	x	x			x		
21	Collaborative planning, forecasting, replenishment (CPFR)				x		x	
22	Dynamic deployment based on constraint-based planning and optimal scheduling							

(continued)

Table A.7 (continued)

		Plan	Plan	Plan	Plan, source, deliver	Plan, make, deliver, return	Source, make, deliver	Source, deliver
	Corrective action	Effective integration of SCM in the organization	Proper supply chain coordination	Efficient interfaces	Effective cooperation and coordination with 3PLs	High customer satisfaction	Accurate forecasting	Satisfactory lead and transit time
23	Exception management (e.g.: unplanned orders are accepted and scheduled only when there is no detrimental impact on overall product delivery plan)						x	
24	Bi-directional digital links (XML, EDI, etc) or internet procurement networks to customer service linkage		x	x	x	x	x	
25	Enterprise-wide planning system for re-balancing of full-stream supply/demand	x					x	

(continued)

Table A.7 (continued)

		Plan	Plan	Plan	Plan, source, deliver	Plan, make, deliver, return	Source, make, deliver	Source, deliver
	Corrective action	Effective integration of SCM in the organization	Proper supply chain coordination	Efficient interfaces	Effective cooperation and coordination with 3PLs	High customer satisfaction	Accurate forecasting	Satisfactory lead and transit time
26	Integrated supply chain or demand planning with point of sale and customer inventory systems		x				x	
27	Eliminate "special deals" (for example to improve forecast accuracy)						x	
28	Enterprise resource planning system (ERP)						x	
29	Vendor managed inventory (VMI)							
30	Integrated demand planning driven by POS; customer movement data	x	x			x	x	x
	Sum of assigned corrective actions	**3**	**4**	**1**	**2**	**3**	**8**	**1**
31	Frequent review and adjustments of inventory targets							

(continued)

Table A.7 (continued)

		Plan	Plan	Plan	Plan, source, deliver	Plan, make, deliver, return	Source, make, deliver	Source, deliver
	Corrective action	Effective integration of SCM in the organization	Proper supply chain coordination	Efficient interfaces	Effective cooperation and coordination with 3PLs	High customer satisfaction	Accurate forecasting	Satisfactory lead and transit time
32	ABC analysis							
33	XYZ analysis							
34	Categorize 100% of total inventory (active, usable, excess, obsolete) for appropriate action							
35	Integrated load planning and building with warehouse management		**x**					
36	Real time inventory control, stock locator, and rules based picking logic							
	Sum of assigned corrective actions	**0**	**1**	**0**	**0**	**0**	**0**	**0**

Table A.8 Assignment of corrective actions to specific objectives (3/6)

		Plan	Plan	Plan	Plan, source, deliver	Plan, make, deliver, return	Source, make, deliver	Source, deliver
	Corrective action	Effective integration of SCM in the organization	Proper supply chain coordination	Efficient interfaces	Effective cooperation and coordination with 3PLs	High customer satisfaction	Accurate forecasting	Satisfactory lead and transit time
37	Advanced shipping notices, e.g. container labeling		x					
38	Automatic identification		x					
	Sum of assigned corrective actions	**0**	**2**	**0**	**0**	**0**	**0**	**0**
39	Consolidation of carriers							
40	Merge-in-transit / hub consolidation							
41	Cross-docking				x			
42	Route scheduling, carrier selection, and rating				x			x

(continued)

Table A.8 (continued)

		Plan	Plan	Plan	Plan, source, deliver	Plan, make, deliver, return	Source, make, deliver	Source, deliver
	Corrective action	Effective integration of SCM in the organization	Proper supply chain coordination	Efficient interfaces	Effective cooperation and coordination with 3PLs	High customer satisfaction	Accurate forecasting	Satisfactory lead and transit time
43	Rules-based carrier selection and actual rate database				**x**			
44	Shipment tracking and tracing				**x**			**x**
45	Integrated inbound/outbound transportation planning				**x**			**x**
46	Carrier agreement							**x**
	Sum of assigned corrective actions	**0**	**0**	**0**	**5**	**0**	**0**	**4**
47	Event-driven supply chain re-planning		**x**				**x**	**x**

(continued)

Table A.8 (continued)

		Plan	Plan	Plan	Plan, source, deliver	Plan, make, deliver, return	Source, make, deliver	Source, deliver
	Corrective action	Effective integration of SCM in the organization	Proper supply chain coordination	Efficient interfaces	Effective cooperation and coordination with 3PLs	High customer satisfaction	Accurate forecasting	Satisfactory lead and transit time
48	Supply chain modeling and visualization system							**x**
		Inappropriate integration of SCM in the company's organization	Poor supply chain coordi-nation	Inefficient interfaces	Poor cooperation and coordination with the 3PLs	Poor customer satisfaction	Forecasting difficulties or inaccuracies	Lead and transit time related issues

Table A.9 Assignment of corrective actions to specific objectives (4/6)

	Corrective action	Make	Make	Make	Make	Deliver	Deliver	Deliver, return	Deliver, return	Deliver
		Appropriate inventory segmentation (sufficient visibility)	Sufficient production capacities	Efficient production capacity utilization	Effective, accurate inventory management	Effective distribution planning	Effective utilization of specific transport modes	Efficient distribution processes	Functioning tracking and tracing	No capacity-related problems with service providers
1	Integrated process modeling and software reconfiguration tools							x		
2	Inter-organizational planning of material flows		x	x	x	x				
3	Integrated supply chain planning system with interfaces to all supply/ demand data sources through digitally enabled supply networks		x		x	x		x		
4	EDI connection (e.g. XML-based) among supply chain members		x							
5	Supply chain advance panning system			x		x				

(continued)

Table A.9 (continued)

	Make	Make	Make	Make	Deliver	Deliver	Deliver, return	Deliver, return	Deliver
Corrective action	Appropriate inventory segmentation (sufficient visibility)	Sufficient production capacities	Efficient production capacity utilization	Effective, accurate inventory management	Effective distribution planning	Effective utilization of specific transport modes	Efficient distribution processes	Functioning tracking and tracing	No capacity-related problems with service providers
6 Supply chain event management systems (SC integration)				x			x		
7 B2B integration and application server systems				x					x
8 Rules-based distribution planning system					x		x		
9 Activity based costing									
10 Proactive education of customers to set expectations and encourage close working relationships									
11 Available-to-promise (ATP) check			x			x			x
12 Integrate customer-focused marketing plans with the management of the supply chain									

(continued)

Table A.9 (continued)

	Make	Make	Make	Make	Deliver	Deliver	Deliver, return	Deliver, return	Deliver
Corrective action	Appropriate inventory segmentation (sufficient visibility)	Sufficient production capacities	Efficient production capacity utilization	Effective, accurate inventory management	Effective distribution planning	Effective utilization of specific transport modes	Efficient distribution processes	Functioning tracking and tracing	No capacity-related problems with service providers
13 Customer relationship management system (CRM)									
14 Business intelligence (BI) software									
15 Joint service agreements (JSAs) between buyers and suppliers									

Table A.10 Assignment of corrective actions to specific objectives (5/6)

		Make	Make	Make	Make	Deliver	Deliver	Deliver, return	Deliver, return	Deliver
	Corrective action	Appropriate inventory segmentation (sufficient visibility)	Sufficient production capacities	Efficient production capacity utilization	Effective, accurate inventory management	Effective distribution planning	Effective utilization of specific transport modes	Efficient distribution processes	Functioning tracking and tracing	No capacity-related problems with service providers
16	Collaborative planning tools with source suppliers			**x**	**x**					
	Sum of assigned corrective actions	**0**	**3**	**4**	**5**	**4**	**1**	**4**	**0**	**2**
17	Frequent review and adjustments of the demand plan									**x**
18	Inter-company resource planning with EDI/Internet communication				**x**					
19	Digital linkage to supplier quoting, planning, configuration and customer service applications							**x**		
	Sum of assigned corrective actions	**0**	**0**	**0**	**1**	**0**	**0**	**1**	**0**	**1**
20	Integrated software systems for matching shelf stock to expectations				**x**					
21	Collaborative planning, forecasting, replenishment (CPFR)									
22	Dynamic deployment based on constraint- based planning and optimal scheduling			**x**						

(continued)

Table A.10 (continued)

		Make	Make	Make	Make	Deliver	Deliver	Deliver, return	Deliver, return	Deliver
	Corrective action	Appropriate inventory segmentation (sufficient visibility)	Sufficient production capacities	Efficient production capacity utilization	Effective, accurate inventory management	Effective distribution planning	Effective utilization of specific transport modes	Efficient distribution processes	Functioning tracking and tracing	No capacity-related problems with service providers
23	Exception management (e.g.: unplanned orders are accepted and scheduled only when there is no detrimental impact on overall product delivery plan)			x						x
24	Bi-directional digital links (XML, EDI, etc) or internet procurement networks to customer service linkage			x						x
25	Enterprise-wide planning system for re-balancing of full-stream supply/demand		x	x						x
26	Integrated supply chain or demand planning with point of sale and customer inventory systems				x	x				
27	Eliminate "special deals" (for example to improve forecast accuracy)			x						
28	Enterprise resource planning system (ERP)			x						x

(continued)

Table A.10 (continued)

		Make	Make	Make	Make	Deliver	Deliver	Deliver, return	Deliver, return	Deliver
	Corrective action	Appropriate inventory segmentation (sufficient visibility)	Sufficient production capacities	Efficient production capacity utilization	Effective, accurate inventory management	Effective distribution planning	Effective utilization of specific transport modes	Efficient distribution processes	Functioning tracking and tracing	No capacity-related problems with service providers
29	Vendor managed inventory (VMI)	x	x		x			x		
30	Integrated demand planning driven by POS; customer movement data		x			x		x		
	Sum of assigned corrective actions	**1**	**3**	**6**	**3**	**2**	**0**	**2**	**0**	**4**

Table A.11 Assignment of corrective actions to specific objectives (6/6)

		Make	Make	Make	Make	Deliver	Deliver	Deliver, return	Deliver, return	Deliver
	Corrective action	Appropriate inventory segmentation (sufficient visibility)	Sufficient production capacities	Efficient production capacity utilization	Effective, accurate inventory management	Effective distribution planning	Effective utilization of specific transport modes	Efficient distribution processes	Functioning tracking & tracing	No capacity-related problems with service providers
31	Frequent review and adjustments of inventory targets				x					
32	ABC analysis	x			x					
33	XYZ analysis	x			x					
34	Categorize 100% of total inventory (Active, usable, excess, obsolete) for appropriate action	x			x					
35	Integrated load planning and building with warehouse management	x	x		x					
36	Real time inventory control, stock locator, and rules based picking logic	x			x					
	Sum of assigned corrective actions	**5**	**1**	**0**	**6**	**0**	**0**	**0**	**0**	**0**
37	Advanced shipping notices, e.g. container labeling							x		
38	Automatic identification				x			x	x	
	Sum of assigned corrective actions	**0**	**0**	**0**	**1**	**0**	**0**	**2**	**1**	**0**

(continued)

Table A.11 (continued)

	Make	Make	Make	Make	Deliver	Deliver	Deliver, return	Deliver, return	Deliver
Corrective action	Appropriate inventory segmentation (sufficient visibility)	Sufficient production capacities	Efficient production capacity utilization	Effective, accurate inventory management	Effective distribution planning	Effective utilization of specific transport modes	Efficient distribution processes	Functioning tracking & tracing	No capacity-related problems with service providers
39 Consolidation of carriers					x		x		
40 Merge-in-transit / hub consolidation		x		x	x		x		
41 Cross-docking							x		
42 Route scheduling, carrier selection, and rating					x		x		x
43 Rules-based carrier selection and actual rate database						x	x		
44 Shipment tracking and Tracing					x	x	x		
45 Integrated inbound/outbound transportation planning					x	x	x		x
46 Carrier agreement						x	x		
Sum of assigned corrective actions	**0**	**1**	**0**	**1**	**5**	**4**	**8**	**0**	**2**
47 Event-driven supply chain re-planning			x		x				

(continued)

Table A.11 (continued)

		Make	Make	Make	Make	Deliver	Deliver	Deliver, return	Deliver, return	Deliver
	Corrective action	Appropriate inventory segmentation (sufficient visibility)	Sufficient production capacities	Efficient production capacity utilization	Effective, accurate inventory management	Effective distribution planning	Effective utilization of specific transport modes	Efficient distribution processes	Functioning tracking & tracing	No capacity-related problems with service providers
48	Supply chain modeling and visualization system		x	x	x	x	x			x
		Inappropriate inventory segmentation (lack of visibility)	Inappropriate production capacities	Inefficient production capacity utilization	Ineffective inventory management	Difficulties in distribution planning	Problems with specific transport modes	Inefficient distribution processes	Difficulties in tracking and tracing	Capacity related issues with service providers

Index

80–20 rule, 182

A

ABC analysis, 56–59, 119, 182, 199
Advancements in technology, 186
After sales service, 165, 233
Agile, 20, 26, 64–68, 73, 77, 94, 96, 97, 102, 117, 118, 120, 129, 131, 134, 135, 163, 189, 191, 196, 197, 217, 222
Allocation of processes, 20
Allocation of resources, 51, 55
Analysis of strategic groups, 40
Analytical hierarchy process, 20, 47, 70, 285
A-priori segmentation, 51
Arm's length, 108, 111, 118, 146, 199, 200
AS-IS situation, 14, 21, 22, 182, 214, 225, 231, 264
Assemble-to-order, 82, 94, 195

B

B2B, 136, 146
B2C, 146
Balance strategy, 114
Bargaining power, 38, 39, 108, 146, 200
Benchmarking, 14, 22, 90, 161, 179, 214, 215, 222, 223, 243, 261, 263, 264, 266
Best practices, 12
Bottom-up estimating, 295
Brand, 184
Brand management, 44
Broad-line producers, 41
Build-to-order, 135
Bullwhip effect, 150
Business diagnostics, 9
Business unit, 20, 22, 68–70, 76, 232
Buyer-supplier relationship, 87, 97, 108–110, 111–115, 118, 143, 144, 146, 208, 258
Buy-or-make decision, 81

C

Capacity utilization, 245, 252, 264, 266
Cash-flow, 36
Cash-to-cash conversion cycle, 43
Category management system, 194
Choice of features, 44
Classification of customers, 20
Co-development, 92, 111
CODP, 71–73, 77, 94–99, 102, 195
Collaborative planning, forecasting and replenishment, 147, 245
Collecting information, 183
Competency approach, 172
Competitive advantages, 7
Competitive priorities, 15, 26, 96, 187, 189, 190, 192, 217, 222, 225, 261, 272
Competitor's situation, 20
Configure-to-order, 43
Content modules, 16, 18–20, 22, 26, 225, 257
Continuous improvement, 147, 160, 161, 212, 214, 243
Conversion costs, 39
Core competencies, 42, 43, 81, 82, 88
Core values, 35
Corrective actions, 15, 18, 22, 70, 217, 231, 236, 244, 245, 252, 255, 260–262, 264–269, 272, 274, 276, 279, 281, 285, 306–336
Cost analysis, 90, 295, 296, 299, 301
Cost comparison method, 286
Cost efficiency, 44, 65, 68, 95, 96, 126, 129

E. Hofmann et al., *The Supply Chain Differentiation Guide*,
DOI: 10.1007/978-3-642-31936-5, © Springer-Verlag Berlin Heidelberg 2012

C (*cont.*)
Cost leadership, 44, 68, 69
Cost optimization, 3
Cost related strategy, 37
Costs of sales, 60
Critical path method, 298
Cross-national segmentation, 61, 62
Cultural conditions, 184
Cultural peculiarities, 66
Customer base, 45
Customer channel, 43
Customer needs, 13, 20, 45, 47, 50, 61, 70, 76
Customer order, 7, 60, 71, 77, 94, 96, 98, 99, 103, 136, 138, 191, 195–197, 207, 225
Customer portfolio models, 55
Customer relationship, 20, 60, 144–146, 149, 154, 155, 164, 208, 210, 211, 233, 241, 279–281
Customer requirements, 4, 6, 7, 14, 26, 43, 47, 67, 74, 96, 138, 172, 173, 182–184, 189, 195, 232, 233, 258, 276, 281
Customer satisfaction, 3, 62, 126, 174, 186
Customer segment, 4, 6, 14, 22, 47, 50–54, 57, 59, 61, 62, 64, 67, 75, 127, 132, 137, 145, 146, 150, 154, 155, 179, 180, 182, 187, 192, 199, 208, 210, 225, 228, 238
Customer segmentation, 20, 22, 50, 51, 54, 55–59, 62, 147, 181, 182, 199, 232, 257, 262, 265, 281
Customer service, 12, 48, 51, 126, 150
Customer structures, 51
Customer-order driven, 196
Customization, 43, 45, 62, 66, 72, 83, 95, 108, 129, 195
Customization of products, 44, 66

D
Decision area, 26
Decision making, 22, 55, 56, 70, 88, 89, 125, 129, 130, 238, 268, 269, 272, 289
Decoupling point, ix–xiv, 7, 25, 26, 53, 64, 71, 73, 77, 94, 98, 102, 136, 191, 195–197, 225, 281
Degree of standardization, 83, 95
Delivery time, 48, 99, 128
Delphi technique, 296
Demand channels, 53
Demanded volume, 183
Demand uncertainty, 66, 87, 150
Demand variability, 66, 75, 150, 183
Demand volatility, 66, 72, 94, 99
Dependency of components, 85
Diagnostic tool, 10, 11
Differentiation strategy, 14, 37, 44
Discount rate, 60
Distribution centers, 73, 196, 203
Distribution channel, 26, 39, 62, 74, 136, 180, 185, 186, 208, 225, 257
Distribution of power, 110, 115, 146, 154
Distribution processes, 20
Distributors, 150, 186, 204
Dominant designs, 40
DWV^3, 51, 52, 64, 74

E
Economies of scale, 39, 54, 83, 84, 87, 127, 128, 183
Economies of scope, 83
Effort estimation, 284, 285, 290
Employee turnover, 168
End customer, 3, 9, 62, 97, 196
Engineer-to-order, 20, 26, 94, 134, 135, 195, 205–207
Enterprise resource planning, 152, 184
Environmental analysis, 38
Exploitation strategy, 114

F
Facility locations, 187
Feasibility study, 284
Fields of activity, 35
Financial resources, 30, 35, 284
Flexibility, 7, 15, 20, 48, 50, 65–67, 76, 77, 82, 83, 94–97, 103, 112, 129, 135, 163, 171, 183, 189, 190, 192, 193, 217, 222
Forecast driven, 71, 72, 196
Forecasting, 65, 72, 147, 168, 183, 245, 279, 280, 302
Fragmentation of markets, 186
Function point analysis, 285
Functional products, 64

G
Gantt chart, 293, 298, 299, 301, 303
Gap analysis, 14, 19, 21, 22, 62, 231, 232, 257, 259–262, 276, 279, 281, 283
Generic strategy, 37, 44, 68, 69

Geographic distribution, 60, 77, 138, 184, 225
Global sourcing, 65
Global supply chain forum, 145
Globally concentrated production, 127, 128
Governance types, 141–143

H
Hierarchical structure, 47, 48, 70
Host-market production, 127, 129
Human resource management, 165–167, 170, 175, 214, 215, 244

I
Idiosyncratic, 83
Implementation process, 167, 168, 268, 283
Industry evolution, 41
Industry structure, 41
Inefficiencies, 10, 12, 90
Information and communication technology, 9
Information sharing, 20, 26, 121, 145, 148–152, 155, 174, 208, 210, 211, 225, 226, 238, 240–242, 258, 259, 263, 276, 277, 281, 302
Information technology, 45, 87
In-house activities, 87, 90
Innovative products, 64
Interdependencies, 83, 91, 200
Intermediary, 186
Internal rate of return, 286
International network design, 129
Inter-organizational boards, 163
Inventory management, 11, 245, 252
Inventory strategy, 187
IT systems, 43, 145, 152

J
Joint venture, 92
Just-in-time, 43, 147

K
Key performance indicator, 179
Key principles, 35

L
Labor market, 168
Leading-edge firms, 214
Lead time, 4, 15, 20, 72, 76, 94, 183, 189, 190, 192, 212, 217, 225, 245, 264
Leagile, 26, 64–69, 77, 96, 129, 258, 276, 281
Lean, 20, 65–68, 73, 77, 96, 97, 102, 117, 118, 120, 128, 129, 131, 134, 163, 189, 190, 196, 197, 217, 225, 258, 276
Learning curve, 54
Level of inventory, 187
Leverage, 26, 101, 109, 115, 118, 121, 138, 139, 154, 201, 211, 225, 226, 259, 276, 281
Location strategy, 187
Logistics service, 62, 66, 184, 245, 252, 287
Long-term capacity, 202

M
Make-or-buy decision, 88, 90, 194, 236
Make-to-order, 6, 20, 26, 94, 134–136, 138, 139, 195, 205–207, 227, 258
Make-to-stock, 7, 26, 94, 134, 136, 195, 207, 225, 258
Manufacturing companies, 7
Manufacturing strategy, 82, 93–99, 102, 103, 125, 132–136, 138, 138, 191–193, 195, 205
Manufacturing theory, 185
Market drivers, 12
Market growth, 35, 40, 55
Market segmentation, 50, 51, 180, 181
Market share, 3, 33, 55, 222
Market-related factors, 72
Mass markets, 44
Material evaluation, 115
Material groups, 20, 81, 92, 93, 193, 194, 202, 236
Maturity level, 21
Methodology-specific pre-requisites, 29
Metra potential method, 298
Modularization, ix–xiv, 81, 83, 86, 92, 109, 193, 194, 236
Module development process, 85
Morphological box, 21
Motivation of purchase, 51
Multi-criteria decision, 70, 269, 272
Multiple channel, 44, 136, 186
Multiplier method, 286
Mutually independent products, 66

N
Narrow model range, 41
Net present value, 286, 293
Network analysis, 293, 298, 301
New to the firm, 84
Niche products, 41

O

Online sales, 76
Operational costs, 7, 266
Operational path, 266
Operations audits, 12
Opportunistic behavior, 151
Order penetration point, 71
Order qualifiers, 67, 185
Order winners, 185
Organizational structure, 30, 288, 289
Original equipment manufacturers, 87
Out of stock situation, 197
Outsourcing, 3, 81, 85, 87–91, 93, 101, 117, 170, 173, 194, 93

P

Packaging, 184
Parametric modeling, 296
Partnership, 115, 118, 143
Percentage method, 286
Perfect competition, 107, 142
Performance metrics, 179, 215, 217, 222
Personalization, 44
PEST-analysis, 38
Pipeline, 47, 67
Pipeline development, 64
Point of sale, 148
Portfolio analysis, 35, 55
Post hoc segmentation, 51
Potential entrants, 38
Power asymmetry, 143
Power balance, 55
Predictability of demand, 60
Preference, 26, 43, 51, 53, 54, 85, 180
Price, 6, 7, 14, 20, 26, 39, 44, 48, 50, 67, 74, 93, 128, 132, 136, 188, 190, 193, 225
Primary needs, 48
Process type, 26, 225
Process-spanning, 252
Procurement, 3, 107, 125, 130, 133, 134, 138, 165, 170, 172, 173, 207
Product architecture, 82–85, 88, 94–96, 101
Product availability, 14, 74, 126, 131, 225
Product characteristics, 20, 54, 70, 76, 180
Product cost leadership, 37
Product designs, 184
Product differentiation, 37, 44, 73, 94, 129, 197
Product life cycle, 29, 36, 53, 64, 75, 183
Product line, 37, 69, 97
Product modularization, 16, 81, 82, 85, 262
Product strategy, 37
Product variety, 73, 75, 97, 183, 196
Production facility, 130
Production flow, 65
Production group, 193, 197, 207
Production-related factors, 72, 94, 96
Profit comparison method, 286
Profit impact, 112, 113, 121, 184, 200, 201
Profitability analysis, 284–286
Program evaluation and review technique, 286
Project management, 16, 20, 29, 30, 159–163, 175, 211–214, 227, 243, 260, 269, 276, 281, 283, 288, 289, 291, 293, 298, 301, 303
Project management institute, 293, 295, 306
Project management maturity model, 159, 212
Project management pre-requisites, 29
Promotion costs, 60
Purchase patterns, 51
Purchasing portfolio, 107, 111, 115, 146, 198, 200
Purchasing structure, 93
Purchasing volume, 57, 119, 199

Q

Qualitative analysis, 54
Quality, 7, 14, 15, 20, 26, 48, 50, 67, 74, 76, 91, 95, 109, 116, 121, 131, 134, 136, 147, 160, 164, 170, 172, 175, 189, 190, 192, 200, 217, 222, 225, 285, 290
Quick response, 152
Quick scan, 9

R

R&D, 48, 83, 92, 127, 130, 131, 132
Relationship management, 23, 143, 208, 211
Reliable delivery, 6
Resource allocation, 22
Resource analysis, 296
Responsibility check, 22
Retailer, 62, 149, 151, 152, 186
Retention of personnel, 21
Risk analysis, 284–286

S

Sales volume, 20
Saturation stage, 183
Scheduling of deliveries, 202
SCOR, 125, 132, 195, 202, 203, 207, 208, 215, 239, 240, 245, 265
Sensitivity analysis, 85

Shareholder value, 145
Shipment validation, 202
Side products, 50
Situational aspects, 51
Small or medium sized enterprise, 27
Source process, 26, 202, 207, 239
Specialist producers, 41
Stakeholders, 29, 163
Standard, 84, 95, 110, 111, 138, 202, 206
Stockholding point, 73
Stock-outs, 150
Strategic alliance, 92, 145, 149, 211, 226, 241, 258
Strategic objectives, 35, 93, 191
Strategic partners, 109, 126
Strategic path, 261, 264, 265, 276
Strategic supply chain orientation, 15, 20, 26, 77, 131, 134, 187, 190, 217, 225, 258, 263
Strategy development process, 51
Substitute products, 38, 39
Subsystems, 82, 84, 193
Sunk costs, 39
Supplier invoices, 202
Supplier management, 108, 109, 111, 115, 147, 198–200
Supplier relationship, 20, 109, 115–117, 143, 146, 149, 154, 155, 211, 259
Supplier segmentation, 20, 107, 115, 119, 179, 198, 199
Supply chain assessment
Supply chain governance, 20
Supply chain partners, 3, 141, 143, 148, 152, 173, 276, 279
Supply chain performance, 5, 151, 166, 214, 215
Supply chain segmentation, 4, 13, 14, 231, 257
Supporting activity, 21
SWOT-analysis, 42, 45
System responsiveness, 126
Systems contracting, 115

T

Tactical needs, 48
Target analysis, 288, 290, 293
Team assembly, 30
Technology adoption life cycle, 54
Third party logistics, 10
Time analysis, 294, 296, 301
Time scheduling, 22
Time-to-market, 83, 84
TO-BE situation, 21, 169, 175, 261
Top management support, 29, 213
Total revenue per customer, 60
Transaction cost, 109, 142
Transit time, 252
Transnational strategy, 128, 129
Transport strategy, 187
Transportation mode, 187
Turn-around times, 207

U

Usage, 51, 60, 95

V

Value adding process, 21
Value chain, 7, 26, 71, 72, 89, 98, 195
Value creating strategy, 90
Value generating, 67, 71, 76, 77, 146
Value network, 25, 26
Value of sold products, 57
Value of the sold product, 20
Value streams, 17
Variety of products, 44, 69, 83, 84
Vendor managed inventory, 147
Vertical integration, 95, 96, 107, 142

W

Weighted score method, 70, 269, 272–274
Window for delivery, 52, 53, 65, 183
Work breakdown structure, 292, 293, 298, 301–303
Working force, 127

Printed by Publishers' Graphics LLC